The Transnational Politics of Corporate Governance Regulation

This ambitious volume explores the politics of recent changes in corporate governance regulation and the transnational forces driving the process. During the 1990s corporate governance became a catchphrase of the global business community. The Enron collapse and other recent corporate scandals, as well as growing worries in Europe about the rise of Anglo-Saxon finance, have made issues of corporate governance the subject of political controversies and of public debate. These debates often overlook the role of public and private regulation in producing a power shift within corporate governance practices at multiple levels.

This book argues that the regulation of corporate governance is an inherently political affair. Given the context of the deepening globalization of the corporate world, it is also increasingly a transnational phenomenon. In terms of the *content* of regulation the book shows an increasing reliance on the application of *market mechanisms* and a tendency for corporations themselves to become *commodities*, 'things' which can be sold and bought on the market. The emerging new *mode* of regulation is characterized by increasing informalization and by forms of private regulation. These changes in content and mode are driven by transnational actors, first of all the owners of internationally mobile financial capital and their functionaries such as coordination service firms, as well as by key public international agencies such as the European Commission.

This book will be of interest to students and researchers of international political economy, politics, economics and corporate governance.

Henk Overbeek is Professor of International Relations in the Department of Political Science of the Vrije Universiteit Amsterdam, The Netherlands.

Bastiaan van Apeldoorn is a Reader in International Relations at the Vrije Universiteit Amsterdam, The Netherlands.

Andreas Nölke is Professor of Political Science at the Institut für Politikwissenschaft of the Johann Wolfgang Goethe-Universität, Frankfurt am Main, Germany.

RIPE series in global political economy

This series, published in association with the *Review of International Political Economy,* provides a forum for current debates in international political economy. The series aims to cover all the central topics in IPE and to present innovative analyses of emerging topics. The titles in the series seek to transcend a state-centred discourse and focus on three broad themes:

* the nature of the forces driving globalization forward
* resistance to globalization
* the transformation of the world order.

The series comprises two strands:

The *RIPE Series in Global Political Economy* aims to address the needs of students and teachers, and the titles will be published in hardback and paperback. ·Titles include:

Political Economy of a Plural World
Critical reflections on power, morals and
civilizations
Robert Cox with Michael Schechter

**A Critical Rewriting of Global Political
Economy**
Integrating reproductive, productive and
virtual economies
V. Spike Peterson

Contesting Globalization
Space and place in the world economy
André C. Drainville

Global Institutions and Development
Framing the world?
*Edited by Morten Bøås and
Desmond McNeill*

**Global Institutions, Marginalization,
and Development**
Craig N. Murphy

**Critical Theories, International
Relations and 'the Anti-Globalisation
Movement'**
The politics of global resistance
*Edited by Catherine Eschle and
Bice Maiguashca*

**Globalization, Governmentality, and
Global Politics**
Regulation for the rest of us?
Ronnie D. Lipschutz, with James K. Rowe

Routledge/RIPE Studies in Global Political Economy is a forum for innovative new research
intended for a high-level specialist readership, and the titles will be available in hardback
only. Titles include:

1. Globalization and Governance*
*Edited by Aseem Prakash and
Jeffrey A. Hart*

2. Nation-States and Money
The past, present and future of national
currencies
*Edited by Emily Gilbert and
Eric Helleiner*

**3. The Global Political Economy of
Intellectual Property Rights**
The new enclosures?
Christopher May

4. Integrating Central Europe
EU expansion and Poland, Hungary and
the Czech Republic
Otto Holman

**5. Capitalist Restructuring,
Globalisation and the Third Way**
Lessons from the Swedish model
J. Magnus Ryner

**6. Transnational Capitalism and the
Struggle over European Integration**
Bastiaan van Apeldoorn

7. World Financial Orders
An historical international political
economy
Paul Langley

**8. The Changing Politics of Finance in
Korea and Thailand**
From deregulation to debacle
Xiaoke Zhang

**9. Anti-Immigrantism in Western
Democracies**
Statecraft, desire and the politics of
exclusion
Roxanne Lynn Doty

The Transnational Politics of Corporate Governance Regulation

**Edited by Henk Overbeek,
Bastiaan van Apeldoorn
and Andreas Nölke**

Taylor & Francis Group

LONDON AND NEW YORK

First published 2007
by Routledge
2 Park Square, Milton Park, Abingdon, Oxon OX14 4RN

Simultaneously published in the USA and Canada
by Routledge
270 Madison Ave, New York, NY 10016

*Routledge is an imprint of the Taylor & Francis Group, an informa
business*

Typeset in Times New Roman by
HWA Text and Data Management, Tunbridge Wells
Printed and bound in Great Britain by
MPG Books Ltd, Bodmin

British Library Cataloguing in Publication Data
A catalogue record for this book is available from the British Library

Library of Congress Cataloging-in-Publication Data
The transnational politics of corporate governance regulation / edited by
Henk Overbeek, Bastiaan van Apeldoorn, and Andreas Nölke.
    p. cm. – (Ripe series in global political economy)
Includes bibliographical references and index.
1. Corporate governance–Political aspects. 2. International relations.
I. Overbeek, Henk. II. Apeldoorn, Bastiaan van. III. Nölke, Andreas,
1963–
HD2741.T63 2007
338.6–dc22   2006102082

ISBN10: 0–415–43172–7 (hbk)
ISBN10: 0–203–94668–5 (ebk)

ISBN13: 978–0–415–43172–9 (hbk)
ISBN13: 978–0–203–94668–8 (ebk)

Contents

Illustrations

Figures

Tables

Contributors

Wladimir Andreff. Professor at the University Paris 1 Panthéon Sorbonne, vice-president of the French Economic Association, honorary president of the International Association of Sport Economists. Andreff has published 22 books and 350 articles in economics journals in the areas of the economics of transition, privatization and corporate governance, the European Union enlargement, foreign direct investment and multinational corporations, and the economics of sports. He recently authored *La mutation des économies postsocialistes. Une analyse économique alternative* (L'Harmattan, 2003); *Les multinationales globales* (La Découverte 2003) and edited *Analyses économiques de la transition* (La Découverte, 2002); *Privatisation and Structural Change in Transition Economies* (Palgrave, 2003); *La transition vers le marché et la démocratie: Europe de l'Est, Europe centrale et Afrique du Sud* (La Découverte, 2006) and, with S. Szymanski, *The Handbook of the Economics of Sport* (Edward Elgar, 2006).

Ian Dewing and **Peter Russell**. Senior Lecturers in Accounting, Norwich Business School, University of East Anglia, Norwich, UK. Research interests include the regulation of financial accounting, auditing and corporate governance, and the supervision of the financial services industry, at national, European and international levels. Recent joint publications are: 'Regulation of UK corporate governance: lessons from accounting, auditing and financial services' (in *Corporate Governance: An International Review*, 2004), 'Accounting, auditing and corporate governance of European listed companies: EU policy developments before and after Enron' (in *Journal of Common Market Studies*, 2004) and *The Role of Auditors, Reporting Accountants and Skilled Persons in UK Financial Services Supervision* (Institute of Chartered Accountants of Scotland, 2005).

Peter Gourevitch. Professor of Political Science, Graduate School of International Relations and Pacific Studies, UCSD, La Jolla, CA. PhD from Harvard in 1969, undergraduate at Oberlin College. Assistant and Associate Professor at Harvard 1969–74, and Associate Professor at McGill from 1974–9, at UCSD since 1979. Author of *Politics in Hard Times: Comparative Responses to International Economic Crises* (Cornell University Press, 1986); winner of Guggenheim Fellowship, Russell Sage Foundation Fellowship, Fellow at the Center for Advanced Study, elected to American Academy of Arts and Sciences. His most recent book is *Political Power and Corporate Control: The New Global Politics of Corporate Governance* with James Shinn (Princeton University Press, 2005).

Laura Horn. PhD student at the Department of Political Science at the Vrije Universiteit, Amsterdam. In the framework of the Amsterdam Research Centre for Corporate Governance Regulation (ARCCGOR), her research focuses on the transformation of corporate governance regulation in the European Union. She is the co-author (with Bastiaan van Apeldoorn) of a forthcoming article entitled 'The marketization of European corporate control: a critical political economy perspective' in *New Political Economy*. Her current research interest is on the role of experts in the regulatory process within corporate governance in the EU.

Bob Jessop. Director of the Institute for Advanced Studies and Professor of Sociology at Lancaster University, UK. He is best known for his contributions to state theory, critical political economy, the regulation approach, and critical realism. He is currently working on the contradictions of the knowledge-based economy. His recent publications include: *The Future of the Capitalist State* (2002), *Beyond the Regulation Approach* (with Ngai-Ling Sum, 2006), and *State Power* (forthcoming, 2007). Further details of his publications and current work are available at his home page: www.lancs.ac.uk/fss/sociology/staff/jessop/jessop.htm.

Andreas Nölke. Professor of Political Science at the Institut für Politikwissenschaft of the Johann Wolfgang Goethe-Universität, Frankfurt am Main, where he teaches international relations and international political economy. He is also Programme Coordinator at the Amsterdam Research Centre for Corporate Governance Regulation (ARCCGOR). His most recent publications include: *Transnational Private Governance* (Routledge, 2007 – with J.C. Graz, eds) and a special issue of *Business and Politics* on the globalization of accounting standards (ed. 2005).

Henk Overbeek. Professor of International Relations in the Department of Political Science of the Vrije Universiteit, Amsterdam. In 2003 he co-founded the Amsterdam Research Centre for Corporate Governance Regulation (ARCCGOR). He received his PhD in 1988 from the University of Amsterdam, where he taught until 1999 when he moved to the Vrije Universiteit. His publications include *Global Capitalism and National Decline: Restructuring Hegemony in the Global Political Economy* (ed.), *The Political Economy of European Employment* (ed.), and *Hegemonie und internationale Arbeitsteilung*.

James Perry is a doctoral researcher in the Political Science department of the Vrije Universiteit, Amsterdam. Working as part of the Amsterdam Research

Centre for Corporate Governance Regulation team, his research examines the link between accounting standards, their governance, and changing patterns of capital accumulation – particularly the growth of the 'knowledge economy' and financialization. Perry's recent research has been published in the *Review of International Political Economy* and *Business and Politics*. He holds an MA in Global Political Economy (Sussex, UK) and also in Economics (CEU Budapest, Hungary).

Antoine Rebérioux. Associate Professor at the University of Paris X – Nanterre, where he received a PhD in Economics in 2002. He is member of the research centre EconomiX in Paris. Current research interests lie at the intersection of corporate governance and industrial relations. In particular, he is interested in the financialization of the business firm and its impact on worker involvement and human resource management. He is the author (with Michel Aglietta) of *Corporate Governance Adrift. A Critique of Shareholder Value* (Edward Elgar, 2005). He also has several articles published in academic journals, including the *Revue Economique* and the *Journal of Common Market Studies*.

Bastiaan van Apeldoorn. Reader in International Relations at the Vrije Universiteit, Amsterdam, co-founder and programme co-coordinator of the Amsterdam Research Centre for Corporate Governance Regulation (ARCCGOR). He received his PhD in the social and political sciences from the European University Institute in Florence in 1999, and was a postdoctoral fellow at the Max Planck Institute for the Study of Societies in Cologne before joining the Department of Political Science at the Vrije Universiteit in 2000. His research focuses on the transnational political economy of European integration wihtin the context of changing global social relations. Van Apeldoorn has published widely in the combined fields of International Political Economy and European integration studies, and is the author of *Transnational Capitalism and the Struggle over European Integration* (Routledge, 2002) as well as of several articles, amongst others, in the *Journal of European Public Policy* and *New Political Economy*.

Arjen Vliegenthart studied political science and history at the Vrije Universiteit, Amsterdam and the Freie Universität (Berlin). Arjan Vliegenthart was junior lecturer at the department of political science of the Vrije Universiteit from 2003 until 2005. Currently he is working within the framework of the Amsterdam Research Centre for Corporate Governance Regulation on his PhD on the political dimension of the developments in corporate governance regulation in Central and Eastern Europe, that is, the former Visegrád group.

Angela Wigger. PhD candidate at the Amsterdam Research Centre for Corporate Governance Regulation at the Political Science Department, Vrije Universiteit, Amsterdam. Her areas of interest and specialization are European and global competition laws and practices, International Political Economy, and European Union Politics. Her most recent publication is in the *Journal of Common Market Studies* (2007)

Series editors' preface

The study of the global political economy has long been concerned with advancing understanding of the nature of the corporation in a changing world. In a world that is said to be globalizing, how are we to comprehend the changing dynamics within which corporations interact – with each other, with banks, accounting houses and other regulatory bodies, with the nation-state and, not least, with shareholders, workers and with societies? In recent times, with high profile crises of corporate governance such as Enron and Parmalat, there has been renewed interest in precisely how it is that particular modes of corporate governance come into being. Yet, despite the obvious need for social science to engage critically with the specific aspects of shifting corporate governance structures, there has been an almost complete absence of attention to the cross-cutting governance structures and norms within which the firm – and indeed production and working practices – are situated. How, for example, is the US Sarbanes-Oxley (Sox) Act concretely reconfiguring the corporate governance terrain? How has the expertise of the 'Big Four' audit houses come to be established as transnational private authority in corporate governance?

What is needed, argue the authors in *The Transnational Politics of Corporate Governance Regulation*, is a detailed analysis of the multi-layered *politics* of corporate governance transformation. In this comprehensive and critical volume we find a refreshing departure from what has become the prevailing 'common sense' knowledge of corporate governance practices. Clearly establishing and critiquing the depoliticized nature of much of the 'law and economics tradition' in corporate governance, the authors intervene in the debates about best practice in corporate governance. Arguing that many contemporary accounts actually bring about the effects – of the primacy of shareholder value, the discipline of market forces, and so on – which they seek to analyse, this volume revalues the contingency of particular modes of corporate governance regulation. How does one route into corporate governance regulation come to achieve transnational influence and authority? What are the specific common trajectories that emerge from diverse contexts?

Here we have an important and fine-grained series of analyses of corporate governance regulation in different settings and from diverse theoretical perspectives. At the same time, the book offers cutting-edge frameworks for thinking through the problems of multiple sites and authorities of corporate governance. What all of the contributions to this volume achieve is a combination of empirically rich and situated analysis and the opening up of new political questions. The book is concerned to ask 'cui bono?' (who benefits?) in the political struggles and contests that shape corporate governance policy. The picture that emerges is one that scholars of the global political economy will find illuminating and challenging – a transnational mode of governance that extends across multiple scales, from the often private regulation associated with the 'global', to the European and national governance arenas. If we are to understand the transnational extension of market principles in the form and content of corporate governance, then this book cautions us to relocate politics at the heart of our analysis.

We are confident that *The Transnational Politics of Corporate Governance Regulation* will be identified with leading edge scholarship in contemporary international political economy and, indeed, across the social sciences. The questions raised here are crucial to our times, they demand our attention and they are certain to open up new areas of debate and new possibilities for inquiry.

Louise Amoore
Randall Germain
Rorden Wilkinson

February 2007

Acknowledgements

The Amsterdam Research Centre for Corporate Governance Regulation (ARCCGOR) was established in the Department of Political Science of the Vrije Universiteit, Amsterdam in April 2004. Funding for research at ARCCGOR comes from the Netherlands Organisation for Scientific Research (NWO) within the 'Shifts in Governance' Programme and from the Faculty of Social Sciences at the Vrije Universiteit. We are very thankful for the help we received in the early stages of drafting the project from Sander Chan, and from Jan Klaassen, our co-applicant in the original application for research funding.

The original idea for this book was born during the inaugural workshop celebrating the establishment of ARCCGOR held in December 2004. Funding for the workshop came from NWO, the Netherlands Institute of Government, the Faculty of Social Sciences and the Department of Political Science at the Vrije Universiteit. In the organization of ARCCGOR as well as in the preparation of the workshop we were greatly assisted by Suying Lai: thank you so much for all your help, Suying!

Most chapters were first discussed as papers at this conference. We are grateful to all participants for their input: in particular we thank (in alphabetical order) József Böröcz, Cees Camfferman, Dagmar Eberle, Meindert Fennema, Luc Franssen, Eelke Heemskerk, Michael Ellman, Martin Höpner, Dimitrios Katsikas, Jan Klaassen, Susanne Lutz, Daniel Mügge, Sol Picciotto, Tony Porter, Stuart Shields and Geoffrey Underhill.

Many contributions to the book have repeatedly been discussed within the ARCCGOR programme. For manifold input the editors are very grateful to Laura Horn, James Perry, Arjan Vliegenthart and Angela Wigger.

We thank Taylor & Francis Ltd, the *Review of International Political Economy* (RIPE) and Colin Hay for permission to reprint Figure 11.1. The figure was first published as Figure 4 in 'Common Trajectories, Variable Paces, Divergent Outcomes? Models of European Capitalism Under Conditions of Complex Economic Interdependence' by Colin Hay in *Review of International Political Economy*, 11(2), 2004. Taylor & Francis Ltd, www.tandf.co.uk/journals, reprinted by permission of the publisher.

Three anonymous referees have provided very valuable comments on an earlier version of the manuscript: we are grateful for their careful and conscientious reading.

We also thank the editors of the RIPE Series in Global Political Economy for their feedback on the manuscript and for their support for the project, and Harriet Brinton and Heidi Bagtazo at Routledge for their efficiency and support.

In the preparation of the manuscript we were awarded an 'NIG Editing Grant' for which we would like to express our gratitude.

Antoinette Lloyd-Wolkowiski and Richard Lloyd are thanked for their invaluable assistance in turning the manuscript into intelligible English. Gea Wijers finally is thanked warmly for her priceless editorial assistance: thank each of you very much!

Finally, the editors wish to acknowledge the support of their families. Given the special burden put on their patience and support by Andreas' long-distance commuting, a special word of thanks is due to Andrea, Anouk and Antonia Nölke.

Abbreviations

ARCCGOR	Amsterdam Research Centre for Corporate Governance Regulation
BCBS	Basel Committee on Banking Supervision
BIS	Bank for International Settlements
BMC	banking and managerial control
CAG	Competitiveness Advisory Group
CAPM	Capital Asset Pricing Model
CEEC	Central and East European countries
CEO	chief executive officer
CFI	European Court of First Instance
CFO	chief financial officer
CIS	Commonwealth of Independent States
CME	Co-ordinated Market Economy
CNC	National Accounting Council (*Conseil National de la Comptabilité*)
COIC	control by an outsider–insider coalition
DG	(EC) Directorate-General
DoJ	(US) Department of Justice
DRSC	Deutsches Rechnungslegungs Standards Committee
EBRD	European Bank for Reconstruction and Development
EC	European Community
ECE	East Central Europe
ECJ	European Court of Justice
ECN	European Competition Network
EEC	European Economic Community
EFRAG	European Financial Reporting Advisory Group
EMU	European Monetary Union
EP	European Parliament
ERT	European Round Table of Industrialists
ESUC	employee and start up control
EU	European Union
EVA	economic value added
FASB	Financial Accounting Standards Board

FCC	foreign corporate control
FDI	foreign direct investment
FIG	financial-industrial group
FSAP	Financial Services Action Plan
FT	France Télécom
FTC	US Federal Trade Commission
GAAP	Generally Accepted Accounting Principles
HGB	Handelsgesetzbuch
HLG	High Level Group of Company Law Experts
IAASB	International Auditing and Assurance Standards Board
IAIS	International Association of Insurance Supervisors
IASB	International Accounting Standards Board
IASC Foundation	International Accounting Standards Committee Foundation
IFAC	International Federation of Accountants
IFRS	International Financial Reporting Standards
IMF	International Monetary Fund
IOSCO	International Association of Securities Supervisors
IPE	international political economy
ISAs	International Standards on Auditing
LME	Liberal Market Economy
M&A	mergers and acquisitions
MBO	management buy-out
MEBO	management and employee buy-out
MSP	Minority Shareholder Protections
MVA	market value-added
NCA	national competition authority
NGO	non-governmental organization
NSA	non-state actor
NWO	Netherlands Organisation for Scientific Research
OECD	Organization for Economic Co-operation and Development
PCAOB	(US) Public Company Accounting Oversight Board
PET	postsocialist economy in transition
PIF	Privatization Investment Fund
QCL	quality of corporate law
RA	regulation approach
R&D	research and development
ROA	return on asset
ROE	return on equity
S&P	Standard & Poor's
SEC	(US) Securities and Exchange Commission
SME	small and medium-sized enterprise
SOA	(US) Sarbanes-Oxley Act 2002
SOE	state-owned enterprise
SPD	Sozialdemokratische Partei Deutschland (Social Democratic Party Germany)

SPE	special purpose entity
TEC	Treaty Establishing the European Community
TNC	transnational company
UMTS	Universal Mobile Telecommunications System
UNCTAD	United Nations Conference on Trade and Development
UNICE	Union of Industrial and Employers' Confederation of Europe
US GAAP	US Generally Accepted Accounting Principles
USGAO	United States General Accounting Office
VBM	value based management
VoC	varieties of capitalism
WACC	weighted average cost of capital
WB	World Bank

1 The transnational politics of corporate governance regulation

Introducing key concepts, questions and approaches

Bastiaan van Apeldoorn, Andreas Nölke and Henk Overbeek

Introduction

Who controls the modern corporation, how is it 'governed' and for what purpose? These central questions of what is now called *corporate* governance have been debated since the modern corporation or joint-stock company became the dominant unit of capitalist production. They are also recurrent questions in the ongoing debates on the nature of contemporary capitalism. They came to the fore again, for instance, in the US in the 1980s when a flurry of takeover activity and so called leveraged buy-outs (Jensen 1993) awakened the dormant market for corporate control and strengthened shareholder power (Useem 1993). Questions of corporate governance received even bigger, and worldwide, attention in the wake of the 2001 collapse of US energy giant Enron and other corporate scandals, for example, Ahold, Parmalat. In the European context, we can now observe an emerging transnational debate (somewhat reminiscent of the earlier US debate) on the role of, in particular, hedge funds and private equity funds in taking control over 'our' (where 'we' is normally defined in national terms) corporations.[1] What is often absent from these debates, however, is sustained attention to the question of what has enabled these apparent shifts in corporate control, or more broadly, corporate governance. The starting point for this book is that a key role here is played by *regulation*, and that here, long before Enron (cf. Hopt 2002; Lannoo and Khachaturyan 2003; Wouters 2000), a major transformation within different socio-economic settings is taking place. Crucially, these regulatory changes take place not only within various national jurisdictions, but also at different and interacting levels of governance.[2]

Whereas much of the corporate governance literature derives from and is focused upon the US and the UK, or presents comparative national case studies, this book has a wider scope. Although by and large restricted to the Organization for Economic Co-operation and Development (OECD) area, its geographical scope extends beyond the usual Anglo-Saxon focus well into the whole European arena and beyond. At the same time, the scope of our research extends beyond the (cross-) national by analyzing regulatory change in transnational and global settings.

At the global level, for instance, private bodies such as the International Accounting Standards Board (IASB) set important corporate governance standards (Dewing and Russell 2004, and this volume), and international organizations like the OECD disseminate norms for good corporate governance (OECD 2004). With regard to European governance, the European Union (EU) is paying increasing attention to the area of corporate governance as part and parcel of its ongoing efforts to integrate Europe's financial markets and to promote the restructuring of European industry as based on market-liberal principles (Bieling and Steinhilber 2002; Bieling 2003). Within the European arena we may note the special position of the Central and East European countries (CEEC) as they have been exposed to multiple transnational pressures by both global institutions and by the EU when developing their corporate governance structures (Grabbe 2003).

Although there is by now an enormous body of academic literature on corporate governance, much of it is either highly normative or focused on corporate governance practices at the level of the firm. This book then, seeks to go beyond this by presenting a number of studies aimed at explaining the current transformation of both the content and mode of corporate governance regulation. We take regulation as our main explanandum as we deem it critical in understanding the practice of corporate governance. Focusing on the regulation of corporate governance, this book thus emphasizes the political nature of corporate governance. Doing so, we believe, takes us beyond much of the current literature on corporate governance, in which many of the changes taking place in corporate governance are rather taken for granted. Instead, this book seeks to explore the political economy of corporate governance regulation by asking how, why and in what form certain regulation has come about.

The point-of-departure for this book has thus been that shifts in corporate governance are to a significant extent shaped by shifts in political governance, that is, by shifts in the regulation of corporate governance set within a broader politico-economic and politico-ideological context. As different regimes of corporate governance (regulation) serve different social constituencies, that is, have a different social purpose, a central question we must thus pose in analyzing the current transformation of corporate governance regulation is whether we can observe a clear shift in terms of who benefits from changes in the way corporate governance is regulated. Indeed, the *cui bono* question is a central concern of this book and informs our analysis of the politics of changing corporate governance regulation. This then expresses a concern with the changing content of corporate governance regulation. In this respect this book draws upon, and seeks to contribute to, the long-standing debate within comparative and international political economy on to what extent globalization (and regionalization, for example, Europeanization) leads to a convergence of (national) models of capitalism (see, for example, Berger and Dore 1996; Drache and Boyer 1996; Crouch and Streeck 1997; Garret 1998; Hall and Soskice 2001a; Ryner 2002; Hay 2004; Crouch 2005). We seek, however, to go beyond most of this vast body of literature in two ways. First, rather than adopting a cross-national comparative perspective describing patterns of convergence or divergence within national corporate governance regimes, this book adopts a transnational and multilevel perspective emphasizing the common elements of structural changes (as they emanate from common origins at different levels of governance) taking place across national varieties, even when recognizing the nationally diverse ways in which this process of transnational transformation manifests itself. Second, rather than merely describing these changes, and assessing to what extent they reveal convergence, we seek to explain these changes.

Another major focus of this book concerns the form or mode of regulation. Indeed, a critical point of departure for our analysis is the observation that in particular the last 15 years or so have witnessed a profound transnationalization of corporate governance regulation inasmuch as some elements of regulation have shifted upward to the regional and global levels (partly in the form of private governance) whereas other elements remain at the national level yet are to a large extent transformed by what is taking place on these other scales of governance. In other words, whereas the regulation of corporate governance used to be a distinctly national affair, it is now increasingly an area subject to both public and private (self-) regulation in multiple arenas. In highlighting the interplay of global, European, and national governance arenas, we build upon, but at the same time move beyond, the various (global, European, multilevel) governance bodies of literature (Held and McGrew 2002; Hewson and Sinclair 1999; Hooghe and Marks 2001). Generally speaking, most of this literature concentrates on the mode of governance, i.e. on the various interlinked levels at which governance occurs (often outside or beyond the sphere of the state and intergovernmental bodies); on the nature of the actors involved in the governance process (concretely, often highlighting the enhanced role of non-governmental actors in governance), and finally on the informality and networked nature of these new forms of governance. What is mostly lacking in these newer governance studies is an awareness of and sustained attention for the idea that form and content are highly interrelated. In our view, the new modes of governance cannot be understood properly unless they are linked integrally to the content, the social purpose, of governance. Form and content, mode and social purpose are intricately interlinked, interdependent and mutually constitutive. A central argument of this book, and one that we will return to explicitly in the concluding chapter, is that both the content and the form of current corporate governance regulation reflect a strengthening of market principles, promoting the mobility of capital.

The remainder of this introductory chapter is organized as follows. The next section clarifies the key concepts that make up the focus of this book. We then briefly review the relevant literature on corporate governance regulation, indicating its limits with respect to the purposes of this book. Building upon that, the third section then presents the core questions and approaches of our own research agenda. The final section outlines how the central research questions will be addressed through the four main parts of the book.

Corporate governance regulation in multiple arenas: defining key concepts

Corporate governance can be broadly defined as the way the modern capitalist corporation is 'governed', that is, by whom (the issue of corporate control) and for whom, to which purpose. As such, it refers to the institutionalized practices that are both the medium and outcome of the power relations between the various actors that have a stake in the modern corporation: shareholders (or more broadly, capital, which may also include creditors) managers, and workers (cf. Aguilera and Jackson 2003: 450; Cioffi 2005: 4; Hopt *et al.* 1999: 5). In other words, corporate governance is a set of practices constituted by underlying power relations within the firm while the latter are at the same time also reproduced by these practices.[3]

Although the discourse of corporate governance has only become popular since the 1990s (cf. Erturk *et al.* 2004), corporate governance issues, as referring to prevailing power configurations within the firm, are as old as the modern corporation, or joint-stock company, itself, that is, what has come to be the dominant unit of capitalist production since the end of the nineteenth century (Roy 1997). It is with the advent of the modern corporation, and therefore with the potential separation of ownership and control (Berle and Means (1991 [1932]), or at least of ownership and management, that, that what is now called corporate governance has come to be regarded by many as a 'problem' requiring certain regulatory and technical solutions. The problem here, at least since the 1970s, has often been defined primarily in terms of how shareholders could safeguard their investment, i.e. prevent management from 'squandering' it, and the solution advocated has thus been that of strengthening 'internal' and above all 'external' shareholder control (see, for example, Fama and Jensen 1983b). Although we reject this neoclassical definition of the problem (see below), and its proposed solution, we share the notion that it is the struggle over control (see, for example, Becht *et al.* 2002; O'Sullivan 2000b; Berle and Means 1991 [1932]) that is at the heart of corporate governance, and that this struggle within capitalism has been primarily a struggle between (different groups of) owners and managers. Hence, in this respect we may deem the shareholder-management relation as central, even if in some regimes of corporate governance labour also exercises real, if limited, control over the strategic decision making within a corporation, and even if, regardless of any institutionalized role of labour, the social relations between both management and workers on the one hand, and shareholders (owners) and workers on the other, are a critical constituent part of the relationship between management and shareholders.

Corporate governance as a practice is, like any social practice, rule-governed. Yet the rules of corporate governance in this sense can be seen as internal to the corporation. Thus there might be certain internal rules that constitute a certain division of power between the executive and supervisory directors. Another internal rule maybe one that sets certain targets with regard to the return on capital (part of what is nowadays referred to as 'shareholder value', see on this Höpner

2003a). If we speak of the regulation of corporate governance we, however, refer to something that is external to the corporation and its governance, yet shapes that governance to a very significant extent. Thus we refer to the regulation of corporate governance practice.

Regulation we here define broadly as all forms of formal and informal rule making pertaining to some collective (nations, groups, sectors) where those rules are either binding to the members of that collective or at least significantly constrain their behaviour. This involves both public and private (self-) regulation, the latter reflecting the rise of what has been dubbed private authority in the global political economy (Cutler 1999; Hall and Biersteker 2002a). With regard to public regulation it includes 'softer' (in the sense of not legally binding) forms of regulation such as policy co-ordination and benchmarking, as practiced most notably by the EU, but also by for example the OECD. Regulation defined this way shapes the framework in which corporate governance takes place. It defines the legal, institutional and discursive parameters, both constraining and enabling the agency of those actors (shareholders, managers, creditors, employees, etc.) that ultimately shape the governance of a particular firm.

In order to clarify the distinction between corporate governance practice and corporate governance regulation, and how the latter affects the former, Table 1.1 below lists a number of examples (most of which are discussed in this book) of regulation of corporate governance and concomitant corporate governance practices. Within the domain of public law, we may include securities (or capital market) law, company law and labour law as the main domains in which regulation directly affects corporate governance. In addition, we may identify different forms of self-regulation. We must note that although these distinctions, such as between public and private (self-) regulation, have some analytical value, the lines between them get, and arguably increasingly so, blurred in practice. Similarly, many forms of regulation extend across several of the domains of public law or are difficult to classify in any one of them. For instance, the European takeover directive, which used to be seen as primarily an instance of (harmonization of) company law, has increasingly been framed as part and parcel of European financial market

Table 1.1 The relationship between corporate governance regulation and practice

Corporate governance **regulation**	Corporate governance **practice**
Securities/capital market law: disclosure rules, proxy rules	e.g. Bank-based or (capital) market-based financial systems
Company law: internal firm structure, take-over regulation	Managerial discretion, shareholder or stakeholder protection
Labour law: co-determination (works council/supervisory board)	Strength/weakness of employees as stakeholders
Private regulation: accounting standards	Degree of transparency of financial reporting for capital markets

Source: adapted and modified from Cioffi (2005).

integration, and thus has also been regarded as an instance of securities or capital market law (see the contribution by Van Apeldoorn and Horn to this book).

As indicated, the regulation of corporate governance takes place in multiple arenas. Here we may distinguish between the global, the regional and the national arena. In all of these arenas we can find examples of corporate governance regulation made by both public and private actors. This is illustrated in Table 1.2 below with some examples taken from the present book. Looking at some of these examples we can indeed see how both the different arenas as well as the public and private modes of regulation are interrelated. Take for instance the case of International Financial Reporting Standards (IFRS). Whereas these standards have, as we have just seen, been set at the global level by a private body (the IASB), they have subsequently been adopted by the public authorities of the EU at the regional level based on the recommendation of again a private committee, the European Financial Reporting Advisory Group (EFRAG), replacing different national accounting standards. Starting at the bottom end, the Sarbanes-Oxley act is an example of purely national regulation with global repercussions (see contributions by Rebérioux and Dewing and Russell to this book).

As indicated, in our view it is 'the transnational' that accounts for how the different levels and arenas are interrelated and interconnected. Thus we argue that in order to capture the multilevel phenomenon of changing corporate governance regulation, we have to move beyond national case studies or cross-national comparisons and adopt instead an integrated transnational approach in which we examine how corporate governance regulation is changing across interacting arenas of governance. What, then, do we mean by transnational? In the context of this book, our understanding of 'transnational' is of a dual nature. In the first instance, building upon the well-known work on transnational politics of the 1970s (see Keohane and Nye 1971), transnational relations are defined as 'regular interactions across national boundaries when at least one actor is a non-state agent or does not operate on behalf of a national government or of an intergovernmental organization' (Risse-Kappen 1995: 3; for an elaboration see Nölke 2004a). This definition focuses primarily on the actors involved in transnational politics. Alternatively, we may also define 'transnational' by focusing primarily on political processes and structures: in this view these are constituted in a social space transcending national borders, i.e. their dynamics are not fundamentally defined by the existence of national boundaries, and occur

Table 1.2 Multiple arenas of corporate governance regulation

	Public	*Private*
Global	OECD principles	International Financial Reporting Standards (IFRS)
Regional	EU Takeover Directive	Recommendation of adoption of IFRS by EFRAG
National	Sarbanes-Oxley	German Corporate Governance Code (Cromme Commission)

simultaneously in sub-national, national and international arenas. As such, 'the transnational' can be viewed as transcending, different (territorial) 'levels'; it is a multilevel phenomenon by definition. In these conditions, the 'national' no longer provides the primary constitutive dimension of politics (for an elaboration see Overbeek 2000, 2003; van Apeldoorn 2004a). In the remainder of this book, both the agency of transnational actors and the salience of transnational processes and structures provide a reference point for the different contributions, albeit in quite different forms, and with different degrees of centrality. Although some of the individual chapters may focus on a particular 'level' rather than integrating those 'levels', the book as a whole seeks to show how corporate governance regulation indeed takes place at different levels, or as we prefer to call it, within multiple and interrelated arenas.

Taking politics seriously: a critique of the corporate governance literature

Within the continuously expanding corporate governance body of literature, we may distinguish two strands of literature that have a direct relevance for the analysis of the regulation of corporate governance. First, we can identify a body of literature, deriving mainly from law and economics, with a highly normative and prescriptive (implicit or explicit) orientation. Rather than seeking to explain (changing) corporate governance regulation, this body of literature seeks to identify the 'best' regulation. In contrast, a second body of literature, extending into various disciplines of the social sciences, adopts a more explanatory perspective, underlining the political underpinnings of corporate governance. Although growing, research of the second type is still relatively scarce, especially research that takes corporate governance regulation as its main explanandum. Even scarcer, we argue, is research that not only offers an empirically grounded explanation of the regulation of corporate governance, but also seeks to extend its analysis across various levels of governance. We will now have a closer critical look at each of these bodies of literature in turn.

Law and economics: Legitimating the 'standard model'

The literature within legal studies is usually the most explicit in its normative and prescriptive agenda. Some authors argue in favour of giving more voice to stakeholders (for example, Blair 1995; Ireland 1996; Deakin 2002). Others, indeed an overwhelming majority, focus on the question of how to (legally) enhance the (property) rights of shareholders (see, for example, Black 2001; Baums and Scott 2003), especially so-called minority shareholders such as institutional investors (see, for example, Black 1992; Baums and Buxbaum 1994; Coffee 1991). A clear illustration of this normative perspective may be found in an often quoted paper that (notwithstanding the weight of divergent legal traditions) predicts the convergence of corporate law on the basis of a strong ideological consensus in favour of (absolute) shareholder primacy. The authors claim that, in the context of growing global competition, this 'standard model' normatively speaking has 'no important competitors' left (Hansmann and Kraakman 2001: 50).[4] On the basis of this normative superiority, then, we will witness the inevitable and at the same time desirable 'end of history for corporate law' (Hansmann and Kraakman 2001; cf. Coffee 1999a; Gordon and Roe 2004).

We may also note that, although some of this literature is comparative, most of it is focused on the US, reflecting that country's longer history of shareholder activism, and, recently, the impact of Enron and the legal reforms (especially the Sarbanes-Oxley Ac) that have been undertaken in response (for example, Coffee 2003). Furthermore, inasmuch as what Gourevitch calls the 'law-and-economics' tradition (see his contribution to this book; and Gourevitch 2003) puts forward any explanatory claims (see especially La Porta *et al.* 1998), it treats existing differences in the legal and regulatory framework as rather exogenous (to the politics of corporate governance), and simply deriving from given differences in legal tradition, such as common law versus civil law. Law here is thus treated as an apolitical realm, an autonomous force that, as such, needs no further explanation (see, for a more elaborate discussion, Gourevitch's contribution to this book).

Although purportedly intended to explain the varied behaviour of firms and the varied performance of economies under different systems of corporate governance, much work in the economics discipline is (implicitly) also rather normative in orientation. Indeed it could be argued that the work of US finance professors in this respect has provided some of the initial key intellectual and discursive underpinnings of the 'standard model' (cf. Erturk *et al.* 2004: 684; Froud *et al.* 2000: 87–8). Around this initial work a strong normative consensus has been emerging since the 1990s (see, for example, the contribution by Rebérioux to this book), although in our view this development is far from inevitable and certainly does not lead to an 'end of history', as if any opposition has been neutralized for ever. Important here is the argument that politically some of the academic work in economics has been rather instrumental in fostering this consensus. Especially so-called agency theory (notwithstanding its elegance and value as an analytical theory) is based on the highly normative assumption that a firm is no more than a piece of property owned by its shareholders (Jensen and Meckling 1976; Fama and Jensen 1983b; Jensen 1993; Shleifer and Vishny 1996) whose rational interest is to maximize the cash flow (i.e. 'shareholder value' (Rappaport 1986)) flowing from those property titles. Any institutional arrangement that makes managers, as the agents of shareholders, behave in a way that does not maximize the interest of the principal, for instance by seeking to serve other interests, such as those of employees or the long-term survival of the firm, as well, is therefore considered a problem.

As a solution to the problem of managers not maximizing shareholders' returns, agency theory puts much emphasis on the external discipline imposed by liquid capital markets and above all an active market for corporate control. Although we do not dispute that, under these conditions, such control mechanisms as identified by agency theorists do indeed shape and constrain the behaviour of managers, the problem with agency theory in our view is rather, as Van Apeldoorn and Horn argue in their contribution to this book, that it tends to treat these mechanisms apolitically and ahistorically – that is, it tends to take them as given, or in their absence, takes their desirability as given rather than seeking to explain how and why they have come about. Indeed, it naturalizes that which in fact is highly political and historically contingent, namely a regime of corporate governance in which the firm, in effect a complex social institution, is treated as representing no more than a nexus of contracts establishing the absolute primacy of shareholders. Given this normative bias, agency theory also fails to account, as Aguilera and Jackson (2003: 448) point out, for the variety (across time and space) of corporate governance regimes, or the different institutional ways in which 'agency problems' are solved. In continental Europe, for example, traditionally, the dominance of large blockholders ensured, and to some extent still does, that owner control can be exercised much more directly (see Gourevitch's contribution to this book). In sum, agency theory simply does not offer any explanation of (the given variety of) corporate governance regulation, or of how and why that regulation may be changing – rather it simply posits the superiority of one particular governance model.

Social science research pertaining to corporate governance

Going beyond the normative concern of much of the law-and-economics literature (which may to some extent theoretically explain the effects of corporate governance regulation on corporate governance practice, but cannot explain the (political) origins of that regulation) there is a gradually developing second body of literature, partly originating in the law-and-economics tradition, but now expanding into political science, sociology and political economy, that adopts a more explanatory approach. As indicated, this body of literature is growing yet still modest in size, especially literature that explicitly takes corporate governance regulation as the *explanandum*.

Much research within the political and social sciences thus far has stayed either at the descriptive level, or has taken corporate governance regulation mainly as the 'independent variable' – as in a number of micro-level, and partly quantitative, studies that seek to analyze corporate governance practices at the level of the firm (see, for example, the ground-breaking research that has been undertaken within the Max Planck Institute for the Study of Societies: Höpner 2001, 2003a; Höpner and Jackson 2001; Jackson 2001; Goyer 2002; Streeck 2001). Although we recognize that ultimately the practice of corporate governance is what counts, and hence acknowledge the significance of such research, we also note that in this research the regulatory environment, as such, usually remains unexplained.

With regard to the more descriptive analyses we may mention several studies that have contributed to, and built upon, what has come to be known as the 'Varieties of Capitalism' (VoC) approach (Hall and Soskice 2001a). This literature has been very useful in developing a typology of (national) regimes of corporate governance but tends to take corporate governance regulation at best as an independent variable, not seeking to explore the politics that bring it into being.

The comparative politics of corporate governance regulation

Going beyond the limits of the above literature we now shift our focus to research seeking to explain the legal and regulatory framework as it shapes the practice of corporate governance. Although an obvious field for political analysis, political science has in fact arrived late on the academic 'corporate governance' scene. Indeed, pioneering work on the politics of corporate governance regulation in fact came from within the law-and-economics tradition, in particular the influential work of legal scholar Mark Roe (1994, 2003, 2004; see also Gourevitch 2003). In Roe's 'politics school' differences in extant national corporate governance regimes are explained in terms of their different 'political roots'. The main explanatory variable here is what Roe terms 'social democracy', which he defines as the extent of government intervention in the economy to serve distributive goals and favour labour over capital 'when they conflict' (Roe 2004: 254; 2003). He thus divides advanced capitalist states into 'social democracies' and nations where social democracy is absent, and argues that whereas in the former a 'gap' (in interests and outlook) between managers and shareholders has historically opened that subsequently has become difficult to close, in the latter (such as the US) such a gap did not arise to the same extent. Given this difference, social democratic regimes have seen the continuing concentration of ownership, with corporate governance dominated by blockholders who deem it often too risky to sell their stakes in a political (regulatory) context in which organized labour has considerable clout, for example through co-determination, and can thus potentially exercise more corporate control if ownership would be fragmented (hence given this incentive structure they choose to hold on to their large blocks). In contrast, in the absence of social-democratic political forces, ownership has become dispersed and equity markets have expanded (on this issue of ownership concentration see also the section below and the contribution by Gourevitch to this book). The causal mechanisms at play in this model are in part premised on a path-dependency argument similar also to that of the abovementioned VoC approach (see also Bebchuk and Roe 2004; Schmidt and Spindler 2004).

Apart from the point that it might be somewhat problematic to classify whole countries as 'social democratic' and attribute solely to left-labour strength the growth of particular institutions and public policies that are often the result of complex historical class compromises and cross-class coalitions (cf. Gourevitch 2003: 1846, 1859–61), work by John Cioffi and Martin Höpner (Cioffi 2005; Höpner forthcoming, Cioffi and Höpner 2006) also indicates that contrary to Roe's model in, for instance, a country like Germany it has been social-democratic political forces that have always been ideologically opposed to a German model dominated by both managerialism and the role of large blockholders, and thus were more inclined to favour more market-oriented reforms, whereas Christian Democrats have been the staunchest supporters of this model and of its concomitant economic elites. In line with this, the Social Democrats while in opposition fervently supported, and later during the first Schröder-government themselves introduced, several key market-liberal reforms of the traditionally non-liberal

German corporate governance regime (Höpner forthcoming; Cioffi 2005: 27–33). Whereas these recent publications by Cioffi and Höpner are among the still rare examples of an empirical analysis aimed at explaining contemporary corporate governance regulation 'reform', Roe's analysis, in contrast, is not concerned with accounting for such (recent) transformations of corporate governance regulation, but only seeks to provide (and test) a theoretical model explaining existing cross-national diversity.

Peter Gourevitch and James Shinn (2005), in a recent book that stands out as one of the few systematic empirical analyses of the politics of corporate governance regulation, take Roe's political analysis several steps further. Whereas Roe restricts his political variables to a simple left-right dichotomy (where the left stands for labour strength) Gourevitch and Shinn offer a more complex interest group model in which different social groups compete and also form (sometimes cross-class) coalitions. In addition, they emphasize the role of political institutions in shaping coalition formation (Gourevitch and Shinn 2005; see also Gourevitch 2003). Backed up by a wealth of statistical data, Gourevitch and Shinn seek to explain how institutionally mediated interest group politics accounts for different outcomes in terms of corporate governance policies across 39 countries (see also Gourevitch's contribution to this book). While the book by Gourevitch and Shinn in this way forms an important contribution to the body of literature, its limitation is that its focus is almost exclusively on the national level, comparing regulation and policies across national states, and, as such, is stronger in explaining historical diversity than in explaining contemporary change (even if it does pay attention there too), in particular given the multilevel character of current corporate governance regulation.

Another important contribution derives from economic sociology (see for instance Fligstein 2001; Aguilera and Jackson 2003; for a more elaborate discussion see Gourevitch's contribution to this book). Economic sociologists not only make the valuable point that all economic practices are always embedded within social relations and associated cultural frames (Fligstein 2001: 145), but also that markets are political constructs, indeed, outcomes of 'state-building' projects (Fligstein 2001; see also Roy 1997). They thus also draw our attention to how politics and public policies shape, for instance, corporate governance. Yet although making the point theoretically, much of the research in economic sociology (Fligstein's otherwise insightful work (2001) on shifting 'conceptions of control' being a case in point) in fact fails to provide much systematic analysis, and empirical evidence, of the politics of corporate governance regulation as such (cf. Fligstgein 2001: 168). Furthermore the empirically most rich and most convincing work within this tradition tends to have a rather historical focus (for example, Roy 1997). With regard to present day capitalism, most analysts are, like Fligstein (2001: 236), mainly interested in explaining why 'national organization of business persists' and diverse 'national capitalisms' are preserved, precisely as an 'overall effect' of a 'state-building process' and associated path dependencies (even if his empirical analysis focuses almost exclusively on the US). In our view, this conclusion tends to miss the qualitative changes that are now actually taking place, and which arguably become more apparent if one adopts a transnational perspective (whereas much economic sociology often remains committed to a methodological nationalism). Similarly, most economic sociological approaches also fail to account for how in fact the 'state' not only is responsible for creating and sustaining the differences but also, at different levels of governance (for instance at the supranational level of the EU as a multilevel polity), can actually be an important agent of radical regulatory change – albeit of course supported by powerful societal interests.

Critical approaches

From a radical political economy perspective, several authors within critical business and management studies have provided interesting political analyses. These authors locate what they view as the corporate governance discourse of the 1990s (as it manifested itself especially within the US and the UK) within the context of a contemporary capitalism characterized by 'financialization', as well as squarely within a political context by seeing it as reflecting a broader governance narrative that is 'part of a more general discursive attempt to combine neoliberalism with social responsibility' (Erturk *et al.* 2004: 677). Although strong in highlighting important political aspects of changing corporate governance regulation within a specific (mainly British) context, this research does not so much seek to explain concrete regulatory change.[5]

The process of financialization, or the rise of 'finance-led capitalism', is also at the heart of the analyses of shifts in corporate governance as made by a number of regulation theorists (see in particular Aglietta and Rebérioux 2005; Aglietta 2000; Boyer 2000b). As Aglietta and Rebérioux argue, regulatory change in the domain of financial market law (in particular the liberalization of financial markets accompanied by '[i]nstitutional reforms undertaken with the aim of favouring the tradability of securities and risks' (Aglietta and Rebérioux 2005: 3)) have radically changed the power relations within the firm (Aglietta and Rebérioux 2005: 1, and *passim*). While this is an important argument, to which we will return below in the context of discussing different ways of understanding the content of current changes in corporate governance regulation, research of this type tells us more about the implications of regulatory change than about its (political) origins.

Beyond explaining cross-national diversity?

In sum, to the extent that the politics of corporate governance regulation is now being taken seriously within the academic literature, most studies, if not merely focused on just one or two countries, are better in explaining existing regulatory variety across national states than in seeking to analyze and explain changes in both form and content in corporate governance regulation taking place at different levels of governance. The cross-national comparative perspective that underlies many of these studies (especially Roe 2003; Gourevitch and Shinn 2005) in our view, although very valuable, ought to be complemented with a perspective that transcends the different levels of analysis, and seeks to explain transformation of corporate governance regulation within and across multiple arenas. Hence this book also includes studies of the European, transatlantic and global arenas, and it examines how these arenas are interrelated, as well as linked to the national level, through transnational political processes.

With respect to the question of transformation, there is some literature emerging in particular out of the aforementioned 'convergence' debate, that is, a convergence of models of capitalism in response to globalization. The limited research that has been undertaken here with regard to corporate governance regulation is either extremely sceptical towards the convergence thesis (for example, Vitols 2001; Bebchuk and Roe 2004), or seems to adopt that thesis rather uncritically (for example, O'Sullivan 2000a; Hansman and Kraakman 2001; Useem 2004; cf. Gordon and Roe 2004). In neither case, however, does the evidence appear to be conclusive. Moreover, this research too does not, explicitly, take into account levels of governance beyond that of the nation-state. In a theoretical paper on the 'cross-national diversity' of corporate governance, Aguilera and Jackson (2003: 461) suggest that given 'multilevel interactions spanning from international to national and subnational policies, [and] most strikingly through the European Union' (as well as transnational interactions of 'stakeholders', such as institutional investors) '[c]onvergence and path dependence (…) may be false theoretical alternatives in trying to understand simultaneous processes of continuity and change across national boundaries'. Yet, in terms of empirical research, both with regard to corporate governance practices and certainly with regard to its changing regulation, the research agenda implied here remains largely unfulfilled.[6] This book attempts to fill this void by presenting a collection that in its entirety (if not in each chapter separately) indeed deals with the transnational multilevel politics of changing corporate governance regulation. In order to lay the theoretical groundwork for this, the next section outlines the basic elements of a transnational political economy framework that enables us to pursue such a research agenda.

Towards a transnational political economy of multilevel corporate governance regulation: Questions and approaches

In contrast to the normative-prescriptive orientation, our aim (though recognizing the important normative dimension of the subject matter) is to explore the reasons for the current transformations of corporate governance regulation. In order to come to such a fuller understanding of what is driving the current transformation of corporate governance it is crucial also to analyze the politics of corporate governance regulation. Which political processes drive the current transformation of corporate governance at different levels of governance? Which political and socio-economic actors are involved? What are their interests, and how are power-relations between them configured? What can we say about the content of the changing regulation: in other words, what is the social purpose of these changes?

We argue that in order to capture the multilevel phenomenon of changing corporate governance regulation, we have to move beyond national case studies or cross-national comparisons and adopt instead an integrated transnational approach in which we examine how corporate governance regulation is changing across interacting arenas of governance.

From this perspective, we formulate the following central question:

What explains the transformation of corporate governance regulation at different levels, and through varying modes of governance?

This central question gives rise to three sets of sub-questions:

A   What is the content of the changes taking place in corporate governance regulation in different arenas (global, EU, CEEC), and do these changes reveal convergence on a particular model or rather a continuing or increased institutional diversity?
B   How, or through what modes of regulation, and at which levels of governance, do these changes take place? Are there significant shifts in governance: from public to private and from the national to the European or global levels?
C   Why is this so? What explains both the changing content of corporate governance regulation and the changing form through which it takes place?

To develop answers for each of these questions, we can make use of a number of conceptual options that are available within the literature. Although these options are not able to provide us with ready-made solutions, they can still serve as building blocks for further conceptual development.

A: Conceptualizing the content of regulatory change

An obvious option for any further research into the content of corporate governance regulation and the question of convergence versus diversity is to identify the most important groups of actors that are affected by this type of regulation. Here we can find a number of dichotomies that structure the corporate governance debate. These are summarized in Table 1.3 below. It has to be stressed at the outset that this table only represents a number of common ideal-types, and is too much of a simplification and too dichotomous to cover the whole scope of the theoretical debate, let alone to cover the complexities of empirical reality. Moreover, it should be stressed that different dichotomies do not necessarily overlap. For instance, what we identify below as owner control may be both control by (minority) shareholders (through the stock market), and control by blockholders, leading to rather opposing models of corporate governance. Nevertheless, the table may serve as a first approximation of the different ways in which to understand the (changing) content of corporate governance regulation and associated practice.

Table 1.3 Alternative conceptualizations of the content of corporate governance regulation

Dominant actors	Owner control	Managerial control
Ownership	Dispersed	Concentrated/blockholders
Locus of control	Outsider control	Insider control
Role of workers	Shareholder primacy	Worker involvement
Variety of capitalism	Shareholder/liberal/ Anglo-Saxon	Stakeholder/coordinated/ Rhenish
Regime of accumulation	Finance-led	Production-led

The most well known of the dichotomies presented in the above table is the one of owner control versus managerial control. The *locus classicus* is here of course Berle and Means's *The Modern Corporation and Private Property* (1991 [1932]), which argued that in the wake of the corporate revolution in the US (and with the stock market developing as a 'mechanism of liquidity' (Berle 1991 [1932]: xxxiiii)) share ownership was becoming more and more fragmented, and as a result control became separated from what remained of the legal owners and ended up in the hands of managers. The managerialist thesis (see Burnham 1975 [1941]) subsequently became conventional wisdom for much of the twentieth century (cf. Scott 1997).

In contemporary literature too, the degree to which ownership is concentrated, respectively fragmented, is still considered a key variable to distinguish different regimes of corporate governance. Thus, a standard dichotomy (see for instance the contribution by Gourevitch to this book) is that between regimes where ownership is generally dispersed and those where it is concentrated into the hands of so-called large blockholders (whether other corporations, banks, families, etc.). However, it is increasingly recognized that the latter situation is not the only one in which owners can exercise control, or at least influence the management of the firm. Indeed, what is nowadays often referred to as shareholder capitalism or the shareholder model (see below) on the one hand refers to a situation in which ownership is fragmented, but at the same time to one in which the interests of shareholders have become primary over those of other stakeholders. Indeed, the problem with the managerialist thesis has always been not only that outside the US (and the UK), ownership remained relatively concentrated, but also, and crucially, that it tended to ignore that under certain institutional conditions the diffusion of ownership can actually lead towards a different form of control, that is, control exercised collectively through the market (what Aglietta and Rebérioux 2005: 81ff. call stock market control). Although shareholder control in this model is neither individual nor direct, it can nevertheless be very effective in disciplining management. Here then, the stock market is not only a mechanism for liquidity but also for external control, especially to the extent that the capital market evolves into a market for corporate control (see the contributions by Van Apeldoorn and Horn as well as Rebérioux to this book).

A related dichotomy in the literature is that between 'insider control', where large blockholders exercise control through voice, versus 'outsider control' where control is exercised by shareholders through their power of *exit* (cf. Nooteboom 1999; Hirschman 1970). Insider control remains a defining feature of many corporate governance regimes. Here, Wladimir Andreff, in his contribution to this book on the introduction of corporate governance in post-socialist economies, defines insider control as a situation in which the owner 'exerts all the prerogatives of an owner/boss, that is as chief executive officer (*usus*), as residual claimant (*usus fructus*) and as possible vendor of his/her enterprise (*abusus*)' (see Chapter 9, p. 162; see also Gourevitch's contribution to this book).

In fact, most observers claim that we are currently witnessing a shift towards shareholder primacy throughout the advanced capitalist world. Owners and management, however, are not the only forces of relevance to issues of corporate governance regulation. Although somewhat less prominent in the public and academic debate nowadays (but see Rebérioux 2002), workers tend to be involved as well, at least in some countries (think of co-determination in Austria or Germany). Thus, another dichotomy unfolds between the poles of workers' involvement and shareholder primacy (cf. Gourevitch's and Rebérioux's contributions to this book). We could thus further specify our research question as to whether we can observe a current convergence of corporate governance regulations that favour shareholder (outsider) control, and, whether as a result we can perceive a general tendency towards an erosion of workers' rights within corporate governance regulation.

An alternative way to conceptualize current changes in corporate governance regulation is to put it into the context of broader models of capitalist production systems. Here, we can distinguish between conceptualizations that distinguish synchronic variations between countries (or regions) and those that rather favour a diachronic differentiation over time. The synchronic perspective is perhaps best represented by the VoC approach (Hall and Soskice 2001) introduced above. A key premise of this analytical approach is the notion of institutional complementarities between different spheres, for example that of industrial relations, which make up divergent production regimes (Hall and Soskice 2001: 17ff.). Corporate governance, or more narrowly corporate finance, that is, the relations between firms (management) and external providers of finance (Vitols 2001: 337), can be seen as one such institutional sphere, interacting with other spheres within national political economies. Viewing varieties of capitalism under this aspect, a common and useful distinction is that between the so-called 'shareholder model' belonging to the Anglo-Saxon capitalist economies premised on the sovereignty of shareholders exercising their power through the stock exchange (constituting a market for corporate control) on the one hand, and on the other hand the 'stakeholder model' prevalent in most continental European capitalist economies, in particular within the so-called 'Rhenish' countries, in which the firm and its management are more embedded in a network of interests (see, for example, Albert 1993; De Jong 1996; La Porta *et al.* 1998; Rhodes and Van Apeldoorn 1998; Dore *et al.* 1999; Hall and Soskice 2001; Vitols 2001; Höpner 2003a; Aguilera and Jackson 2003; Aglietta and Rebérioux 2005: Chapter 3 and 4).[7]

The varieties-of-capitalism perspective has so far hardly been applied outside Western Europe and the US. For conceptualizations of corporate governance regulation in (semi-)peripheral modes of capitalism, other models are being applied, such as externally dependent neoliberal capitalism. Sometimes the early work of Alain Lipietz is referred to as an example of an attempt to categorize socio-economic orders in semi- peripheral countries (for example, Holman 2004). Although properly speaking Lipietz can not be identified as a VoC author, his work on the concept of peripheral Fordism to characterize the variety of dependent and externally oriented capitalism in such places as South America, East Asia and Southern Europe during the late 1970s and early 1980s (see Lipietz 1982, 1987) may indeed serve as a starting point for further discussion.[8]

If we wish to adopt a diachronic perspective, much of the VoC literature is (given its

a-historical focus) less helpful.[9] To the extent that the question of the transformation of corporate governance regulation across the boundaries of different varieties is addressed, the causes of change (usually discussed in terms of a possible convergence on the Anglo-Saxon model) are often treated exogenously, for example, internationalization. Following on from the notion of institutional complementarities, the VoC approach furthermore stresses that a transformation in one area, such as corporate governance, will have destabilising effects on the whole system (cf. Höpner 2003a; Lane 2003; Whitley 1999). Yet, in general, most studies adopting a VoC approach tend to stress the continuing institutional diversity across national systems.

We may finally identify a growing body of research that relates the current transformation of corporate governance regulation to the financialization of contemporary capitalism. The distinction between what we here identify as finance-led capitalism and production-led capitalism draws upon four interrelated sets of literature and theoretical approaches:

1   A literature dealing with what can be termed 'household financialization' emphasizing the way the mass of the population is both economically and politically involved in and affected by the financialization process (for example, Erturk *et al.* 2005a, 2005b; also Harmes 2001a, b);

2   A literature drawing upon the French regulation school emphasizing, and criticizing, finance-led capitalism as an alternative to the Fordist growth regime (for example, Boyer 2000b; Aglietta and Rebérioux 2005; see also Jessop in this book);

3   Research done within what has been called the Amsterdam International Political Economy Project (Van Apeldoorn 2004b) emphasizing the shift from a corporate-liberal 'concept of control' centred around a productive capital perspective to a neoliberal 'concept of control' centred around a money capital perspective; and

4   A literature drawing upon the World-System perspective identifying structural changes within the capitalist world economy associated with the rising dominance of finance (cf. Arrighi 1994; Arrighi and Silver 1999). </List>

Although financialization constitutes a transnational process bound up with the restructuring of global capitalism, according to some, implying a shift away from a more 'productionist' paradigm of accumulation, this process manifests itself to varying degrees and in varying ways within different national capitalist regimes – being the most advanced in the US and in the UK, and still weaker, although growing, in continental Europe and elsewhere (Erturk *et al.* 2004; Aglietta and Rebérioux 2005).

B: Conceptualizing the mode of regulatory change

If we turn to the mode of corporate governance regulation, two fundamental dichotomies that may help us to conceptualize current changes in corporate governance regulation are those between public and private as well as between national and global regulation. As with most other dichotomies, empirical developments more often than not fall between these poles. What, for example, is the character of the German Corporate Governance Code – developed by a private commission and backed by the federal government, not a law, but always under the threat of public regulation? Similarly, many regulations spill over the boundaries of distinct (national) jurisdictions, but still do not have universal global applicability. The most obvious example of this would be EU regulations, but the accounting standards as developed by the IASB too have a less than truly global character as of yet (see also Table 1.2 above).

Based on these very broad dichotomies, some more nuanced differentiations are possible. In particular the study of public regulation provides us with several conceptual tools. For instance, we may distinguish between 'regulatory harmonization' and 'regulatory competition' as representing two different regulatory strategies within, in particular, the European arena of corporate governance regulation (see the contribution by Van Apeldoorn and Horn to this book). These different strategies represent two distinct modes of 'Europeanization' of the latter, the one through supranational law-making and the other through encouraging (within a regulatory framework that advances marketization) market actors to bring national standards more in line with each other. A similar conceptualization is the one between proactive and reactive regulation. The adoption of the US Sarbanes-Oxley Act 2002 in reaction to the Enron crisis and similar scandals may here serve as an example of the latter (see the contribution by Dewing and Russell to this book). A clear example of a pro-active role played by public authorities in devising a (new) regulatory framework for corporate governance can be seen in the attempts of the EU to promote the marketization of corporate control (see the contribution by Van Apeldoorn and Horn to this book).

Finally, public regulations can also be classified regarding their predominant source of initiation. Here, the distinction between market-driven and legislation-driven regulation is particularly helpful for an analysis of corporate governance regulation in Eastern Europe. Here, contemporary developments in corporate governance regulation are particularly affected by the dialectic between rules-based regulation as imposed by the *acquis communautaire* governing the Single European Market and the impact of interests related to foreign direct investment (especially in the banking sector) on corporate governance regulation on the other hand (for further elaboration see the contribution by Vliegenthart and Overbeek to this book).

Turning to private modes of corporate governance regulation, we have a more limited arsenal of conceptual tools available, reflecting the early stage of the debate on private regulation within international affairs (with the literature being less than a decade old: for example, Cutler *et al.* 1999c; Hall and Biersteker 2002a). One basic distinction concerns the difference between private norm development (as in the case of accounting standards) and private enforcement (as in the case of competition policy). While private actors substantially write the content of accounting standards within the IASB, they serve as watchdogs for the supervision of competition laws (for further elaboration see the contributions by Wigger as well as by Nölke and Perry to this book).

C: Explaining changes in mode and content of corporate governance regulation

For answers to our third and most important question, namely the explanatory one, we cannot easily rely on established conceptualizations and approaches. As we concluded from our critical review of the literature, those studies seeking to explain corporate governance regulation are mostly focused on explaining existing (national) diversity and less apt in accounting for regulatory changes taking place in shifting modes (and at different levels) of governance. This book therefore approaches this question somewhat more inductively (we will return to the 'why question' in the conclusion). Yet, in seeking to deepen our understanding of why both the content and mode of corporate governance regulation are changing the different contributions of this book we depart from similar questions such as: Which political processes drive the current transformation of corporate governance at different levels of governance? Which political and socio-economic actors are involved? What are their interests, and how are relations of power between them configured? How are these different constituencies organising and mobilising themselves? Which political coalitions can we identify in the field of corporate governance regulation? How and why do they succeed against counter-alliances? How do these processes interact with intervening variables such as (inter-)national structures and institutions?

We focus on explanations that combine actors and structures, as well as domestic and international political and economic factors, i.e. contribute to a transnational political economy perspective. We assume that the current transformation of corporate governance regulation is above all driven by politics, which in turn is linked and being reconfigured by structural changes in global capitalism, such as the globalization of securities and equities markets. In terms of actors we focus *inter alia* on the following social constituencies:

- Transnational capital market actors such as multinational banks, pension funds and other institutional investors;
- Professional service firms such as the Big Four auditing companies or transnational law firms;
- Public authorities on the national and/or the international level (national governments, European Commission, World Bank, OECD).

We focus in particular on the role of broad social constituencies that might be internally divided, such as managers or workers. Here the general argument about labour being opposed to current changes in the content of corporate governance regulation needs to be qualified, since we might need to differentiate between different groups of workers, some whom may actually benefit (at least financially) from the industrial restructuring engendered by the re-orientation of firms to the maximization of shareholder value (for example, by boosting their pension fund assets), whereas others may either lose their job or accept that they have to work longer hours for less pay. Managers may also not necessarily be the losers of a process that purposively intends to increase owner control. Indeed, what managers may lose in autonomous control over the production process they may very well win in income (for instance through stock options packages), prestige and international career mobility (that is at least as long as they manage to push the market value of their firm upwards).

Corporate governance regulation in diverse arenas: The structure of the book

The regulation of corporate governance increasingly takes place at different but interacting levels: at the global level through bodies like the IASB, at the European level – where, in addition to the process of financial market integration, attempts are undertaken to create a regulatory framework for a more market-driven corporate governance, and at the national level, where we still find much country-specific regulation, albeit challenged by the governance efforts at these other levels. In other words, the changing nature of corporate governance regulation is by definition a *transnational* and multilevel phenomenon and therefore in our view also requires a transnational approach that recognizes how the different levels, regions and (public/private) forms of governance are interrelated.

The book is divided into five parts. Part I addresses (both theoretically and empirically) a number of general questions and themes common to the transformation of corporate governance regulation across different arenas, and which as such are central to this book. The subsequent three parts of the book then each examine in more detail some of the changes in corporate governance regulation in the three interrelated arenas of governance that we identified before. Part II offers an analysis of regulatory changes taking place within the supranational and transnational European arena. Although not necessarily entirely supplanting national regimes, supranational governance in the EU, it will be argued, is increasingly transforming the regulatory framework of European corporate governance regimes. The EU, furthermore, does not operate in a vacuum but in a transatlantic and global context where it has to negotiate its choices with both state (mainly the US) and non-state actors. This global arena is examined in Part III, in particular by examining the role of private authority in setting standards (such as accounting standards) for business. Part IV focuses on those countries where the influence of the EU and other international institutions on the changes in corporate governance regulation is perhaps most clearly felt, namely the CEEC. Part V seeks to synthesize the major arguments of the individual contributions to this book in a concluding chapter.

First, in spite of these evolving multilevel governance structures, the nation-state still retains its role as an important location for the contestation about the design of corporate governance regulation. Peter Gourevitch's contribution paints a comprehensive picture of the domestic politics of corporate governance (regulation). He demonstrates that these politics may best be understood as the outcome of different coalitional line-ups between owners, managers and workers. These different configurations of political forces according to Gourevitch largely explain the observed divergence of corporate governance regulations in different (groups of) countries. Bob Jessop too rejects a simple convergence thesis and instead observes a 'complex, path-dependent, materially-conditioned, and politically contested pattern of convergence-divergence'. However, he puts more emphasis on the structural forces at work in the process of globalization that explains for him the ecological dominance of neoliberal forms of regulation. In this way these contributions provide a challenging reformulation of the *problématique* of convergence versus divergence to which we will return in the concluding chapter. Inasmuch as convergence is argued to take place, the literature generally assumes that this would be on the Anglo-Saxon model of shareholder primacy. The contribution by Antoine Rebérioux provides a penetrating theoretical critique of this model as based on an analysis of Enron and similar scandals and of the regulatory responses to them. Rebérioux argues that the roots of these financial scandals actually lie in the Anglo-Saxon shareholder model as premised on external control. Paradoxically, Rebérioux claims, this model, while privileging shareholders in theory, has empowered managers in practice. Rather than trying to strengthen external control mechanisms, as the new regulations seek to do, a more appropriate response would be to come to a re-appreciation of the (continental) European insider model.

Second, the development of a European regulatory framework for corporate governance becomes more and more salient. The contribution by Bastiaan van Apeldoorn and Laura Horn argues that analysing regulatory initiatives taken by the EU, and comparing this to earlier efforts (in the 1970s) pertaining to the creation of European-level company law, a fundamental change can be observed in the social purpose of European corporate governance regulation. This change can best be described in terms of the emergence of a European project that seeks to advance the marketization of corporate control. This shift in social purpose is seen as concomitant to a shift from a regulatory approach aimed at the harmonization of company law in order to prevent regulatory competition, to a regulatory framework advancing a market-oriented corporate governance regime in part through promoting market-based forms of regulation, that is, making use of regulatory competition as brought on by market forces. The contribution by Angela Wigger demonstrates how recent reforms in the European regime of competition control (which has a strong affinity with corporate governance regulation in a more narrow sense) also indicate a growing marketization, both in the substance of regulation and in its governance. With regard to the substance, the EU competition authorities increasingly rely on microeconomic analysis as premised on the Chicago School type of free-market economics, whereas with respect to the mode of governance, formal (*ex ante*) public control has given way to *private* enforcement with regard to anti-competitive conduct. Wigger concludes that as anti-trust enforcement increasingly comes to depend on market mechanisms, a process of regulatory convergence on the Anglo-Saxon model and away from the Rhenish co-ordinated type of capitalism is indeed taking place.

Third, the regulation of corporate governance is not only limited to national laws or EU regulations, but also comprises of private regulations. The most well-known case of private regulation are accounting standards as devised by the IASB. Accounting standards are a crucial ingredient of corporate governance regulation, since they provide critical information for shareholders. While accounting standards traditionally were regulated at the national level, the IASB is increasingly able to muster global support for its standards. So far, the US has been a major exception to this rule, but as the contribution by Ian Dewing and Peter Russell shows, there are increasing tendencies towards a convergence between IASB and US standards. This convergence might further empower the private authority of the IASB and of the Big Four auditing companies that are its most important collaborators. The rising prominence of co-ordination service firms within corporate governance regulation is not restricted to the Big Four and accounting. The contribution by Andreas Nölke and James Perry demonstrates considerable parallels between auditing companies and the activities of rating agencies. Both types of co-ordination service firms derive their role as standard-setters for transparency regulations, which are a major precondition for the external control of corporations (by debtors and investors) from similar features, such as a high degree of market concentration and a premium on very specific technical expertise. Finally, both types of co-ordination service firms contribute to the ongoing erosion of the Rhenish variety of capitalism, strongly supported by their incorporation into EU legislation.

Fourth, the influence of the EU and other international institutions is most clearly felt in CEEC: these countries are exposed to multiple (and partially conflicting) demands as they are developing their corporate governance structures. The contributions to this section highlight specific aspects of this ecological dominance of EU and other external regulation, each posing the question whether there exists such a thing as a Central European model of corporate governance. Wladimir Andreff makes a detailed comparative study of the introduction of the capitalist market economy in the post-socialist states and concludes that due to the accession process of the EU a gulf has opened up between those post-socialist states that have entered, or are near entering, the Single European Market, and those (primarily the countries of the Commonwealth of Independent States) that have, and will, not. Arjan Vliegenthart and Henk Overbeek, finally, taking as a point of departure the externally dependent nature of Central and Eastern Europe's recent economic development, distinguish three phases in the introduction of capitalist corporate governance in the region. They conclude that it is not the dependence on foreign capital *per se*, but in particular the domination of the banking sector by foreign (mostly West European) capital (which occurred in a particular phase of the crisis of the global capitalist economy) that gives the Central European model its distinctiveness.

Notes

1 For instance, in Germany, the then chairman of the Social Democratic Party (SPD), Franz Müntefering introduced the notion of 'locusts' ('Heuschrecken') to describe the growing role of (Anglo-Saxon) private equity investors (first in a public speech on programmatic renewal of the party on 22 November 2004, but becoming famous through his interview with the weekly 'Bild am Sonntag', 17 April 2005). The same metaphor was later also used, referring to both private equity funds and hedge funds, by the Dutch minister of economics, Joop Wijn (*NRC Handelsblad*, 21 August, 2006). Although these examples underline the potential controversial nature of some of the changes in corporate governance currently taking place, this is not to imply that for instance policy-makers thus far have done much to slow-down some of these developments. On the contrary, as several chapters in this book will show, these developments have been critically enabled by regulatory changes set in motion at different levels of policy-making.

2 When referring to 'governance', rather than 'corporate governance' we obviously refer to the political science usage of the term, which comes close to how we will define regulation below, although emphasizing that one may govern without government (but also, through for example, private actors, see, for example, Hall and Biersteker 2002a). Whereas corporate governance refers to governance of the firm by relevant stakeholders within the firm, governance as a generic term refers to processes of collective choice taken beyond and above the (micro-level of the) firm. As such we might also speak of 'the governance of corporate governance'. But as this sounds confusing we prefer the phrase 'the regulation of corporate governance' (see also the next section). In discussing shifts in corporate governance regulation we do, however, draw upon the political science literature on governance, distinguishing between different levels and arenas of governance.

3 This definition is much broader, more 'sociological' (see Jackson 2001), than the conventional definition of the neoclassical agency theory (see also below), which focuses solely on the relation between the so-called principal (shareholders) and the so-called agent (management), and moreover assumes that the former, regardless of institutional arrangements and prevailing configurations of power, always has only one interest, which is, 'to get the managers to give them back their money' (Shleifer and Vishny 1996: 4). As we shall emphasize later on, 'capital', however, is not a homogenous category, but different types of owners may in fact have different identities and interests. Moreover, even if we also focus on the shareholder-management relationship, we refrain from treating labour acting as a direct stakeholder capable of exercising real control (for example, through the supervisory board) as an anomaly the way neoclassical agency theory does (by simply excluding it from its normatively-biased models). Our definition also deviates from some of the critical

political economy literature on 'financialization', which tends to analyze corporate governance above all as a 'narrative', that is, a discursive practice situated moreover in a specifically Anglo-Saxon politico-economic context of the 1990s stock market boom (Erturk *et al.* 2004). In contrast, we treat corporate governance primarily as a set of objective social relations (even if this may have important discursive dimensions) concomitant to the very existence of the modern corporation itself, and existing in different varieties across time and space.

4   Hansmann and Kraakman do raise the *cui bono* (in whose interest) question with respect to this triumph of the so-called standard model. Their answer is straightforwardly that of course 'corporate enterprise should be organized and operated to serve the interests of society as a whole', but that these general interests happen to coincide with the interests of shareholders, i.e. that managers work to maximize shareholders' wealth – 'logic and experience' showing (although no empirical substantiation whatsoever is given here) that this is the best way to promote 'aggregate social welfare' (Hansmann and Kraakman 2004: 42–3).

5   This applies even more to some other work of the same group of researchers. Froud *et al.* (2000) for instance offer a critical analysis of the role played consultants as 'key intermediaries' in transforming corporate governance practices, in particular by the selling of 'shareholder value' as a consultancy product. Although this highlights an important dimension (including its commodifying aspects) of the politics of changing corporate governance practices, it does not examine the politics of corporate governance regulation, upon which this book focuses.

6   There are of course some studies focusing on the regulation of corporate governance beyond the national level, in particular focusing on the EU. Here we may mention, for instance, Story and Walter 1997, Rhodes and Van Apeldoorn 1998, Lannoo 1999, Rebérioux 2002, Callaghan and Höpner 2005, and Perry and Nölke 2005, and 2006. Of these studies, only the most recent, which also have a more specific empirical focus, offer an empirically informed explanation of (the politics of) changing transnational corporate governance regulation.

7   Hall and Soskice (2001a) use the conceptual dichotomy of Liberal Market Economies (LMEs) and Co-ordinated Market Economies (CMEs) which arguably covers a wider geographical scope than is suggested by the opposition of Anglo-Saxon versus Rhenish capitalism. Nevertheless in several chapters of this book (for example,. by Wigger as well as Nölke and Perry) the latter dichotomy is preferred since the changes they observe in particular apply to the 'Rhenish variety' of the co-ordinated market economies. To this we may add that we realize that for other purposes, whatever the terminology, this dichotomous classification may not be adequate (see also Aguilera and Jackson 2003). For instance, it gives us only a limited understanding of the more detailed variety within (Western) Continental Europe (Rhodes and Van Apeldoorn 1998) while its applicability to the new market economies of Eastern Central Europe is also questionable (for this, see the contribution by Vliegenthart and Overbeek to this book).

8   Over the last few years a number of contributions have appeared that have tried to relate the VoC concepts to the CEEC; see, for example, Cernat (2006), Lane and Myant (2006), Nölke and Vliegenthart (2006).

9   An important exception here is formed by Streeck and Yamamura 2002 whose edited book explicitly seeks to explain the origins of different models. More recently, others have also criticized the VoC approach for being too static and unable to account for change and innovation, while at the same time holding on to its central notion of (national) capitalist diversity, see especially Crouch 2005, see also Morgan *et al.* 2005).

Part I
Themes and approaches

2 Explaining corporate governance systems

Alternative approaches

Peter Gourevitch

Why do corporate governance systems vary around the world? Awareness of this variance is relatively recent, despite a rich literature on comparative capitalism (Schonfeld 1965), and with it has come a vigorous debate about explanation. This chapter explores how several research traditions deal with explanation of divergence among corporate governance models. We can identify three very broad research strands of vigorous debate, one focusing on politics, another on law, and a third on sociology.

Overlaying all three is an argument about levels: do patterns follow largely national variables, or international ones? Certainly we see substantial linkage across national boundaries: 'flows' of money, goods, people and technology/ ideas cut across boundaries; 'structures' link governments into supranational institutions; transnational processes link people into a kind of global civil society. All of this certainly places nations into an international framework into which national processes must fit and which influence national structures substantially (Gourevitch 1978). The processes can fruitfully be analyzed from this perspective exploring the autonomous contribution of each level of decision making (local, national, and supranational) and each strategic actor (business, labour, multinationals, investors, politicians, non-government organizations (NGOs), interest groups), as does Jessop in this book. At the same time, there is value in sustaining a national perspective. Key regulations continue to be nationally determined: laws and their enforcement rely on countries; international agreements are generally delegations by countries – for example, the EU is still debating a take-over law, where national differences are of great importance (Callaghan 2005, 2006; see also the contribution by Van Apeldoorn and Horn to this book). The globalization processes are thus refracted through national prisms which continue to deserve attention.

Corporate governance patterns: what is to be explained?

The dominant way of characterizing and measuring the dependent variable of corporate governance patterns is shareholder concentration (blockholding) versus shareholder diffusion, although an earlier tradition measured bank debt versus equity. These are crude proxies for the dichotomy between 'stakeholder

' and 'shareholder' models (Albert 1993; Dore 2002). In the latter, the claims of shareholders have primacy over suppliers, workers, local communities and 'society' writ large; in the former, shareholders are but one claimant in the community of interest, participating with the others in the distribution of benefits and decisions about the firm. Blockholding (concentration of ownership) overlaps with the concept 'stakeholding' although in principle one could have blockholding without stakeholding.

Measurements of diffusion/blockholding show considerable variance around the world. The US and UK rank at the highly diffuse end, Chile at the other end, with a great range of variance in between.

Table 2.1 Ownership concentration

Concentration	Country	Concentration	Country
4.1	Japan	49.0	Venezuela
5.0	China	51.5	Belgium
15.0	United States	51.9	Thailand
20.0	Netherlands	52.0	South Africa
23.6	United Kingdom	52.8	Austria
24.6	Ireland	55.0	Israel
27.0	New Zealand	55.8	Spain
27.5	Australia	58.0	Turkey
27.5	Canada	59.6	Italy
31.8	South Korea	60.3	Portugal
37.5	Denmark	63.0	Brazil
38.6	Norway	64.6	Germany
42.6	Malaysia	64.8	France
43.0	India	66.0	Mexico
44.8	Singapore	67.3	Indonesia
45.5	Taiwan	71.5	Hong Kong
46.4	Philippines	72.5	Argentina
46.9	Sweden	75.0	Greece
48.1	Switzerland	90.0	Chile
48.8	Finland		

Note: This is drawn from Table 2.1 in Gourevitch and Shinn (2005) where the sources and the data set are explained. The numbers measure the percentage of firm shares owned by the given number of block holders, so that the larger the number, the more shares are owned by that number.

What explains that variance?

We can identify three answers to this question: political processes; law and economics; and economic sociology. The three contest each other as alternative explanations, but also overlap in some ways, differ internally, and attract people who cross the boundary lines. But it is perhaps more useful here to emphasize the distinctions rather than the overlap – each 'strand' of work has its own 'centre of gravity' of concerns and preoccupations.

The primacy of politics

Pride of place is given here to the politics approach. The politics tradition explains corporate governance by the rules and regulations which are generated by political processes in each country. Corporate governance patterns reflect incentives on whether to accept (reject) a minority shareholder position in a firm. The incentives are shaped by laws, regulations and enforcement, and these in turn are shaped by politics. The relevant laws include the formal rules on corporate and securities law (Minority Shareholder Protections or MSP) but also a set of interacting policies (labour market, price and wage setting, education and training, trade unions, anti-trust, economic openness) which shape the firm. Divergence among countries reflects divergence in political processes – the politics which sustains one form of 'patterned capitalism' rather than another (the neoliberalism of Thatcher–Reagan or the co-ordinated economies of Germany and Japan (Boyer 2001; Hall and Soskice 2001)). Politics is in turn a product of political parties, elections, interest groups, ideologies, class, and political institutions (Rajan and Zingales 2003a; Roe 2003; Gourevitch and Shinn 2005).

Law and economics

The law and economics school stresses the autonomous role of law and regulation, apart from political processes (La Porta *et al.* 1997, 1998, 1999, 2000). It focuses the arena of law more narrowly to those that deal explicitly with organization of the firm, securities regulation, and finance to argue that where MSP is provided by law, we find diffusion. To explain high quality MSP, the dominant tradition in law and economics looks to 'legal family' – common versus civil law – where common law is more favourable to shareholder diffusion.

Economic sociology

The third approach embeds the firm in a system of social roles: norms, practices, institutions, relationships that define the possible and the permitted. The social practices that shape the firm are national in character, having substantial local variance, and not universal. Variance across countries expresses differences in their 'national scripts' on how firms should be run (Dobbin 2004).

Let us examine these different approaches in greater detail. We begin by examining the key intermediate variable: MSP. Most directly, the three schools disagree on how to explain this variable. Indirectly they disagree as well on its 'sufficiency' as an explanation, and on which other processes influence corporate governance outcomes besides MSP. Both the politics and the law and economics schools start with a rationalist framework, which sees corporate governance systems responding to a set of economic incentives that deal with the problem of managerial agency costs. The relevant players in the firm (managers, owners, investors, and workers) are pursuing a strategy of optimizing their utility function for control of the firm's cash flow. Institutions, rules and 'private bonding' arrangements shape those incentives. According to the logic of this approach, then, variation in corporate governance outcomes reflects some variance in incentives across countries.

But which incentives? In recent years, attention has focused on MSP, an expanded version of 'quality of corporate law' (QCL). Investors seek protection from moral hazard: the ability of managers to take advantage of owners, and the ability of insiders to exploit minority shareholders. The essence of the governance problem lies in the incomplete contacts between owners and managers (Shleifer and Vishny 1997). Without protections for minority shareholders, investment will be low and shareholding will be concentrated in blocks. Where MSP is strong, financial markets are deeper, investment is higher, and shareholding is more diffuse.

If MSP is strong, shareholder diffusion occurs; if MSP is weak, blockholding prevails. In the 'law matters' school, strong MSP leads to deeper financial markets. What explains the provision of MSP? Political processes (elections, parties, interest groups, political institutions) argues the politics school. Legal family, according to the dominant view in law and economics. National traditions and 'cultural scripts', according to the economic sociology group.

A second level of disagreement among the schools concerns the sufficiency of MSP as an explanation. Other incentives besides the formal corporate governance ones influence investors and the other players: labour market relationships, economic competition (Roe 2003), education and skill development, all impact the economic system. These variables have a bearing on the choice among corporate governance systems, argues the French regulation school (for example, Boyer 2001), and the *Varieties of Capitalism* authors (Hall and Soskice 2001; Roe 2003) for example, note that diffusion is strongest in countries with vigorous product market competition (thus low trade barriers and strong anti trust), weak labour market protection, high income inequality and weak trade unions. Competition drives down the 'surplus' firms have and makes them vulnerable to agency problems. Labour strength creates a power block in the firm that induces owners to retain share blocks, so that they can bargain more effectively. These ideas rest on the logic of 'institutional complementarities', whereby one set of structures reinforces another (Milgrom and Roberts 1990), so that economies cluster around one pole or another (Scharpf and Schmidt 2000a; Schmidt 2002).

Table 2.2 Minority shareholder protections index

Country	Information	Oversight	Control	Incentive	Total MSP	
US	86	100	100	100	97	US
Singapore	89	71	80	97	84	SIN
Canada	83	71	100	78	83	CAN
UK	81	60	100	53	74	UK
Australia	75	71	80	59	71	AUS
Hong Kong	85	14	100	81	70	HK
Ireland	69	71	80	59	70	IRE
Malaysia	84	36	80	69	67	MAL
South Africa	73	43	100	41	64	SAF
Chile	35	14	100	66	54	CHIL
France	64	37	60	47	52	FRA
New Zealand	56	71	80	0	52	NZ
Argentina	48	0	80	72	50	ARG
Spain	57	14	80	50	50	SPN
Israel	74	29	60	31	48	ISR
Norway	66	29	80	16	48	NOR
Sweden	67	36	60	22	46	SWD
Finland	60	36	60	16	43	FIN
Venezuela	49	14	20	81	41	VEN
India	50	7	100	0	39	IND
Switzerland	59	36	40	16	38	SWT
Japan	66	0	80	0	37	JPN
South Korea	65	21	40	22	37	SK
Denmark	44	43	40	16	36	DEN
Netherlands	57	0	40	47	36	NED
Philippines	74	7	60	0	35	PHL
Taiwan	74	7	60	0	35	TAI
Belgium	43	32	0	59	34	BEL
Germany	44	29	20	41	33	GER
Thailand	78	7	40	6	33	THA
Brazil	27	0	60	41	32	BRZ
Austria	40	36	40	6	30	AUT
Greece	53	14	40	0	27	GRC
Mexico	59	14	20	9	26	MEX
Portugal	43	0	60	0	26	POR
Italy	69	7	20	0	24	ITAL
Turkey	51	0	40	0	23	TURK
Indonesia	45	0	40	0	21	INDO
China	25	0	20	0	11	CHIN

Note: This is Table 3.1 of Gourevitch and Shinn (2005) where the sources are explained. Each column averages measures from different data sources of each element of corporate governance. These measures include: information (disclosure and audit), oversight (board independence), control rules (voting processes), and managerial incentives (executive pay). The higher the level of MSP, the more supervision of managers, the more reassured are investors.

A theory of corporate governance must therefore explain two closely connected policies: the supply of High (or Low) MSP and the degrees of co-ordination in market economies (LME versus CME). The various schools examined here offer differing interpretations of those policy patterns.

Political explanations

The political explanation looks at the interaction of social preferences with institutions, as modelled in this diagram.

Policies are made by the politicians. In democracies, these reflect the preferences of interest groups, voters, and political parties, as refracted by the mechanisms of aggregation (political institutions). Following the work of the much of the finance literature, we can stylize preferences by grouping the members of the firm into owners, managers and workers (Zingales 2000). From the logic of their position in the firm, they have preferences about corporate governance. The political question is how they translate those preferences into public policy.

We begin with the actors within the firm identified by finance theory (owners, managers, and workers) and the preferences for corporate governance practices of each group. The three actors contend with each other over the resources of the firm each with a varying set of claims against the firm's revenue and profit stream. Each set of actors has a range of preferences that set up a range of trade-offs, thus of possible alignments with the other players.

Workers seek good wages, job stability in the face of lay-offs, even at the expense of profitability; and protection of their pension claims on the firm. They are in conflict with managers and owners over wages and with managers over agency costs that benefit only them. They may be relatively indifferent to expropriation costs that help one set of shareholders at the expense of other shareholders (but they will oppose them) unless self-dealing by a blockholder

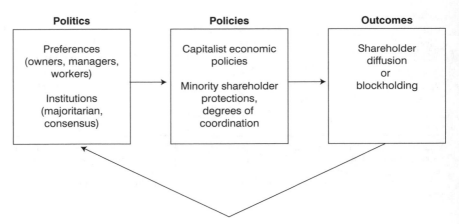

Figure 2.1 Causal schema (Source: Gourevitch and Shinn 2005: Table 2.1)

Table 2.3 Political coalitions and governance outcomes

Coalitional lineup	Winner	Model name	Predicted outcome
Pair A: Class Conflict			
Owners + Managers vs. Workers	Owners + Managers	Investor	Diffusion
Owners + Managers vs. Workers	Workers	Labor	Blockholding
Pair B: Sectoral			
Owners vs. Managers + Workers	Managers + Workers	Social Bargain	Blockholding
Owners vs. Managers + Workers	Owners	Oligarchy	Blockholding
Pair C: Property and voice			
Owners + Workers vs. Managers	Owners + Workers	Transparency	Diffusion
Owners + Workers vs. Managers	Managers	Managerism	Diffusion

Source: Gourevitch and Shinn (2005) Chapter 2.

threatens the financial viability of the firm thus jobs and its ability to cover its pension claims.

Managers seek income, job security, and managerial autonomy. They will want high payments of various kinds, from salary to options, and the greatest autonomy in directing the resources of the firm – which also gives them the greatest leeway to shirk. They dislike expropriation costs at the expense of the firm, for reasons similar to those of workers. Thus they have common interests with workers against some kinds of owner action, and common interests with owners against worker claims.

Owners prefer to minimize all the forms of agency costs paid to managers and workers, fearing that each of these is able to divert resources from profits, requiring the firm to pay above market prices to these groups. Owners may be concentrated or diffused. Concentrated owners incur a portfolio risk of exposure to a single firm, compared to diffuse owners who can spread out the risk of their equity investment over a variety of firms and assets. On the other hand, blockholders can help themselves to a variety of expropriation costs at the expense of minority shareholders. Diffuse owners do not share in expropriation costs; they focus on getting the best risk-adjusted rate of return on their investment, and a diversified equity portfolio. Some subset of owners may have common interests with workers against the expropriation claims of blockholders, while in other situations, blockholders may make common cause with managers and workers (Becht, Bolton *et al.* 2003/revised 2005).

We see three possible alignments. Each group can make a bargain with another. This requires resolution of the internal struggle within each – which cleavage principle dominates? Or more accurately, each group can divide, one faction going in one direction, another faction the other. This helps us understand 'coalitional potential', the possible alliances combinations of the intra firm players as they move outside to politics. Which one coalesces in a given country, and which side wins, cannot be understood only by knowing the preferences. In order to translate these preferences into real coalitions, however, we must understand the forces at work that decide which coalitions will coalesce. Here we explore three coalitional patterns: class conflict, sectoral conflict and transparency alignment.

Class conflict, left versus right. Mark Roe (Roe 1994, 2003) developed one of the first overtly political interpretations of corporate governance in looking at a classic line of reasoning in political economy – left versus right, or the partisan manifestation of class conflict. Patterns of policy are produced by the balance of power between left and right. Where the left is strong, we get policies that support blockholding and the ancillary package of labour employment protections and income equality. Where the right is strong we get policies that support shareholder diffusion, weak employment protection and income inequality. Roe argues this effect on corporate governance is independent of the degree of MSP: that is, even where shareholder protection is relatively strong, as in Scandinavia, we find blockholding because strong labour inhibits diffusion.

Sectoral conflict: labour (manager) blockholder bargains. Another way of interpreting the political cleavages looks at cross class alliances and conflicts.

Roe's statistics contrast left governments versus right governments; his carefully done country case studies suggest a somewhat different pattern: countries differ on the extent to which bargains are struck across the class divide. The CME/ blockholder/stakeholder outcome reflects arrangements made among certain subsets of managers, workers and some kinds of owners to preserve a system in which they share power and benefits: the firm is protected, and all those who work and invest in it are able to retain their jobs, be this the workers or the managers, while the owners are sheltered from hostile takeovers and instability. This contrasts with the diffuse shareholder model where the fluidity of asset mobility is protected; the rights of the external shareholder to the cash flow of the firm, to reduce 'the agency costs of cash flow' (the firm retaining its earnings) and to exit. Policy outcomes reflect in this way cross class bargains (Gourevitch 1986; Rogowski 1989; Hiscox 2002). Pagano and Volpin (Pagano and Volpin 2001, 2005) model a bargain in favour of blockholding as an accommodation among managers, workers and inside owners against a regime of external capital holders. What Roe labels as Social Democracy are often bargains of this kind involving labour with management and capital: Christian Democracy in Germany and Italy look like this. So do the coalitional foundations of the bargains in Scandinavia which involve farmers and workers in 'red–green' alliances (Swenson 1989, 2002).

Transparency coalitions. The class and sector alignments are quite familiar to students of political economy, as they appear in the literature on trade disputes (tariffs), social policy and other issue areas. Less familiar is a third coalitional alignment: the link of labour to minority shareholders against managers and insider capital. Labour pushes for transparency (via minority shareholder protections) as a way of monitoring managers (Höpner 2003a) and to defend pension investments (Cioffi and Höpner 2006; Gourevitch and Shinn 2005). Examples can be found in Germany: the Social Democrats and Free Democrats aligned to push through various reforms facing opposition from the Christian Democrats, the defenders of the Rhenish model of CMEs. In the US and the UK, we find labour related pension funds (CalPERS, Hermes and TIAA/CREF) as leaders in the effort to push for strong shareholder protections in the regulatory process, and which challenge managers in the boardrooms.

Political institutions. We have identified the alternative coalitional line-ups that support one or another regulatory policy posture leading to alternative governance outcomes. What explains the triumph of one coalition over another? Political resources and leadership to be sure – Tiberghein (Tiberghein 2002, 2003, 2006) is developing a political leadership model using cases studies of France, Japan and Korea, Culpepper *et al.* stress the choice specific actors faced with ambiguous incentives (Culpepper *et al.* 2006). Resources and leadership matter, but are hard to operationalize across a larger number of countries. What can be measured more readily are political institutions: structures influence the aggregation of preferences (they increase or decrease the chances of one or another coalition winning. Gourevitch and Hawes (Gourevitch and Hawes 2002) and Pagano and Volpin (Pagano and Volpin 2005) examine electoral systems) proportional representation favours blockholding, single member first-past-the-post favours diffusion models. Following such writers as Lijphart (Lijphart 1999), Beck *et al.* (Beck *et al.* 2001) and Shugart and Carey (Shugart and Carey 1992), Gourevitch and Shinn (2005) incorporate electoral laws into a broader typology of political systems – Majoritarian and Consensus. High levels of MSP and a liberal production regime correlate with Majoritarian political institutions. Low levels of MSP and an organized or regulated production regime correlate with Consensus institutions.

Majoritarian systems magnify the impact of small shifts of votes, thus allow large swings of policy; consensus systems reduce the impact of vote shifts by giving leverage to a wide range of players through coalitions, thus have lesser swings of policy. Consensus systems have many 'veto-players', Majoritarian ones have few. In a Consensus system, a wide range of opinion has to be included in decisions. The coalition nature of the government assures this, as all participants in the cabinet have to agree to important decisions. In a Majoritarian system, large blocks of opinion can be overridden by a narrow majority, thus small shifts of votes can have big consequences. In Lijphart's (1999) classification, the UK is closest to a pure Majoritarian model, where a single party controls a cabinet that controls the legislature. Consensus systems (in Scandinavia, Austria) also have cabinet dominance over the legislature, but within the context of a multiparty system. The connection between institutions and outcomes emerges clearly by examining the impact of electoral rules. Electoral rules have a big impact on how preferences are articulated and represented (Cox 1997). Single member districts, with victory to the plurality winner, reward coalition formation before an election. Groups of varying opinions have an incentive to combine forces so as to get the plurality need for victory. Conversely, proportional representation systems reward the articulation of divergent preferences at the time of election. It is after the election that combinations or coalitions are formed. The electoral system is not the only logic at work – there are some strong cleavage lines of preference, such as religion or multiple cleavages in the population that do not follow this logic, but it does have substantial force.

Gourevitch and Shinn (2005) adapt the measures of Lijphart, Beck and others into a particular measure of Consensus systems exploring 'veto points'. A high score on 'political cohesion' means Consensus systems. A low score produces Majoritarian systems. We then correlate political cohesion with blockholding. We find that consensus systems favour corporatist coalitions, low minority shareholder protection, and blockholding. Majoritarian systems inhibit corporatist coalitions, correlate negatively with blockholding and positively with MSP. In authoritarian regimes or weak democracies, most of which are outside Europe, we find that strong governments, with few veto players, have high capacity for policy change and predation, thus correlate positively with blockholding, even if they correlate positively with shareholder protections. Weak governments, with many veto players, are ineffective in responding to crises, also frightening investors, thus correlate positively with blockholding (MacIntyre 2001). These findings are summarized in this figure from Gourevitch and Shinn (2005).

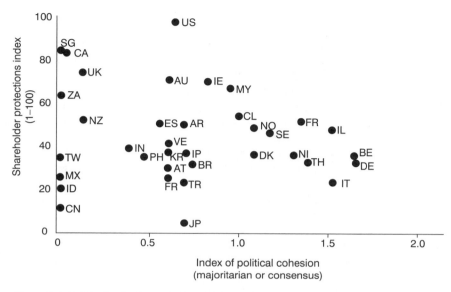

Figure 2.2 Political cohesion and shareholder protections

Economics and law: the legal family argument

The law and economics tradition pioneered comparative work on corporate governance by measuring ninority shareholder protections and shareholder concentration across a wide range of countries. To this, it adds a particular explanation of why MSPs, and therefore corporate governance patterns, differ across countries: 'legal family', i.e. common law versus civil law. Common law, it is argued (La Porta *et al.* 1998; Djankov *et al.* 2002; Botero *et al.* 2004) is more favourable to shareholder protection than is civil law, hence the correlation with MSP and diffuse shareholding. This body of work has created the contemporary comparative literature on corporate governance, a great contribution, but at the same time has shunted the explanatory discussion onto the legal family distinction. As such it has provoked considerable criticism. Among the most noted critics are Rajan and Zingales (2003b) whose 'great reversals' paper notes that countries have shifted over time in the level of MSP and the degree of diffusion/concentration, without changing legal families; Roe (2003), who says legal family has omitted variable bias, as diffusion is strongest in countries that have vigorous product market competition (thus low trade barriers and strong anti-trust), weak labour market protection, high income inequality and weak trade unions. Berkowitz, Pister *et al.* (2003) note a transplant effect, where law is sharply altered by the process of moving from one place to another, so that legal family is altered by local conditions.

While the legal family school provides an intriguing stylized fact that compels attention (the correlation between MSP and legal family) it leaves some important problems to be resolved. If civil law is more regulatory, why does that regulation appear to favour blockholding rather than supply effective shareholder protection? A regulatory system could be a strong MSP one. The fact of higher regulation does not establish by itself the content thereof. If the mechanism is judicial discretion, legal family authors themselves note that judges could apply their discretion in different ways to protect insiders as much as outsiders, or to bar all intervention. Common law countries can pass legislation that suffocates markets, and civil law countries can pass laws that protect MSP if they so choose. Common law Britain became more interventionist under a Labour government in 1945, while civil law France became less regulatory after 1985. Common law countries can have effective rule of law, or weak rule where the common law legacy does not protect against extensive political interference with markets and courts – Pakistan for example, and several countries in Africa. Legal tradition can evolve in different directions, depending on the politics that shapes legislation and enforcement. La Porta *et al.* (2000) note that while it may be true that 'political factors affect corporate governance through channels other than the law itself [...] the law remains a crucial channel through which politics affects corporate governance'. Indeed, law is a channel, but this confirms the point about the centrality of politics: politics picks the law and shapes its enforcement.

Law and regulation come from politics. If Pakistan has weak shareholder protection and thus blockholding, while the UK has the opposite, the difference lies in the political use of their common law tradition (Glaeser *et al.* 2001). What changes over time within countries of any legal tradition are politics and political processes. Is legal family in fact a political interpretation then? Only in the initial move to pick a legal family. At some point decision makers selected a legal tradition – voluntarily in some cases, through coercion (colonialism) in others. At that moment we could say there was a political process that influenced corporate governance. But a weakness of the legal family school is that political processes disappear after that single moment. How it comes about that certain laws are enacted and enforced to give higher or lower protections disappears from the analysis. Judges seem to make decisions because of the logic of the tradition, but this too is insulated in analysis from politics. La Porta *et al.* study laws and regulations (extensively, again a major contribution) but they offer no account of why and when these laws are passed or enforced. It all flows from legal family, thus a single political act in a distant past. Legal family interpretations seem to leave countries trapped in their initial founding moment. It cannot explain 'the great reversals' (Rajan and Zingales 2003b), the changes that have taken place within one country over time. It has odd policy implications: does it mean no civil law country can develop effective MSP? If not, then legal family cannot be so decisive in its impact. Legal family is thus not a political model – it is single formal event and it can not incorporate political processes that generate the policies that shape corporate governance (Gourevitch 2005b).

Legal family, it should be noted, is but one branch of the way the law and economics tradition treats corporate governance, albeit the most well-known. Other specialists develop arguments over: the role of private bonding (Cheffins 2001; Coffee 2001; Cheffins 2002), sequencing (did shareholders come before shareholder protections?) (Franks and Mayer 1997; Morck 2005), general tort law versus a specially designated regulator (Glaeser, Johnson *et al.* 2001; Romano 2005). Another important theme is that over competition among securities markets: does competition among rival jurisdictions and regulatory markets produce convergence up, toward higher quality standards (Romano 1993), or convergence down, toward lower standards (Bebchuk and Roe 1999; Bebchuk and Hamdani 2002; Kahan and Kamar 2002).

Economic sociology

Economic sociology shifts our attention away from the rationalist concern with incentives of both the economics/law and politics schools – which quarrel over the source of the incentives, but not their primacy. These researchers share with political science the desire to locate economic practices and behaviours in social processes, and thus not in a separate logic of efficiency. They differ in stressing sociological processes, norms, networks, socialization and culturally constructed patterns, or scripts.

Valuable work in this tradition includes studies of changes in corporate forms (Fligstein 2001), the influence of investors in the break-up of conglomerates in the 1980s (Fligstein and Markowitz 1993; Useem 1993; Davis, Diekmann *et al.* 1994; Useem 1996), the diffusion of poison pill and anti take-over laws (Meyer and Rowan 1977; Davis 1991, 1996; Thomson and Davis 1997; Davis and Robbins 2005; Davis and Useem 2002); the role of law firms in the development of high technology industry in Silicon Valley (Suchman and Cahill 1996), the emergence of the Chief Financial officer in American firms (Zorn *et al.* 2004), shareholder activism as a social movement (Davis and McAdam 2000), the role of networks in developing and enforcing norms (Davis and Thompson 1994) labour market and labour training in shaping production systems (Streeck 1984), international corporate governance patterns (Aguilera and Jackson 2002; Aguilera and Federowicz 2003; Aguilera and Jackson 2003), the diffusion of corporate governance structures (Guillen 2000; Djelic 2001; Djelic and Quack 2003) and the role of legitimacy versus efficiency in the spread of governance codes (Cuervo-Cazurra and Aguilera 2004; Fiss and Zajac 2004).

A growing number of people across several disciplines see this point about 'embedded' economies. Some specialists in law and finance and corporate governance have been examining the role of interest groups, electoral systems and political institutions, social structures, the media, human capital issues (Krozsner 2000; Grossman *et al.* 2002; Perotti and Von Thadden 2003; Persson and Tabellini 2003; Rajan and Zingales 2003; Rajan 2003; Pagano and Volpin 2005), institutions and social structures (Lazonick and O'Sullivan 2000; O'Sullivan 2000); while others examine the interaction of social structures and path dependence on the evolution of institutions (North 1981; Acemoglu *et al.* 2001; Acemoglu and Johnson 2005; Acemoglu and Robinson 2005).

Conversely, many sociologists studying the economy explore the impact of incentives and utilitarian calculations on economic behaviour. As examples Davis, Dobbin, Useem all note the way changes in antitrust policy by the Reagan administration and the development of financial institutions following important legislation helped set loose processes that undermined the conglomerates that had emerged in the Second World War. Streeck's work on labour and training systems (1984), Dobbin (2004) on railroad building in the US, France and the UK, Aguilera and Jackson on corporate governance, all pay careful attention to the incentives of actors, but seek to embed them in a social context. Sociologists contribute important quantitative work on ownership patterns, on connections across firms among directors and the diffusion of practices across firms. Davis and MacAdam (2000) examine the politics of shareholder activism and locate it in the framework of social movements. Ensminger (Ensminger 1992) shows how norms, social structure and institutions fuse to make markets.

But while there is often substantial overlap, there are differences in emphasis among the disciplines of sociology, economics and political science and in some places those differences are substantial. There are disagreements on two key points. If regulations and policy matter, and these shape economic action, rather than arise form some independent economic calculus, what explains the content of policy and regulation? In this book we stress politics and political processes. Many economic sociologists also point to political processes and resource mobilization, but quite frequently they subordinate politics as a sub-system of a larger society and social action. This is an old quarrel among the social sciences. We do not make an effort to resolve boundary issues among politics and other social processes, but only wish to point out the difference in emphasis. Our goal is to clarify just where political choices are operative.

The second disagreement has to do with incentives and interests. Do economic incentives sufficiently capture the richness of the motivations of economic actors? Many sociologists challenge this. Drawing on the work of John Meyer and others, Dobbin (2004: 4) writes in a major literature survey 'Sociology's core insight is that individuals behave according to scripts that are tied to social roles'. Dore (2002: 5) questions the adequacy of 'allocative efficiency' in explaining behaviour. 'It requires only a small amount of reflection', Margaret Blair (Blair 2003: 14) has written recently,

> to realize that financial incentives and enforceable legal constraints cannot possibly be what holds most cooperative relationships together. They simply do not bind tightly enough. Most business relationships involve, and indeed require, a substantial amount of voluntary cooperation and trust among participants in the enterprise.

Shareholder value, a core concept in the 'nexus of contracts' approach, is 'constructed' for these theorists (March and Olsen 1998; Schmidt 2001; Hancke 2002; Schmidt 2002; Berger 2003; Katzenstein and Shiraishi 2006).

Here the politics school differs from the sociological approach. The political school stresses incentives and interests in shaping policies and the response to them. MSP and the rules of the production system *do* influence behaviour. On that the politics school agrees with the finance economists, the legal family school and those economic sociology colleagues who study the impact of policies upon economic behaviour. The disagreement in emphasis is in explaining the origins of those rules (politics versus legal family, or the 'autonomous' economy pure and simple), and on which rules matter (tort law alone, or MSP and/or rules of the production system). The politics school agrees with Roe, the *Varieties of Capitalism* authors, some of the sociologists, and some of the finance economists in saying that the broader set of rules matter. Where the politics approach disagrees, at least in emphasis, is on the inadequacy of an incentive model (namely the economists) and the sufficiency or separateness of 'scripts' (namely the sociologists).

The politics school stresses change within countries over time over their regulatory regime and its practices. To the extent the idea of 'national script' explains behaviour, does it explain change in a country over time? Ideas about Confucian patterns or the French model, or the American one, do not capture the way those countries changed. Some economic sociologists have written extensively about the self-interest of various actors in bringing about change: the financial analysts who made money encouraging conglomerates, then by breaking them up. The swirl of competing interests both makes a case for 'scripts' – in confusing situations, one's 'priors' are a guide to action (and against them) in confusion, actors advance their particularistic goals. Either way, some abstract concept of optimum efficiency has substantial weaknesses as an explanation.

Conclusion

Three broad families of interpretation have been set out here. Each has generated substantial scholarship on corporate governance patterns and practices. The interaction among them is often limited, as each school refers internally to its colleagues and often does not cut across boundaries. Just how to integrate these alternative arguments remains an open theme for the future. There are advantages to specialization, to having each school working out the logic of its inquiry, and then comparing and contrasting each. That seems better than assembling all the pieces into a collage or a laundry list of factors.

This chapter stresses politics. Corporate governance goes to the heart of power in market economies. It links deeply with income distribution, job security, social services, employment and competition. Analysis overlaps with evaluation. Many see convergence: investors demand strong transparency and MSP; in a world competing for international capital, investors will get what they want and so convergence will occur. Writers on the left condemn this as bad for workers;

conservatives applaud it. Both see the same causal mechanism (the power of capital) but evaluate it differently.

Reality and rhetoric make it hard at times to evaluate what changes are really taking place. Shareholder value rhetoric sweeps the world, companies open offices of shareholder relations, everyone adopts codes of governance that sound alike, resonating with OECD principles, those of CalPERS, Hermes, TIAA-CREF, etc. But what actually happens in these countries may vary considerably. In many places with codes, law has changed little, and enforcement even less. In companies with shareholder relations offices, have practices really changed much – do the managers respond to what shareholders want, or is the PR better?

Important distinctions get neglected: the talk about the power of financial institutions sweeping the world overlooks important differences among them. CalPERS and Hermes for example are quite proactive on corporate governance issues in the US, while Merrill Lynch and Fidelity are not, at least not publicly. The latter have conflicts of interest that may inhibit them from being pro-active: they do consulting and provide services to the firms whose managers they could be monitoring on behalf of their investors. Funds which do not derive income from such sources, and thus do not have to please the managers who award the contracts, lack this conflict: these include public employee funds and union based funds. These are in turn accused by their critics of serving social and not fiduciary goals (Romano 2004). Hedge funds have also become substantial players in the governance system. Some of them acquire shares to force managerial changes – in that way, a governance function. Others influence liquidity and stability, but not governance in any direct way. Hedge funds have become controversial in both respects, attracting the ire of managers, but also the fear of investors for destabilizing the system (Geithner 2006).

We know little about these institutional differences. As private pension funds grow in importance, it is important to study just how the institutions of pension funds are actually structured and controlled – the pension funds and the governance systems interact in important ways (Gourevitch *et al.* 2006). Thus financialization is an important force, but the way it works can vary considerably from country to country.

Corporate governance expresses rules, regulations, preferences, cultures and politics. These vary considerably round the world. Indeed it may be that having a different system can be a comparative advantage – so that systems can differ as they specialize in one form of activity rather than another. The power of globalization forces is considerable: capital, goods, people and culture move around the world, some at great speed. And yet that process may reward diversity as much as force convergence. Different strategies of putting the pieces of production together allow for divergent forms of economic organization, including corporate governance. Convergence happens only if there is no reward for heterogeneity, and no social barriers to it. Political jurisdictions and levels of government refract social processes in divergent ways, leaving considerable space for regulatory differentiation. The logic of Adam Smith's market is specialization, and that means differentiation of form within a common structural frame.

3 Regulation- and state-theoretical perspectives on changes in corporate governance and metagovernance

Bob Jessop

Corporate governance and its regulation are continuing concerns in modern market economies. Nonetheless the salience of these issues varies – conjuncturally according to the incidence of scandals at the level of the firm or sector and structurally with the outbreak of crises in the overall design and implementation of corporate governance regimes and their regulation. This temporal differentiation is linked to variations across economic sectors and varieties of capitalism. Responses to crisis also vary in these terms. In the spirit of the present book, this chapter develops a general meso- and macro-level account of corporate governance and its regulation (or metagovernance) that builds on complementary perspectives on the political economy of the economy and the political economy of the political. These are the regulation approach in evolutionary and institutional economics and the strategic-relational approach respectively. Both adopt a methodological relational approach and recognize the continued relevance of the critique of political economy. It is nonetheless worth distinguishing them because one is more sensitive to the logic of the profit-oriented, market-mediated process of accumulation and the other to the logic of the policy-oriented, territorially-grounded exercise of political power. The relative importance of these logics, their structural coupling and their strategic coordination are crucial issues for a coherent account of the form and function of corporate governance regimes, which are located at the intersection of the political economy of the economy and the political.

Theoretical perspectives

This is not the place for an extended account of these two approaches. But it is worth noting some key theoretical points about the regulation approach even at the risk of caricature in order to situate corporate governance (see Boyer and Saillard 2002 and Jessop and Sum 2006 for more elaborate analyses) and about the strategic-relational approach to government and governance to situate my claims about governance failure (for more details, see Jessop 1990, 2002a).

First, the regulation approach (RA) starts from the improbability of stable capital accumulation because of the inherent structural contradictions (or, at least, inherent tensions) involved in securing the complex, spatio-temporally and institutionally differentiated, sets of economic and extra-economic conditions necessary for relatively stable expansion of the anarchic, profit-oriented, market-mediated, and conflictual circuit of capital. Second, in this context, it focuses on the trial-and-error selection and consolidation of complementary sets of institutional forms and regularizing practices that provide a suitable, albeit temporary, extra-economic framework for the operation of profit-oriented, market-mediated economic activities. Third, for Parisian regulationists, the enterprise form and forms of competition constitute just one of five key sites of regulation (or, better, regularization) of capital accumulation: the others are the capital–labor relation, monetary and financial systems, the state, and international regimes. Fourth, given the contradictory, conflictual, and dilemmatic nature of capitalism, any accumulation regime and its mode of regulation will necessarily be provisional, partial, and unstable, their reproduction being more or less permanently vulnerable to uneven development and disruption. Fifth, whilst disruptions and minor crises can often be handled within the basic rules of a given accumulation regime and its mode of regulation, repeated problems and more serious crises will sooner or later initiate a search for a new accumulation regime and corresponding mode of regulation. Sixth, owing to the interconnectedness of different institutional forms, this search process must sooner or later address the enterprise form, forms of competition, and corporate governance.

Regarding the state, my first point is that, like capital, it is best interpreted as a social relation. Thus, just as the course of capital accumulation is a form-determined condensation of the changing balance of forces involved in the capital–labor relation and the wider struggle for differential accumulation, state power is a form-determined condensation of the changing balance of forces concerned with shaping policy, politics, and the nature of the polity as territorialized political power. Second, the exercise and impact of state power depend on state organization in its broader sense of 'political society + civil society' (Gramsci 1971) or, more appropriately in the present context, 'governance in the shadow of government'. Third, the legitimacy of state power depends on its articulation to a political imaginary, that is the capacity of the leading political forces to persuade other forces that the prevailing policies are oriented to the common interests of the imagined political community associated with a given form of state and political regime. Fourth, notwithstanding the temptations of methodological nationalism, there is no necessity to the national form of sovereign state allegedly characterizing the Westphalian state system. Indeed, there are many ways to institute the territorialization of political power and many challenges to territorialization as the basis for realizing common interests. This is why, fifth, it is important to consider the relative weight of different modes of governance, including not only the principle of hierarchy that finds its ultimate embodiment in the sovereign state but also the anarchy of the market, the heterarchy of networked forms of coordination, and the solidarity of unconditional commitments in real or imagined communities. This is an important issue in the light of claims that a shift from government to governance also applies to corporate governance and its regulation.

Corporate governance and metagovernance

One of the questions posed in the conference from which this chapter derives was whether corporate governance regulation reflects an efficiency drive in the face of globalization. Given the transnational historical materialist approach of its organizers, this question is clearly rhetorical and borders on the ironic. If seriously posed, it assumes short time horizons, an economistic reading of corporate governance, and a naïve belief in its efficacy. Yet corporate governance and its regulation have long been contentious, must be related to the periodization of capitalism and its varieties, depend on changing legal, political, social, and moral frameworks, and, like all forms of governance, are prone to failure. Thus we should rephrase this question by asking why there has been a recent, concerted effort to change forms of corporate governance. A regulationist would focus on the crisis in the dominant enterprise form associated with the prevailing accumulation regime and its mode of regulation.

This is best understood in terms of the hierarchy of institutional forms in the Fordist mode of regulation insofar as the initiatives for corporate governance reform (and, in particular, neoliberal forms of shareholder value) originated primarily in the heartlands of the uncoordinated varieties of Atlantic Fordism. In heavily stylized terms, the two dominant institutional forms in Fordism were the wage-relation and money form. The Fordist mode of regulation presupposed the coincidence of interest of industrial capital and the core working class insofar as increasing productivity led to increased wages and thence to more demand for industrial goods, which generated increased profits for investment in another round of production. This virtuous circle was possible because of the relatively closed nature of national economies that were managed by national states in the interests of their citizens. Keynesian economic steering and the welfare state involved in turn the management of money primarily as national money rather than as one among many international currencies. Post-war international monetary institutions were designed to facilitate this by providing overall stability in the monetary and currency systems at the same time as permitting gradual adjustments where imbalances became too great. In equally stylized terms, the enterprise form was dominated by large oligopolistic firms based on the separation of ownership and control and oriented to economic strategies premised on the supply-driven constraints of mass production and the corresponding need for expanding markets. Competition among small and medium-sized enterprises and a more or less significant role for state-owned and/or state-regulated enterprise provided sources of flexibility to facilitate this expansion. This was reflected in Berle and Means's classic account of the enterprise form (1991 [1932]), Galbraith's account of the division between monopoly capital and the competitive sector and the concerted stabilizing role of the politico-economic 'technostructure' (1967), and Shonfield's analysis of public power in the mixed economy (1965).

However, as the post-war Atlantic Fordist economies became internationalized and were challenged by reviving or emerging economies elsewhere, it became harder to sustain this institutional hierarchy. In particular, the wage was increasingly seen as a cost of international production rather than a source of domestic demand; and money increasingly circulated as international currency that could escape national state control. This opened the space for the assertion of a neoliberal 'money concept of control', to use the language of the Amsterdam school of transnational historical materialism, against the productive concept of control that shaped the institutionalized national compromises between industrial capital and organized labor. The call for grounding corporate governance in shareholder value reflects this neoliberal concept because it focuses one-sidedly on the interests of money capital in moving freely between different sites of investment in order to maximize monetary returns for its ultimate owners. This is the only basis for viewing this new form of corporate governance as efficient. From a productive viewpoint concerned with material use-values and interdependencies, its efficiency appears badly flawed and marginalizes other stakeholders whose cooperation is needed for the relatively smooth functioning of the technical and social division of labor.

This is not to deny that Atlantic Fordism was in crisis when the neoliberal assault on its mode of regulation occurred – declining productivity, saturated demand, declining profitability, stagflation, fiscal crisis, trade union and social unrest, and many other economic and political indicators attest to this. Nor is it to deny that globalization contributed significantly to Fordist destabilization for the reasons noted above. But the manner in which these causes were narrated in neoliberal discourse and were then translated into economic and political strategies one-sidedly favored finance capital and mobile industrial capital. Economic efficiency was largely understood in Ricardian terms of allocative efficiency (hence returns to factors of production) and/or static comparative advantage. Globalization was likewise narrated as an inevitable force of nature that obliged all economic and political actors to adapt or die in an increasingly intense global competition. Atlantic Fordism had indeed become allocatively inefficient and an emphasis on shareholder value might be a suitable response thereto. But it was also proving inefficient in the Schumpeterian terms of dynamic competitive advantage – to which the one-sided money concept of control is no long-term solution. It is also clear that internationalization weakened the structural coherence of the Fordist mode of regulation – but this was in part due to the destructive effect of hypermobile, superfast financial capital oriented to shareholder value on that mode of regulation. In short, while there is a material basis to claims that new forms of corporate governance had become necessary, the neoliberal solution was not inevitable, let alone the sole guarantee of increased efficiency. Thus the dominance of neoliberalism reflects structural, strategic, and discursive forces that had little direct connection to the Fordist crisis in general terms.

A more complex, multicausal analysis would need to look at conflicting opportunities for the redefinition of corporate governance that were created by the Fordist crisis. If new industrial paradigms created the space for a redefinition of the firm (increasingly interpreted as a set of core competencies independent of particular forms of material production in particular places) and a transnational spatial and scalar division of labor, they also created the space to reassert the material interdependencies in that division of labour and the increased importance of extra-economic factors to dynamic competitive advantage in global competition. And, if time–space compression and time–space distantiation highlighted the challenges of global competition, they could also be interpreted as calling for greater solidarity and new forms of welfare state to help adversely affected workers, sectors, and regions to adapt positively rather than to reinforce patterns of uneven development and a race to the bottom. Likewise, if the mixed economy model of Atlantic Fordism had been seen to fail, the answer was not necessarily a return to liberal market forces as the principal steering mechanism – with the inevitable return of market failure and the weakening of state capacities to steer, rather than plan, economic development. That there were alternatives to the neoliberal regime shift, financialization, and shareholder value is shown by the relative success of economies that chose to make neoliberal policy adjustments in order to maintain their inherited neocorporatist and neostatist models. The more recent turn from shareholder value to corporate social responsibility and new forms of public–private partnership is one indicator of its one-sided irrationality (on the rhetorical aspects of corporate social responsibility as part of the audit culture that gives globalization an 'auditable' face, see Sum 2005).

Convergence on neoliberalism?

A second question posed at the inaugural conference, and in fact underlying this book, is whether we should expect corporate governance to converge towards neoliberal shareholder capitalism. There was certainly an apparent convergence towards neoliberalism in the 1990s because of the conjunctural coincidence of neoliberal system transformation in post-socialist economies, neoliberal regime shifts in uncoordinated market economies, and more modest neoliberal policy adjustments in coordinated market economies. But neoliberal system transformation has largely failed and been rejected in many post-socialist economies and neoliberal regime shifts have encountered growing difficulties for predictable reasons. Thus, while neoliberalism may have been selected from among many alternatives in the 1980s and 1990s, there is less evidence that it has been consolidated into a monovalent system of corporate governance. To explain this complex, path-dependent, materially-conditioned, and politically contested pattern of convergence–divergence we must examine the limits of liberalism and the causes of the continued variegation within global capitalism.

Ideologically, liberalism claims that economic, political, and social relations are best organized through the formally free[1] choices of formally free and rational actors who seek to advance their own material or ideal interests in an institutional framework that, by accident or design, maximizes the scope for formally free choice. This claim plays an important role in the ideological justification of shareholder capitalism and its associated forms of corporate governance, in particular through the assimilation of the corporation to the natural person. Economically, liberalism endorses the expansion of the market economy, that is, spreading the commodity form to all factors of production (including labor power and, more recently, knowledge) and formally free, monetized exchange to as many social practices as possible. In turn this increases the scope for the owners of the most important factors of production to shape economic dynamics and, as commodification penetrates into more and more areas of social relations, the dynamic of the wider social formation. Politically, liberalism argues that collective decision making should involve a constitutional state with limited substantive powers of economic and social intervention and a strong commitment to maximizing the formal freedom of actors in the economy and the substantive freedom of legally recognized subjects in the public sphere. The latter is based in turn on spontaneous freedom of association of individuals to pursue any social activities that are not forbidden by constitutionally valid laws. These three principles often come into conflict and the relative balance of economic, political, and civic liberalism depends on shifts in an unstable equilibrium of compromise.

The resonance of liberalism (and neoliberalism) is rooted in four features of capitalist social formations. First is the institution of private property, that is, the juridical fiction of 'private' ownership and control of the factors of production. This encourages individual property owners and those who dispose over fictitious commodities such as labour-power, natural resources, or knowledge to see themselves as entitled to use or alienate their property as they think fit, without due regard to the substantive interdependence of activities in a market economy and market society. In this realm 'rule Freedom, Equality, Property and Bentham, because both buyer and seller of a commodity, say of labour-power, are constrained only by their own free will' (Marx 1996: 186). This is a key part of the rationale for the primacy of shareholder value in corporate governance. Second, there is the appearance of 'free choice' in consumption, where those with sufficient money choose what to buy and how to dispose of it. This reinforces the primacy of shareholder value on the grounds that firms that neglect their 'sovereign' customers cannot maximize profits. Third, the institutional separation and operational autonomies of the economy and state make the latter's interventions appear as external intrusions into the activities of otherwise free economic agents. This may initially be an unwelcome but necessary extra-economic condition for orderly free markets but, if pushed beyond this minimum nightwatchman role, it appears as an obstacle to free markets and/or as direct political oppression. This is a key element in the justification for neoliberal attempts to roll back the interventionist states that characterized Atlantic Fordism, export-oriented growth in East Asia, import-substitution industrialization in Latin America, and failed states in Africa. Fourth, the institutional separation of civil society and the state encourages the belief that state intervention is an intrusion into the formally free choices of particular members of civil society once the conditions for social order have been established. This also supports shareholder value if corporations have the same rights as natural persons.

Opposition to liberalism may also emerge on the basis of four other features of capitalist social relations. First, growing 'socialization of the forces of production' despite continued 'private ownership of the means of production' suggests the need for *ex ante* collaboration among producer groups to limit market anarchy, through top–down planning and/or various forms of self-organization. Second, there are the strategic dilemmas posed by the 'shared interests of producers' (including wage-earners) in maximizing total revenues through cooperation and their 'divided and potentially conflicting' interests over how these revenues are distributed. Various non-market governance mechanisms have a role here helping to balance cooperation and conflict. Third, there are the contradictions and conflicts posed by the coexistence of 'the institutional separation and mutual dependence' of the economic and state systems. This leads to different logics of economic and political action, at the same time as it creates a need to consult on the economic impact of state policies and/or the political repercussions of private economic decision-making. And fourth, problems are generated by civil society as a sphere of 'particular interests' opposed to the state's alleged embodiment of 'universal interests'. This indicates the need for some institutional means of mediating the particular and universal and, since this is impossible in the abstract, for some hegemonic definition of the 'general interest'. In this context, of course, shareholder value privileges private ownership, capture of revenues, the formal primacy of the market despite the substantive mutual dependence of the economic and the political, and the sphere of particular interests.

This suggests that, if liberalism can be interpreted as a more or less 'spontaneous philosophy' rooted in capitalist social relations, one should also recognize that it is prone to 'spontaneous combustion' due to tensions inherent in these same relations. Polanyi noted this in his critique of late nineteenth-century liberalism, arguing that, in response to crisis-tendencies in *laissez-faire* capitalism, many social forces struggled to re-embed and re-regulate the market. The eventual compromise solution was a 'market economy' embedded in and sustained by a 'market society' (Polanyi 1957). The same point holds for neoliberal capitalism. Thus, after the efforts of 'roll-back neoliberalism' to free the neoliberal market economy from its various corporatist and statist impediments, attempts are now being made to secure its medium-term viability by embedding it in a neoliberal market society. This can be seen in increasing resort to supplementary measures to flank, support, and sustain the continued dominance of the neoliberal project in those social formations where it has been associated with radical neoliberal system transformation and/or neoliberal regime shifts. In the case of corporate governance, for example, 'society' has fought back through its demands for a stakeholding society, corporate social responsibility, the greening of the corporation, and a new ethical approach to economic issues.

This said, different principles of corporate governance seem more or less well suited to different stages of capitalism and/or its contemporary variants. Thus, *laissez-faire* was probably more suited to the pioneering forms of competitive capitalism than to later entrants onto the capitalist world market (cf. Gerschenkron 1962); and it is more suited to uncoordinated than coordinated market economies, for which corporatism and statism seem better (Coates 2000; Hall and Soskice 2001; Huber and Stephens 2001). Different stages, forms, and varieties of capitalism may therefore have distinctive institutional attractors (or centres of gravity) around which forms of governance oscillate. So it is crucial to study 'actually existing neoliberalisms' (Brenner and Theodore 2002) to understand how their dynamic and viability are shaped by specific path-dependent contexts, competing discourses, strategies, and organizational paradigms, and the balance of forces associated with different projects. This leads us directly to the question of the so-called varieties of capitalism.

For, although capitalism is increasingly organized on a global scale into an ever-more integrated world market, it still remains quite variegated in form, dynamics, and overall performance. There is no single best way to organize and govern capitalism and, notwithstanding claims about long-term convergence, several varieties of capitalism persist due to the heterogeneity of the goods and services (including fictitious commodities) produced for sale and due to the inevitable embedding of capitalist production and markets in broader sets of social relations. Such variation is evident in the wide range of capitalist firms, industries and sectors, complexes and clusters, localities, regions, national economies, plurinational systems, transnational networks, and trading blocs. Advocates of neoliberalism tend to ignore these constraints. For, from a neoliberal perspective, which prioritizes exchange relations, the circulation of capital, and the 'money concept' of capital, commodities are reduced to exchange-values, obstacles and frictions to circulation can be overcome through creating the conditions for a 'space of flows', and capital is reducible to a liquid sum of money available for investment anywhere and at any time in the global economy. From the viewpoint of productive capital, however, use-value also matters, production has priority over circulation, and capital is in the first instance a stock of assets that must be valorized in a particular place and time. Thus neoliberalism is inclined to support shareholder value and to resist restrictions on the free flow of money capital. In contrast, neocorporatist and neo-statist positions emphasize the specificities involved in producing particular use-values, the complex material interdependencies within production and its extra-economic conditions, and the spatio-temporal complexities of productive capital. From a neoliberal perspective, varieties of capitalism represent path-dependent frictions that offer opportunities for arbitrage, business re-engineering, and neoliberal rollback to enhance economic efficiency, shareholder value, and freedom of choice. From a productive capital viewpoint, however, variation represents the path-dependent economic and extra-economic legacies of specialization in producing and marketing different types of commodity and different forms of insertion into a multi-scalar and still-fragmented world market.

This leads to a general tension between current neoliberal demands to accelerate the flow of abstract (money) capital through an increasingly disembedded space and 'timeless time' (that is, abstract time rather than the concrete modalities of first and second nature and substantive production), and the need for the more concrete forms of capital to be 'fixed' in time and place as well as embedded in specific social relations as a condition for their valorization. Other contradictions are also exacerbated by the neoliberal form of globalization. They include a growing short-termism in economic calculation associated with a system of corporate governance based on shareholder value versus the increasing dependence of valorization on extra-economic factors that take a long time to produce; and the contradiction between the development of an 'information economy' based on the generalization of intellectual property rights and the need to develop an 'information society' in which knowledgeable workers expand the intellectual commons, knowledgeable consumers can use intelligent products and services, and informed citizens can develop a new solidaristic mode of regulation that can overcome the digital divide and other forms of social exclusion and polarization associated with neoliberalism.

Whilst there are important material and institutional factors behind the survival and, indeed, continued development of variegated capitalism, that is, an interdependent set of varieties of capitalism within an integrated world market, we should also note the pressures associated with the 'ecological dominance' of the neoliberal variant. In crude terms, ecological dominance can be described as the capacity of one mode of societal organization to cause more problems for the stabilization of other modes than pursuit of these modes can cause for the ecologically dominant mode (for a more nuanced account, see Jessop 2002a). This is an important element in the spread of neoliberal forms of corporate governance. The ecological dominance of capitalism in general over other logics of societal organization is closely related to the extent to which its degrees of freedom, opportunities for self-reorganization, scope for time–space distantiation and compression, externalization of problems, and hegemonic capacities can be freed from confinement within limited ecological spaces policed by another system – such as a political system segmented along Westphalian lines into mutually exclusive sovereign territories. This is where globalization, especially in its neoliberal form, becomes significant for the relative ecological dominance of capital accumulation. For it powerfully reinforces the always-tendential ecological dominance of capitalism in at least five interrelated respects. First, it is associated with an increasing complexity of the circuits of capital and an increasing flexibility in its response to perturbations. Second, it enhances capital's capacity to defer and displace its internal contradictions, if not to resolve them, by increasing the scope of its operations on a global scale, by enabling it to deepen spatial and scalar divisions of labor, and by creating more opportunities for moving up, down, and across scales. These enhanced capacities reinforce uneven development as the search continues for new spatio-temporal fixes that can resolve the tension between time–space distantiation and time–space compression. Third, it appears to emancipate the exchange-value moment of capital from extra-economic and spatio-temporal limitations. This extends the scope for capital's self-valorization dynamic to develop in a one-sided manner at the expense of other systems and of the lifeworld until crises forcibly re-impose the substantive as well as formal unity of the circuit of capital and its extra-economic supports. Fourth, neoliberal globalization magnifies capital's capacity to escape the control of other systems and to follow its own procedures in deciding how to react to perturbations. This is particularly associated with its increased capacity for discounting events, its increased capacity for time–space compression, its resort to complex derivative trading to manage risk, and its capacities to jump scale. Fifth, it weakens national states' capacity to confine capital's growth dynamic within a framework of national security (as reflected in the 'national security state'), or national welfare (as reflected in social democratic welfare states), or some other national matrix. Corporate governance oriented to shareholder value is a particularly powerful force in pushing the ecological dominance of the logic of capital accumulation as the primary principle of societal organization.

This does not mean that capitalist ecological dominance is unilateral and uniform. The political system, which is currently materialized above all in the institutional architectures of national states and international relations and linked to the lifeworld through public opinion, has important reciprocal influences on the development of the capitalist economy. Indeed it poses the biggest challenge to the latter's ecological dominance. For, whilst the state system is responsible for securing certain key conditions for the valorization of capital and the social reproduction of labor power as a fictitious commodity, it also has overall political responsibility for maintaining social cohesion in a socially divided, pluralistic social formation. The always-problematic relationship between these functions generates risks and uncertainties for capital accumulation. So does state failure. This is why struggles over political power are so crucial to the reproduction-regulation of capital accumulation and why the state is so central to securing spatio-temporal fixes that enable relatively stable accumulation. And it is why globalization, especially in its neoliberal form, represents such a challenge to the actually existing institutional architecture of the political system. For it tends to weaken the typical form of the national state in advanced capitalist societies as this developed during the period of Atlantic Fordism and to disrupt the spatio-temporal fixes around which both accumulation and the state were organized.

It is in this context that Boyer discusses the hierarchies that characterize the arrangement of the five key institutional forms identified in the regulation approach in periods of relative stability and periods of transition between such periods. He writes that, in periods of stability, the dominant institutional form is the one that imposes structural constraints on the configuration of other institutional forms (Boyer 2000a: 291); conversely, in periods of transition,

> [a]n institutional form may be said to be hierarchically superior to another if its development implies a transformation of this other form, in its configuration and its logic. Unlike the earlier definition, the latter does not imply that the mode of *régulation* which emerges from this complex of transformations will be coherent.

Implicit here is a distinction between what we can call the 'structural dominance' of a given institutional form over other forms in a structural configuration during periods of stability and what we can call the 'ecological dominance' of a given institutional form during periods of transition and/or instability marked by lack of coherence. At stake is the question: 'under what conditions does an embryonic, "marginal" form of organization impose itself on the whole of the system, to the point where it fashions its overall logic?' (Boyer 1990: 108). In the current era of globalization, Boyer believes that the ecologically dominant form is international finance[2] whose increasingly global operations are enabled by international economic integration more generally (Boyer 2000a: 311–19). Guttman even describes this pattern of ecological dominance, with its volatile exchange rates and high interests rates, as a new mode of regulation because it destabilizes the Fordist mode of regulation (Guttman 2002: 61–2). However, it would be better to see this dynamic not as a (possibly transitional) mode of regulation but as the 'work of crisis' engendered by the contradictions of the previous mode of regulation and creating thereby a space for struggles over the constitution of a new mode of regulation (cf. De Bernis 1988: 101–5; Peck and Tickell 2002). And it is the reaction to this 'creative destruction' introduced by 'roll-back neoliberalism' (Peck and Tickell 2002) and by neoliberal forms of corporate governance that is responsible, in part, for the search for alternative forms of solving the continuing crises in the enterprise form, in the relations between financial and productive capital associated with financialization and the ecological dominance of hypermobile, superfast money capital, the deleterious effects of downward pressure on wages and the social wage (including pensions) as international costs of production, and the growing disjunction between the turnover time of productive as well as money capital and the rhythms of the natural world.

From public–national to private–global regulation?

A third question (as indicated in the first chapter) relates to the modes and levels of governance: it conflates two key tendencies in the development of corporate governance, namely, the de-statization of governance (public–private) and the de-nationalization of the juridico-political regulation as one form of territorialized power (national–global) among others. Both tendencies should be defined relative to the post-war period rather than earlier periods and both are limited in their present reach. Indeed, even if we accepted that these trends were adequate descriptions of recent shifts compared with the primacy of public–national regulation in advanced capitalist economies in les trente glorieuses of the post-war Atlantic Fordist boom, each trend still requires qualification in its own terms and must also be linked to important counter-trends. For the de-territorialization of regulation involves downwards and sideways as well as upwards movement; and de-statization in turn involves a wide range of old, revived, and new forms of governance, often combined in new hybrid forms. In addition, variegated capitalism and variations in state capacities also pose important questions about the scope for neoliberalism to expand and about the differential capacities of states to halt or reverse neoliberal 'ratchet effects' in countries where neoliberalism has been introduced.

The first trend implies a turn from public to private forms of corporate governance. This must be qualified in two respects. First, public power has rarely penetrated formally, let alone substantively, into the heart of the corporation as a productive organization. It has created different forms of enterprise and established different forms of corporate governance but it has not abolished the legal right of owners and managers to manage the enterprise within these limits and has also found it difficult (even where the collective or political will was present) to police and punish infringements of prevailing restrictions. This is especially clear in the uncoordinated varieties of capitalism but is a general reflection of the difficulties of directly controlling any self-organizing system from outside using resources belonging to another system. For, in a profit-oriented, market-mediated capitalist economy, there may be strong economic incentives to engage in efficient breach of law, avoidance of fiscal obligations, neglect of political directives, denial of social duties, and so forth. This is reflected in the tendency for states to use indirect methods of steering corporations even where a strong institutional, organizational, and interpersonal separation exists between state and market. And, second, the current fashion for the de-statization of the political reflected in the often-noted shift from government to governance is accompanied by a shift from government to metagovernance. This is reflected in the commonplace that de-regulation is usually coupled with forms of re-regulation. But it can be generalized to the hypothesis that, as states at different scales reduce their role in imperative coordination through the use of their sovereign powers, they seek to extend their capacities to engage in indirect steering through re-designing the institutional architecture of markets and organizing the conditions of self-organization. Following Dunsire (1996), Jessop (1998), and Kooiman (2003), this response can be called 'collibration' or 'metagovernance'. It involves the judicious mixing of market, hierarchy, and networks to achieve the best possible outcomes from the viewpoint of those engaged in metagovernance. Governments have a key role to play here but metagovernance is also fallible.

The de-nationalization of governmental and governance regimes also demands both historical qualification and recognition of important counter-trends. Thus, historically, governments have always operated at multiple sites and on multiple scales as well as in relation to multiple policy fields and multiple time horizons. The dominance of the national scale is the product of a specific socially-constructed coincidence of the national economy as an object of economic management, the national state as a sovereign territorial state, and the emergence of 'national societies' largely contained within national territorial borders. Even in the heyday of national economies, states, and societies, however, state powers were exercised locally, regionally, and inter- or trans-nationally. Moreover, with the 'relativization of scale' that has accompanied the crisis of Atlantic Fordism, East Asian exportism, Latin American import substitution, and so on, no other scale has gained the same dominance that was previously held by the national state. On the contrary, there is a continuing struggle over which scale of government-governance, if any, should be dominant. In this context, we find that national states are heavily engaged in interscalar management, that is, efforts to shape which powers go up, sideways, or downwards, and, in addition, to influence the form and content of international regimes that will then be interpreted and applied at lower levels (for a case study of competition law, see Wigger 2005). In contributing to multi-scalar metagovernance in this way, state actors draw on a wide range of sources to construct international regimes, soften hard law, harden soft law, use economic incentives, develop specialized bodies of intelligence and knowledge, set up international standards and benchmarks, and so forth (cf. Picciotto 2004).

The emerging system should not be described simply in terms of 'global–private governance' but recognized instead as a complex, multi-scalar, hybrid, and tangled system of metagovernance that operates in the shadow of post-national statehood. Moreover, the very complexity of the interweaving of different forms of governance and government on different scales means that the resulting system is more complex than any social force can conceive and its overall evolution lies beyond the control of any social force. This risks adding governance failure to market failure and state failure, if only through their unforeseen and/or unintended consequences and side-effects, as problems to be confronted by regulatory agencies. The largely unknowable and uncontrollable activities of the rapidly evolving system of hedge funds provide just one telling illustration of this more general problem and the collapse of long-term capital management shows the extent to which regional, national, and international governmental as well as non-governmental agencies had to be mobilized in order to prevent economic meltdown. This in turn poses important questions about the possibility and prospects of developing global forms of metagovernance that would not themselves be prone to metagovernance failure.

This is by no means a simple task. Indeed, unless we recognize that the object of corporate governance is inherently contradictory in structural terms, poses major strategic dilemmas, and is subject to all manner of paradoxes, we will never fully understand the complexities of governing capitalism (including corporate governance) and the inherent tendency for all forms of governance to fail. This is reflected in the re-emergence and transformation of the basic contradictions inherent in capitalism following the neoliberal turn prompted in part by growing signs of state failure. Likewise, where the limitations of neoliberalism (including the shareholder value model of corporate governance) have been recognized, attempts to develop networked forms of governance or public–private partnerships that stress interdependence and 'stakeholder' interests have also proved contradictory, dilemmatic, paradoxical, and hence fallible, in their turn. All forms of governance generate fundamental problems of collective action as well as more or less acute dilemmas for individual economic or political actors. Indeed, even where the problems generated by the contradictory nature of the capital relation are relatively easy to resolve at the individual firm level because of the nature of their inputs, products, or markets, the pursuit of individual solutions need not produce a coherent collective solution even in the long run.

Elsewhere I have distinguished four specific factors behind governance failure. First, the conditions of successful action may have been oversimplified and/or there may be deficient knowledge about the many causal connections affecting the object of governance. This raises the 'governability' problem, that is, the issue of whether the object of governance could ever be manageable, even with adequate knowledge (Mayntz 1993). The capital relation appears to fall into this class of 'ungovernable' objects on a global scale, even if there are partial and temporary zones of relative stability that are enabled by the displacement and deferral of contradictions and crisis tendencies elsewhere and/or into the future (cf. Jessop 2002a, 2002b). At best one finds the partially successful governance of delimited objects of governance within specific spatial and temporal horizons of action – at the expense of deliberately neglected or unrecognized costs elsewhere. Neoliberal corporate governance is a good (or bad) illustration of this problem because it creates short-term stability for protected groups at the expense of exacerbating instability elsewhere and in the future. Second, coordination problems may occur within and across the interpersonal, interorganizational, and intersystemic levels where governance is adopted. These levels are often related in complex ways. The one-sided emphasis on shareholder value is a classic illustration of this, leading to unintended consequences for the overall integration of the technical and social division of labor and the political ecological order more generally. Third, gaps can open between representatives engaged in communication (networking, negotiation, etc.) and those whose interests and identities are being represented. This is common in corporatism, political parties, and social movements and raises questions of legitimacy, effectiveness, and resistance. It is, of course, at the heart of the heated debates about principal–agent conflicts in the field of corporate governance and there is no neat technical or legal fix to this problem. Fourth, where several distinct governance arrangements exist to deal with interdependent issues, problems can also arise due to inconsistent definitions of the objects of governance, different spatial and temporal horizons of action, and their association with different interests and balances of force. The co-existence of corporate governance and many other governance regimes that bear on economic performance illustrates this well.

Cui bono?

Finally let us briefly address the question who benefits from these transformations. The preceding theoretical analysis suggests that corporate governance based on shareholder value primarily benefits finance capital and hypermobile productive capital. It also depends on the development, dissemination, and adoption of new forms of economic calculation and benchmarking that are the specialized field of the symbolic analysts of the audit culture. This category benefits not only from the primacy of shareholder value in the private sector but also the translation of these principles into new public management, with its watchwords of economy, efficiency, and effectiveness or, more succinctly, value for money. This involves not only privatization but also the adoption of market proxies in the residual public sector based on contestability and/or market testing. For a time some regulationists suggested that shareholder capitalism was a viable alternative to the Fordist accumulation regime provided that workers shared in the increase in stock markets driven forward by the emancipation of firms from out-dated regulation – just as they previously shared in the benefits of productivity based on economies of scale through wages that were indexed to productivity gains and inflation. But subsequent modelling of the preconditions for such a new virtuous circle showed that it was inherently implausible in the medium-term and certainly infeasible in the longer term (for example, Aglietta 2000; Boyer 2000b). The collapse of the 'new economy' bubble reinforced this conclusion as has the trend towards growing inequalities in wealth and income in the most neoliberal economies compared with competitive economies (such as the Scandinavian economies) that have maintained much of their welfare states whilst reorienting and recalibrating them (cf. Scharpf and Schmidt 2000a, 2000b).

Conclusions

In contrast to other contributions to this book, mine has not focused on corporate governance per se but has attempted to put corporate governance in its place. This has involved two parallel lines of argument. First, I have used the regulation approach to locate corporate governance primarily within one of five sites of institutional arrangement and regulatory (governance) practices and to argue that the importance of these different sites varies across different accumulation regimes and their modes of regulation. The hierarchy of institutional forms in Atlantic Fordism privileged the wage and money forms with meso- and macro-patterns of corporate governance and regulation subordinated to the discursively constructed and materially based requirements of national economic management in line with a 'productive concept of control'. The crisis of Atlantic Fordism created the space for the reassertion of a money concept of control more favorable to internationalization and the neoliberal prioritization of shareholder value. However, while the hierarchy of institutional forms in Atlantic Fordism was conducive to relative stability, the primacy of hypermobile financial capital and its ramification through the financialization of corporate control has undermined the institutional hierarchy of Atlantic Fordism without creating an equivalent hierarchy of institutions conducive to relatively stable growth on a world scale. On the contrary, the primacy of shareholder value has had a destructive impact on global economic order, enhancing uneven development, promoting the polarization of incomes and wealth, and promoting increasingly unsustainable imbalances in the global economy. Second, drawing on a strategic-relational approach to government and governance, I have highlighted the tendency for all modes of governance (broadly defined) to fail, the resulting need for 'collibration' or metagovernance, and the tendency of metagovernance also to fail. This implies that the neoliberal form of corporate governance should be seen as one element in a broader institutional architecture of economic governance and that, faced with the destructive medium-term impact of the dominant neoliberal form of shareholder value and its associated financialization and securitization of economic activities, we can expect a Polanyian 'double movement' that seeks to redress the balance between different forms of governance and to re-assert one or another form of substantive rationality over the formal, procedural rationality of a one-sided emphasis on exchange-value.

Notes

1 I use the concept of formal freedom here to draw an implicit contrast with the lack of full 'substantive' freedom due to the multiple constraints that limit free choice. The institutionalization of formal freedom is nonetheless a significant political accomplishment and a major element in liberal citizenship, as well as a precondition for market economies.

2 I have rephrased Boyer's argument here. He writes that, in contrast to the dominance of the capital–labour nexus in the Fordist era, in the 1990s integration into the international economy plays 'the cardinal role in the context of opening up to broader world trade, of increasing productive investment abroad, and, especially, of creating particularly active globalized financial markets' (Boyer 2000: 291). But, in Boyer's own terms, integration into the international economy is not an institutional form but constitutes a potential change in accumulation regimes. International regimes and money are institutional forms, however; and it is clearly money that is at stake in this transformative process rather than international regimes as conventionally interpreted by the regulation approach.

4 The paradoxical nature of shareholder primacy

A re-consideration of the Enron-era financial scandals in the US and the EU

Antoine Rebérioux

The rise to power of market finance since the mid-1970s has radically altered the characteristic traits of contemporary capitalism. This process of 'financialization' is driven by two movements (cf. the introductory chapter to this book). The first is the growth in the liquidity of capital markets, expressing increases in the breakdown and transfer of risks. The second is the upsurge, in these same markets, of investment funds, responsible for the management of continually increasing collective savings. Far from remaining limited solely to the financial sphere, theses changes have, as Van Apeldoorn and Horn argue in their contribution to this book, induced a process of 'marketization of corporate control'. In this respect, the doctrine of shareholder value has played, and continues to play, an essential role. The basic idea is that the sole objective of corporate executives and directors is to serve the interests of the shareholders. The main actors behind the resurgence of this (classical) doctrine for corporate governance were US institutional investors, for whom the maximization of the value of their holdings was synonymous with the defence of (minority) stockholders. In addition, shareholder primacy received much support from law and economics scholars (see, for example, Easterbrook and Fischel 1993). However, the major theoretical argument put forward to support it (the idea that shareholders are the only residual claimers) does not stand up to economic analysis. As has been convincingly argued by, amongst others, Williamson (1985), Blair (1995), and Zingales (1998) non-shareholder constituencies (and in particular workers investing in specific human capital) do bear risk when contracts are incomplete.

Yet a more pragmatic justification for shareholder primacy is commonly used by its proponents: shareholder primacy is considered to be the most effective way to foster managerial (corporate) accountability. In other words, stock market control of non-financial firms is described as efficient. The main reason is that it assigns a clear objective to managers (the maximization of the market price of shares), together with numerous disciplinary and incentive mechanisms. By contrast, a stakeholder approach would dilute managerial accountability and lead to a (sub-optimal) politicization of the board of directors (see for example, Bainbridge 1993; Hansmann 1996; Tirole 2001).

This chapter casts doubt on the validity of this doctrine, by arguing that shareholder primacy and stock market control of corporations lead to a *decline* in managerial accountability. In the first section, this decline is illustrated by an unprecedented series of accounting irregularities by champions of US and (to a lesser extent) European stock markets and a huge rise in executive compensations in the US. In the second section, we review the standard explanation of this process, which accounts for the failure of the supervising actors (gatekeepers and directors) in terms of inappropriate incentives. Shareholder primacy as such is hardly ever questioned. However, in the third section we argue that an exclusive control of the business firm by the stock market has a congenital defect. Hence we are led to consider the following paradox: shareholder primacy, usually described as a disciplining device, in fact favours erratic, deceptive behaviours on the part of corporate insiders. Following this analysis, in the fourth section we critically assess the legislative measures taken in reaction to corporate scandals, on both sides of the Atlantic. We show that these measures are deeply influenced by the primacy of shareholder ideology. Accordingly, the diffusion of this doctrine is an important (and by definition transnational) mechanism explaining the current evolution of corporate governance regulation and practices. We conclude, by stressing the role that (organized) labour might play to encourage and enhance corporate accountability.

The Enron-era scandals in the US and in Europe

On 2 December 2001, Enron was placed under bankruptcy. At \$63 billion in assets, this has been the largest bankruptcy in US history. In terms of stock market capital gone up in smoke, the loss inflicted upon shareholders was considerable: at the end of November, the stock traded at 26 cents. For Enron's 27,000 employees, the damage was just as heavy. They lost their jobs, and their retirement fund evaporated. The in-house pension fund, based on a so-called 401(k) Plan and thus exempted from the Employment Retirement Income Security Act imposing diversification, had been 60 per cent invested in Enron shares (Bratton 2002). Besides, heavyweights of the US financial industry numbered among the actors compromised by this bankruptcy. The various investigations will show that accounting frauds and manipulations were systematic:[1] heavy recourse to off-balance-sheet accounting and creative accounting on the income statement all contributed to the misuse of value for the benefit of few executives.

Much has been written on this high-profile corporate scandal. Yet we would like to insist on one particular point: the compliance, in rhetoric and in practice, with the principles of shareholder value creation by Enron executives. This compliance allowed for a continual increase in Enron share prices; in turn, this favourable valuation sustained external growth through hostile takeovers and the use of stock options for white collars and executives. For example, in 2001, the year of bankruptcy, the Chief Executive Officer (CEO) made \$9.6 million from stock options in two months (he was replaced in February); the Chief Financial Officer (CFO) made \$3 million. Numerous signs of this compliance with shareholder value might be pinpointed. For example, Enron developed a flat structure, weakly hierarchical, and organized around profit centres judged on their ability to meet financial requirements. Moreover, the board of directors was composed of 12 independent members out of a total of 14. As argued below, the independence of directors is one of the most basic requirements of a shareholder-friendly governance mode. Last but not least, asset-light strategy became the cornerstone of Enron's strategic orientation in the second half of the 1990s. Simply put, this strategy consists in acquiring assets in a given industry (broadband, textile, bulk and agricultural chemicals, etc.), using them to trade commodities in those industries, and finally selling the assets at a profit. In so doing, Enron was, again, obeying the commandments of 'Value Based Management' (VBM): the reduction of assets involved in the productive and commercial activity increases by definition the return on capital and 'shareholder value' (see below). If Enron's success at risk management in the energy sector is indisputable, its rapid expansion and its collapse are closely related to this asset-light strategy. One of Enron's particularities was to have instituted this as a permanent strategy for ensuring long-term profit (Chatterjee 2003).[2] The concrete application of this principle leads to a policy of asset repurchasing and large-scale investment. Indeed, to sell, one must acquire assets beforehand. This was so much the case that Enron, in its last years, was much less an energy sector corporation than a firm specialized in the trading of very diverse assets, from which it derived more than two-thirds of its profit. Enron's inordinate profit growth was due less to its choice of investments than to its policy of covering up the inevitable losses inherent in this type of activity. Its policy essentially consisted of transferring the most devalued assets, *a priori* unmarketable, to Special Purpose Entities (SPEs) which appeared at first glance to be autonomous, but which were in fact controlled by Enron.[3] Heavy use of off-balance-sheet accounting and deconsolidations, allowing Enron to undervalue its debt and to dispose of troublesome assets, became the company's trademark. Enron used a galaxy of almost 3000 SPEs. If SPEs are fairly common in the US, there were three particularities in the Enron case: the number of SPEs, the extent of deconsolidation[4] and the misuse of company property to allow for substantial personal enrichment.

Astonishing as it sounds, it was not an isolated case. In the months that followed Enron's collapse, massive scandals of listed companies in the US followed one after the other. The telecommunications sector was hit especially hard by the bankruptcies of Qwest, Global Crossing, and WorldCom. WorldCom's June 2002 bankruptcy even surpassed Enron's in scale – $104 billion in assets and $41 billion in liabilities. In each case, accounting frauds and manipulations became systematic, to guarantee favourable stock market valuations. For example, Global Crossing, created in 1997, used its inordinate market capitalization (more than $40 billion at the end of 1998, just months after being listed) to pursue a particularly aggressive acquisition policy. But all sectors were involved. In 1998, 158 listed companies were the objects of earnings restatements; in 2000, this number rose to 223, a 43 per cent increase. According to a report published by the General Accounting Office in October 2002, between January 1997 and June 2002, nearly 10 per cent of listed companies in the US restated their earnings at least once due to accounting irregularities. Moreover, a recent study conducted by the Huron group demonstrates that earnings restatements following financial irregularities are on an upward trend:[5] they reached a peak in 2004, with a total number of 414. Ultimately, the 1990s and the first half of the 2000s witnessed a dramatic increase in financial irregularities, together with a growing sensitivity of corporate executives to investor interests.

Recent decades also witnessed a huge rise in executive compensations in the US. According to Holmström and Kaplan (2003) overall CEO compensation increased by a factor of six during the 1980s and the 1990s. Most of this increase took the form of incentive pay – primarily stock options. This process has resulted in a deepening of intra-firm inequalities, of which the *Business Week* executive pay survey, regularly carried out, gives an idea: in 1980, the average income of CEOs of the largest firms in the US was 40 times the average salary of a worker. In 1990, it was 85 times greater, and in 2003, it jumped to 400 times greater. From a strict economic standpoint, such an increase raises serious concern: it is hard to explain on the basis of incentive factors alone, despite the effort made by some authors (see in particular Jensen and Murphy, 2004). Rather, a process of rent extraction by corporate managers is highly plausible (Bebchuk and Fried 2004; Bratton 2005). As such, this process might be considered together with the wave of financial scandals and accounting irregularities. Both are the most visible marks of a structural phenomenon: a decline in corporate management accountability.

Even if the US was particularly affected by scandals related to the management of listed companies, European countries did not escape unscathed. Various examples can be cited, though none having the magnitude of the US crisis: Vivendi Universal and France Télécom (FT) in France, Ahold in the Netherlands, and Parmalat in Italy all contributed in varying degrees to undermining confidence in finance-led capitalism. However, European CEO compensations did not increase to the same extent as the US ones, the main reason being the smaller diffusion of stock options.[6]

Parmalat, declared insolvent on 27 December 2003, has been considered as the 'European Enron'. And indeed, the concentration of ownership did not in the least prevent an Enron-like scenario. The largest food-processing corporation in Italy, quoted on the Milan Stock Exchange, was 51.3 per cent held by the family of the founder who was accused of having misappropriated more than one billion euros. The CFO/majority shareholder simply played the part of the managerial team in misappropriating assets. Even if some differences might be pinpointed between the two scandals (Coffee 2005) Parmalat would include most of the ingredients of the Enron affair. In particular, in the 1990s, the company launched an intensive policy of acquisition and diversification, accompanied by the raising of large amounts of cash on the US and European stock and bond markets. Parmalat contracted 26 bond loans starting in 1996, for an estimated debt of seven billion euros by the time insolvency was declared. And as with Enron, Parmalat had a multitude of offshore fronts designed to ease the balance sheet – a practice that would particularly increase beginning in 1998.[7]

In the case of FT, it is again the reliance on stock markets in order to implement a policy of accelerated development which is the direct source of its difficulties. Nevertheless, this case differs from Parmalat and Enron in that fraudulent accounting practices were never uncovered.[8] In 1995, the president who arrived to restructure FT was given the responsibility of preparing the state-owned operator for the opening up of its capital and for the liberalization of the telecommunications sector in Europe, scheduled for 1998. A policy of large-scale acquisitions was immediately embarked upon, particularly well received in a period of rising stock markets. The policy was rewarded: in June 1999, FT was placed first in France in the Economic Value Added/Market Value Added ranking made by the Parisian branch of the firm Stern, Stewart & Co. Vivendi Universal (whose conduct perfectly mimicked the American style of external growth based on stock price increase) was placed fourth. Much of these ingredients may be found in the case of Ahold.[9] The Dutch company pursued an aggressive external growth strategy through acquisition, mainly in the US, with an objective of a 15 per cent annual growth in earning per shares during the 1990s. Just like FT, Ahold was awarded for its shareholder-friendly business conduct (De Jong *et al.* 2005): from 1990 to 2001, Ahold was designated seven times as the best company during the Day of the Share. Returning to FT, the year 2000 saw no pause in the activity of acquisition, in spite of the reversal in capital market trends. FT acquired 28.5 per cent of MobilCom's capital and bought Orange from Vodafone. This policy of international development, as well as the acquisition of Universal Mobile Telecommunications System (UMTS) licences, was expensive: in the year 2000 alone, FT's debt quadrupled to 60 billion euros. The debt-to-equity ratio reached 180 per cent. The company thus engaged in a policy of non-strategic asset disposal in the hopes of easing the pressure. Balance sheet restructuring was impeded by continued depreciation of the company's stock market price, which lost 65 per cent of its value between January and September 2001. FT found itself trapped in a dynamic of debt appreciation/equity depreciation: stock market deterioration calls into question debt reduction by asset disposal, which reinforces the decline of stock market prices. In spite of this, FT continued to acquire, buying the Polish company TPSA in return for four billion euros more in debt. At the end of June 2002, the debt reached 70 billion euros, making FT the company with the highest debt in the world. In September, the CEO of FT was replaced.

Upon closer inspection, the repeated financial scandals on both sides of the Atlantic reveal a common rationale: the use of stock markets in a framework of aggressive acquisition policies with no obvious economic logic. Enron, Parmalat, FT and Ahold were favourably evaluated by stock markets and investor relations became a crucial component of their strategy. As such, these four companies bring to light a paradoxical affinity between managers' desire to expand and the defence of shareholder primacy. This paradox is even more accurate when one considers the dramatic increase in CEO compensation in the US. In sum, never have managers been as powerful, or at least so well-remunerated, as they have been since the return in force of the shareholders. The rest of this chapter provides some insights into this striking paradox, at the very heart of finance-led capitalism

Financial market requirements and control

Essentially, the increasing power of investment funds is expressed by the imposition of constraining criteria of financial returns on listed companies. The competition among funds to attract collective savings is transferred onto the companies, which are judged on the basis of their ability to meet the financial demands imposed on them.

Following this process of financialization, VBM is now a common practice for listed companies (Cooper *et al.* 2000). While the wealth going to shareholders is normally measured by net return (that is the profit once the employees have been paid and the debts serviced), VBM is based on the assumption that value actually created for shareholders comes from surpluses relative to the profitability demanded by the capital market. This value has been termed the Economic Value Added (EVA) by the Stern & Stewart consulting firm at the beginning of the 1990s, which copyrighted it. If all the listed companies have not adopted the EVA model as such, it has nonetheless, by virtue of its widespread dissemination,[10] contributed to legitimating and to theoretically grounding the investment funds' demands for financial returns.[11]

The assumption that there are no tax deductions or exceptional results simplifies the calculation, so that the current result merges with the net result. Let us denote R the net result, D the book value of debts, r their average costs, EC the book value of equity capital, k the equilibrium return on equity capital as determined by the Capital Asset Pricing Model (CAPM),[12] K the total book value of the assets $(D + EC)$ and $WACC$ the weighted average cost of capital.[13] The simplest expression of a company's EVA is then the following:

$$EVA = R - k \cdot EC \tag{1}$$

By denoting ROE the return on equity (R / EC) and ROA the return on assets (R / K), expression (1) is rewritten as follows:

$$EVA = (ROE - k) \cdot EC = (ROA - WACC) \cdot K \tag{2}$$

Equation (2) brings out the specific nature of the EVA: if the effective return on investment (the ROE) is the rate k, which correspond to the equilibrium market return for that class of risk, then the EVA model considers that no 'value' has been created (EVA=0). Likewise, if the investment is ultimately remunerated at a rate n with $0 < n < k$, then there is destruction of value: there is some return on investment, but less than the market has the right to expect. The difference is identified as a loss, even if shareholders are paid for their investment. The market return at equilibrium (k) becomes a minimal return or an opportunity cost, 'always to be exceeded' (Batsch 1999: 36).

As such, the creation of shareholder value originates in a logic of imbalance transformed into a permanent objective. The macroeconomic inconsistency of this principle is obvious: all the (listed) companies cannot create value for their shareholders, whatever the quality of their management. At a microeconomic level, methods for doping financial returns beyond what the companies' economic potential would permit are sustained by elevated stock-exchange prices. These methods combine the increase of the debt-to-equity ratio if the interest rate r is below k (decrease in the $WACC$), the asset-light strategy (increase in ROA), the repurchase of shares (increase in ROE) and external growth.

These methods have been extensively used by Enron's, Parmalat, FT and Ahold's officers. Clearly, none of them are sustainable in the medium to long-term. These are short-term strategies aiming at fostering financial returns (ROE) beyond the market equilibrium (k). As such, they are highly risky and encourage bold innovations flaunting acceptable standards of caution: hence the necessity to have efficient controlling (supervising) devices, especially in a period of stock market bubble.

The board of directors constitutes the main internal control device. Following Fama and Jensen (1983a), shareholder primacy proponents depict the board as an institution whose function is to reduce agency costs by monitoring and ratifying the actions of the managerial team on behalf of the shareholders. The 'strategic' role of the board, as an organ supporting executives in their choices (Roberts *et al.* 2005), is minimized. This conception has a crucial consequence: non-executive directors' independence from the management is recognised as a cardinal value, preventing conflicts of interests. Therefore, board failure to control corporate executives in the various scandals has been most often interpreted as a consequence of a lack of independence for directors. In other words, the failure, we are told, originates in poor incentives: directors were not in a good position to supervise managers not because they could not, but because they were not willing to do so.

The same argument is put forward to account for the failure of 'gatekeepers', held responsible for verifying the honesty and the relevance of financial statements as well as for using the information to give the best advice possible to investors. Three different actors are mainly concerned: external auditors (who verify and certify companies' accounts), securities analysts (who compile information in order to make buy-and-sell recommendations on securities) and ratings agencies (which assess companies' solvency). The auditors and the financial analysts are those whose responsibility in the high-profile scandals has been the most emphasized. According to Coffee (2002), who provides the most convincing thesis on that point, auditors' and analysts' failure is due to misappropriate incentive or conflict of interests running through these professions. Concerning auditors, the conflicts arose as firms began to provide consulting services to their clients – beyond auditing. Not wanting to lose this lucrative consulting activity, audit firms tended to be more indulgent toward the accounts presented. These conflicts of interest were nothing new, but it seems they became particularly widespread over the course of the 1990s: according to the Panel on Audit Effectiveness, from 1990 to 1999, earnings from consulting rose from 17 per cent, to 67 per cent of total fee income. Coffee (2002) also underlines the fact that, in the 1990s, a series of legal decisions made legislation on auditors' responsibilities more flexible. Thus the cost of error was relatively weak. Conflicts of interest are also presented as the main driver of analysts' adrift: securities analysts most often worked for investment banks offering advisory services to the corporations they analyse. Under these conditions, it can prove to be a costly move (both for the bank and the analyst's career) to issue a recommendation to sell. The mounting force of conflicts of interest may be properly appreciated by looking at the ratio of buy recommendations versus sell recommendations, issued by all of the analysts in the US: whereas in 1991 the ratio was six to one, by 2000, it had risen to 100 to one. Ratings agencies seem to have been less concerned with conflicts of interests; yet one may wonder why, in such circumstances, they gave such an excellent credit rating to Enron up until December 2001.

If the failure of these actors (directors and gatekeepers) is obvious, the reason behind it remains open to discussion. The next section offers an original point of view on that question, one that emphasises cognitive rather than incentive concerns.

The limits of external control

The fact that incentive concerns (lack of independence) contribute to the decline in managerial accountability is indisputable. Yet one may doubt that this explanation is sufficient in accounting for the paradox previously put forward, according to which the power of corporate executives seems to increase together with the extension of shareholder primacy. As a consequence, we would like to offer a complementary explanation: we argue that cognitive problems, intimately linked to shareholder primacy, are the main driver behind the decline in managerial accountability. To do so, we rely on the seminal work of Berle and Means (1991 [1932]).

Few books have caused as much stir as *The Modern Corporation and Private Property*, written in 1932 by Berle and Means. The 'separation of ownership and control' is still a key concept in academic debates on corporate governance (see on this also the introductory chapter to this book). Berle and Means observed that shareholder primacy, as a social and economic fact, was over: a majority of US listed companies were under managerial control because of share dispersion. This empirical observation was presented in Book I of the *Modern Corporation*. Book I remained, by far, the most famous. However, Book II, devoted to an analysis of the jurisprudence of the time, offers deep insights concerning the relationships between firm and finance that have been largely overlooked by subsequent commentators.

The analysis developed in Book II demonstrated that US jurisprudence still espoused the doctrine of shareholder primacy as a normative, guiding principle. As such, it considered that managerial power was an abuse that should be remedied. This revealed a certain lag in the legal order in relation to the social and economic reality, as well as underscoring the failure of the legal order to discipline corporate managers. Indeed, detailed analysis of the jurisprudence showed that the stacking of legal measures, with the aim of ensuring shareholder control despite the dispersion of equity capital, was totally insufficient for restoring shareholder power:

> As the power of the corporate management has increased, and as the control of the individual has sunk into the background, the tendency of the law has been to stiffen its assertion of the rights of security holder. The thing that it has not been able to stiffen has been its regulation of the conduct of the business by the corporate management. And this omission has resulted, not from lack of logical justification, but from lack of ability to handle the problems involved. The management of an enterprise is, by nature, a task which courts can not assume; and the various devices by which management and control have absorbed a portion of the profit-stream have been so intimately related to the business conduct of an enterprise, that the courts seem to have felt not only reluctant to interfere, but positively afraid to do so.
>
> (Berle and Means 1991 [1932]: 296)

This quotation clarifies the reasons behind the legal system's incapacity to control effectively the misappropriation of corporate wealth by managers: these misappropriations proceed, for the most part, from the very process of management itself. It is, for example, by choosing to take over a given firm or to invest in a given market that the executives increase their wealth and power at the expense of shareholders. Managers can always justify their choices by invoking industrial strategy, a justification that is practically impossible for the law to contest. And the reason is simple: courts are exterior to the firm as much as the shareholders concerned with preserving the liquidity of their shares. Ultimately, cases of pure embezzlement, objectively perceptible by the law (insider trading, for example, or misuse of corporate property), are relatively rare.

This analysis of the courts' structural inability to discipline managers did not receive much attention, as compared to the free riding problem stemming from the dispersion of ownership.[14] However, it has profound insights for current debates on corporate governance. Berle and Means (1991 [1932]) did not only emphasise the difficulty for 'liquid' (small) shareholders to control corporate executives; they also underlined the intrinsic limits of purely external control. Courts have the (legal) power to discipline executives, but they do not have reliable information to do so in a rational manner. Because they are remote from day-to-day business conduct, courts lack the knowledge of business conduct, of the firm as a productive entity, necessary to discipline corporate executives in the name of stockholders. *In fine*, Berle and Means (1991 [1932]) shed light on the cognitive limitations of courts as a corporate management controlling device.

This argument is particularly interesting as it can be extended to the case of gatekeepers and directors. Just as courts, the gatekeepers are exterior to the firm. Being outside the firms, they can only monitor a firm's behaviour *ex post*, the limits of which were evident in the Enron-era financial scandals. If they did fail in these high-profile scandals, cognitive reasons may be at least as important as incentive concerns: by nature, the gatekeepers are limited in their ability to evaluate the origins of corporate profits. As a consequence, it is misleading to put the full responsibility of corporate control on their shoulders.

At first sight, the case of the board of directors is different. According to institutional investors as well as shareholder primacy proponents, the *raison d'être* of this internal organ is the control of the managerial team on behalf of distant stockholders. Following this line, independence – as a way to prevent collusion between the controllers (board members) and the controlled (managers) – came to be a cornerstone of corporate governance reforms. The difficulty is that it is hard to give a precise content to the concept of independence. Yet institutional investors need clear signs, visible from a distance. Among these signs, the absence of relationships with management is favoured. But as Roberts *et al.* (2005) note, such an approach of independence tends to limit the involvement and engagement of non-executive directors in corporate affairs. In turn, this means a rather weak knowledge of the firm and its productive and commercial dynamics. The assessment of the board of directors offered by the doctrine of shareholder primacy is therefore paradoxical in that it advocates an increasing exteriority for this internal mode of control. As argued before, this exteriority reduces the effectiveness of the board as a controlling device. But it is even more damaging for its strategic role, that remains (contrary to the claim of the agency theorists) an essential part of the job. The in-depth study conducted by Roberts *et al.* (2005: 19) demonstrates that if independence is a crucial feature for non-executive directors, it should be understood as a 'willingness to exercise independence of mind in relation to executive strategy and performance'. And this willingness is only possible if directors' knowledge about the company and its management is strong enough. Accordingly, as Roberts *et al.* logically conclude: '[…] the advocacy by institutional investors, policy advisors and the business media of greater non-executive independence may be too crude or even counter-productive' (ibid.). The Enron case is a good example of this upshot of independence: Enron's board, composed of 12 independent directors of a total of 14, saw nothing of what was going on inside the corporation.

Ultimately, the information used by stock markets to evaluate business conduct and performance is produced by actors that are, by their very nature, outside the firm – that is, by actors that are not directly involved in business conduct or productive activity. As such, they suffer from intrinsic cognitive limitations. Reliable knowledge on the business firm is to be acquired, in a large part, inside the firm as a going concern, combining specific competences and tacit knowledge – a point that Berle and Means (1991 [1932]) did already note. By trying to empower liquid investors, shareholder primacy contributes to the externalization of the sources of information and control on business conduct. *In fine*, those who are supposed to be sovereign, those whose interest should be served, are in a structurally weak position to properly evaluate the accuracy of the business conduct. Accordingly the deficiency of control is a congenital defect of shareholder primacy, rather than a failure that can be corrected. A purely external control on the business firm, through liquid stock markets, suffers from cognitive limitations, beyond incentive concerns. The fact that Europe has been hit by corporate fewer scandals and that the surge in CEO compensation is to a much lesser degree than in the US is because the financialization of the business firm is less advanced.

Let us sum up our argument so far. The growing implementation of the doctrine of shareholder primacy has two consequences. On the one hand, it results in high financial demands, with a logic of imbalance. On the other hand, shareholder primacy leads to an exteriorization of supervising devices, which means a rather weak form of control. As a consequence, capital markets have increased their ability to obtain results (in terms of financial return) but they are structurally limited in their ability to appreciate the way these requirements are met. This contributes to make managerial power less accountable: financial irregularities multiply and executive remunerations explode. Shareholder primacy fails exactly where it strives to succeed: it reinforces the discretionary power of managers rather than limiting it.

US and European regulatory responses

The Sarbanes-Oxley Act (SOA), promulgated on July 2002 less than 10 days after WorldCom's bankruptcy, was the explicit response to the loss of confidence in US security markets. This legislation addresses two main issues. First, the SOA strengthens the auditors' regulation in order to limit conflicts of interests. From now on, audit firms are forbidden from providing certain services to the firms they are auditing – appraisal or consulting services, creation and operation of financial data processing systems, etc.[15] Note that despite their ineffectiveness as gatekeepers from 1997 to 2001, securities analysts are the objects of fairly inconsequential clauses aimed principally at preventing conflicts of interest. The Act does not deal with ratings agencies. Second, the SOA reaffirms the disciplinary role of the board of directors. The most significant rule concerns the audit committee. The Securities Exchange Commission is authorized to strike a company off the exchange if its audit committee, 'directly responsible for appointing, paying and supervising' the external auditor, is not entirely composed of independent members. Note that even if the text does not specifically anticipate the obligation to put an audit committee into place, it does specify that in the absence of such a committee, all clauses dealing with this committee (notably the independence of its members) must be applied to the board of directors as a whole. The constrictive character of this clause leads one to conclude that the majority of listed companies will create an audit committee. Despite increasingly virulent criticism, the subject of stock options is not even broached.

In short, the SOA can be summed up as follows: shareholder value is good, but its monitoring system failed. And this failure is considered to be due to conflicts of interests, inside the board of directors and audit firms. As such, the SOA does not call into question the source of the problem – a mode of governance focused exclusively on satisfying financial markets. From this point of view, one may doubt on the ability of the SOA to reduce the growing inequalities inside listed companies.

Confronted with the weakness, which the US market crisis revealed, of an oft-cited model of excellence, European regulatory authorities have most often been reactive rather than proactive. At the European level, the choice in favour of the IFRS for corporate accounting, with the adoption of Regulation 1606/2002/CE, is willingly presented by the European Commission as its principal preventative measure.[16] However, the Anglo–American orientation of the accounting system developed by the IASB, raises serious concerns. In the US, the first conceptual norm (Statement of Financial Accounting Concept 1), published in 1978 and devoted to the objectives of accounting information diffused by quoted companies, recognizes explicitly that the privileged users are the shareholders (current or potential) and creditors. Accounting must help them to evaluate the cash flow perspectives. The vision of accounting as working within a larger project of capital market efficiency is very palpable in this first standard (Aglietta and Rebérioux 2005). In continental Europe, until the choice in favour of IFRS, accounting information was destined *a priori* for a broader public than simply financial investors. The French example is a good one. If there are no conceptual norms explicitly indicating the privileged users of corporate accounting, the process of accounting standardization is a sign of a stakeholder rather than a shareholder approach. The elaboration of accounting rules both for quoted and non-quoted companies was the business of the National Accounting Council (*Conseil National de la Comptabilité*, CNC). The CNC has about 50 members, representing the accounting profession and public administration, but equally the various unions – workers and employers. Accordingly, the elaboration of standards follows a process of negotiation between the different members of the CNC. The EU's choice of IFRS for listed companies replaces this stakeholder approach of corporate accounting by a pro-shareholder one: the conceptual framework of the IASB clearly favours stockholders (see also the contributions by Nölke and Perry, and Dewing and Russell to this book). As a consequence, rather than consolidating elements particular to the European model, this choice brings Europe closer to US practices at the very moment these appear most fragile. For example, the 'fair value' method (the warhorse of the IASB) is at the root of numerous accounting manipulations.[17]

Faced with an ever increasing number of scandals across the Atlantic, in April 2002, the European Commission decided to entrust the drafting of a report on desirable reforms in EU law to the hands of a 'high level group' of experts in business law. Chaired by Jaap Winter, the group had been formed several months earlier with the purpose of reflecting on how to respond to the defeat of Directive XIII on takeover bids (see also the contribution by Van Apeldoorn and Horn to this book). A first report, called 'Winter I' (Winter 2002a), was made on this issue in January 2002. In November of the same year, the 'Winter II' report appeared (Winter 2002b), proposing 'a modern regulatory framework for company law in Europe'. The general orientation of the report, favourable to shareholder value, is clearest in the following lines:[18]

In a proper system of corporate governance, shareholders should have effective means to actively exercise influence over the company. As we emphasised in our Consultative Document, shareholders are the residual claimholders (they only receive payment once all creditors have been satisfied) and they are entitled to reap the benefits if the company prospers and are the first to suffer if it does not. Shareholders need to be able to ensure that management pursues – and remains accountable to – their interests. Shareholders focus on wealth creation and are therefore, in the Group's view, very suited to act as 'watchdog' not only on their own behalf, but also, in normal circumstances, on behalf of other stakeholders.

(Winter 2002b: 47)

Inspired in large part by the SOA, but having to take European specificities into account, the report's conclusions are fairly modest. The report proposes that the board of directors be made collectively responsible for the accuracy of the financial statements; moreover, the report looks favourably on harsher punishment for fraud, most notably banning a guilty party from working as a director anywhere in Europe. The structure of ad hoc nomination, audit and remuneration committees within the board of directors poses its own particular problems.[19] Conscious of the US model of governance, the report insists on the advantages of the independence of board members who head committees. The report immediately notes, however, that this arrangement would be difficult to adapt to Europe. It would automatically exclude majority shareholders and employee representatives, because their involvement in the firm would be incompatible with the notion of independence. Yet majority shareholders are present all over Europe, and board-level participation of employee representatives is characteristic of many member countries. Not only can the insistence on board members' independence be criticized *per se* (see above); it also does not fit very well with the European model of corporate governance, in which workers as well as blockholders do play a role. Thus the report adopts a moderate position, one of fairly limited scope: *ad hoc* committees should constitute a majority (not a totality) of independent members. The most daring clause in the report, which clearly differentiates itself from the SOA, is that it proposes stronger regulations on stock options. The group argues that shareholders should be better informed as to the use of stock options as a tool, as well as to the way they are recorded in accounting, but without proposing any particular method.

To sum up, the 'Winter II' Report (Winter 2002b) illustrates the reaction of European regulatory authorities. They did not use the US crisis to reaffirm the specificities of the continental European model. Instead, they were content to copy measures taken in the US, exploiting the relative quiet of the European landscape to justify less ambitious clauses.

Conclusion

Shareholder primacy originates in a misleading conception of the firm, as a standard financial asset. This conception finds an operational content through the EVA/MVA metrics: indeed, these metrics support the idea that investment in firms implies a constant comparison of *ex ante* defined opportunity costs. This is a purely financial conception of the firm that denies its productive dimension: profit (or value) creation is the result of a temporal and social process (production), rather than something that can be defined and required *ex ante*. Besides, this conception relies on the belief of the efficiency of a purely external control by stock markets. This belief is a fallacy that forgets, once again, the productive dimension of the firm: profits originate in the pooling and coordination of complementary and specific assets (human, tangible and intangible), that cannot be observed solely from the outside. The practical consequences of the implementation of shareholder primacy are damaging: managerial accountability declines rather than increases.

At the theoretical level, an alternative conception of the corporation and its governance is needed, one that recognizes both the specific nature of the firm as a productive entity and the role played by workers in this entity. Employees, by definition, have access to specific and tacit knowledge, the foundation of effective monitoring. As such, the institutionalization of the views of the workforce within companies' decision-making procedures can be portrayed as a structural safeguard against the misalignment of financial and productive interests (Moore and Rebérioux 2007). This should, in theory, enable some degree of non-shareholder input into important strategic decisions (for example mergers or major financial restructuring projects) on an *ex ante* basis, thus vesting employee representatives with the formal role of policing controversial exercises of managerial prerogative.

At the political level, the preceding analysis should lead to a renewed attention to the European (continental) mode of corporate governance. Indeed, the European continental model is characterized by worker involvement in corporate governance (Rebérioux 2002):[20] as a constituent element, workers have the right to be informed and consulted about the main issues in the functioning of the firm. Possibly, they may be granted a power of co-determination on a more or less wide range of subjects, through elected representatives. Through these rights, managers are induced (or forced) to take the interests of employees into account when making their decisions. Corporate governance is directly affected: these rights to information, consultation and co-determination contribute, when they exist, to the definition of a specific aim for the exercise of power within companies, in which the maximization of the well-being of shareholders is not taken to be the required norm. And these rights provide at least some internal countervailing powers that may foster corporate accountability.

Notes

1 The Powers Report (2002) remains the authoritative reference. See also the US Senate Report (Permanent Subcommittee on Investigations of the Committee of the Governmental Affairs United States Senate, 2002).

2 As reported by Chatterjee (2003), Enron's executives announced in August 2001 – a few months before the bankruptcy – plans to sell 4 billion in assets over the following two years.

3 A Special Purpose Entity is a legal structure, created at the instigation of a company for multiple purposes: to avoid paying taxes on foreign transactions, to make risk transfers and, in the case of Enron, to make off-balance-sheet deconsolidations. The parent company is not liable for the debt of the SPE providing it holds less than 50 per cent of its equity capital.

4 In April 2000, 50 per cent of assets were non-consolidated.

5 Cited by Coffee (2005).

6 Coffee (2005) gives the following indications: in 2004, CEO compensation was 531 times greater than the average employee compensation in the US, 16 times in France and 11 in Germany

7 At the centre were the Bonlat Financing Corporation and the Epicurum funds, both registered in the Caiman Islands. The announcement by the Bank of America, on 19 December 2003, of a 'black hole' of 3.95 billion euros in Bonlat's accounts precipitated the company's downfall: these liquid assets, registered to the account of the offshore company with the Bank of America, only existed because of a false document. The revelations which followed increased the estimate of the black hole to between seven and 13 billion euros, close to one per cent of Italy's gross domestic product. The hole was simply virtual assets compensating for real debt.

8 One of the reasons may be the large stake held by the French state.

9 For a detailed account of the Ahold case, see De Jong *et al.* (2005).

10 See special issue of the *Journal of Applied Corporate Finance* for the USA, Cooper *et al.* (2000) for the UK and Hossfeld and Klee (2003) for German and French firms.

11 Yet, as argued earlier, financial requirements should not be considered as a pure constraint on corporate executives. The regular fulfilment of these requirements – the creation of value for shareholders – induces a continuous rise in stock prices. In turn, this rise is the pre-condition for a strategy of large scale acquisitions that enables a high-speed (external) growth. Besides, positive stock market valuation allows for a considerable increase in compensation, through share options schemes.

12 The CAPM, developed in the 1960s permits the calculation of the premium which rational investors expect for holding risky assets (with high volatility).

13 By definition, we have $WACC = k \cdot EC / K + r \cdot D / K = k - (k - r) \cdot D / K$.

14 When equity capital is widely dispersed, shareholders have weak incentives to get involved in the internal affairs of the company. For each shareholder possessing an insignificant fraction of the capital, the effort necessary to get executives to adopt their views is much greater than the expected gain, implying a typical case of free riding.

15 In addition, the Public Company Accounting Oversight Board – a new supervisory body created by the SOA, in charge of implementing the peer review system in the profession – has the authority to extend this list of forbidden activities in order to guarantee the stability of these 'Chinese walls'.

16 For an in-depth analysis of the transformation of accounting standards following Enron-era financial scandals, see the contribution by Dewing and Russell to this book.

17 The 'dark fibres' example, in the Enron case, is particularly illustrative. Enron invested in an enormous network of high-speed fibre optics cable of which a large part had not been activated. Internally valued at $33 million, this embarrassing asset was sold to an SPE for $100 million. Enron saw a $67 million profit on the transaction. It was

a classic example of Enron's practices, making a fictive capital gain by passing off depreciated assets onto affiliates at arbitrarily fixed prices. Yet the story does not end there. Not content with making a profit on a poorly performing asset – the result of a disastrous investment – Enron took the opportunity to re-evaluate all of its assets that were similar to the 'dark fibres'. Shrewdly arguing that this operation revealed the 'fair value' of its assets, in other words their market price, Enron's management had but to apply 'marked to market' in order to increase the value. In corporate accounting, the principle of 'marked to market' advocates to value an asset at the price that one would obtain for it on a liquid market, even if there is no intention to sell it. This principle opposes the historical cost method, according to which an asset is valued at entry (so called historical) cost, taking into account of its progressive depreciation.

18 In particular, one should note the use of the classical (yet misleading) argument in defence of shareholder primacy according to which stockholders are 'the residual claimers'.

19 Concerning external audit, the European Commission issued a recommendation on 16 May 2002, arguing for a clear separation between account certification and consulting activities.

20 Considering only the supranational regulation (EU level), the following directives are worth noting: Directives 98/59 and 77/187 on the information and consultation of workers in cases of collective lay-offs and establishment transfers, Directive 2002/14/CE establishing a general framework relating to information and consultation of employees, Directive 94/45/CE on European works councils and Directive 2001/86/CE on worker involvement in the European company.

Part II
European corporate governance regulation and the politics of marketization

5 The transformation of corporate governance regulation in the EU

From harmonization to marketization

Bastiaan van Apeldoorn and Laura Horn

The virtual unification of national company laws in all essential aspects [...] is a deliberate act of policy on the part of the Community. In fact, it is a political act necessitated by the desire to accomplish the aims of the Community.

(Schmitthof 1973: 89)

The responsibility of the regulator is to set up the framework, which then enables the markets to play their disciplining role in an efficient way.

(Bolkestein 2003a)

Introduction

Corporate governance regulation forms an integral part of the socio-economic configuration of the EU. Within the EU, national corporate governance regulation has developed along trajectories of path-dependence and institutional complementarities (see Hall and Soskice 2001). Yet while institutional diversity remains considerable, there have been far-reaching and fundamental changes in the Member States' approaches to corporate governance regulation. At the same time, with the progression of market integration in the EU, the regulation of corporate governance at the European level has become more significant both in scope and in impact on national systems. In particular over the past five years or so, a broad range of regulatory initiatives with regard to company law and corporate governance has been taken by the European Commission. These efforts, we shall argue, mark both a continuation (with respect to some of the issues involved) and a fundamental break (regarding both form and content) with earlier attempts at company law harmonization within the European Community (EC). This transformation of corporate governance regulation at EU-level, then, may be seen as a reflection and at the same time as an important cause of a broader, transnational transformation of corporate governance regulation in the European political economy. Indeed, the argument that the European integration process is a significant driving force of changes in national regimes of corporate governance is well established in the literature (Story and Walter 1997; Rhodes and Van Apeldoorn 1998; Lannoo 1999; Bieling and Steinhilber 2002).

Given the obvious importance of corporate governance regulation at the EU level, it is somewhat surprising that thus far little attention has been given to the nature and origins of this emerging European regulatory framework (but see Bieling and Steinhilber 2002 for an important partial exception). With regard to its nature, most analyses remain limited to the question whether or not current changes imply a convergence of the Rhenish national varieties of capitalism on the so-called Anglo-Saxon model (Albert 1993; Hall and Soskice 2001), or whether we are witnessing a new, 'hybrid' form of European corporate governance (Cernat 2004; Rebérioux 2002). Although this is an important debate, it tends to bypass a more thorough understanding of the nature of the European project itself, in particular of its specific socio-economic and political content. This is all the more the case since, to the extent that an attempt is made to explain changing corporate governance regulation, whether at the EU or at the national level, it is seen as due to exogenous pressures stemming from 'globalization' in general, and recent corporate scandals in particular (Lannoo 1999; Lannoo and Khachaturyan 2003). What this argument ignores, we suggest, is the fundamentally political and ideological nature of the regulatory initiatives on the part of EU pertaining to corporate governance.

This chapter seeks to set a first step towards filling these lacunae in the literature by moving beyond the 'convergence debate', outlining and interpreting the development of and changes in corporate governance regulation at the EU-level, and by showing that they in fact constitute part of a broader political project of socio-economic restructuring in the EU. This perspective acknowledges the political underpinnings of the changes in corporate governance regulation, rather than merely perceiving them as inevitable results of reactive processes. Analyzing, then, what we see as the pro-active nature of the EU's efforts to create a regulatory framework for European corporate governance, and analyzing the political trajectory of the policy and regulatory developments preceding these recent initiatives, will provide a more thorough understanding of how and why the regulatory framework is evolving the way it does. The analysis thus undertaken will show that we have witnessed a shift from a regulatory approach aimed at the harmonization of company law in order to prevent regulatory competition in this area to a regulatory framework aimed increasingly at the establishment of a market-oriented corporate governance regime, in part through promoting market-based forms of regulation (compare the case of competition policy as analyzed in Wigger's contribution to this book).

The central argument we put forward is thus that the social purpose of EU corporate governance regulation has changed. We view this changing social purpose in terms of a transnational European political project aimed at a fundamental socio-economic restructuring of European capitalism. In essence, this project can be described as a neoliberal marketization project, which, in the area of corporate governance, is aimed at turning (pieces of) corporations into commodities freely sold on an integrated capital market, which can thus effectively discipline both management and workers in terms of orienting them to the maximization of so-called investor returns. This *marketization project* is neither caused by an exogenous globalization process nor by the obvious superiority of market-based corporate governance (cf. Hansman and Kraakman 2001), but rather must be understood in terms of the outcome of political contestation in what Gramsci (1971) called the realm of hegemony.

This chapter is structured as follows. The next section presents a brief outline of the theoretical framework guiding our interpretation of the changes in corporate governance regulation. While on the one hand drawing on Polanyi and critical political economy approaches to the issue of corporate governance, and to what we interpret as the marketization of corporate control, we also turn to a neo-Gramscian understanding of the process of European integration as a political project of socio-economic restructuring. Adopting this perspective, the main body of this chapter then comprises a delineation and interpretation of key developments in European corporate governance regulation in the last decades. Taking as a starting point the initial attempts by the European Commission to harmonize European company law, we show how this approach has fundamentally changed in later years, with the launch of the neoliberal integration project through the completion of the Single European Market and, most of all, its blueprint for financial market liberalization, the *Financial Services Action Plan* (FSAP). A prime example of how the underlying principles and rationale of the regulatory framework for corporate governance are reoriented to the interests of transnationally mobile 'investors', is here formed by the Takeover Directive. As part of this shift, company law is increasingly subordinated to the wider objectives of financial market integration and thus to capital market law. This also transpires from the Corporate Governance Action Plan, published by the European Commission in 2003, which will provide the framework for an analysis of some other key recent developments and initiatives in corporate governance regulation. The conclusion we draw from this analysis is that these developments indeed constitute a political project, aimed at the marketization of European corporate governance.

Marketization as a political project

The European regulatory framework pertaining to corporate governance currently taking shape is in our view aimed at the 'marketization of corporate control', which we define as: 'a process through which who controls the corporation and to what purpose it is run becomes increasingly mediated by the stock market, that is, through the share price as the regulative mechanism' (Van Apeldoorn and Horn 2006). The issue of corporate control (which came into being with the modern corporation or joint-stock company) is in fact at the heart of what has now come to be known as corporate governance (on this, see also the introductory chapter to this book). In fact, it goes to the heart of the debate on the nature of capitalism inasmuch as private ownership and therefore control over the means of production can be seen as the defining feature of a capitalist market economy. The debate on corporate control goes back at least to Berle and Means who in their classic study *Modern Corporation and Private Property* (Berle and Means 1991 [1932]) advanced the thesis that with the rise of the modern corporation, or joint-stock company, ownership has been separated from control as the former had come into the hands of countless small shareholders unable to overcome their collective action problems, and control shifted to a new class of professional managers (see also Burnham 1975 [1941]; Chandler 1977; Dahrendorf 1959).

In the ubiquitous neoclassical economics understanding, corporate governance serves as a mechanism to mitigate the agency costs arising from this alleged separation of ownership and control. The firm or corporation is seen as a 'nexus of treaties' (Jensen and Meckling 1976: 8) between rational agents in which shareholders have the contractual right to residual profits, and, accordingly, the control rights over the way the corporation is run. Here, the 'market for corporate control' serves as the external corporate governance[1] mechanism *par excellence* to ensure the protection of shareholder interests, by aligning managerial strategies with the latter (Jensen 1993). It is a market in which control over a corporation (in the sense of a majority of vote-carrying securities) can be bought through a variety of methods, ranging from open market purchases to negotiated share swaps (Bittlingmayer 1998). Analytically a distinction can be made between capital markets and markets for corporate control (Höpner 2003b: 104 ff.). In practice, however, the two largely overlap (Windolf 1994). We argue that capital markets and markets for corporate control, whereby the development of the former is also a necessary condition for the emergence of the latter, together form an integral part of the 'marketization of corporate control'. Marketization here has to be understood to mean that the market-based mode of control, that is, control by 'outsiders' who are mobile and can 'vote with their feet' by selling their shares, is being strengthened. Shares then become property titles that not only give the right to a dividend but also to (potential) control over a firm's governance. In the market for corporate control, the firm as a whole becomes a commodity (Windolf 1994: 90). The marketization of corporate control thus puts the firm, its management, and workers more firmly under the discipline of the capital markets.

The share price thus becomes a disciplinary device *vis-à-vis* management inasmuch as '[t]he lower the stock price, relative to what it could be with more efficient management, the more attractive the take-over becomes to those who believe that they can manage the company more efficiently' (Manne 1965: 113). The evaluation of company performance takes place purely on financial criteria – any technical or structural barriers to takeovers are thus perceived as detrimental to shareholder interests, and to undermine the efficient allocation of capital. Since shareholders allegedly value 'good corporate governance' at a premium (McKinsey 2002), it is assumed that in a functioning market there will be a 'natural' process towards the corporate governance system which brings about the most 'shareholder value' (Hansman and Kraakman 2001). Public intervention in corporate governance systems is only tolerated where it serves to ease market failures. Any further public involvement potentially leads to market distortions in the assumedly apolitical market equilibrium, since regulation is perceived as captured by specific interests (Jensen 1988: 45).

Although we share the emphasis of the neo-classical perspective on the market for corporate control as critical to what can be called an exit- (and hence market-) based system of corporate governance (see also Nooteboom 1999), we reject its normative commitment to this model, that is, the way, the disciplining of management by liquid capital markets is presented as a 'natural' and rational solution to the so called agency problem. We reject this discursive move as it presupposes the very fact that needs to be explained, which is that the shareholder is seen as sovereign with respect to the (control over the) firm (see the contribution by Rebérioux to this book). Here, corporate governance is thus reduced to the problem of 'how investors get the managers to give them back their money' (Shleifer and Vishny 1996: 4). In our view, such a definition of the problem reflects a particular conception of the firm, and is as such highly political and ideological. Furthermore, and, critical with respect to the current analysis, the extent to which that conception can be put in practice must be seen as dependent on a prior regulatory framework. The latter in turn requires a political explanation.

Our point of departure here is a Polanyian understanding of markets as political and social constructs (Polanyi 1957; cf. Fligstein 2001). Thus, in contrast to the tendency of neo-classical agency theory to view regulation as intervening in the efficient allocation of capital through the market, we stress here the indispensability of public regulation in establishing this market (that is, a well-functioning capital market and a market for corporate control) in the first place. Markets do not create themselves, nor are they the spontaneous outcome of man's allegedly innate entrepreneurial habits. Rather, they are created through the state, which needs to establish the necessary pre-conditions (such as the alienability of certain objects, that is, their capacity to be sold on the market and thus function as commodities; secure property rights; money as a medium of exchange and a sufficient degree of competition) for markets to emerge and develop (for a further conceptualization and analysis of these pre-conditions see Van Apeldoorn and Horn 2006). Drawing on Polanyi's insight that markets are always embedded in a societal context, and that the perception that the capitalist mode of production, and the capitalist market system, function outside society and provide a space for organizing economic life without any interference of social forces thus constitutes a 'stark utopia' (Polanyi 1957: 3), we argue that changes in corporate governance are by no means inevitable processes driven by apolitical market forces. Rather, as markets are always social and political constructs, the current marketization of corporate control must be understood in terms of a 'political project'. Below we will apply this notion to the European arena and outline how we may theorize such a project within an EU context.

The European marketization project

Adopting a neo-Gramscian perspective, and applied to the European arena, we define a political project as an integrated set of 'initiatives and propositions that, as pragmatic responses to concrete national and European problems, conceptually and strategically further the process of socio-economic, societal and institutional restructuring' (Bieling and Steinhilber 2002: 41, our translation). As indicated in the introduction, within Europe it is no longer the national states that exclusively provide the regulatory framework of corporate governance – rather, increasingly, a key role here is played by the EU and by the process of European integration. In analyzing this role we adopt a transnational perspective (Van Apeldoorn 2002, 2004a; see also the introductory chapter to this book) in which the institutional intergovernmental and supranational governance structures of the European multi-level polity are seen as embedded within a transnational political economy and a transnational civil society (see also Van Apeldoorn *et al.* 2003). Such a political project reflects the agency of a dominant set of transnational social and political forces. Concretely, a political project is articulated ideologically through the discursive and political practices of a multitude of (transnational) associations, lobby groups, think tanks, private forums and planning groups, and, as we shall see, in the case of corporate governance regulation, increasingly so-called 'expert groups', experts who are far from autonomous (inasmuch as such a thing exists) but are often directly linked to concrete (transnational) social forces. Through the transnational networks constituted by these actors (cf. Nölke 2003) certain interests are brought to the fore and come to underpin the EU's policy discourse and shape the content of the regulatory framework it seeks to put in place.

From this perspective, then, the European Commission, although indeed an important supranational public actor, whose role as policy-entrepreneur is also very much confirmed by our case of European corporate governance regulation, must not be interpreted as an autonomous actor in the way some 'supranationalist' accounts of European integration tend to do (for example, Sandholtz and Stone Sweet 1998). Rather, the European Commission can arguably be viewed as a key public actor within the EU as a 'multi-level state formation' (Jessop 2002a: 205; cf. Caporaso 1996), and as such embedded in a particular configuration of transnational social forces, and a concomitant (potentially hegemonic) construction and articulation of interests.

In capitalist societies generally, it is of course capitalist interests that are privileged through these processes. In the current EU as a system of asymmetric socio-economic governance establishing a 'free space for capital' (Van der Pijl 2006: 32) it is in particular those interests bound up with the most transnationally mobile fractions of capital that are privileged (see also Van Apeldoorn 2002). At the same time this emphasis on the structural primacy of transnational capital must not be taken to imply that political projects, notwithstanding their presentation as coherent programmes, are free from contradictions and therefore uncontested. Hegemony in a Gramscian sense is in fact never complete, and subordinate groups and classes may always struggle to redefine the terms of the dominant discourse and transform underlying social practices.

We thus claim that a critical role, both directly and indirectly, is played by the process of European integration, which, in our view, since the end of the 1980s has been driven by a broader (neoliberal) marketization project, of which the project of a marketization of corporate control must be seen as part and parcel. We do not, however, claim that the regulatory changes with regard to corporate governance exclusively emanate from the EU. Rather, this regulatory transformation must be viewed as a transnational process where changes take place simultaneously at different levels. What we see as a project of market liberalization at the EU level here is both an expression and a constituting force of this transnational process. In this sense many of the recent regulatory changes on the national level can only be explained in the context of the European integration process.

Yet at the same time, the European project of market liberalization can only be understood against the backdrop of a global capitalist restructuring process that has taken place since the 1970s and that has engendered a deepening of the transnationalization of capital. Focusing on financial liberalization in particular, the European drive to integrate capital markets only makes sense in a global context. The collapse of the Bretton Woods system was accompanied by a worldwide financial deregulation wave in which finance became once more detached from the real economy and liquid capital gained a new transnational mobility and hence exit power. The globalization of capital markets, in conjunction with the globalization of product markets, leads to a competition between firms to suit the interests of transnationally mobile investors (Jackson 1998; Rhodes and Van Apeldoorn 1998: 413). Although crucial as a context, globalization or global restructuring is at the same time also partly constituted by the European regionalization process, and the political choices made therein.

Corporate governance regulation in the EU – analyzing an emergent project

In this section, developments in corporate governance regulation and company law in the EU are delineated and contextualized. We argue that a shift has taken place from a regulatory regime aimed at the harmonization of company law (with corporate governance still perceived as mainly a policy issue pertaining to company law) through public intervention and regulatory practices, to an increasingly market-regulated and market-based corporate governance system, the goals of which are defined in terms of financial efficiency and competitiveness.

Harmonizing European company law

There seems to be a consensus in the body of (political economy) literature that, as for instance Dewing and Russell state, 'until relatively recently, the EC had not concerned itself with corporate governance issues' (Dewing and Russell 2004: 299). This perception might hold true when taking corporate governance as the comprehensive and interdisciplinary concept as it is used today, pertaining to securities as well as company law, to business and management studies as well as to political economy. Yet it can be argued that this perspective on corporate governance is itself a result of changes in the socio-economic configuration of capitalist market systems, inasmuch as corporate governance practices and regulation shape and in turn are shaped by changing conceptions of the role of the firm and how, and to which purpose, it should be run.

We argue that corporate governance issues have in fact been part of the European market integration process from an early stage on, albeit in a narrower sense than in the recent discussions. The European Commission's attempt at harmonizing company law in the 1970s and early 1980s represents an early key development in this regard. As the Commission points out in the Corporate Governance Action Plan of 2003, most of the initiatives taken at EU level in the area of company law have been based on Article 44(2)g (ex 54) of the Treaty establishing the European Community. Accordingly, the freedom of establishment within the EU is to be guaranteed 'by co-ordinating to the necessary extent the safeguards which, for the protection of the interests of members and others, are required by Member States of companies or firms within the meaning of the second paragraph of Article 48 (ex 54), with a view to making such safeguarding equivalent throughout the Community' (European Commission 2003: 6; see also Wouters 2000). The first harmonization directive in the field of European company law was adopted in 1968 (Wouters 2000: 257), and until 1989 a total of nine directives and one regulation pertaining to the harmonization of company law were enacted (European Commission 2003: Appendix). Among the initiatives promoted by the Commission were proposals for a Takeover Directive and the European Company Statute. As the Commission argued, the harmonization of company law was strongly conducive to the further integration of European markets. 'Unity of law would not only promote integration, but would also give enterprises easier access to foreign capital markets, [...] and to acquire an interest in or merge with enterprises from other Member States' (European Commission 1965: 106).

At the same time, the regulatory focus within the company law harmonization strategy was aimed at avoiding regulatory competition (Wouters 2000: 282). In a then authoritative textbook on European company law, it is argued that 'unless the national company laws in the European Community are identical in all aspects, a movement of companies to the state with the laxest company law will take place in the Community. If it may be said without giving offence to our friends in the US, 'the Community cannot tolerate the establishment of a Delaware in its territory' (Schmitthof 1973: 9). The fear of a 'European Delaware', in this regard, referred to the (re)incorporation of companies in Member States where company law provisions stipulated lower capital requirements and shareholder and creditor protection in general. To avoid the erosion of company law standards, and to achieve harmonization of company law, substantive regulation through legislative instruments was thus deemed necessary. To this end, the culinary strategy of the 'salami tactics' was to be employed, according to which:

> one slice of national company laws after the other will be harmonized, uniform minimum standards will be established in the national company laws of the Community with respect to all important areas. As these minimum requirements will be fairly detailed, what is taking place under the guise of harmonization is in fact a virtual unification of national company laws, leaving to different national regulation only unimportant matters of detail.
>
> (Schmitthof 1973: 7)

Yet while the harmonization of company law progressed in the 1970s, the process came to a grinding halt in the 1980s. As Lannoo and Katchaturyan (2003: 5) argue, 'the more they tried to harmonize corporate governance the less successful they were' (see also Wouters 2000: 271). In the 1985 White Paper, the European Commission argued that the regulatory strategy 'totally based on harmonization would be over-regulatory, would take a long time to implement, would be inflexible and could stifle innovation' (European Commission 1985: 18). Harmonization, it argued, should rather be substituted by mutual recognition of national regulations and company laws, based on competition (in the sense of regulatory arbitrage by firms) as a mechanism for convergence rather than centralized top–down regulation.

Concomitant to a broader political struggle over the direction and aims of European integration (see Van Apeldoorn 2002), the strict harmonization approach to company law (and thus to corporate governance) was abandoned due to mounting intergovernmental contestation. The further harmonization had advanced, the more Member States realized how integral their national corporate governance configuration was to their national socio-economic system. Member States' concerns against and contestation of the harmonization approach, and the European Commission's changing strategy have thus led to an approach to corporate governance regulation favouring mutual recognition over centralized coordination. As Rhodes and Van Apeldoorn argue:

> One of the reasons for the acknowledgement of subsidiarity at Maastricht was the battle waged in the 1980s and early 1990s over attempts to introduce a uniform system of corporate governance. Harmonization had been advocated from various quarters, but in fact the directives regulating European corporate space have either been blocked by national disagreements over surrendering national sovereignty or have been issued in a form that allows a degree of national diversity.
>
> (Rhodes and Van Apeldoorn 1998: 422)

At the same time, increased transnationalization of business, and in particular an unprecedented increase in takeover activities in Europe in the late 1980s, led to a surge in public attention to corporate governance issues (Skog 2002: 302). Corporate governance regulation became more and more an issue of political contestation within the process of European integration. What explains this rising salience? Some downplay the role of the EU as such, by arguing, as Wouters for instance does, that 'unlike the 1960s and 1970s, the impetus for new company law no longer comes from Brussels, but from the practical needs in the Member States, and (particularly as far as corporate governance is concerned) from the globalization of financial markets' (Wouters 2000: 306). Yet as we would maintain, explaining the changing trajectory of corporate governance regulation on the basis of pressures emanating from the 'globalization' of financial markets means to ignore the role of political agency at the European level in 'translating' and formulating these (perceived) pressures into a regulatory framework. Here, the role of the European Commission has been crucial for the re-orientation of corporate governance regulation.[2]

Rather than advocating a 'positive' harmonization approach, the European Commission's approach has become increasingly based on identifying and subsequently eliminating obstacles to the free movement of companies and capital. Whereas corporate control used to be very much located in the domain of company law, subject to 'positive' harmonization, it has become increasingly regulated under aspects of capital and financial markets law. In the next section, then, the shift of corporate governance regulation as a subfield of company law towards the regulatory overlap between, on the one hand, securities and financial market law, and corporate governance and company law on the other, will be examined.

Framing corporate governance regulation – the Financial Services Action Plan

Financial market integration has been an integral part of the single market programme from the start. The speed with which financial market integration was implemented was at first rather impressive, helped along by the 'Europhoria' in the second half of the 1980s. However, it was only in the second half of the 1990s that the attempt to create an integrated European financial market really picked up speed and developed into a core project of European socio-economic governance (see also Bieling 2003). This next phase of the EU's drive to deepen financial market integration must be seen against the background of the following four factors. First, in spite of the earlier progress made, the integration of European capital markets was far from complete (Story and Walter 1997). Second, at the same time, the creation of EMU, the success of which was far from certain at the time, was expected to deepen capital market integration provided the right regulatory environment was put in place (see also Bieling and Steinhilber 2002: 48–9), and thus served as an impetus to further financial market integration. The single currency was expected to lower the transaction costs for cross-border trade in stocks and bonds and thus to lead investors to diversify their portfolios across the Eurozone, promoting the development of a pan-European capital market (Lannoo 1999; OECD 1998). Third, those neoliberal forces that sought to advance this market liberalization project first needed to overcome the crisis of confidence in the relaunched European integration process that beset the European Community in the early 1990s in the context of an economic recession and the troubles regarding the ratification of the Maastricht Treaty, as well as growing social unrest in the face of rising mass unemployment (Van Apeldoorn 2002: 161ff.; Bieling and Steinhilber 2002: 45).

Finally, and most importantly, the neoliberal project itself needed to be consolidated (reinforcing its societal consent) before financial market integration could be further advanced. Although the neoliberal discourse had been shaping European policy debates from the 1980s onwards, it was only in the second half of the 1990s that the neoliberal project fully took shape and rose towards hegemony, at least at the level of the European elite discourse (Bieling and Steinhilber 2002: 43). As Van Apeldoorn (2002) has argued, the neoliberal project first needed to neutralize the challenges posed by contending transnational projects, in particular that of a supranational social democracy as promoted by the Delors Commission, and a neo-mercantilist project promoted by those sections of European industry that wanted to use the internal market as a protected home market in the face of growing global competition. In contrast, the neoliberal project put the emphasis on enhancing the (microeconomic) efficiency of European industry through market liberalization in the context of a globalizing European economy.

At the discursive level, the ascendancy of this neoliberal project, and thus its (temporary) triumph over rival conceptions of the relaunched integration took place through a shift (effectuated in part through the transnational class agency of the European Round Table of Industrialists (ERT)) from a 'neo-mercantilist' 'competitiveness discourse' advocating a strengthening of European industry through non-market means in order to enable it to better withstand the forces of global competition to a neoliberal competitiveness discourse in which competitiveness is precisely seen as benefiting from an unprotected exposure to global competition, in product as well as in capital markets (see Van Apeldoorn 2002: 173–80, also 2003). In this discourse, then (which effectively neutralized the opposition of alternative projects through the ideological appeal of the goal of competitiveness itself – an objective shared by social-democrats, neo-mercantilist and neoliberals alike), globalization is constructed as an inevitable reality against which one cannot and should not (wish to) protect oneself and as a challenge that needs to be confronted head on through an ongoing process market liberalization allegedly necessary to enhance competitiveness in the face of global competition. Complying with the perceived needs of global markets has hence become the primary goal of European socio-economic governance. What Watson and Hay (2003) have called 'rendering the contingent necessary', the European Commission has thus increasingly come to legitimate its project in terms of promoting competitiveness defined in neoliberal terms.

In this context, a reinvigorated neoliberal project in the form of a number of new initiatives has been undertaken by the EU to accelerate and complete the creation of the single financial market. This project started with the Cardiff Council of 1998, which called for the Commission to develop an action plan for removing the remaining obstacles to an integrated financial market (see Bieling and Steinhilber 2002). With this the Council followed a proposal from the Competitiveness Advisory Group (CAG), a transnational group of 'experts' and representatives from labour and above all from transnational business, which was created in 1995 following an initiative of the ERT (Van Apeldoorn 2002: 175–6). The CAG, like the ERT (ERT 1998), argued that financial market integration not only promoted efficiency of resource allocation but also would enhance the flexibility and the competitiveness of the European economy (Bieling and Steinhilber 2002: 49). These developments then led up to the European Commission's FSAP drawn up in 1999 (European Commission 1999b). This plan, which turned financial market integration into one of the EU's top priorities, contained a blueprint for the realization of an integrated financial market by 2005, and has as its clearly defined rationale that 'integrated capital markets would enhance pressures for a market- and competition-oriented modernization of the whole mode of capitalist reproduction' (Bieling 2003: 212).

The FSAP also gave new impetus to the attempt to create a more market-driven European corporate governance regime. In fact, the latter was seen as an integral part of the former, that is, of the EU's strategy for financial market liberalization. This framing of corporate governance within the FSAP constitutes an important shift in the EU approach to corporate governance regulation. Corporate governance issues are increasingly articulated in the discourse of financial integration rather than solely in company law terms. Thus, for instance, the Takeover Directive became part of the legislative programme contained in the FSAP and was deemed crucial to 'facilitate the restructuring of the financial industry [...] and mark an important milestone in the emergence of an open market in EU corporate ownership' (European Commission 1999b: 4). In other words, regulatory initiatives in the realm of corporate governance, also within what previously was rather narrowly conceived in terms of Europeanizing company law (like the Takeover Directive (see below)) were now discursively and politically integrated into a comprehensive plan for financial market integration. The latter goal moreover became clearly embedded within the 'master' policy discourse of neoliberal competitiveness.

The following quote from the then internal market Commissioner Frits Bolkestein provides a good illustration of the way the European Commission invokes this competitiveness discourse. Referring to the FSAP, and articulating financial market integration with the need to create a European shareholder capitalism, Bolkestein argued that:

> Without a fully integrated financial services and capital market in Europe we shall be unable to release the economic opportunities that will underpin the Union's new competitiveness. Because the cost of capital will remain too high and the yields on assets unnecessarily low. The availability of pan-European risk capital will be sub-optimal and the attractiveness of IPOs (initial public offerings) limited.
>
> (Bolkestein 2000)

In other words, integrating financial markets is about 'sufficiently rewarding' holders of liquid assets. It is thus about redistribution from stakeholders to 'shareholders', though at the same time the claim is upheld that financial market integration 'will lead to a higher quality of life for all European citizens. A large, more liquid capital market in Europe will create investment, more growth, more innovation, more jobs and higher incomes' (Bolkestein 2000). Similarly, Alexander Schaub, then Director General of the European Commission's Internal Market Directorate, stresses that:

The growing importance of corporate governance on the political agenda is not just a response to the recent wave of scandals in the US and in Europe. *First and foremost it is a key component of a strategy* to boost business' competitiveness and to foster efficiency in a modern economy.

(Schaub 2004, emphasis added)

We argue that by turning the establishment of a European regulatory framework for corporate governance into an integral part of its overall drive for the integration and liberalization of Europe's capital markets, and articulating this discursively with the overarching goal of promoting European competitiveness in the face of globalization pressures, the Commission has both changed the social purpose of European corporate governance regulation *and* widened its basis for organizing consent for this project. This way, earlier regulatory initiatives that got stuck because of a lack of intergovernmental consensus, acquired a new impetus. Issues that previously proved too politically sensitive in some Member States were depoliticized, or rather re-articulated in a different political project that, however, was presented in apolitical terms, that is, as objectively necessary to boost European competitiveness.

After being approved by the Council at the critical Lisbon summit of March 2000 (see below), the implementation of the project of the integration of European capital markets was further advanced (and, at the same time, depoliticized by turning it into a matter of seemingly apolitical, 'technical' regulation best left to experts) through the creation of another transnational 'expert group', the so called Committee of Wise Men (*sic*) on the regulation of European securities markets under the chairmanship of Belgian banker Alexandre Lamfalussy (Lamfalussy *et al.* 2000; see also Bieling 2003; Bieling and Steinhilber 2002).

The Lisbon summit and the subsequent so-called Lisbon strategy, itself also marked another key step in the development of the EU's marketization project, with financial market integration being a fundamental part of the comprehensive socio-economic agenda adopted in the Portuguese capital. The Lisbon strategy, proclaiming the goal for the EU to become 'the most competitive and dynamic knowledge-based economy in the world by 2010' (European Council 2000), articulates the goal of competitiveness with that of social cohesion, but in a way of making the latter subordinate to the exigencies of the former as defined by the neoliberal competitiveness discourse (see Van Apeldoorn 2006). The Lisbon 'reform process' has recently come under much criticism because of the lack of progress with respect to its implementation. We maintain, however, that at the level of formulating an elite policy discourse and an integrated programme that can muster the consent within European transnational civil society, and that can thus carry the project of neoliberal European socio-economic governance forward, Lisbon has been rather successful. Moreover, the implementation of the Lisbon agenda is not lagging equally behind in all areas. Thus in the spring of 2004, some 70 directives had been adopted under the Lisbon process, mainly in the area of the internal market. Although transposition of these directives has been lagging, most progress has in fact been made in the area of financial market integration under the heading of the FSAP (see European Commission 2004a: 13, 2004b). As the Commission announced, nearly all legislative measures of the FSAP have been completed on time (European Commission 2004c); a first evaluation will soon be followed by an impact assessment of transposition and implementation. Thus, what Commissioner Bolkestein (2000) considered to be 'the core of the Lisbon strategy' remains intact. The promotion of market-driven corporate governance reform constitutes an increasingly central element of the European Commission's overall strategy towards (financial) market integration in the European arena.

The Takeover Directive

The Takeover Directive may serve as an illustration of how the framing of corporate governance regulation within the context of the FSAP has re-oriented policy. Although, formally, the Takeover Directive is a directive on company law and part of the company law harmonization process, 'at the same time, it seeks to regulate an important element of the functioning of capital markets. Many features of the draft directive have been driven much more by capital market concepts than by company law thinking [...] The reach of capital market law over subjects that traditionally fall within the realm of company law is expanding' (Winter 2004: 106). The directive seeks to regulate important elements of the functioning of capital markets, in particular the process of bidding for the majority or all of the shares of a listed company.

The 'never ending story' (Skog 2002) of the Takeover Directive, that is, its legislative history, started back in the 1970s with the European Commission's plan to harmonize takeover regulation within the European Community.[3] Various legislative initiatives by the Commission stranded, until, in 1989, it published its first draft proposal for a Takeover Directive. Following objections of the European Parliament (EP) and the European Council, the European Commission subjected the directive proposal to 'a drastic shot of subsidiarity therapy' (Wouters 2000:263). Whereas the European Commission argued that the Directive would create a 'level playing field' for takeover bids in the EU, several Member States (notably Germany and Sweden) argued that, due to their national regulatory framework for corporate governance, implementation of the Directive would put them at a comparative disadvantage *vis-à-vis* other Member States' regulations. The proposal that was eventually put to vote in the EP in 2001 contained several compromises and references to national regulatory exceptions, but was nonetheless rejected in a tied vote.

After the defeat in the EP, a High Level Group of Company Law Experts (HLG) (both from academia and business and chaired by Dutch company law professor and legal advisor for Unilever Jaap Winter) was installed by the European Commission with the mandate to 'point out a new direction for the future' of European Company Law and Corporate Governance (Winter 2004: 98) and thus prepare the ground for a reformulation of the Takeover Directive that would be able to break the political deadlock.[4] The European Commission, in its subsequent 2002 Takeover Directive proposal (European Commission 2002c) and the ensuing Action Plan on Corporate Governance published in 2003 (European Commission 2003a), followed most of the recommendations and issues raised by the HLG. Indeed, the role and influence of the HLG was far more extensive than just the provision of nitty-gritty company law expertise to figure out the very details of new proposals – rather, by setting policy options and recommendations in a framework which entailed a considerable shift towards a more market-based corporate governance regulation they significantly shaped the parameters of the corporate governance regulation debate in the EU (see Horn forthcoming). Although the new proposal by the European Commission again met considerable objections in the European Council and the EP, a diluted form eventually passed in the EP, and the Takeover Directive came into force in May 2004.

As the above brief account indicates, while it is important to acknowledge the intergovernmental dimension of the struggles over the Takeover Directive, including, indirectly, of the struggle taking place in the EP (cf. Callaghan and Höpner 2005), it is crucial to appreciate both the European Commission's role in pushing for the market-liberal content of the Takeover Directive, as well as the role of transnational private 'expert' groups in providing the 'epistemic' underpinnings (that is, producing the discourse and ideas and concomitant concrete policy proposals) of the marketisation of corporate control that the European Commission had been promoting since the 1990s. As such, the struggle over the Takeover Directive serves as an example of the political nature of the changes in European corporate governance regulation. While Member States increasingly seek to safeguard their interests with regard to national corporate governance regulation, the European Commission's objective is to create and promote international investment opportunities and market integration. It has repeatedly expressed its belief in the efficiency of the market for corporate control, or, as Frits Bolkestein put it, a market where 'the good can take over and improve the bad' (Bolkestein 2003b).

As pointed out above, the final form of the Takeover Directive is characterized by a compromise that has watered down its original market-liberal content.[5] Whereas the directive includes provisions on the neutrality of the board and the abolition of voting restrictions and multiple voting rights in the case of a takeover bid (Articles 9 and 11, respectively), Article 12 renders these potentially far-reaching provisions as optional. This means that Member States can decide whether they should be implemented when transposing the Takeover Directive into national law. This compromise form has led most observers to argue that the Takeover Directive was, in the words of the *Financial Times*, toothless and 'a missed opportunity for open markets' (Dombey 2003). Arguably, however, the Takeover Directive, albeit not quite the far-reaching instrument for the marketization of European takeover regulation that the European Commission envisaged, does in fact represent a stepping stone towards the further marketization of corporate control in the European arena (for a more elaborate account see Van Apeldoorn and Horn 2005). While it will only become clear after the full implementation of the directive in all Member States in how far the optional arrangements have actually been enforced,[6] the Takeover Directive indeed includes a number of provisions that do not fall under the optional specifications, such as broad transparency and disclosure provisions and a mandatory bid rule to enforce (minority) shareholder protection. As Maul and Kouloridas argue, 'transparency and disclosure is considered, beyond any doubt, as a cornerstone of the effective operation of capital markets and the market of corporate control' (Maul and Kouloridas 2004).

Its significance notwithstanding, the Takeover Directive is nevertheless but one example of the developments in corporate governance regulation within the EU. In the following section, the European Commission's 2003 *Corporate Governance Action Plan* and several regulatory initiatives in its framework further illustrate the changes in regulatory orientation. They also serve to emphasize the political nature of the marketization project.

Modernizing company law and enhancing corporate governance? The Company Law Action Plan

The European Commission's 2003 Action Plan for 'Modernizing company law and enhancing corporate governance' is partly based on a report from the same group of company law experts that has played a critical role in the development of the Takeover Directive (High Level Group of Company Experts 2002). Klaus Hopt points out the 'close connection' between the FSAP and the Company Law Action Plan:

> Mr. Bolkestein [Commissioner for the Internal Market] was highly successful with the former, but company law harmonization was unsuccessful for decades. Bolkestein's ingenious idea was to link both fields and both regulatory schemes by using the experience with and the political success of the Financial Markets Action Plan for progress in company law. This was politically very skilful and has also worked out well legally and economically.
>
> (Hopt 2005: 5)

The Company Law Action Plan frames corporate governance reform in the same notions of competitiveness and efficiency that also underlie the Commission's agenda for capital market integration:

> A dynamic and flexible company law is essential for deepening the internal market and building an integrated European capital market. [...] An effective approach will foster the global efficiency and competitiveness of business in the EU [...] and will help to strengthen shareholder rights.
>
> (European Commission 2003b)

As Bolkestein pointed out, the European Commission sees itself in a key position for this reform agenda. '[O]ur challenge is to lead the debate in the European Union and beyond, and to adopt the right policy approaches to the different issues' (Bolkestein 2004). The Company Law Action Plan is based on a comprehensive set of proposals on corporate governance, capital maintenance, corporate pyramid structures and other corporate governance related issues. Within the framework of this plan, two different objectives have to be distinguished. On the one hand, most of the short-term measures introduced in the Plan are indeed very much aimed at re-establishing investor confidence after corporate scandals such as Parmalat and Ahold. This is reflected in the short-term priorities – enhancing the quality and independence of audit,[7] increasing the responsibility and independence of the board and making directors' remuneration more transparent. On the other hand, the overarching objective of the European Commission remains the strengthening of shareholder rights and the fostering of efficiency and competitiveness of business (European Commission 2003a). Rather than just containing measures to prevent other corporate scandals, the Company Law Action Plan has thus a far more fundamental purpose, in tune with the overall political project of European integration (for an analysis of how these two objectives might be contradictory, as shareholder primacy has in fact been a cause of the corporate scandals rather than that it can be part of the solution, see the contribution by Rebérioux to this book.) As Charlie MacCreevy, Commissioner for the Internal Market, points out:

> The context in which we will set our priorities for the second phase is very different. The impetus for what we do next at EU level must now be the tandem of: 1) improving the competitiveness of EU companies – the so-called Lisbon agenda; and 2) the EU's push towards better regulation.
>
> (MacCreevy 2005a)

Although the Company Law Action Plan itself is not very concrete on medium- to long-term measures (for an overview, see European Commission 2003a: 25–26), there is a whole range of initiatives already initiated within the broader framework of regulatory reform.[8] While the European Commission has repeatedly stated that it does not envisage a unified 'European code of corporate governance' (MacCreevy 2005b), it appears to be confident about a trend towards convergence of national corporate governance codes:

> Corporate governance practices vary among Member States because of their different economic, social and legal traditions. Nevertheless, there is a clear market-driven trend towards convergence in Europe. […] Market participants, including investors, have every interest in taking the view that such convergence is vital for integration of our capital markets – and even for economic growth.
>
> (MacCreevy 2005b)

Member States are expected to establish unified national corporate governance codes that their companies will be obliged to apply (Maul and Kolouridas 2004: 1293). To promote the discussion and, ultimately, dissemination of 'best practice' of these national codes, it has set up an expert group in 2004, the European Corporate Governance Forum. Next to academics (often with links to the corporate world, though), the membership of this forum is predominantly made up of representatives of Europe's largest transnational corporations as well as, and even more so, representatives of financial capital (institutional investors; shareholder associations).[9] A similar bias in terms of membership can be found in the Corporate Governance Advisory Group, which the European Commission has set up to provide it with 'technical advice'.[10]

The transnational politics of the transformation of European corporate governance regulation

As the above analysis shows, the European Commission has been at the forefront of a number of EU-level regulatory initiatives constituting a political project aimed at the marketization of corporate control. At the same time, the Commission's push has been facilitated and encouraged by a transnational network of interests and private bodies, most visibly in the form of so-called expert groups, in which the experts, however, often have ties to, or directly represent the interests and ideas of European transnational, and predominantly financial, capital (see also Wigger's analysis of the role of transnational law firms in her contribution to this book). Next to the powerful interests from which their members are drawn, the significant role of these transnational expert groups may also be understood (linking form and content) in the light of how in the push for a more market-driven European corporate governance regime they usefully depoliticize what in fact is deeply political, and therefore often prevent overt political conflict, or, as was the case with the Takeover Directive, break the political deadlock over certain (potentially) contentious aspects of the marketization project.

The ideational shift underlying the changes in company law and corporate governance regulation in the EU has thus in part taken place through the agency of these transnational expert groups (for a more detailed analysis see Horn forthcoming). While these expert groups, on the one hand, represent the European Commission's ambition (under the heading of the 'better regulation' approach) to consult with 'stakeholders' on regulatory initiatives, they, on the other hand, (re)produce and consolidate the dominant discourse on market-driven regulation. The European Commission's focus on facilitating cross-border transactions and the establishment of a truly integrated market to enhance the investment opportunities for transnationally mobile capital is partially instigated, and at the same time reinforced, by incorporation into the early phases of the regulatory process of these experts *cum* representatives of transnationally mobile capital – in particular, capital market actors. The European Commission's initiatives, to a large degree, articulate the discourse engendered and disseminated by such transnational networks.

All in all, it appears that the European Commission has indeed fully taken on a 'negative harmonization' approach to corporate governance regulation. Rather than insisting on concrete and definite regulatory coordination, it seeks to strengthen the position of shareholders, and ultimately the role of the market, by removing 'technical' obstacles such as multiple voting rights or facilitating cross-border transactions. The objective behind this is clearly that 'in the medium to long term our actions must respond to the needs of the market (MacCreevy 2005b). Apart from the European Commission's push for a 'shareholder democracy' (European Commission 2005b), increased transparency and disclosure of corporate governance issues are supposed to advance the functioning of market control. As Frits Bolkestein argued: 'disclosure elements are a highly effective market-led way of rapidly achieving results [...] better disclosure will help the markets to play their disciplining role' (Bolkestein 2004). Within EU financial market and corporate governance regulation, several regulatory initiatives have been aimed at improving transparency and disclosure, most notably the 2003 Prospectus Directive (2003/71/European Commission) and the 2004 Transparency Directive (2004/109/European Commission).

In the field of regulating corporate governance, the EU thus increasingly only intervenes and provides a regulatory framework in cases where the market cannot provide for the conditions necessary for its proper functioning, which means that regulatory activities are increasingly assigned to the market and thus further removed from democratic control. National regulatory arrangements of corporate organisation are subjected to the scrutiny of the market in an environment of increasing regulatory arbitrage. As Jaap Winter contends, 'the picture emerges that the original legislative approach to harmonize company laws in Europe, in order to avoid 'bad' competition between Member States, has been supplemented by a judicial approach explicitly allowing for competition between the company laws of Member States' (Winter 2004: 107). From a market perspective, even regulation that might be considered 'efficient' in a national context ceases to be efficient if it does not provide for a basis for the further integration of a liquid transnational market. In the words of the HLG, 'these more and less developed markets must be integrated on a European level to enable the restructuring of European industry and the integration of European securities markets to proceed with reasonable efficiency and speed' (High Level Group of Company Experts 2002: 23). This means we are dealing with a process of transnational marketization, arguably disembedding the socio-economic organization of the EU.

Conclusion

In this chapter we have sought to show that the EU has not only increased its attention to corporate governance regulation, but that, in terms of its *content*, the European approach to regulating the governance of corporations has shifted from a focus on harmonization, aimed at the prevention of regulatory competition, to a focus on promoting the marketization of corporate control, in part making use of market-based regulatory mechanisms. We have argued that this shift cannot be simply explained either as a result of exogenous globalization pressures or as response to the recent wave of corporate scandals, but has to be interpreted as bound up with a coherent transnational political project constructed from the late 1980s onwards. This project can be understood both more broadly as a neoliberal project aimed at the marketization of the European socio-economic order in general (that is, promoting the market mechanism as the organizing principle (Polanyi 1957) of this order) and, more narrowly, as a project aimed at the marketization of corporate control. As we have seen, the latter has been increasingly articulated with, and made an integral part of, Europe's strategy for creating a single financial market.

The currently hegemonic neoliberal policy discourse, subjecting the governance of corporations to the discipline of capital markets, and ultimately turning corporations themselves into commodities, is supposed to enhance the global competitiveness of the European economy in general. In other words, increasing the exit power of transnationally mobile shareholders and 'sufficiently' rewarding these 'investors' for the risks they have taken ('shareholder value') is presented as necessary in order to let Europe survive in the globalized world economy. Elsewhere in this book, several arguments have been advanced to cast considerable doubt on this kind of logic (see especially the contributions by Rebérioux and Jessop). Here we have mainly claimed that this kind of discourse shows the ideological underpinnings and political contingency of the EU's attempt to create a European regulatory framework for corporate governance. At the same time, we have underlined the key role of EU regulation, and regulation in general, in constructing and promoting the development of markets. In as far as European corporate governance becomes more market-based and reveals some convergence among diverse national systems, this is not spontaneously brought about by market forces. Regulation, in providing the key pre-conditions for markets to arise and develop, is central here. The EU has set this task for itself with an impressive zeal. Paradoxically, as policy makers increasingly seek to 'leave things to the market', the state, or in this case the multi-level polity of the EU, has to play an increasingly pro-active role in order to achieve this state of affairs. Partly for this reason the idea of a self-regulating market is ultimately, as Polanyi (1957) argued, a utopia. It is also a utopia because the destructive forces that the free market and its commodifying logic unleash will require a more protective role of the state as well, if the capitalist system is not to break down entirely. However, this part of the Polanyian 'double movement' is as yet far from apparent at the level of EU socio-economic governance.

Notes

1 To avoid conceptual confusion, the concept of 'external corporate governance' differs from what Rebérioux (in this book) calls 'external control'. While he refers to an 'exteriorization of supervising devices' as in auditing and an independent board of directors, this paper uses 'external corporate governance' as a shorthand for the influence and power of holders of control rights tied to shares.
2 The role of the European Court of Justice (ECJ) and several decisions have also been of significance for the trajectory of company law, and thus of corporate governance, in the EU. In several decisions in recent years, the ECJ has put the freedom of movement of capital and companies (as legal persons) above national configurations of company law and corporate governance systems (for recent overviews, see Winter 2004; Armour 2005).
3 For detailed accounts of the legislative history of the Takeover Directive, see for example, Skog (2000); Berglöf and Burkart (2003); Wooldridge (2004).

4 For a more detailed account of the role of the HLG, see Horn forthcoming. For a list of members and published reports see http://ec.europa.eu/internal_market/company/advisory/index_en.htm.

5 Directive 2004/25/EC of 21 April 2004 on takeover bids; for a detailed overview and discussion of the provisions see Maul and Kolouridas (2004); Wooldridge (2004).

6 Implementation of the Directive has been rather slow (see Buck 2006). For an overview of the implementation process and which Member States have followed the optional arrangements, see a study conducted by the European Group for Investor Protection, available at www.egip.org/docs/Updated%20version%20of%20EGIP%27s%20survey%20on%20the%20implementation%20of%20the%20EU%20Takeover%20Directive.pdf (last accessed 11 September 2006).

7 Agreement has recently been reached on the eighth company law directive on statutory audit (IP/05/1249).

8 The European Commission has recently conducted a consultation on the 'future priorities' of the Company Law Action Plan. For the report of the consultation, see http://ec.europa.eu/internal_market/company/docs/consultation/final_report_en.pdf (last accessed 11 September 2006).

9 For the list of members see: http://ec.europa.eu/internal_market/company/docs/ecgforum/members_en.pdf (last accessed: 22 September 2006).

10 For information on the membership of this group and for its reports see: http://ec.europa.eu/internal_market/company/advisory/index_en.htm (last accessed: 22 September 2006). In terms of the composition of both these groups, it is remarkable that labour organisations are only represented by one member in each group.

6 Towards a market-based approach

The privatization and micro-economization of EU antitrust law enforcement

Angela Wigger

Introduction

An important flanking device of the contemporary transformation of corporate governance regulation is constituted by the developments of EU-level competition or antitrust policy.[1] Consisting of laws and regulations, competition policy generally pertains to the structure of market power and market integration. Situated at the heart of modern capitalist economies, it typically sets the conditions of market concentration and access, the scope of commercial freedom to conclude cooperative ventures with other companies, and more generally the distinction between the public and the private realm. Apart from the genuinely public market interventionist nature, competition policy can come in different shapes and serve a broad range of conflicting interests. Biased by the wider enforcement philosophies and competences of competition authorities, established practices and procedural rules, and most notably, interest group influence, it can both enable and constrain private market power, be more or less market-interventionist, more or less business-friendly or free market-orientated. Consequently, competition policy needs to be understood as 'a product of the prevailing economic and political thinking of the times' that is both constituted by and constitutive to the structural power relations in a political economy (Gavil *et al.* 2002: 69).

It is not be immediately obvious, but there is an intimate connection between competition policy and corporate governance. The stringency in which competition laws are interpreted and enforced can have important repercussions on the patterns of ownership and corporate control. It can boost investor sentiments in procuring corporate equity, and influence strategic decision making with regard to mergers and acquisitions (M&A), financing capital, research and development (R&D) investment, joint ventures and other forms of cooperative business contracts. The interface of competition law enforcement and corporate governance is manifold. A range of studies suggests linkages between announcements of anticipated mergers between listed companies and share price increases, filed antitrust lawsuits and negative share price reactions of defendant companies, or overall lower shareholder returns, and in the worst case even bankruptcy resulting from financial distress caused by litigation costs and liability payments (Bhagat *et al.* 1994; Bittlingmayer and Hazlett 2000; Alexander 1999; Bhagat *et al.* 1998; Bizjak and Coles 1995). Again other studies attempt to demonstrate how shareholder initiated antitrust class actions can provide a powerful disciplinary tool to achieve boardroom reform and enhance corporate performance and managerial efficiency (cf. Gande and Lewis 2005).

Here the focal point of analysis is the wider significance of the transformation of antitrust regulation at the EU-level with respect to one key aspect within corporate governance, namely the power relations between shareholders and management (see the introductory chapter to this book). Regulatory reforms constitute important signposts for analyzing the *Zeitgeist* of competition policy as they mark the end of certain ideologically held beliefs and the consolidation of new ideas brought forth by dominant political forces in the time before the finalization. What is commonly termed 'the Modernization' comprises a package deal of both substantive and procedural reform measures that came into force on 1 May 2004 (European Commission 1999a). According to former Competition Commissioner Mario Monti it is tantamount to 'a revolution in the way competition rules are enforced in the European Union' (Monti 2004a). This chapter highlights the combined impact of the newly introduced Regulation 1/2003, and the increased reliance on neoclassical microeconomics in the assessment of anticompetitive conduct. The new regulatory framework concerns the enforcement of EU cartel law and the prosecution of other forms of restrictive business behaviour as spelled out in Article 81 (TEC) (hereinafter antitrust law). It brought about a regulatory shift away from a centralized administrative *ex ante* public control model for commercial intercompany agreements towards a decentralized *ex post* private enforcement model, which refers to the 'application of antitrust law in civil disputes before the courts' and implies that private actors can litigate observed anticompetitive conduct before the courts as complementary to public antitrust enforcement (European Commission 2005c: 4). The reform seeks in many ways to enhance the levels of private enforcement in the EU. The launch of a Green Paper proposes the introduction of new judical tools to render private actions more worthwile for claimants.

The chapter demonstrates that behind seemingly technocratic and detailed legal issues in the arcane field of antitrust control lurk important political questions regarding the distribution and concentration of economic power, not only between corporations, but also within the organizational structure of corporations. It attempts to reconstruct the interest constellation and the structural forces in the political economy that informed this process by paying close attention to the question of *cui bono*. This concomitantly helps to explain why it was conducted and how it relates to the power balance within corporate governance. It will be argued that the new regime of private enforcement plays into the hands of a more shareholdervalue-orientated market economy by opening up windows of opportunity for groups of shareholders to increase their voice options in the governance of corporations and to redistribute economic power in their favour. Moreover, a range of additional consequences are identified that come to the fore, such as the withdrawal of public market surveillance in an important field of competition control, and a growing market-reliance on the application of antitrust law. Reinforcing this trend is the institutional anchoring of the use of microeconomic theories and ever more sophisticated econometric techniques to model anticompetitive conduct and market performance – a process that has been ongoing for a couple of years and that finds its consolidation in the reform measures. It will be argued that similar to the transformation of EU corporate governance regulation (see the contribution by Van Apeldoorn and Horn to this book), the reform of EU competition policy has been orientated towards a profound neoliberal restructuring – entailing a political predisposition towards more competition, more market-based regulatory approaches and a general inclination towards fostering corporate efficiency.

The chapter is organized as follows: the first section introduces the substance of the regulatory shift and locates its importance in the variety of capitalism debate by drawing on the Rhenish and the Anglo-Saxon categories as a point of departure. The following two sections interpret the reform against the backdrop of intersecting and mutually reinforcing features: the growing market-reliance in the application of antitrust law prompted by private enforcement, the consolidation of a process of 'microeconomization' and the combined impact of the latter. Section four zooms into the interest constellation that has driven the reform. Next to those directly involved in the reform process, that is, transnational business, the European Commission and private practioners, the particular interests of a diffuse group of shareholders are highlighted, which alongside the antitrust reform lobbied for class action litigation and criminal sanctions as means to gain more corporate control. In conclusion the chapter discusses the parallels of the substantive changes of corporate governance and antitrust law and underscores the contradictoriness of the interest motives of the different transnational forces that sought enhanced market-integrating and market-based regulatory solutions.

The reform of EU antitrust law enforcement

The administrative ex ante *Notification Regime – A 'Rhenish' peculiarity*

For more than 40 years the EU antitrust enforcement operated as a market-correcting regime following the rationale that the European Commission's Competition Directorate-General (DG Competition) monitors the market for anticompetitive conduct before it actually takes place. Regulation 17 from 1962 provided the interpretative and procedural framework regulating cartels and other restrictive business practices prohibited under Article 81 (TEC), as well as Article 82 (TEC) on the abuse of dominant positions. Its central component was an administrative *ex ante* notification regime according to which companies above a certain turnover threshold could notify envisaged intercompany agreements to the European Commission.[2] Each of these notifications was reviewed on the basis of whether the intended deal had the object or the effect of 'prevention, restriction or distortion of competition within the common market' stipulated in Article 81(1).

Entrusted with far-reaching executive powers, the European Commission could either prohibit or allow a deal, ask for amendments, or grant exemptions. The latter could be done individually, on a case-by-case basis or as block exemptions in the form of regulations specifying whole groups or sector-specific categories of agreements that were not considered anticompetitive, provided that the conditions set out in Article 81(3) were fulfilled. These conditions entailed that the agreement needed 'to improve the production or distribution of goods, or then promote technical or economic progress that ultimately allows consumers a fair share of the resulting benefit'.

Notifying a proposed transaction provided companies with a safe-harbour mechanism regarding the various forms of agreements that could potentially fall into the category of a cartel or restrictive business practice and ensured legal immunity from prosecution. Apart from crude price-fixing and market-sharing, the agreements under concern could take the form of production and R&D joint ventures, patent licensing, franchising contracts, strategic alliances in marketing and sales, distribution, information exchange and other cooperative activities, concerning either direct competitors (horizontal agreements) or companies involved in the different stages of the production, distribution, or marketing process (vertical agreements).

The wider significance of an administrative *ex ante* notification regime for commercial intercompany agreements in particular, and for the way in which capitalism is organized more generally, often tends to be neglected. Commercial intercompany agreements and strategic alliances are a much more common business practice in modern market economies than the more easily observable concentration developments through M&As, which stand more frequently in the limelight of scholarly and media attention. The boundaries are often blurred: intercompany agreements can integrate major long-term business goals and include far-reaching equity joint ventures, minority holdings and equity swaps (Ullrich 2003: 211–12). Similar to the wave of mergers during the 1990s, commercial agreements between companies rose considerably in number and often involved a cross-border dimension. Estimates for the OECD indicate an increase from 1050 in 1989 to 8660 in 2000, with a sudden jump to 4000 in 1990 and a temporal peak of 9000 in 1995 (Ullrich 2003: 210). The vast magnitude of such agreements reveals that the neoclassical notion of atomistic or perfect competition according to which discrete companies with clearly separable interests compete one by one is misleading. In the market reality the concentration of economic power through a web of ever more indiscernible linkages of agreements and strategic alliances seems prevailing, in particular in times of harsher competition resulting from an accelerated pace of ongoing liberalization of trade and financial markets as is the case since the 1990s.

The administrative *ex ante* notification and exemption system of controlling commercial intercompany agreements constitutes a peculiar characteristic of the European antitrust model and reflects in many ways the central features of the Rhenish model of capitalist organization (cf. Albert 1993; Hall and Soskice 2001; Crouch and Streeck 1997). It was designed by leading representatives of the ordoliberal school, home-based at the Freiburg University in Germany, which enjoyed a long-standing influence on the institutional design of the EU antitrust regime, enforcement philosophies and attitudes towards anticompetitive conduct (cf. Gerber 1998).[3] Central to the ordoliberal idea is that capitalism needs to be organized through the creation of a 'thoroughly and continuously policed competition order' (Budzinski 2003: 15), in which many competitors compete on equal and fair terms. Franz Böhm (1980), one of the leading proponents, suggested to understand competition as a cultivated, rather than a naturally grown plant. The establishment of a proactive, powerful and governmentally independent institution of market surveillance protecting and controlling corporations from the harmful and destructive forces of the free market was considered essential. Only by means of a long-term orientated and balanced market interventionist strategy the ordoliberal proviso of 'complete competition' could be accomplished – a state of affairs in which no company has the power to coerce the conduct of another (Eucken in Gerber 1998: 245). From this macroeconomic vantage point, an enduring market structure with many equally powerful players was considered more important than the short-term market performance of individual companies.

The ordoliberal legacy of an ideal market structure manifested itself in Article 82 prohibiting the abuse of a dominant position. However, apart from the current prosecution of Microsoft this law remained largely underenforced. Instead, the ordoliberal doctrine of many competitors was translated in the safeguarding of the diversity and entrepreneurial freedom of small- and medium-sized enterprises (SMEs), which received special attention in EU antitrust practice.[4] Moreover, the notion of strong public market intervention and supervision is reflected in the wide-ranging powers of the European Commission in antitrust matters, which can act as investigator, prosecutor, judge and jury in antitrust matters. The notification and exemption regime is a case in point, as it provided the European Commission with much interpretative leeway. Primarily concerned with the long-term goal of the European economic integration project, the European Commission tradionally applied antitrust laws to break up national market barriers in order to provide access to new market entrants and to stimulate the broader project of economic integration. Cross-border cooperation agreements were considered conducive to this goal. As exemption regulations expanded cumulatively, they came to include a broad range of agreements: a few vertical agreements, R&D, specialization, and standardization agreements, and technology transfer agreements, as well as specific agreements in the car distribution sector or the insurance sector (Cini and McGowan 1998: 98).

The overwhelmingly administrative character of the notification and exemption regime provided the business community with a high degree of legal certainty and an avenue for lobbying for a *laissez-faire* treatment with regard to transactions that otherwise would have been forbidden. Occasionally exemption rules were even applied to counterbalance the competition focus with wider socio-economic and redistributive goals, such as the alleviation of employment problems of certain regions (Jarman-Williams 2001). Moreover, industry could anticipate the benevolence of a public actor in the pursuit of long-term orientated restructuring measures in times of economic downfall, such as in the early 1970s when cutthroat economic competition was generally considered a danger for the economy and the social order. Declining industries (that is, sugar, steel and shipbuilding) were allowed to deal with chronic overcapacities by jointly moderating production levels rather than competing each other to death and drastically reducing employment (Pollack 1998: 230; Fox 1997: 342). Therefore, due to permissive interpretations of the exemption rules, the toleration of the temporary establishment of so-called 'crisis cartels' has been no exception in Europe.

The rather generous stance towards contractual agreements allowing companies to combine their resources and explore new profit opportunities contributed to the development of a variety of capitalism in which (hostile) takeovers were relatively less common (cf. De Jong 1989; Hudson 2002) – arguably together with a range of other important 'Rhenish' features: the existence of major banks providing patient capital in form of long-term loans, and the lesser need for stock market quotations as a form of corporate finance rendering the acquisition of shares by potential bidders less of an option, as well as structural barriers for hostile takeovers in most corporate governance regimes, such as the issuance of priority shares with multiple controlling rights, and veto rights by banks, the state, or employee representatives (Cernat 2004: 153–5; Nölke 1999). In marked contrast to the systemic aversion to hostile takeovers in most European countries, in the Anglo-Saxon type of capitalism (most notably that of the US and the UK), the criminal prosecution of price-fixing and market-sharing agreements, in other words 'cartels', encouraged companies to merge instead (Gaughan 2002: 23). In addition, this predisposition to mergers was also furthered by the predominance of stock market capitalization, the supremacy of shareholder interests and relatively few limitations for predatory raids in corporate governance regulation.

The abolition of the notification regime – a step of convergence towards the US model

One of the central components of the 2004 EU antitrust reform package is the replacement of Regulation 17 with Regulation 1/2003, according to which notifications for Article 81-type agreements are no longer possible. In addition, the conditions for block exemptions have been expanded, and the whole of Articles 81 and 82 declared directly applicable 'if trade between the Member States is affected'.[5] The latter implies that the EU antitrust enforcement regime has become decentralized: national competition authorities (NCAs) and national courts have to apply EU antitrust laws for commercial transactions of EC-dimension in parallel to their own distinct competition laws. The abolition of this long-standing tradition of administrative and supervisory market control for commercial intercompany agreements means that companies cannot rely anymore on the European Commission's official decision prior to concluding an agreement, nor can they seek individual exemption. This reflects a retrenchment of the European Commission and marks the introduction of a system of private enforcement. With the removal of a public warranty to proceed with a transaction, companies have to assess themselves whether a particular cooperative agreement breaches EU antitrust law, or whether it falls under the revised system of block exemptions for Article 81(3). It entails further that companies are increasingly exposed to the risk of being litigated by other market actors, a jeopardy that so far has constituted a relatively alien feature in EU antitrust control. The reform seeks in many ways to enhance the levels of private enforcement, which reflects a major step of convergence towards the Anglo-Saxon antitrust model, in particular towards that of the US. The federal antitrust authorities, the Department of Justice (DoJ) and the Federal Trade Commission (FTC), never played a similar comforting role as the European Commission, nor was there an equivalent of the EU notification regime for commercial agreements in the US. Instead, under the US model of *ex post* private enforcement hitherto more than 90 per cent of all formal antitrust actions are brought to the courts by private litigators (James 1999; Kemper 2004: 9; Wils 2003: 477).[6] Although private entities have always played an important role in the enforcement of EU antitrust law (the European Commission received on average more than 100 private complaints per year (Paulis and Smijter 2005: 12)) private litigation as complementary to public enforcement has never become a widely applied practice: in less than five per cent of the cases did private litigators take the initiative to invoke a claim at the European courts (Kemper 2004: 9).

The *ex ante* notification regime provided little ground for private actors to bring legal actions to the courts: once the European Commission cleared a case or granted exemption, companies enjoyed legal immunity from further prosecution, leaving for claimants only the option of challenging the Commission's decision before the European courts. Positing a case at the European Commission's desk was far more appealing as most civil law schemes plaintiffs needed to collect the relevant evidence and prove that a certain business conduct infringed the law, as well as cover the alleged costs of suing (Pirrung 2004: 97). In addition, most of the legal features that make it attractive to initiate legal proceedings against corporations in the US were absent in the EU system: successful plaintiffs were not awarded three times the damage suffered on top of the costs of suing, nor was there a possibility for class actions in which several plaintiffs group together and sue collectively. Moreover, 'no-win, no-fee' or contingency fees offered by most US law companies (according to which professional litigators representing the plaintiffs in court make their profit dependent on the monetary award) are prohibited in most European legal systems. Hence, the absence of these judicial tools renders the legal landscape of the EU a rather hostile environment for private antitrust action, which is why in the European setting a claimant's culture with exorbitant compensation payments, like that of the US, is a rather alien feature.

Even though the 2004 reform does not directly touch upon further legal modifications, the current discussion on a range of legal instruments for private plaintiffs is likely to render the reform a stepping-stone in a much broader process of enhanced convergence towards the US model of private enforcement. In particular the creation of stronger incentives for private litigation has achieved high agenda status. Commissioner Kroes is quite overt in this respect: '[…] the comprehensive enforcement of the competition rules is not yet complete – not enough use is made of the courts' (Kroes 2005c). In December 2005 the European Commission presented its ideas on how to 'increase the scope for private enforcement' in a Green Paper promoting the introduction of 'Damages Actions for Breach of the EC Antitrust Rules' (European Commission 2005c). As a point of departure, the current situation of damage claims for antitrust infringements in the EU-25 was noted to present a picture of 'total underdevelopment' and 'astonishing diversity' (European Commission 2005c). Whether or not a facilitated damage relief system should be introduced at all did not form part of the European Commission's 36 options specifying its implementation. Once a system of damage relief is introduced, the Commission expects private parties to go much further in bringing actions to the courts than competition authorities (Monti 2004b). Moreover, the gradual raise in private law suits and facilitated court access is expected to increase the overall level of enforcement and render it at least 'as effective as in the US, if not more so' (Philip Lowe cited in Dombey 2004). The next section highlights why private enforcement unequivocally stimulates a more market-based antitrust regime.

Towards a more market-based regime

With the emphasis on private enforcement the centre of gravity shifted from the European Commission's desk to the proactivity of market participants. Companies are not only expected to watch over themselves but also their competitors, distributors and suppliers and to bring antitrust breaches to the courts. The same is expected from consumers, employees and other possible private litigants. Even though competition authorities continue to be entitled to intervene in private market conduct, the system has become more market-based: it attempts to evoke a situation of mutual control by market actors, and henceforth a deterrent to anticompetitive behaviour: the fear of litigation should prevent companies to engage in unlawful agreements and ensure a better compliance with antitrust laws.

An essential effect of the new regime is that the retrenchment of a public authority creates a whole new avenue for professional services firms specialized in antitrust regulation, also called law companies, to assist other companies in the decision whether a planned business transaction produces anticompetitive effects, or whether it belongs into the category of block exemptions. Although legal experts have played already significant counselling roles under the notification procedure, with the introduction of private enforcement the demand-side for judicial advocacy in antitrust matters increases, in particular as most companies do not possess in-house expertise on complex antitrust matters. Professional service companies find a new market for a whole range of products, such as tailor-made compliance programmes, economic analyses on market structures and market shares as a basis for assessment, targeted lobbying activities at the EU and the national regulatory institutions, and in case of litigation, corporate lawyers representing their clients at the courts. Whereas the European Commission's decision provided companies with a legal check free of charge, under the new regime specialized legal advice needs to be purchased on the market similar to any other commodity, reflecting a case in point of an overall 'deepening commodification', which started in the late 1970s and is marked by 'expanding market relations and possibilities for private profit pursuit into ever further spheres and dimensions of human activity and existence' (Overbeek 2004a: 4). This development is likely to be reinforced by the ongoing trend towards more 'microeconomics' in antitrust enforcement, which will be addressed in the next section.

The 'microeconomization' of EU antitrust enforcement

The 2004 reform is concomitant to a steady trend towards the use of ever more sophisticated neoclassical economic principles and econometric evidence in the assessment of anticompetitive conduct. The sheer number of economists and financial analysts that were employed to assist the legal experts in the EU has been growing in the past few years. Arguably it should not be a surprise that a regulatory field located at the interface of law and economics attracts personnel with an interdisciplinary academic background, including legal experts and lawyers, paralegals, economists, industry specialists and accountants and the like. Traditionally more lawyers and legal experts than economists have occupied the field of antitrust enforcement in the EU (Cini and McGowan 1998: 50). Correspondingly, judicial interpretations of anticompetitive conduct were predominant. Again, this marks a strong contrast to the US, where economic principles and the collection of quantitative econometric data in the investigation phase forms the epitome of antitrust decision making (Scheffman and Coleman 2001; Katz 2004).

From the from the 1960s onwards, generations of US antitrust practioners were influenced by the maxims and analytical concepts of the Chicago School of Law and Economics, which emerged as a Monetarist response to Keynesianism and celebrated its heyday under the Reagan administration in the 1980s (cf. Gerber 1998; Budzinski 2003). Adherents of the Chicago School propagated neoliberal deregulation and further liberalization of markets by drawing on the neoclassical economic assumption of self-regulating markets, according to which the free interplay of market mechanisms results in an optimal and effective resource allocation, and ultimately benefits consumers with lower prices.[7] In this view, any regulatory steering of the market should be the exception and antitrust law enforcement restricted to safeguarding price competition and efficiency improvements at the company level. In the Reagan era, mergers were no longer contested. Market concentration was assumed to create a situation of economies of scale, and therefore greater allocative and productive efficiency, and thus, lower prices for consumers – a perspective that ushered in a 'hands-off' approach at the federal level (Motta 2004: 4). When some of the leading exponents of the Chicago School were elected as judges at the US Supreme Court and when the Chicago Trainee Program 'educated' about half of the federal judges in antitrust law enforcement under Reagan's presidency, Chicagoan theorems penetrated antitrust jurisprudence and so became a deeply engrained philosophy (Schmidt and Rittaler 1986: 11–12). Although so-called Post-Chicago scholars eventually took a slightly more interventionist stance, the yardsticks of narrow efficiency concerns and the focus on price reductions as a conceptual benchmark for consumer welfare maximisation remain unchallenged until today. This is likely to be fortified by the re-employment of the Chicago-brigade under the presidency of George W. Bush.[8] Over time the Chicagoan heritage resulted in highly sophisticated economic modelling to measure market efficiency and consumer welfare based on neoclassical economic theories, supported by econometric analyses and specific algorithms for the definition of markets and market boundaries and rational-choice game theories as a foundation for detecting rent-seeking cartel behaviour (Fox 1997: 340). Moreover, the use of price theories and price modelling as a central reference point for determining anticompetitive conduct quintessentially gives precedence to a microeconomic perspective and to short-termism: the focus on prices limits the perspective to single company behaviour in relation to consumers at a particular point in time and disregards macroeconomic issues like market power concentration and market structure.

Narrowing the gap: From Freiburg to Chicago

Currently about half of the qualified officials working at the Commission's DG Competition have an academic degree in economics (Röller and Friederiszick 2005). Under the legacy of former Commissioner Mario Monti, an economist himself, the *economic* sophistication of antitrust law enforcement received a major boost. Also his successor Neelie Kroes repeatedly announced that further reforms facilitating high-quality economic analyses will also be at the top of her agenda (Kroes 2005a, 2005b). As one of the chief architects behind the 2004 'modernization', Monti's role was pivotal in reorganizing the professional nature of the European Commission's competition department. As Monti himself noted: 'One of my main objectives upon taking office […] has been to increase the emphasis on sound economics in the application of the EC antitrust rules, in particular to those concerning different types of agreements between companies […]' (Monti 2001). Similar to the US model, a post called the 'Chief Competition Economist' was established, which had the mission to scrutinize the European Commission's antitrust investigations with a 'fresh pair of eyes' and 'independent economic viewpoints' (Monti 2002). Accompanied by an entourage of experienced economists called the Economic Advisory Group, the Chief Economist guides the work of the regular staff of lawyers and other economists on a case-by-case basis in all fields of competition control, that is, mergers, antitrust and state-aid cases and advises on the future development of competition policy (Röller 2005: 6).

Apart from the numerical transformation of competition officers with a background in economics, a range of indicators lay bare that the kind of competition economics that made its entry is grounded in microeconomics, analytically premised on methodological individualism, and home-based in the neoliberal free market ideology. The new creed of economists maintains strong transatlantic links indicating that the substance of economic theories that has become prevailing in

EU enforcement practice is likely to be streamlined with that dominant in the US. Bilateral meetings where 'past case work' and 'economic methodology' are discussed with economists working at the FTC and the DoJ take place on a regular basis (Röller 2005: 6). In this vein it seems no coincidence that Professor Lars-Hendrik Röller, who was appointed Chief Competition Economist in July 2003, was educated in competition economics in the US.

Although differences in the legal instruments remain, the European Commission is increasingly using 'the same micro-economic analytical tools as the US' (Schaub 2002: 3). Monti heralded the silent process of convergence as the 'most important success story in the transatlantic relationship' and argued that EU competition policy is now clearly grounded in 'sound microeconomics' (Monti 2004b). He observed:

> [...] (w)e share a common fundamental vision of the role and limitations of public intervention. [...] We are both grappling with the same evolving economic realities and are both exposed to the same evolution in economic thinking.
>
> (Monti 2004b)[9]

This 'common fundamental vision' entails that the ultimate purpose of public intervention into the marketplace is to ensure that competitive prices are not harmed. The enhanced emphasis on prices together with the declaration of consumer welfare as the predominant task of competition control, indicates that the macroeconomic orientated vision inspired by ordoliberal economic thinking is vanishing in one of its last strongholds. This has a profound impact on the scope and nature of antitrust control in a regime of private enforcement and the overall corporate climate in the EU as the next section will show.

'Microeconomisation' in a system of private enforcement

Economic principles and econometric analyses are predicated upon ideologically-held beliefs on how economic reality functions. Recalling that 'theory is always for someone and for some purpose' (Cox 1981: 128) reminds us that there is no such thing as neutral theory. The reduction of real-world complexity into econometric modelling and analyses, the subsequent operationalisation and assessment of empirical data has as a consequence that the parameters excluded, so-called exogenous variables, simply remain unnoticed in the decision making. Mathematical economics merely measures what it can measure. If price calculations to indicate consumer welfare are prioritized, the welfare of employees and employment aspects, the restructuring of certain industries in times of economic downfall, or the protection of the environment are less likely to be considered as decisive factors in the final decision making. Moreover, there is no such thing as testing against what Joseph Schumpeter (1942) called 'the cold metal of economic theory'. Assessing a particular business transaction as anticompetitive conduct is always based on a speculative judgment of collected evidence, which derives from paradigmatic beliefs about market realities.

Private enforcement in a decentralized enforcement regime is likely to bring the speculative character of antitrust enforcement to the fore. In the decentralized enforcement regime of the EU, no less than 26 jurisdictions with thousands of tribunals will have to set the yardsticks and evaluate the soundness of technically complex empirical material used in accusations and court defences. In the absence of specialized competition courts, 'ordinary' judges will award damage compensation and impose fines, and in Member States where competition law infringements are prosecuted under criminal law, even imprison CEOs for their unlawful activities. The chances for deviant interpretations are very high and the legal forum-shopping for claimants may become common. As competition laws often tend to be formulated in loose and imprecise terms, due process of law according to established rules and principles is difficult to maintain. The frequency of so-called 'borderline' cases constitutes part of the reason why the devolution of antitrust enforcement competences to national courts has led to many controversies.[10]

In combination with enhanced possibilities of private enforcement, the 'microeconomization' of competition law enforcement becomes all-pervasive. Future claimants may rely upon legal precedents, which has the potential effect that the growing body of judge-made case law looks in certain economic data-gathering methods as the standard for decision making. In sum: whereas before a public authority could balance the decision making in antitrust matters according to broader political macroeconomic goals, individual private claimants by definition are more likely to be driven by self-interest when invoking a claim. Similarly, national judges proceed on a case-by-case basis without taking into account the wider political economy. In combination with the trend towards more microeconomics, the new regime is likely to prelude a political bias towards narrower and more short-term conceptions of competition. This then, brings us to the question of who, given this content, benefits from the new antitrust regime, and to what extent those who have an interest also have been driving the reform.

Cui bono? The driving forces and their agendas

The mixed emotions of 'corporate Europe'

The *ex ante* notification regime did not cause widespread public dissatisfaction that would explain why the reform was conducted. On theoretical grounds one could expect companies subject to the reform, including management boards and shareholders alike, to be strong proponents of the reform: with the removal of a burdensome administrative straightjacket, the leeway to make use of the freedom of contract and to engage in all types of commercial agreements without being immediately controlled by the European Commission's interventionist arm increases. Indeed, the business community represented at the EU-level, the Union of Industrial and Employers' Confederation of Europe (UNICE), and the ERT, were to some extent in favour of 'modernizing' the application of the EC antitrust rules (Union of Industrial and Employers' Confederation of Europe 1995, 2001, 2002). CEOs in particular repeatedly criticized the European Commission's far reaching powers that themselves were not subject to judicial control (European Round Table of Industrialists 2001: 3). Cumbersome, in-depth antitrust reviews in which the European Commission needs to be persuaded that a deal should go through on the basis of elaborate rock-hard economic data and legal analyses is neither in the interest of executive boards nor shareholders.

Transnational companies (TNCs) are genuinely interested in lifting regulatory barriers that hamper the free flow of capital accummulation, or what in Eurojargon euphemistically came to be translated as 'creating a level playing field'. Rigid reviews of cross-border intercompany agreements involving several jurisdictions increase transaction costs and the probability of conflicting results. Therefore, the regulatory system offering the most favourable structure tends to be preferred. In this vein, the ERT encouraged the European Commission to embody a more economics-based interpretation of antitrust law and 'to emulate the US more fully' in this respect, in particular with regard to measuring efficiency improvements in antitrust analyses (European Round Table of Industrialists 2002). A range of reasons account for the strong preference for the US model. In the 1990s, about half of all strategic partnerships had a transatlantic dimension, whereas only a quarter concerned pure intraeuropean deals (Ullrich 2003: 210–1). Moreover, US antitrust officials and business representatives repeatedly criticized the European Commission's weak commitment to sound economic evidence in its decision making especially after a series of divergent rulings by the Commission in high-profile cases between US companies.[11] Severe criticism came also from the Court of First Instance (CFI) and the ECJ, which overruled three high-profile decisions taken by the DG Competition on the grounds that the economic evidence that underpinned the prohibitions was deemed insufficient and its economic logic not convincing (that is Airtours–First Choice in 1999, Schneider–Legrand and Tetra Laval–Sidel in 2002). After these embarrassing court defeats, the hiring of economists and the convergence towards US-style economic thinking received a major boost. Director-General Philip Lowe, an economist himself, concluded that the reliance on economic foundations in competition matters brings 'comfort on the robustness of the decisions' (Lowe 2003). A large part of this 'comfort', however, can be ascribed to the fact that since 2002 most of the transactions have been cleared anyway.

The use of microeconomics in antitrust matters is also grounded in the vested interest of transnational corporations to keep certain stakeholders away from the negotiating table. The ERT quite overtly argued that the greater involvement of groups like consumers and employees 'risks diverting the attention from the competition focus of the European Commission's analysis and increasing both uncertainty and delay' (European Round Table of Industrialists 2001: 4). With the focus on 'competition only' building upon short-term orientated econometric evidence more diffuse societal interest are unlikely to be expressed. Additionally, it may bestow a regime an arm's length basis and provide managers with an avenue for less stringent enforcement. Concepts such as 'dynamic efficiency improvements' leave ample room for gerrymandering the decision making in the wished-for direction. Already prior definitions on 'relevant product markets' or delimitation of one product *vis-à-vis* another can be used for 'moulding' evidence to support a particular claim. Moreover, as one commentator has argued, estimations of future competitve impacts assessed on the basis of defined confidence intervals are tantamount to an 'intuitive judgment in deciding whether a test is passed or not' (Dobbs 2002: 3).

Nevertheless, the support of 'corporate Europe' is not straightforward. On the contrary, emotions are mixed and certain elements of the reform have been fiercely criticized. The administratively burdensome, but secure way of the notification regime has had its proponents especially among UNICE, which comprises the whole range of European companies including SMEs. With respect to the regime change it argued that 'the complexity of the rules requires extensive expert advice' and 'substantial management time' (Union of Industrial and Employers' Confederation of Europe 1999, 2001). This contrast to the argumenation of the Commissioner Monti justifying the reform by saying that the European Commission's role, as an antitrust enforcer, was not to give comfort, and that 'after forty years of experience the application of European competition law should be sufficiently clear to business' (Monti 2004a). Elsewhere he compared the notification procedure to parking a car in a town: 'citizens must know where to park a car and shouldn't have to go to the police station to check first' (Monti 2004b). The fact that antitrust law enforcement is far more complex than Monti's car parking allegory suggests forms part of the discontent of the business community, in particular as the fines imposed on cartel cases exceed those of traffic offences. Also among the selected group of TNCs represented in the ERT the formal safe harbour regime constituted a much cherished good – provided that 'speedy and straightforward processing' was guaranteed (European Round Table of Industrialists 2002). Judicial advocacy by corporate lawyers cannot provide for the wished-for legal certainty in a competitive environment of ever-shorter amortisation periods of new technology products – so the argument. Generous interpretations on corporate alliances such as investment-sharing, R&D partnerships and the like have always been welcomed (European Round Table of Industrialists 2002).

In marked contrast to enthusiasm for a more microeconomics-based approach, the novel risk of litigation and the exposure to compensation payments alarmed the management boards of companies organized in the UNICE and ERT alike. The reason seems obvious: potential fines, damage compensation payments to private claimants and the costs of defending can cause significant reductions in a company's wealth (cf. Bizjak and Coles 1995). Although the 2004 antitrust reform does not immediately mean the advent of an US-style litigation culture, CEOs from the European business community have been very much aware of this scenario. Moreover, the new regime of decentralised private enforcement, which allows private litigants to bring breaches of EU antitrust law to national courts, has been deemed to 'accentuate inconsistency, a lack of transparency and unpredictability' (cf. Union of Industrial and Employers' Confederation of Europe

1999; European Round Table of Industrialists 2002). In a range of position papers during the preparatory stages of the reform, business organizations sought to limit the exposure to law suits by advocating inbuilt legal safety measures in the form of *ex ante* reasoned opinions by competition authorities and national jurisdictions. The issuance of such advices would come close to the reintroduction of the notification regime. In response, the European Commission promised merely the occasional provision of general 'guidance letters' published on its website. Only in 'genuine cases of uncertainty', it will grant case-specific informal guidance (cf. Recital 38 of Regulation 1/2003). This loosely defined assent by the European Commission has been very much regretted by business, which pleaded for guidance, in particular in cases of commercial agreements that 'are ancillary to, or involve a financial risk, capital investment, or an effect on shareholder value' (Union of Industrial and Employers' Confederation of Europe 2001: 5; European Round Table of Industrialists 2002). The latter is important in the context of the current transformation of corporate governance regulations. The next section addresses private antitrust enforcement in terms of its potential impact on the corporate power balance of management *vis-à-vis* shareholders.

Enhanced antitrust litigation to pursue corporate governance goals?

Commissioner Kroes presents the enhanced antitrust litigation possibilities 'as a right for consumers and individual businesses in Europe who have lost out as a result of the anticompetitive behaviour of others' (Kroes 2006). The generalization that society is constituted by either consumers or competitors that might have an interest in rectifying abusive corporate behaviour downplays the existence of other stakeholders, such as labour and environmentalists. Moreover, diffuse groups such as labour, consumers and individual businesses, face high administrative costs to organize claims against corporate fraud. Instead, another category of plaintiffs is more likely to make use of the facilitated antitrust litigation possibilities, namely shareholders, in particular institutional investors and hedge funds prioritsing short-term profits. As the reform explicitly hinges upon enhanced private antitrust litigation, so-called 'voice options' for shareholders increase (cf. Hirschman 1970). At a first glance, the reform and shareholder activism in antitrust litigation may not appear to be related. However, apart from accounting manipulation or securities fraud in cases of inaccurate disclosure of information, a wide range of other events can account for legal actions induced by shareholders. These include breaches of contract, patent infringements, product failures, bankruptcy issues, slander, marketing, distribution and franchise disputes and notably, also antitrust violations (cf. Bizjak and Coles 1995; Kahan and Rock 2006). As a rule of thumb, the more regulatory fields become subject to private enforcement, the more rent-seeking private investor groups are provided with new windows of opportunity to alter the corporate power balance in their favour and to pursue corporate governance goals. Challenging mismanagment and fraudulent behaviour of CEOs at the courts may serve as a means for vetoing inauspicious decisions by CEOs and for intervening into decision making in cases of sharevalue loss, altering the composition of the management, allocating monetary awards compensating for past harmful board actions or conducting hostile take-over bids by litigating target companies. Shareholder activism in antitrust matters may expose management boards to new risks regarding long-term investment strategies and in the worst case bankruptcy, which makes an easy prey for hostile take-overs. The institutional anchoring of short-term performance indicators in antitrust assessments provides additional ground for litigation. Already the mere threat of suing may discipline company boards to deliver higher returns on investment in the short run.

A number of shareholder rights organisations and institutional investors, such as public pension funds, have long urged national governments in Europe to introduce a range of legal modifications in the litigation procedures, such as class actions and criminal sanctions (cf. Hollinger 2005; Allen 2005; Sherwood and Tait 2005). Quests for more 'market justice' have in particular intensified with recent corporate scandals in the accounting sector, such as in the case of Enron, Parmalat and Ahold, or in the turmoil of ABN AMRO's acquisition of controlling stakes in Banca Antonveneta. Investor plaintiffs in Europe have a stake in getting the same leveraging powers as investors in the US (cf. Allen 2005). However, shareholders neither speak with one voice, nor is there a clear-cut interest coalition of shareholders to identify. Different categories of shareholders have different interests: whereas, for instance, hedge funds may follow an aggressive strategy of short-term profit maximization, banks (investment), insurance companies and (certain) pension funds may be more inclined to more secure long-term investment. Moreover, the interests of the shareholders of one company are not equivalent to those of another company. The reason seems obvious. The exposure of a company to high damage compensation payments and in the worst-case even bankruptcy or hostile takeovers eventually renders economic life more precarious for all stakeholders involved, including shareholders.

In view of the current proposals for facilitated shareholder litigation in the EU Member States, one is tempted to conclude that those shareholder demands opting for the Anglo-Saxon litigation practice find themselves on the winning side: while Sweden and the UK have already introduced the possibility for class action lawsuits in general, Germany specifically included a range of measures that facilitate private actions into its seventh amendment of competition law. As a part of the attempt to make Germany a global financial centre with 'a stock market as a viable avenue for investment', two government proposals were launched on 14 March including a bill on shareholder class actions and a bill on shareholder derivative lawsuits (Kamar 2005: 17–18). Similarly, in Italy shareholder rights have been strengthened and made conceptually reminiscent of US corporate legislation to attract US investors (Kamar 2005: 22). Also in Finland, the Netherlands and France, the issue of facilitated shareholder litigation has reached agenda status. For instance in France President Chirac has recently instructed his government to put forward initiatives for the introduction of class actions against abusive market practices – an incremental move which fits into the political landscape of the competition law overhaul.

Professional service companies – the beneficiaries of the reform?

Private antitrust practioners working at professional services companies, commonly termed law companies, are often underrated as a political force in antitrust matters (cf. the contribution by Nölke and Perry to this book on the role of coordination service firms, of which law firms may be considered an example). They form part of the epistemic community surrounding the DG Competition, which is marked by a dense fabric of professional linkages: private practioners work on the same antitrust cases as public officials, although representing antagonistic positions when defending a client, and they gather at the same conferences. Hence, they are socialized to speak, write and think about antitrust technicalities in the same idiosyncratic way (Slaughter 2004: 253). Moreover, they provide for a source of staff recruitment and inspiration with regard to the future development of competition policy.

Professional service companies will always profit from private antitrust enforcement as it increases the demand for judicial advocacy. The contemporary legal services landscape in the EU demonstrates that the phenomenon of law companies with a specialization in antitrust issues is no longer a phenomenon restricted to the Anglo-Saxon type of capitalism. Countless law companies with ever expanding numbers of lawyers and economists have established offices throughout Europe and in particular in Brussels – all tuned to profit from the booming market of antitrust counselling in Europe. Not to be underestimated is the sheer number of law companies originating from across the Atlantic. As an US antitrust lawyer observed: 'Some firms think Brussels will be the next Washington' (cited in Henning 2003).[12]

As regular and influential guests in the preparatory stages of the reform, private law companies displayed their expertise in the form of advisory reports to European Commission officials: their share of official comments on the 'White Paper on the Modernisation' and on the 2005 Green Paper outnumbered that of business and labour organisations, or NCAs (European Commission 2006). Again, a significant share of commentators originated from the US, which is illustrative of a strong interest from across the Atlantic to create similar market conditions in Europe. Professional service companies also took the lead in the formulation of possible avenues to promote enhanced private litigation in the EU. A comparative study conducted by Ashurst – a transnational law company specialized in EC competition law provided the intellectual basis for the Green Paper, which apart from a detailed account on the possibilities for damage actions in the EU covered a wide range of other litigation-related measures, such as the introduction of class actions (cf. Waelbroeck *et al.* 2004).

While the business community in Europe is expected to keep watch over itself and its competitors by seeking counselling support of professional law companies, the European Commission has embarked on its own agenda as the next section will illustrate.

The stakes of the European Commission>

The political ideas and the steadfast commitment of the DG Competition were an essential driving force of the reform. The European Commission's agenda comes to the fore through the decentralisation of antitrust enforcement, which implies that now also NCAs and courts have to apply Articles 81 and 82 for cases with an EC-dimension, something that previously was the exclusive prerogative of the European Commission. Although it initially may sound counterintituive, the decentralisation was deliberately shaped to expand the DG Competition's status quo of antitrust competences. Following Wilks (2004) the reform is exemplary of an 'audacious coup' by the European Commission to 'extend its powers and to marginalize national competition laws' or, what George Orwell in his seminal book *1984* expressed with 'decentralization is centralization' (Wilks 2004: 12).

As a part of the decentralization endeavor the European Competition Network (ECN) was established to provide a forum for NCAs and courts to cooperate and warrant legal consistency when enforcing Articles 81 and 82. As the nodal point within the ECN, the European Commission reserved for itself far-reaching supervisory powers: the opening of every new case needs to be reported to the Commission and in the event of conflicting decisions the Commission can retrieve cases again (that is Articles 11(6) and 16 of Regulation 1/2003). These provisions allude that there is only one reference point for the interpretation of EC antitrust law, namely that of the European Commission. The ongoing discussions on introducing facilitating legal features in a decentralized private enforcement regime leave the tentative conclusion that the harmonization of litigation systems may reach high on the Commission's future agenda. Although inconsistency in the enforcement of EU antitrust law is likely to be the order of the day for the reasons outlined earlier, the ECN as a mode of governance to cope with decentralization needs to be understood as an attempt at diluting the significance of the diverse national competition laws and practices in the long run. Thereby the project of an 'ever-closer Union' intruded into a policy domain in which a harmonization never was politically feasible due to the strong resistance of the Member States to give up one of the last bastions of national market intervention (cf. Pollack 1998; Nugent *et al.* 2001). In the light of the tolerant stance of the European Commission with regard to the freedom to cooperate, a harmonization towards the EU antitrust model fully complies with the free movement interests of companies and capital.

However, rather than making itself obsolete, the European Commission hopes to refocus its staff resources on cracking down cartels more vigorously on a global level (eventually it can impose fines that amount to 10 per cent of a company's annual turnover) and leave smaller cases to private trustbusters and national jurisdictions. The incentive to patrol the globe for hard-core cartels needs to be placed in the context of a range of prominent price-fixing cases in the late 1990s that marked a 'golden age' of US cartel prosecution, which resulted in highest fines ever and the imprisonment of CEOs (Litan and Shapiro 2001: 27). In the absence of a 'world competition authority', the European Commission tries to expand its powers beyond the borders of the EU and fight transnational cartels in duopoly with the US agencies. The impetus goes further than the prestige- and competence-seeking of a regulatory body that long suffered from the image of being the junior partner of the US agencies. Instead, the antitrust reform was announced to convey 'a world class regulatory system' (European Commission 2002), which forms part of expediting and fostering the broader European project of neoliberal market integration that takes places against the background of the reinvigorated discourse surrounding the Lisbon Agenda of 2000 (on the latter see the contribution by Van Apeldoorn and Horn to this book). The aim to make the EU 'the most dynamic knowledge-based and competitive economy by 2010', in other words, to economically outperform the US and the rest of the world, is according to the dominant neoliberal view best achieved by downsizing Brussels' 'regulatory jungle'. With the privatisation and decentralisation of important aspects of EU antitrust enforcement, the reform seems no longer deviant from the prevailing tenet.

Conclusions

This chapter demonstrated that the 2004 reform exposes antitrust law enforcement to market mechanisms and introduces a more microeconomic reasoning in the assessment of anticompetitive conduct. With the abolition of the administrative public control model and the concomitant decentralization of Articles 81 and 82, the primacy of enforcement has shifted to the proactivity of private parties who are expected to bring observed antitrust breaches to the national courts. Private enforcement together with the institutional anchoring of enhanced microeconomics narrows the scope of antitrust enforcement to short-term efficiency criteria and price indicators, which can be construed as a considerable step of regulatory convergence towards the Anglo-Saxon style of organizing private market conduct, and the erosion of what has commonly been termed the Rhenish model of a coordinated market economy (on the latter see also, in particular, the contribution by Nölke and Perry to this book).

The new regime produces a whole range of cross-purposes. In the absence of significant political opposition, private antitrust enforcement is likely to be further strengthened by subsequent reform steps as the 2005 Green Paper indicates. The costs of suing may be unaffordable for certain potential plaintiffs, in particular SMEs, employees, consumers, or more diffuse interests of society at large, which has as a consequence that the new regime is likely to be predisposed towards those who can afford 'sound' economic analyses and are willing to take the effort of suing. Shareholder interest groups, most notably large institutional investors or hedge funds with a strong interest in short-term payoff rather than long-term profitability, constitute one category of actors that is likely to profit from the new antitrust litigation possibilities. Although their agency cannot be derived from the actual reform in a minutely detailed way (their presence is merely confined to lobbying efforts regarding the introduction of criminal sanctions and class action litigation) and even though there is no transparent common agenda of shareholders to to identify – this chapter maintains that the EU antitrust reform opens up a window of opportunity for powerful shareholder interests to gain more corporate control. Antitrust litigation may serve as a means to alter the power constellation of the internal corporate governance structure, in particular to influence the business strategies of the management or the ouster of underperforming board members, as well as to facilitate predatory take-overs. Thereby the antitrust reform parallels in many ways the regulatory reforms of corporate governance regulation in Europe designed to strengthen the position of shareholders vis-à-vis the management, as well as other corporate stakeholders.

The political forces that dominated the reform process (the DG Competition and its wider epistemic community of private practioners from the professional services sector) are also expected to benefit from the new regime, albeit for different reasons. The heightened demand for antitrust counselling and litigation services resulting from the retrenchment of a public authority provides intermediary law companies with a lucrative business. The European Commission, in contrast, embodies a broader agenda of enhanced neoliberal market integration, which reflects the view of 'less regulation is better regulation' and market-based solutions are superior to the interventionist arm of a public authority. The involvement of private market actors as complementary controlling instances of the competitive process has been intended as an encouragement to tougher competition, which is believed to feed back on overall economic welfare and the goals defined in the Lisbon Agenda. Furthermore, those subject to antitrust control, the transnational business community, have a strong stake in legal certainty and a high degree of economic freedom, which implies uniform laws and practices in a common market. However, whereas the increased emphasis on microeconomic instruments in the assessment of anticompetitive conduct can work to their advantage, the increased private litigation activity at the expense of the secure notification procedure poses severe risks; in the worst case the advent of a claimants culture similar to that of the US, with significant consequences regarding the distribution of corporate wealth.

Notes

1 The term 'antitrust policy' is generally used among US practioners and academics, whereas in Europe the generic analogue 'competition policy' is more widespread. Here, the term 'antitrust' is used to specifically refer to the fight against cartels and restrictive business practices.
2 The requirement to notify the European Commission excluded SMEs anticipating an inter-firm agreement as their actions were considered of minor importance to trade and competition within the Internal Market.
3 Whereas the overall influence of German ordoliberal scholars in other economic regulatory policies has waned since the 1960s, it continued to have a remarkable stronghold in EU competition policy (cf. Budzinski 2003; Hölscher and Stephan 2004). Officials of German origin and trained in German competition law have traditionally held strategic positions in the DG Competition (cf. Hooghe and Nugent 2002).
4 The European Commission repeatedly emphasized that '[…] [it] takes a favourable view of aid to small and medium-sized enterprises, given their structural handicaps as

compared with large undertakings and their potential for innovation, job creation and growth' (European Commission 1996a: 34).

5   The following preconditions need to be fulfilled: 'the agreement must lead to an improvement in the production or the distribution of goods, or the promotion of technical or economic progress; it must allow consumers a fair share of the resulting benefit; restrictions should be indispensable to the attainment of these objectives; and the agreement must not afford such undertakings the possibility of eliminating competition in respect of a substantial part of the products in question'. These rather elastic notions are further clarified by lengthy guidelines issued by the Commission (see also Communication of the Commission, Guidelines on Vertical Restraints, 2000/ C291/01, JOCE n° C 291/1, 13/10/2000).

6   The high level of private enforcement in the US is also due to the fact that all cases of infringements with US antitrust law have to be prosecuted in the courts, including those initiated by US authorities. However, as this is a timely and costly procedure, more than 80 per cent of the US government cases are either abandoned, or modified through voluntary settlements prior to involving the courts (Venit and Kolasky 2000).

7   The artificial situation of perfect competition is taken as a benchmark and the premises underpinning methodological individualism extrapolated to company boards: rationally behaving managers are assumed to generate economies of scale and scope in order to achieve efficiency gains and to maximize profits. Once efficiency gains are achieved, marginal production costs are expected to decrease, and – due to the competitive environment in which rival companies offer similar products – passed on to consumers.

8   For example, Mr Muris, Chairman of the FTC since 2001 had already served under Reagan in the early 1980s where he became famous for his *laissez-faire* view according to which, not corporations, but governments were considered a threat to competition. He particularly displayed the Chicagoan attitude in the lax enforcement of the Microsoft monopolization case (Tomand and Lister 2001)

9   Elsewhere Monti concluded: '[i]t is fair to say that the far-reaching policy shift which occurred in US antitrust enforcement during the 1980s – namely, the shift towards a focus on the economic welfare of consumers – has been mirrored in the policy priorities of the European Commission during the 1990s' (Monti 2004c). The heightened emphasis on consumers is attested by the creation of a post within the European Commission's DG Competition called 'Consumer Liaison Officer' in December 2003. The task ascribed to this new institution is to ensure a permanent dialogue with European consumers and alert consumer groups to competition cases 'where their input might be useful' (European Commission 2003b).

10   Mr Justice Ferris, an English judge specialized in antitrust law expressed his concerns as follows: '[Judges] cannot make value judgments, except in a very limited field, certainly not in relation to general economic questions […]. The Court should not have any part to play […] in deciding whether an agreement or course of conduct contributes to improving the production or distribution of goods or promoting technical or economic progress […] I cannot see any court as we know it making a satisfactory job of that task' (cited in Forwood 2003: 2).

11   The divergent rulings in 2001 on the GE-Honeywell merger fuelled the controversies. According to Charles James, former Assistant General of the US DoJ, the contradictory rulings are due to a 'fundamental, doctrinal disagreement over the economic purposes and scope of antitrust enforcement' (James 2001).

12   Compare the observations made by Nölke and Perry (to this book) on the growing role of Anglo-Saxon credit-rating agencies and accounting firms in Europe.

Part III

The role of private authority in corporate governance regulation

7 Coordination service firms and the erosion of Rhenish capitalism

Andreas Nölke and James Perry

Introduction

Research on transnational private authority is coming of age. More than 10 years ago, a first round of studies placed the topic on the agenda of International Political Economy (Cutler 1992; Haufler 1993; Porter 1993; Sinclair 1994). Since then a number of major collaborative efforts have broadened the issue area and firmly established its importance (Cutler *et al.* 1999a; Higgott *et al.* 2000; Ronit and Schneider 2000; Hall and Biersteker 2002a). As well as explorative case studies, these books introduced more thorough conceptualizations of transnational private authority, namely typologies of the different forms of authority (see in particular Cutler *et al.* 1999b; Hall and Biersteker 2002b). However, given the diversity of empirical cases, it remained difficult to draw overall conclusions that could explain the evolution of transnational private authority (Cutler 2002: 40). More recently the body of literature on transnational private authority has grown rapidly, particularly that on financial sector (self) regulation and corporate social responsibility (for a review see Nölke 2006). Meanwhile, a number of in-depth studies of specific cases of private authority, such as transnational merchant law (Cutler 2003) and credit rating agencies (Sinclair 2005) have been published.

This chapter singles out the mid-range concept of coordination service firms for more detailed investigation. Coordination service firms are a specific sub-group of the wider issue of transnational private authority, thereby allowing for the development of more meaningful theoretical conclusions. At the same time, coordination service firms are a more general category than the specific case of, for example, rating agencies or merchant law, thereby allowing somewhat broader generalizations to be made. We demonstrate that a particularly important role of coordination service firms is the private regulation of corporate governance. Coordination service firms are a characteristic component of the Anglo-Saxon variety of capitalism. The growing role of coordination service firms thus introduces elements of Anglo-Saxon capitalism into the Rhenish system and, in doing so, erodes core elements of this variety of capitalism, such as the *Hausbanken* system.

Coordination service firms set and enforce the standards of behaviour for other firms. Law firms, insurance companies, management consultancies, credit-rating agencies, stock exchanges, and financial clearing houses have all been offered as examples (Cutler *et al.* 1999b: 10; Cutler 2002: 28). In contrast to other forms of cooperation among firms, such as production alliances, subcontractor relationships or cartels, coordination service firms govern across sector lines. Their relevance is not limited to their own sector alone, but rather affects the wider private economy. Coordination service firms therefore have the potential to be the most fundamental, 'infrastructural' (Sinclair 2001) form of transnational private authority.

When compared to other forms of transnational private authority, coordination service firms clearly are under-researched. Only credit-rating agencies have been explicitly analyzed as coordination service firms (Sinclair 1999), in addition to some more limited references to this function of insurance companies (Haufler 1999). Neither have the other examples of coordination service firms been analyzed from this perspective, nor is there any systematic conceptual treatment of this type of private governance. One of the reasons for this neglect appears to be the low degree of institutionalization of coordination service firms, when compared with other types of private authority. In contrast to, for example, private regimes or business associations, there is no central institution that exercises authority, but rather a number of decentralized agents. Consequently, coordination service firms represent a radical departure from conventional international organizations or regimes, the traditional form of international cooperation. This perhaps partly explains why coordination service firms are rarely considered a worthy object of research in the field of international studies.

A second reason for the neglect of coordination service firms may be related to definitional issues. Not all of the common examples of coordination service firms are clear cases of transnational private authority. Management consultancies are coordination service firms, but at the same time lack important features of private authority, such as the backing of public authority. The very broad definition of coordination service firms utilized in the literature dilutes the concept and makes it difficult to study in a systematic manner. If we use a somewhat more narrow definition of coordination service firms that limits the term to those types of firms that clearly are *in authority*, then we can identify rating agencies and accounting firms as the two most important cases.

This chapter argues that rating agencies and accounting firms can indeed have a deeply infrastructural impact on the economy. However, the impact of these firms is not all pervasive, it is bound to certain circumstances. In each case we can identify a similar set of conditions under which coordination service firms exert most influence. First, an inter-temporal comparison demonstrates that these firms are linked to a phase in the development of capitalism in which financial markets are increasingly influential. Second, an inter-regional comparison shows that not all 'varieties of capitalism' are equally affected by coordination service firms, since the latter are far more favourable to the Anglo-Saxon variety. Lastly, an inter-sector comparison between types of coordination service firms demonstrates that features of the coordination service sectors themselves (particularly the degree of concentration and the mobilization of specialized analytical resources) are also crucial determinants of their importance.

From a political perspective, the role of coordination service firms (over time, in certain regions and business sectors) raises considerable normative concerns. These concerns not only relate to the shift from public to private authority (and the corresponding issues of democratic legitimacy) but also to the substantial impact on, for example, particular categories of labour. By identifying this impact as well as the corresponding mechanisms and conditions, this chapter tries to put coordination service firms into the context of current changes in the international political economy.

Definition: coordination service firms with transnational private authority – but also without it

A popular analytical concept always runs the risk of becoming more and more diluted by frequent and imprecise use, until it finally may lose most of its content. An example of this development is the broadening of the original concept of transnational private authority by Rodney Bruce Hall and Thomas J. Biersteker. They argue that the concept should be extended beyond the realm of international political economy and 'market' authority, to also include the 'moral' authority exercised by non-governmental organizations and transnational religious movements, as well as the 'illicit' authority of mafias and mercenaries (Hall and Biersteker 2002b: 7). This suggestion not only erases the distinction between transnational private authority and transnational actors in general (Risse-Kappen 1995, 2002), but also clearly contradicts the core concept of private authority that is based on legitimacy instead of coercion: what differentiates authority from power is the legitimacy of claims of authority. That is, there are both rights claimed by some superior authority and obligations recognized as legitimate on the part of subordinates or subjects to that authority (Hall and Biersteker 2002b: 4).

It is difficult to see how the exercise of brute force by organized crime or private mercenaries incorporates this legitimacy (Graz 2005: 6).

It makes good sense to reserve the use of the concept of transnational private authority (in contrast to private power or private influence) to the more narrow definition as originally defined by Clair Cutler, Virginia Haufler and Tony Porter. According to these authors, transnational private authority may be empirically identified based on three criteria:

> First, those subject to the rules and decisions being made by private sector actors must accept them as legitimate, as the representations of experts and those 'in authority'. Second, there should exist a high degree of compliance with the rules and decisions. Third, the private sector must be empowered either explicitly or *implicitly* by governments with the right to make decisions for others.
>
> (Cutler *et al.* 1999b: 19 emphasis in original).

Besides highlighting the importance of consent (instead of coercion) for the exercise of transnational private authority, this definition emphasizes the importance of compliance with private rules. Given the voluntary character of private (in contrast to many cases of public) authority, this is a crucial distinction from the mere proclamation of rules by private actors. Finally, the empowerment by governments is included because transnational private authority does not exist independently of the state, or even against it. Instead, private authority should be understood having a mutually constitutive relation to state authority.

If we apply these three criteria to the broad category of coordination service firms it becomes clear that not all of them can be said to exercise transnational private authority. For example, management consultancies coordinate the behaviour of business in other sectors, based on their representation as experts. But the degree of compliance with their decisions is far from assured, and their empowerment by governments is largely absent. A similar assessment could be made for law firms, although one could argue that the reliance on a culture of litigation as an instrument of competition policy is a form of empowerment of private (law) firms (Wigger 2004; and in this book). Other types of coordination service firms such as banks or institutional investors clearly coordinate the behaviour of other companies across sector lines, but do so mainly based on their economic power (Nölke 2004b: 164–6), and much less on the consent they mobilize as experts and by empowerment through public authorities. Stock exchanges do fulfill the latter criteria, but have a rather limited impact. And the transnational private authority exercised by insurance companies is mainly focused on risk-regulation within their own sector (Haufler 1999: 203); their authority over other industries, particularly on environmental issues, is more limited.

However, two types of coordination service firms clearly can be identified as carriers of substantial transnational private authority, namely accounting firms and credit rating agencies. Both types govern the behaviour of actors in other sectors. In both cases consent is clearly based on the expert authority of the coordinating firms. Consequently there is a high degree of compliance, but also in recent years both rating agencies and accounting firms have been explicitly empowered in their authority by governments: Rating agencies are empowered by the new guidelines for capital adequacy (Basle II) and accounting firms by the adoption of IFRS throughout the EU. Given these properties, accounting and rating agencies are the most promising candidates for a more detailed study of the workings of coordination service firms as a case of transnational private authority.

Theoretical framework: combining critical and institutionalist perspectives

Although the literature on transnational private authority is burgeoning, theoretical development has been somewhat muted. One reason for this may be the fragmentation of the discussion between critical political economists on the one side and more institutionalist global governance scholars on the other.[1] While the critical discussion focuses on cases of private self-regulation in what may be termed 'business infrastructure' – such as law, finance and technical standards (Cutler 2003; Graz 2002; Sinclair 2005), the governance branch is primarily occupied with the activities of NGOs and business to promote corporate social responsibility (Haufler 2002; Kollman 2003; Pattberg 2004; Rieth 2004; Wolf 2002). And while the critical discourse is strong on historical context and on explanations based on power relations, it is rather weak in coming up with some kind of empirically testable theory of transnational private authority, or with concrete proposals how to use this authority for a transformative agenda. The governance discourse, on the other hand, has a clear advantage in the concrete analysis of institutional mechanisms and the identification of practical proposals, but fails to provide a comprehensive explanatory and normative concept, instead offering a rather descriptive and mostly inductive picture. In order to overcome this state of affairs, theories on transnational private authority have to combine both discourses, in particular the more historical arguments about structural forces and power relations of critical political economy with the wealth of institutional details and pragmatic issues that is provided by the governance perspective (Nölke *et al.* 2003: 6–7).

The VoC concept can in some ways be considered as a mediator between the two broad debates sketched above. While placing capitalist systems in their specific historical context, the VoC concept at the same time provides a rather detailed model to analyze the institutional interdependencies of contemporary capitalism. By locating the role of coordination service firms within the different varieties of capitalism it is possible to assess the significance of this very specific type of economic regulation.

Institutionalist perspectives: the governance debate

The point of departure for the governance debate is the perception that some problems of transnational economic regulation cannot be solved by governments (alone). Particularly the cooperation between companies and civil society actors in the context of concepts such as 'corporate social responsibility', 'business ethics' and 'corporate citizenship' has attracted great attention. From the perspective of the governance approach, these forms of private voluntary cooperation might be able to compensate for the inability (or unwillingness) of governments and international organizations to cater for global business regulation. The governance approach suggests that transnational NGOs should replace national civil societies and governments as a counter-weight against irresponsible business behaviour, whereby so-called 'externalities' such as environmental degradation and the mistreatment of workers can be limited by standards developed and overseen by private institutions. Given the voluntary character of these institutions, the core task then becomes one of identifying the conditions under which private actors obey norms that are not set by states. The governance discussion has already tentatively identified a number of these conditions. Some are specific to the issue of corporate social responsibility, such as the vulnerability of big manufacturing companies with well-known brand names that can easily be punished by customers (Haufler 2002: 11), or the fact that improving social and labour practices can be very costly, whereas improving environmental performance may be less expensive

– and even profitable in the long run through eco-efficiency gains (Kollman 2003: 34–5). However, other factors are less specific and can be applied to the case of coordination service firms. One such factor is the network of resource dependency that forms the backbone of inter-firm cooperation.

Private actors only conform to standards set by other private actors if they can get access to crucial resources through this cooperation (Nölke 2004b: 163). Given the consensual nature of transnational private authority and the fact that this authority (by definition) has to be based on the legitimacy of coordination service firms, we can surmise that substantial analytical resources (information, expertise, etc.) are crucial for the working of coordination service firms. Another important factor that determines compliance with private standards is the degree of concentration within a particular coordination service sector. Private norms are difficult to enforce under conditions of strong competition between firms (Haufler 2002: 10), whereas the dominance of a single company or an oligopoly of coordination service firms makes enforcement much easier.

Critical perspectives: the political economy debate

Critical political economy places these observations in the more general framework of the development of capitalism, and the structural forces and power relations involved in this development. The recent rise of private authority here is based on the parallel development of the competition state, the deterritorialization of capital and the related process of flexible accumulation (Cutler 2003: 28–32). Furthermore, it is connected with the rise of neoliberalism as a political ideology in which the private sector is assumed to be inherently more efficient than the public sector and measures such as privatization and deregulation free private business from unnecessary state controls, leaving a rationalized core of controls which are supposed to be more efficient and responsive to a fast-changing business environment. The evolution of transnational private norms thus can be perceived as an attempt to permanently weaken the role of public international regulation of business, as has been shown to have occurred with other forms of contemporary global governance (Overbeek 2004b). Having corporate codes of conduct in place legitimizes the retreat of the state, or at least its unwillingness to tackle certain issues by intergovernmental regulation. As such, the existence of these codes could be used as a shield against popular calls for business re-regulation if widespread discontent with economic globalization were to occur. Phrased another way, the form and the content of regulation should not be treated separately from each other. Thus, we should not analyze the mechanisms and forms of private governance without taking into account the role that this type of regulation plays in the development of global capitalism. In this context, coordination service firms have the essential function of aiding the deterritorialization of capital by providing basic analytical services for the mobile trans-border investors that stand central to the current evolution of capitalism (Van Apeldoorn and Horn 2005: 7; see also the contributions by Van Apeldoorn and Horn as well as Rebérioux to this book). By exercizing transnational private authority, coordination service firms spread the basic preconditions for the operation of financialised capitalism. In particular the ongoing process of disintermediation of finance (away from traditional banking and towards corporate finance via bonds or shares) requires considerable investments in business intelligence in order to avoid information asymmetries.

The 'variety of capitalism' contribution

However, capitalism is not a homogeneous whole, but rather exhibits national and regional variations in its operations. One of the clearest ways of conceptualizing these variations is to distinguish between the Rhenish and the Anglo-Saxon 'variety of capitalism' (Albert 1991; Hall and Soskice 2001; see also the contribution by Gourevitch to this book). The role of coordination service firms in each emphasizes the most important differences between these varieties of capitalism. Owing to the different intensities of financial disintermediation, the activities of coordination service firms fit more easily with the Anglo-Saxon than with the Rhenish one.[2] Core features of the Rhenish model traditionally are the fairly balanced and consensual relationship between labour and capital and the availability of patient capital being provided by major banks ('Hausbanken') and, to a more limited extent, internally generated funds. Management has to meet an arrangement with well-organized representatives of both labour and capital that often participate directly in the decision making process. Decision making may therefore take a long time but the implementation of the resulting consensus is relatively smooth. Moreover, the Rhenish model of corporate finance leads to a comparatively long-term perspective with regard to the economic well-being of firms. 'Hausbanken' are less interested in short-term price movements on the stock markets than in the long-term solvency of their loans. The same long-term perspective applies to other sources of investment capital such as investors who hold large blocks of shares in a company, so-called 'blockholders'. At the same time, stable ownership structures provide firms with considerable protection against take-over. All of these factors also support the long-term investment in human resource development that is crucial for the Rhenish specialization in high skill and high quality products. However, these advantages may now be eroded by a weakening of the Hausbanken model and the increased influence of transnational financial markets. Coordination service firms are empowered by the latter process and, at the same time, contribute to financial disintermediation in the Rhenish model, thereby deepening and institutionalizing this erosion (Nölke 2004b).

Towards a synthesis

If the three strands of reasoning outlined above are combined, an empirical study of the exercise of transnational private authority by coordination service firms emerges. There are four factors; the first two focus on the actors, the second two focus on the structural context in which these actors find themselves:

- the type and volume of the analytical resources of the coordination service firms;
- the degree of concentration within the coordination service sector;
- the relationship with different types of capitalism;
- the role within recent developments of capitalism as a whole – in particular towards financial disintermediation.

The basic assumption is that the role of coordination service firms is not all-pervasive, but rather is limited to firms that (a) control a large proportion of the necessary analytical resources, that (b) stem from an sector with a high degree of concentration, and that (c) benefit from financial disintermediation. A fourth factor, usually taken as granted by all studies of transnational private authority, is (d) the at least implicit support of this authority by public actors (see section two above). Within these parameters, coordination service firms are seen to have a deeply infrastructural impact on the workings of contemporary capitalism, and in particular an eroding impact on the Rhenish variety.

In order to give some empirical backing for these theoretical claims, we will now explore the two most important types of coordination service firms that are able to exercise transnational private authority: rating agencies and accounting firms. In contrast to the rather comprehensive studies on rating agencies by Timothy Sinclair (1994, 1995, 1999, 2001, 2003, 2005; King and Sinclair 2001), the transnational private authority of accounting firms has only recently become a major subject of study (Botzem and Quack 2005; Dewing and Russell 2004; and in this book; Eaton 2005; Martinez-Diaz 2005; Perry and Nölke 2005, 2006; Porter 2005).

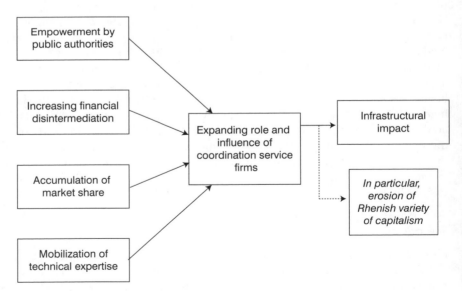

Figure 7.1 A theoretical model for the analysis of coordination service firms

By systematically comparing coordination service firms in rating and accounting, we attempt to compensate for a major shortcoming of the existing literature on coordination service firms, namely its strongly inductive character which bases most theoretical development on the case of rating agencies only. Still, given the early stage of research on accounting authority, the study will be limited to '... the examination of a number of cases with the goal of showing that a particular model or sets of concepts usefully illuminates these cases. No real test of the theory occurs, but rather the goal is the *parallel demonstration of theory*' (Collier 1993: 108, emphasis in original). Additional research will be necessary, in particular to test the arguments developed above against other cases of coordination service firms that fail to produce a similar amount of transnational private authority. Thus, in future, one might want to study whether the failure of management, law or insurance companies in this respect could be attributed to the more limited degree of concentration within their respective sectors and/or to their association with financial disintermediation.

Rating agencies: framework conditions and impact

Empowerment by financial disintermediation

The authority of rating agencies is a product, and a core element, of an ongoing process of the disintermediation of finance that diminishes the role of commercial banks in the provision of capital (cf. King and Sinclair 2001: 5–8). Banks traditionally function as financial intermediaries in that they bring together the users and suppliers of financial resources. Alternatively, suppliers and users can also come to an agreement without the intermediation of banks (that is, via capital markets), thereby avoiding the overhead costs involved. However, this process of disintermediation creates an information problem for investors, since they have to carry the risk of default repayments themselves. This is when rating agencies come in, because they take over the task of collecting dispersed information on the financial situation of borrowers and condensing it into a single measure.

Resource base

Rating agencies derive their authority from their analytical resources and the legitimacy that is derived from the expert character of these analytical resources as perceived by market participants. The demand for the analytical output of rating agencies stems from the overwhelming quantity of information available to market actors. Rating agencies condense this information into a standardised metric (a 'rating'), which is then used as a benchmark for other market actors. Although the latter may choose not to follow the recommendations implied by these ratings, they nevertheless set standards by which other actors operate (King and Sinclair 2001: 4ff.). However, analytical resources are somewhat less stable than financial resources, since they may be severely affected by perceived rating miscalls. Thus the reputation as global experts for debt quality, developed by rating agencies over decades, can be rapidly undermined, as demonstrated by the Mexican and Asian financial crises of the 1990s (King and Sinclair 2001: 10). Resource dependencies exist both between rating agencies and investors, and between rating agencies and the companies whose debts are rated. While investors depend on the analytical resources of rating agencies for their investment decisions, the rated companies depend on the legitimacy of these agencies for their access to capital.

Concentration within the sector

Rating agencies are assisted in their exercise of transnational private authority by a high degree of concentration within this business sector. Although there has been intensified competition and an increasing number of players in the credit rating sector since the 1990s, two major agencies (Moody's Investor Service (Moody's) and Standard & Poor's (S&P)) continue to dominate the market. Other agencies occupy niche markets, such as Fitch Ratings for municipal and financial institutions. The dominant role of Moody's and S&P is not limited to the US, and it is their transnational authority over European and Asian market actors that has caused the most controversy (King and Sinclair 2001: 12). This controversy has been intensified by the Basle II capital adequacy proposals which mandate specific risk metrics which are to be provided by the leading rating agencies (cf. King and Sinclair 2001: 17–25). The justification for these proposals is that banking insolvencies have frequently been shown not to be limited to a bank's country of origin, but rather to have spilled-over to impact the financial systems of other countries. Still, given the level of competition in the banking sector and the mercantilist behaviour of many governments, banks have long had a strong incentive to take greater risks than might be considered optimal. While the first Capital Adequacy Accord in 1988 (Basle I) addressed some of these issues, a second accord (Basle II) currently is in its final round of ratification. Rating agencies play a core role in Basle II, because less sophisticated banks are obliged to calculate the amount of capital to be held against the risk of credit default based on external ratings. Private authority here becomes enmeshed in a public–private system of multi-level governance.

Structural impact

Credit rating agencies exercise their authority in two ways (cf. King and Sinclair 2001: 4): First and foremost, they shape the behaviour of market participants by limiting their thinking to a range of legitimate possibilities. Second, they can occasionally exercise an explicit veto over certain options, by using a ratings downgrade. Rating agencies have received most attention for their evaluation of public institutions, because this assessment forms one of the most obvious cases where transnational private authority has a direct impact on public actors (cf. Hillebrand 2001; Sinclair 2003: 151–5), although the principal task of rating agencies is to assess the 'quality' of other companies' debts. It is here that rating agencies exercise their authority over other private actors, since most companies cannot afford a low ranking and will therefore consider changing their behaviour to suit the preferences of a rating agency. The authority of rating agencies over the basic organization of capitalist economies should therefore not be underestimated. Even if a company that is issuing a bond does not agree with a particular assessment, it has to take account of other market actors who will be acting upon that particular rating (King and Sinclair 2001: 11). Given the public character of rating up/downgrades, the impact of these agencies is far more infrastructural than the confidential assessment of banks in a system of intermediated finance *à la* Rhenish capitalism. Correspondingly, rating agencies can be considered a core element of a new form of 'financialized capitalism' in which the owners of liquid capital and their investment analysts occupy an increasingly powerful position (Sinclair 1999: 158).

Erosion of Rhenish capitalism

Insofar as the epistemic authority of rating agencies favours the US system of disintermediated finance, it is not politically neutral, but rather actively favours a specific socio-economic model which is very much in line with the short-term investment horizon of the Anglo-Saxon approach (Sinclair 1994: 149). Third-party enforcement of credit rating has a long history in the US and some other Western countries (cf. Kerwer 2001; King and Sinclair 2001: 14–17), but has now gone global. These most recent developments have not only been criticized due to the practical problems involved, but also because they may further undermine the Rhenish model, in this case especially the financing structure of many '*Mittelstand*' companies, one of the backbones of Rhenish capitalism. Currently, German small and medium sized business feel this threat very strongly because of the limited availability of internally generated funds and their strong reliance on long-term loan financing for investment. Basle II and the increasing role of rating agencies will make this financing model even more difficult since highly indebted companies will face a steep increase in credit costs due to their 'problematic' risk profile under Basle II. In effect, many of these companies are being forced to mobilize funding by going public or selling themselves to private equity funds, referred to by critics in especially continental Europe as 'locusts'.[3] This may, in turn, lead to the familiar 'pressures of 'short-termism' that plague American and British companies – pressure from shareholders to maximize dividends by concentrating on quarterly results and short-range return on investment variables' (Sally 1995: 69), and to a more conflictive relationship with the representatives of labour. An increasing role of rating agencies, therefore, may threaten the very basis of the Rhenish capitalist model, because its elements are highly interdependent and may not be easily transferred and exchanged.[4]

Accounting firms: framework conditions and impact

Empowerment by financial disintermediation

As coordination service firms, the accountants occupy an especially privileged position since they alone have the authority and legitimacy to validate the accounting information provided by corporations in their financial statements. Without such validation (auditing), the corporations cannot fulfil their statutory obligation to publish annual financial statements. Accounting information is an essential anchor around which production and distribution are organised in a market-based economy. The measures of profit, wealth and value provided in companies' annual financial statements are the primary means by which society is able to compare the efficiency of different production techniques. This is true in both the public and private sector. In the former, national government statistics on economic growth, and also on the contribution of various industrial sectors to that growth, draw substantially on accounting numbers produced at the firm-level. Such statistics inform policy decisions not only in corporate governance, but also in other arenas such as fiscal and trade policy. In the private sector investors allocate financial resources on the basis of accounting information that they receive both directly and via intermediaries who process and analyse the data for specific purposes. Among these intermediaries are not only the specialized financial news media, but also the rating agencies discussed in the previous section that rely on financial statements for comparable data describing the performance and solvency of the companies whose creditworthiness they are assessing.

The authority of accounting companies as coordination service firms is strengthened by the widespread adoption of international accounting standards, as developed by the private IASB. Traditionally, accounting standards were developed on the national level, under the supervision of national governments. However, international economic integration and the disintermediation of finance have led to increasing demands for the harmonization of national standards. The assessment of the quality of stocks traded on international capital markets relies on accounting: international financial investors not only need transparent company accounts in order to make their resource allocations on a sound basis, but also the standardization of such information in order to compare their investment options in different countries without major difficulties. In the absence of international harmonization of accounting standards, financial investors have shown a clear preference for the shares of firms audited by the global accounting firms, that is, the Big Four (Strange 1996: 137). In the system of bank-intermediated finance, prevalent under Rhenish capitalism, internationally harmonized accounting standards were less important, partially because of the domestic focus of many banks, but also because banks frequently had alternative ways of assessing the financial situation of their major clients, due to their insider status, for example as blockholders.

Resource base

Internationally harmonized accounting standards are also important for the legitimacy resource base of the whole profession, because it increasingly becomes obvious that different national standards lead to dramatically different results for the same company (Sundgren 1997: 15), thereby threatening to call into question the reliability of accounting data, and with it the authority of the profession. Following failed intergovernmental efforts to harmonize EU accounting standards, and in the face of several large EU-based corporations applying US accounting standards in order to list on US-based stock exchanges during the 1990s, the European Commission decided to adopt IASB standards for all exchange-listed corporations in the EU from 2005, taking the total coverage to 92 countries (Tweedie and Seidenstein 2005). The US has not adopted IASB standards, instead retaining those set by the Financial Accounting Standards Board (FASB). However, the IASB and FASB have been engaged in a long-term convergence project since 2002 (the 'Norwalk Agreement') and the two organizations are now developing many standards jointly by default.

The ongoing process of international accounting harmonization can be seen to have strengthened the position of the Big Four accounting firms in several respects. First it has reduced the threat that divergent national standards, and the corresponding differences in company earnings, pose to the authority of their main product – audited financial statements. Second, harmonization also gives the Big Four even greater scale advantages in capturing national markets that were hitherto regulated by local standards. Unsurprisingly therefore the Big Four are the major source of funding for the International Accounting Standards Committee Foundation, a non-profit Delaware corporation which is the parent body of the IASB, and which funds and directs the work schedule of the standard setter. The Big Four accounting firms also occupy key positions on the IASB's committees and working groups, as do many financial-sector actors, which may go some way to explaining the content as well as the form of regulation (Perry and Nölke 2005).

Concentration within the sector

The development of powerful transnational private authority in the form of accounting firms was already highlighted by Susan Strange in her seminal study on the 'Retreat of the State' (1996, chapter 10). Strange focused on the extreme concentration of the market for accounting services, where the biggest six firms (referred to as the 'Big Six') had market shares of more than 95 per cent in the most important national markets, thereby giving them considerable structural power. In the meantime, concentration within the sector has progressed even further, with the Big Six becoming the Big Four (PriceWaterhouseCoopers, KPMG, Deloitte & Touche, and Ernst & Young). A study by the US General Accounting Office (2003, cited by Porter 2005: 6) revealed that these four firms audit over 78 per cent of US public companies, virtually 100 per cent of major listed companies in the UK, over 80 per cent in Japan and 90 per cent in the Netherlands. This heavy concentration within the accounting industry is, *inter alia*, being supported by the ongoing process for the development of international accounting standards, as highlighted above. At the same time, the powerful role of the Big Four together with the current harmonization of international accounting standards intensify the structural impact of this type of coordination service firms.

Structural impact

Central to the IASB's new standards is the move from historic cost to fair value accounting. Historic cost accounting values assets at the cost of acquisition whereas fair value accounting uses current market prices – if no such market exists, a model is used to arrive at a simulated market price. The move from historic cost to fair value reduces the discretion of management in valuing assets, especially for assets with active markets. It also compresses the future into the present in a manner that is both volatile and which changes the reference point for understanding both the value, and the workings, of a company.

An asset is valued by buyers and sellers based on the present value of the future expected profits which will arise from owning it. With historic-cost accounting, this process impacts the asset's accounting value only once, when it is acquired. The result is that the asset is thereafter seen more for its productive capacity, and less for its acquisition/disposal value. Under fair value-accounting the re-evaluation of an asset's worth is an almost continuous process. As such, the current use of the asset has to be regularly justified in terms of its current market value. Fair value accounting therefore gives external forces (that is, influential financial market actors) more leverage with which to set the parameters for economic decision making within the firm, a practice which is in line with the relationship between finance and production in the Anglo-Saxon variety of capitalism.

Erosion of Rhenish capitalism

Accounting standards are an integral foundation of a particular variety of capitalism. Thus, the rather conservative, creditor-oriented accounting standards in Germany (the Handelsgesetzbuch (HGB)) complement the strong role of the German banks during the development of the Rhenish variety of capitalism in which the HGB was designed. For example, the German accounting standards which enabled the building of substantial 'hidden' reserves by German companies should be seen as an expression of the priority German banks gave to ensuring the safety of their long-term lending to enterprises. In contrast, IASB financial statements now employ so-called fair value accounting (the IASB's preferred measurement technique for new accounting standards), giving shareholders the wherewithal to demand that every corporate asset is put to its most profitable use, as judged by market benchmarks (Barlev and Haddad 2003). In defining what constitutes a profitable use, shareholders are likely to adopt a much shorter-term perspective than managers so IASB standards can be expected to make conservative (Rhenish) financial planning rather more difficult, and thereby serve to discourage the longer-term business strategies which depend upon it.

It should be stressed however that accounting standards are not the root cause of such changes and pressures – rather they are a complimentary factor alongside others such as the deregulation of the financial sector, and the corresponding rise of shareholder value from a management consultant's tool to a corporate governance paradigm. Nevertheless, IASB accounting standards are playing a key role in institutionalizing changes in the structure of capitalism. As in the case of credit rating, regulation based on the Anglo-Saxon variety of capitalism is contributing to an erosion of the Rhenish variety. It is probably the realization of this fact which recently led to the foundation by major German companies of a German committee for accounting standards (Deutsches Rechnungslegungs Standards Committee (DRSC)), with the specific purpose of wielding greater influence in the IASB's policy network. So far the DRSC has not been very successful, as evidenced by its comprehensive reorganization after only a short period of operation.

Conclusion

The infrastructural importance of coordination service firms lies in their effects on the balance of power within the political economy of modern capitalism. They contribute to a 'commodification' or 'marketization' of business functions (Van Apeldoorn and Horn forthcoming). In contrast to the functioning of the firm as a more autonomous entity, coordination service firms place sub-firm assets under greater scrutiny of the financial markets. Whereas managers previously retained a certain ability to mould their companies' financial statements for long-term strategic purposes, the shift to IFRS gives external analysts a closer insight into the composition of these statements (Perry and Nölke 2006). Similarly, the external rating of company bonds is far more transparent to most capital market actors than the cosy relationship between management and '*Hausbanken*' in the old system of intermediated finance. These changes thus strengthen the negotiating position of mobile investors (and the accounting and rating specialists who, in effect, supply these investors with much of their information) to the disadvantage of management and employees. Correspondingly, the exercise of transnational private authority through coordination service firms not only constitutes a shift in the mode of governance (from public to private authority) but also alters its content.

Although this process has already gone a long way, it is important to remember that there is nothing inevitable about it. The process of financial disintermediation was initiated (or at the very least supported) by governments. Governments also tolerate the high concentration of market shares in the coordination service firm sector. And governments have given coordination service firms important regulatory functions, such as via the Basle II accord and by adopting IFRS. Somewhat ironically, in both cases the EU and its Member States were core drivers of a process that mainly benefited US-based coordination service firms and the

Anglo-Saxon variety of capitalism in general (see also Dewing and Russell 2004; and in this book). Activities that are intended to enhance the competitiveness of European economies may in the end undermine the very basis of the competitive advantage of European-style capitalism. Furthermore, those most fundamentally affected by these regulations still have not even begun to address their implications. Labour unions in particular should pay much more attention to the activities of coordination service firms. Unfortunately, the allocation of regulatory tasks to transnational private authority has in many respects made this task more difficult since, by shifting regulation from public deliberation in national parliaments to transnational private expert bodies, the supervision of the economy has been further isolated from broad public scrutiny. Likewise, the implications of the rise of coordination service firms for the organization of capitalism have so far gone mostly unnoticed and not become the object of societal contestation.

Notes

1   This section of the article draws on an argument that has first been published in Nölke (2006).
2   Since the exact character of the variety that is evolving in the emerging markets of the East and South still is unclear (see Vliegenthart 2005 as well as the contributions by Overbeek/Vliegenthart and Andreff in this volume), it will be neglected here.
3   The notion of locusts ('Heuschrecken') has most prominently been introduced in 2004 by the then chair of the German social democratic party, Franz Müntefering, within German domestic politics.
4   More trouble for the Rhenish model has recently surfaced in the context of the International Accounting Standards Board's IAS32. By reclassifying the internal capital (Eigenkapital) as borrowed capital, many small- and medium-scale enterprises become heavily indebted (in accounting terms). Together with Basle II, this could strongly increase their credit risk premium (see *Frankfurter Allgemeine Zeitung*, 28 November 2005, p. 20).

8 The role of private actors in global governance and regulation

US, European and international convergence of accounting and auditing standards in a post-Enron world

Ian Dewing and Peter Russell

Introduction

Discussions of international economic and financial governance have generally focussed on the role of international institutions set up by governments, such as the International Monetary Fund (IMF), the World Bank and the Bank for International Settlements (BIS). However, the collapse of Enron and other financial scandals in the US, the demise of the global accountancy firm Andersens, and, more recently, major financial scandals involving European companies such as Ahold, Allied Irish Banks and Parmalat, have focussed attention on national, EU and international frameworks for setting, monitoring, and enforcing compliance with accounting and auditing standards. A key factor in stimulating current debates at national, EU and international level has been the controversial US Sarbanes-Oxley Act 2002. The Act was designed to improve US accounting, auditing and corporate governance practices post-Enron. However, the Act has had a considerable impact on other jurisdictions (see Dewing and Russell 2004).

International accounting and auditing standards are an essential, though often overlooked, aspect of the international financial architecture. Post-Enron hitherto obscure private actors,[1] with links to the accountancy profession and concerned with technical accountancy practices, have been subject to an unprecedented degree of attention and scrutiny, not least by academics and policy-makers. Key accounting and auditing standard bodies at the international level are the IASB, which assumed its present role from 1 April 2001, and the International Auditing and Assurance Standards Board (IAASB), which assumed its present role from 1 April 2002.[2] The IAASB functions as independent standard-setting body under the auspices of the International Federation of Accountants (IFAC). The IASB sets IFRS and the IAASB sets International Standards on Auditing (ISAs). At the EU level, after long and complex debates, all EU listed companies are required to prepare consolidated financial statements in accordance with IFRS from 2005 (European Parliament and Council 2002), and the European Commission has issued a proposal that all statutory audits in the EU should be undertaken in accordance with ISAs (European Commission 2004d).

The *de facto* alternative to international accounting and auditing standards are the equivalent US standards. A major reason for this is because non-US companies seeking a stock exchange listing in the US are required to comply with US listing requirements, which includes providing consolidated financial statements prepared and audited according to US accounting and auditing standards. The powerful US Securities and Exchange Commission (SEC) is the federal agency that regulates US capital markets. US accounting standards are set by a private body, the FASB, and are known as Financial Accounting Standards. The collection of recognized accounting standards and practices are often referred to as US Generally Accepted Accounting Principles (US GAAP). US auditing standards are set by the Public Company Accounting Oversight Board (PCAOB), a private body created by the Sarbanes-Oxley Act, and are known simply as Auditing Standards. The FASB and the PCAOB are recognised by the SEC as the relevant standard-setting bodies. The US has consistently chosen not to recognize international accounting and auditing standards as equivalent to its own. However, with the EU's move to endorse international standards and the weaknesses of US standards exposed by Enron and other financial scandals, one of the key issues is the extent to which US and international procedures for setting, monitoring, and enforcing compliance with accounting and auditing standards will converge post-Enron. An important related question is the nature of any convergence.

The objective of this chapter is to explore the extent to which US and international accounting and auditing standards will converge post-Enron, and the nature of any convergence, and the role of key private and other actors in the process. The chapter is structured as follows: the first section outlines recent efforts to increase accounting harmonization, both at EU level and internationally, including the implications of the post-Enron, Sarbanes-Oxley Act; the second section investigates the nature of two key private actors, the IASB and IAASB, in international accounting and auditing standard-setting; the third section discusses the nature of convergence between US and international accounting standards; the fourth section is a wider discussion of the role of key private and other actors in the global governance and regulation of accounting and auditing. The final section is a conclusion.

Towards convergence

Accounting harmonization pre-Enron

The importance of high quality financial reporting and rigorous auditing to good corporate governance has been recognized for more than a decade. For instance, in the UK the Cadbury Committee on corporate governance was set up in response to concerns about 'the perceived low level of confidence both in financial reporting and in the ability of auditors to provide the safeguards which the users of company reports sought and expected' (Cadbury Report 1992: para. 2.5). Indeed, the Cadbury Committee viewed the annual audit as one of the 'cornerstones' of corporate governance, a position echoed by the European Commission with the audit identified as 'an essential element' of the system (European Commision 1996b: para. 4.18). In the 1990s one response to the low level of confidence in financial reporting and auditing was that concerted efforts, both at EU level and internationally, were made to pursue a policy of accounting harmonization based on IFRS and, latterly, auditing harmonization based on ISAs. Accounting harmonization pre-Enron is considered further below.

In 1995, the IASB and the International Association of Securities Supervisors (IOSCO) agreed to work on a 'Core Standards' programme whereby financial statements prepared in accordance with IFRS could be used in cross-border stock market offerings and listings as an alternative to national standards. At the same time the European Commission also proposed a new strategy for EU accounting harmonization based on international accounting standards developed by the IASB (European Commission 1995b). Considerable progress was made and in 2000 the Presidents' Committee of IOSCO recommended that IOSCO members permit multinational issuers to use the 30 'IASB 2000' standards to prepare financial statements for cross-border offerings and listings (International Organization of Securities Commissions 2000). In 2002 the EU adopted a regulation requiring EU listed companies to prepare their consolidated financial statements in accordance with IFRS from 2005 onwards (European Parliament and European Commission 2002). Including the EU member states, by 2005 almost 100 countries in six continents are using IFRS, or aligning their national standards with IFRS.

The US is the most important country that does not yet recognize IFRS. During the work on the IASB/IOSCO core standards programme the FASB published the results of an IASB-US comparison project and the SEC, building on the FASB's work, issued a concept release on international standards for comment (Financial Accounting Standards Board 1999; Securities and Exchange Commission 2000 respectively). Although this release signalled concerns *inter alia* about accounting standards, post-Enron there has been a concerted effort on the part of the FASB and the IASB, supported by other national standard-setters, such as the UK Accounting Standards Board, and encouraged at intergovernmental level by, for example, the EU and IOSCO, to seek convergence between US and international accounting standards.

Post-Enron developments

The Sarbanes-Oxley Act 2002 was designed to remedy deficiencies in accounting, auditing and corporate governance that were revealed by Enron and other financial scandals. The Act has had a major influence on practices in the US, and directly and indirectly on practices in other jurisdictions. Faith in US accounting standards hitherto regarded as the 'best in the world' was shaken. In October 2002, not long after the passage of the Sarbanes-Oxley Act, the IASB and the

FASB announced a memorandum of understanding (the 'Norwalk Agreement') whereby: 'each acknowledges their commitment to the development of high quality, compatible accounting standards that could be used for both domestic and cross-border financial reporting' and that each would use 'their best efforts to (a) make their existing financial reporting standards fully compatible as soon is practicable and (b) to coordinate their future work programs to ensure that once achieved, compatibility is maintained' (Financial Accounting Standards Board/ International Accounting Standards Board 2002). This initiative was strongly encouraged and supported by the European Commission, and Commissioner Frits Bolkestein enthusiastically welcomed the announcement stating it was: 'a very positive move towards a single worldwide set of high quality, best of breed, principles-based financial reporting standards, which would dramatically improve the efficiency of global capital markets...' (European Commission 2002a).

The IASB proceeded with two main developments: first, to complete the '2005 standards', so that by the end of March 2004 the IASB would have a broad set of high quality standards in place that could be adopted for use by the EU from 2005; and, second, to work on the eventual convergence of US and international financial reporting standards. As regards the former, the IASB's aim was to produce a 'stable platform' whereby only those standards issued prior to March 2004 would apply in 2005. Any standards issued after that date would not be applicable until 2006. Thus, there would be 'period of calm' for about 21 months such that there would be no changes to standards during the period of changeover from national to international standards in the EU. As regards the latter, the IASB and FASB have set up a joint 'short-term convergence' project to examine differences between US and international standards that may be capable of resolution within a relatively short time. If convergence in the short term proves to be too difficult, consideration of the topic is deferred to a discrete project.

The next section considers the processes for setting international accounting and auditing standards and discusses issues that have emerged from attempts to seek convergence between US and international standards.

International standard-setting

International Accounting Standards Board (IASB)

The International Accounting Standards Committee Foundation (IASC Foundation) is the oversight body for the IASB. The objectives of the IASC Foundation are stated in its constitution as:

   (a)   to develop, in the public interest, a single set of high quality, understandable and enforceable global accounting standards that require high quality, transparent and comparable information in financial statements and other financial reporting to help participants in the world's capital markets and other users make economic decisions;

   (b)   to promote the use and rigorous application of those standards;

(c) in fulfilling the objectives associated with (a) and (b), to take account of, as appropriate, the special needs of small and medium-sized entities and emerging economies; and

(d) to bring about convergence of national accounting standards and International Accounting Standards and International Financial Reporting Standards to high quality solutions.

(International Accounting Standards Committee Foundation 2005a, para. 2)

The constitution of the IASC Foundation provides that the trustees shall appoint 14 members of the IASB and shall: 'select members of the IASB so that it will comprise a group of people representing, within that group, the best available combination of technical expertise and diversity of international business and market experience in order to contribute to the development of high quality, global accounting standards' (International Association for Statistical Computing Foundation 2005a: para. 19).

The IASB has a due process for developing and approving IFRS. The structure of the IASB is 'designed to support those features that are regarded as desirable in establishing the legitimacy of a standard-setting organisation, its members are technically expert, represent the wider community and are independent'.[3] An IFRS requires the approval of nine of the 14 IASB members (International Accounting Standards Committee Foundation 2005a: para. 30) voting on a 'one member, one vote' basis. The IASC Foundation and the IASB are advised by a Standards Advisory Council which consists of about 40 members, each appointed for a period of three years, and provides a forum for organisations and individuals with an interest in financial reporting.[4]

International Auditing and Assurance Standards Board (IAASB)

Before considering the IAASB, it is necessary briefly to consider its parent body, IFAC. IFAC is the worldwide organisation for the accountancy profession. It is made up of over 160 member organizations in 120 countries.[5] IFAC's mission is:

To serve the public interest, strengthen the worldwide accountancy profession, and contribute to the development of strong international economies by establishing and promoting adherence to high-quality professional standards, furthering the international convergence of such standards and speaking out on public-interest issues where the profession's expertise is most relevant.

(International Federation of Accountants 2006: 2)

To carry out its mission it works closely with 'members bodies and regional accountancy organisations' and, in addition, obtains 'the input of regulators, standard-setters, governments, and others' who share IFAC's commitment 'to creating a sound global financial architecture'.[6] The IAASB is part of IFAC but acts on its own authority. IAASB's objective is:

To serve the public interest by setting, independently and under its own authority, high quality standards dealing with auditing, review, other assurance, quality control and related services, and by facilitating the convergence of national and international standards.

(International Auditing and Assurance Standards Board 2006: 1)

The structure of the IAASB comprises of 18 members, 10 of whom are put forward by member bodies of IFAC, five are put forward by the Forum of Firms[7] and three public members. The public members may be members of IFAC member bodies but may not be in public practice. Advice to the IAASB is structured differently to the way advice is provided to the IASB. The IAASB is advised by a total of 15 technical advisers. In addition, the IAASB has its own Consultative Advisory Group that comprises 25 members drawn from international organisations and trade associations (International Auditing and Assurance Standards Board 2006: 23).[8]

The mission of the IASC Foundation/IASB, IFAC and IAASB include serving the public interest and furthering the international convergence of standards set by the respective bodies. Of crucial importance is the extent, and nature, of convergence of international and US standards.

Convergence of US and international standards

An important question regarding the convergence of US and international accounting standards is: will it be towards US GAAP, or will there be a genuine dialogue whereby alternatives receive genuine consideration and recognition?

The principal criticism of the US approach is that it is 'rules-based' rather than 'principles-based'. The advantage of a rules-based approach is that requirements are set out in detail and compliance with the rules can be more easily monitored and enforced; the disadvantage is that there are strong incentives to create financial transactions and accounting treatments designed to avoid the rules and corresponding disclosures (see Dewing and Russell 2004: 301). The advantage of a principles-based approach is that it allows greater scope for professional judgement in evaluating the overall effect of a series of individual transactions and disclosures;[9] the disadvantage is that decisions are not so obviously clear cut and there is scope for professional disagreement. In practice, both approaches are needed but different legal and institutional environments have resulted in a rules-based emphasis in the US and a principles-based emphasis in the UK, a significant difference in what is often perceived to be an undifferentiated Anglo-Saxon approach.

Therefore, whether convergence is rules-based or principles-based is an important one. An interesting aspect of the Sarbanes-Oxley Act was section 108(d) which required the SEC to conduct a study on the adoption in the US of a principles-based accounting system, and stated that the study should include an examination of:

- the extent to which principles-based accounting and financial reporting exists in the US;
- the length of time required for change from a rules-based to a principles-based financial reporting system;
- the feasibility of and proposed methods by which a principles-based system may be implemented; and
- a thorough economic analysis of the implementation of a principles based system.

The SEC duly reported in July 2003. It acknowledged there was room for improvement, but argued neither US GAAP nor international standards are representative of the 'optimum type of principles-based standards'. The SEC clarified its 'optimal paradigm' for an accounting standard as follows: first, there should be a concise statement of the substantive accounting principle or the 'accounting objective'; second, there should be an appropriate amount of 'implementation guidance'; and, third, the standard should be consistent with, and derive from, a coherent conceptual framework of financial reporting. To distinguish its optimal approach from other less well-defined approaches, the SEC referred to its approach as 'objectives-oriented standard setting' (Securities and Exchange Commission 2003: 5). Thus, by proposing a carefully charted middle course, the SEC (2003: 6) was able to advocate a variety of benefits, including facilitating convergence between US GAAP and international standards, which it painted in glowing terms:

> Standard setters can come to an agreement on a principle more rapidly than they can on a highly detailed rule. The benefits of convergence include greater comparability and improved capital formation globally. We believe that neither current US GAAP nor the current array of international standards strike an optimal balance in the various trade offs inherent in standard setting, and thus we see convergence as a process of continuing discovery and opportunity to learn by both US and international standard setters.

This view was confirmed in a speech by Donald Nicolaisen, Chief Accountant of the SEC in which he stated that: 'Convergence is a two-way street... Said another way, convergence does not mean convergence to US standards. ... In converging standards, the standard-setters should always choose the better model' (Nicolaisen 2004). In practical terms, following the Norwalk Agreement, the FASB and IASB are working together on several major projects, as well as on a 'short-term' convergence project. Thus far, progress has culminated in a 'roadmap', agreed by both the European Commission and SEC, towards establishing equivalence between IFRS and US GAAP (European Commisson 2005a; Securities and Exchange Commission 2005, 2006). The roadmap established the goal of eliminating the need to reconcile IFRS prepared accounts to US GAAP by 2009 at the latest. The importance of accounting standards was also highlighted in the Joint Declaration at the EU–US Summit held in Washington on 20 June 2005, with 'promoting convergence of accounting standards as soon as possible' identified as an area of focus (EU–US Initiative, 2005). The signs are promising that there will be a genuine convergence or 'friendly merger' of US and international accounting standards as opposed to a 'hostile takeover' by US GAAP. Indeed, in February 2006 the FASB and IASB issued a joint Memorandum of Understanding reaffirming their commitment to developing 'high quality, common accounting standards' and removing the existing reconciliation requirements, but recognising that this 'will require continued progress on the boards' convergence programme' (Financial Accounting Standards Board/International Accounting Standards Board 2006: 2).

Discussion

There cannot be many private actors that can expect the rules they propose to be speedily adopted into the laws or regulations of nearly 100 countries, and countless companies across the globe be required to comply with them, including 7000 companies approximately in the EU alone and many of the world's largest multinationals. From 2005 this is the case for international accounting standards set by the IASB for the regulation of financial reporting. The US will shortly be the only significant economy where international accounting standards are not recognized. Moreover, it is expected that another set of rules established by another private actor, the IAASB, a subcommittee of IFAC, will soon be setting international auditing standards for the regulation of the audit of financial statements on the same basis. As Whittington (2005: 151) points out, IFRS need to be 'effectively and consistently implemented' in which auditors play a 'critical role'. Thus, within a few years, as international and US accounting (and auditing) standards are set to converge these, or comparable standards, are likely to be accepted by the US and applied to US companies. The aim of the discussion is to investigate how this has come about. The discussion is taken forward in three main parts and considers: the factors underpinning the recent momentum behind convergence of accounting standards; the role of state, private and 'mixed' actors operating at national, regional and international levels; and the extent to which convergence is based on US hegemony and/ or projection of US power, or whether a genuine international debate is taking place.

Recent momentum behind convergence of accounting standards

There are a number of factors that have led to the recent momentum behind convergence of accounting standards. Whittington (2005: 128) points to the internationalization of capital markets since the 1970s and the consequent need for common accounting standards to aid comparability between companies to make the preparation of group accounts easier. Thus between 1973 and 2002 Whittington (2005: 129) characterizes the development of international accounting standards 'as a product of the marketplace'. Indeed, Whittington views the EU's decision to adopt international accounting standards in 2001 in a similar way – to provide shared accounting to EU capital markets, especially in the context of EU enlargement. Perhaps the only other credible alternative for the EU, given the need for comparable accounting standards would have been US GAAP. Whittington points to the difficulty that this would have presented for the EU in that US standards are designed to meet the needs of the US economy, not those of the EU, and, moreover, the EU would have no influence in the setting of US standards – hence the EU's decision to adopt international standards.

The notion of market power is also used by Simmons (2001) to explain harmonization of accounting standards. However, Simmons argues that the dominance of the US capital markets, and the consequent lack of incentive (pre-Enron at least) for the US to embrace international standards, led the IASC[10] to produce standards close to those of the US to increase the likelihood of them being accepted by the SEC. Thus, Simmons argues (2001: 611) 'the IASC has provided the cover of multilateral legitimacy to mostly US standards'. For Simmons the reason for the EU deciding to adopt international standards was that it provided 'a politically more palatable tactic than accepting US GAAP without any pretence of multilateralism' (Simmons 2001).

If market power was the primary driver for convergence towards international standards at EU level pre-Enron, one question that arises is: Does this also explain the proposed convergence of US GAAP and international standards post-Enron? Pressure from international capital markets is an important factor but also important is the demand by multinational companies for one set of rules. As David Tweedie, Chairman of IASB, states: 'The IASB's main thrust is now on achieving the convergence of its standards with those of other standard-setters, and particularly those of the FASB. We have been told repeatedly by multinational companies that this must be our most important objective' (International Accounting Standards Committee Foundation 2005b: 4). Interestingly, Robert Herz, Chairman of the FASB, reports being asked by analysts and investors and by foreign and US multinationals 'Why is international convergence taking so long?', although this is balanced by a comment from many US preparers of accounts 'I'm in favour of convergence, but make them do it our way' (Financial Accounting Foundation 2005: 12). The latter comment perhaps indicates a typical US viewpoint, but with the growth in authority and stature of the IASB and IAASB resulting from recognition by the EU and other jurisdictions, and exposure of the inadequacy of US accounting and auditing standards as revealed by Enron and others, international convergence has moved up the agenda. The next issue to explore is why private actors have moved to centre-stage in determining a crucial component of the international financial architecture and to consider the extent to which US hegemony is weakened or, paradoxically perhaps, strengthened in the process.

The role of private actors

Originally established by the worldwide accountancy profession, recent reforms of IASB and IAASB and other developments have had the effect of distancing these bodies, at first sight at least, from the accountancy profession. This has occurred in a variety of ways: oversight and advisory mechanisms have been strengthened by increased representation from outside the profession; they are able to issue international standards on their own authority, without reference back to the professional bodies; and their deliberations and pronouncements are subject to greater prominence and scrutiny by others, partly because of the globalization of financial markets, partly because IOSCO and the EU have either already recognized, or are set to recognise, their standards, and partly because the main alternative, US standards, have been found wanting post-Enron.

The question to be explored is – how have hitherto obscure private actors, the IASB and IAASB, achieved their current authority and legitimacy? Following Strange (1994, 1996) it can be argued that the source for their authority and legitimacy is the shift from relational power, that is power held by governments and states, to structural power, that is power held by markets, and, in particular, to the knowledge structure, that is power-based on organized expertise, in this case of the accountancy profession (see Dewing and Russell 2004: 309–10). However, possession of organized expertise by private actors does not of itself automatically lead to a position of dominant power and influence. Indeed, to understand the dominant role of private actors in setting international accounting and auditing standards, it is essential to consider the role of states.

In this context professions are key.[11] The bargain between states and professions is that in return for the state granting special recognition over an area of expertise to a professional body, the profession agrees to regulate its members and to act in the 'public interest', that is to maintain professional standards and not to exploit its privileged position. The state confers legitimacy, the price is accountability. A not dissimilar bargain is struck between states and limited liability companies – the state confers limited liability, the price is independently audited accounts made publicly available. The state authorizes that only members of recognized professional accountancy bodies may undertake audits of limited liability companies.

In this context it is helpful to refer to a study by Moran (1991) who investigated the financial services revolution of the 1980s in the US, UK and Japan from a political science perspective. From this study of trends in financial services regulation in the 1980s involving a greater role for private actors in the regulatory process, 'a public function done by private interests' (1991: 14), Moran noted, *inter alia*, a 'bias' to mesocorporatism marking 'a compromise struck between demands to regulate private power and wealth, and the needs of privileged private interests to have protection against democratic politics' (1991: 15). Mesocorporatism differs from traditional corporatism and has the following key features: 'the appropriation of a regulatory role by private interests; the transformation of private, voluntary associations into authoritative bodies; the restriction of economic and political competition' (Moran 1991: 15). Several international financial crises and several 'failure followed by reform' cycles have since confirmed and strengthened Moran's findings of the bias to mesocorporatism in financial services regulation with an ever increasing role for private actors.

As mentioned above, the oversight of commercial activity rests on accounts, independently audited by private accountancy firms, and oversight of accountants and accountancy firms is entrusted to a private body, the accountancy profession. The state has granted recognition to the professional accountancy bodies, thereby granting hitherto private associations the status of authoritative bodies. Economic competition in the provision of accountancy and auditing services is likely to be restricted as international accounting harmonization strengthens the position of the Big Four (see the contribution by Nölke and Perry to this book). The subsequent growth in the size, complexity and interdependence of global financial markets has served only to intensify the trends identified a decade and a half ago by Moran.

Thus, the details of accounting and financial reporting and auditing of limited liability companies are entrusted to a profession having special expertise which, to retain its privileged position, regulates its members and has regard to the public interest. A government department is given ultimate oversight of the accountancy profession and of limited liability companies. The result is a civil society or, alternatively, market arrangement of self-regulation within a statutory framework whereby the state consciously recognizes the accountancy profession and consciously grants it a monopoly over limited liability company audit. Regulation of other areas of commercial activity, for example, stock exchanges, supervision of financial services firms such as banks and insurers, though having their own statutory framework with oversight by different government departments or other agencies, rests on independently audited accounts of limited liability companies. The result is that the accountancy profession, and accounting and auditing firms, although private actors are in effect agents of the state.[12]

Therefore, although on the one hand steps have been taken to reduce the influence of the accounting and auditing profession, such as by independent oversight, on the other hand its influence remains pervasive because of its knowledge and expertise and its organizing power. As the history of financial scandals demonstrates, the accountancy profession and accounting and auditing firms are more than capable of pursuing their own interests. States regularly have to step in to reform matters. Indeed, Enron is simply the latest in a long line of 'failure followed by reform' (see also Dewing and Russell 2002).

It follows that the fundamental reason why the IASB and IAASB as private actors have achieved global prominence is that states are simply doing at a global level what they do at a national level, that is, taking advantage of the standard state/profession bargain whereby the state grants special recognition over an area of expertise to a profession, and the profession agrees to regulate its members and to act in the public interest. It is not without good reason that 'public interest' occurs in the first line of statements of the mission or objectives of the IASC Foundation, IFAC and IAASB. Nor is it without good reason that the only organizations having membership of both the IASB's and IAASB's advisory groups are precisely those intergovernmental organisations in charge of the international financial architecture, namely, BCBS, IAIS, IMF, IOSCO and the World Bank.[13] International accounting and auditing standards are at the very heart of the international financial architecture.

US hegemony – weakened or strengthened?

The initial signs are that the US, or at least the SEC, is prepared to view convergence towards high quality, objectives-oriented accounting standards as a 'two-way street', the question remains as to what will be the nature of the outcome. US hegemony prevails over intergovernmental organisations, see for example Foot *et al.* (2003), and it can be argued that US hegemony will also prevail over private actors in international accounting and auditing. This may occur for a variety of reasons. First, individual members of the IASB and IAASB come from a background that, if not predominantly US, is predominantly Anglo-Saxon (Nobes and Parker 2004: 102–3) which, in spite of certain differences of emphasis because of different legal and institutional environments, is based on a market-driven, shareholder-focused model of accounting. Second, members of the advisory groups are precisely the intergovernmental organisations that stand accused by Foot *et al.* of being dominated by the US, especially the IMF and the World Bank. Third, standing behind the accountancy and auditing profession are the Big Four global accountancy firms,[14] which dominate the market for listed company audit and the national professional bodies and associated institutions. The Big Four, and virtually all other large and medium sized accountancy firms that have an international practice, have strong Anglo–American origins. Neither should it be forgotten that many of those who qualified and worked for the Big Four and other accountancy firms, move into positions of responsibility and influence elsewhere, including occupying key positions on the IASB's committees and working groups (see the contribution by Nölke and Perry to this book).[15] Certainly the Big Four take advantage of this fact and cultivate their alumni as assiduously as any ivy-league university or business school. Indeed, Nölke and Perry (in this book) go so far as to argue that the process of international accounting harmonization has strengthened the position of the Big Four by increasing the 'authority' of financial statements as differences arising from national standards are eliminated, and by giving scale advantages to capture national markets. Fourth, the US is the largest and therefore most significant global capital market. Regulatory changes in other regimes, even in those of London or Frankfurt, are therefore unlikely to have the same impact as those in the US.

The result of these factors is that US accounting and auditing practice is commonly regarded without question as 'best practice', thereby achieving US hegemony without the US needing to try very hard. In financial services Moran (1991: 121) argues that during the 1980s there was a bias towards mesocorporatism and an 'increasing "Americanization" of financial services' with American regulatory practices 'successfully exported' (1991: 122). A similar trend may be evident in the harmonization of accounting standards. This possibility is reinforced by the SEC's continuing belief that, in spite of acknowledged limitations, US accounting standards, even post-Enron, are still the 'best' in the world: 'In the staff's view US generally accepted accounting principles ("GAAP"), despite being the historical product of a mixture of standard-setting approaches, constitutes the most complete and well developed accounting standards in the world' (Securities and Exchange Commission 2003: 5).[16] Thus, although the SEC may state that convergence between US and international standards is a two-way street, in practice the presumption may continue to be that even with the cards stacked in its favour, it is the US view that should count in the event of disagreement. This is why the initial European Commission 'carve out' to achieve acceptance for International Accounting Standard (IAS) 39 *Financial Instruments: Recognition and Measurement* (International Association for Statistical Computing 1998)[17] is potentially damaging to convergence between US and international standards since if the EU is not prepared to accept even agreed international standards, it also opens the door for other countries, such as China and Japan, to seek their own opt outs.

Ultimately, the US can still choose to achieve its aims by acting unilaterally, and even in accounting and auditing can 'project' its power. The most dramatic recent illustration of this is the Sarbanes-Oxley Act 2002. For instance, the Act required the establishment of a PCAOB with which accountancy firms must register if they prepare or issue audit reports for financial statements filed in the US, whether for US or non-US companies. By 31 December 2005 646 non-US accountancy firms were registered with the PCAOB from 80 countries (Public Company Accounting Oversight Board 2006: 6). Such registered firms are subject to the PCAOB's oversight, including the inspection and enforcement regimes, notwithstanding they are based in a non-US jurisdiction. The PCAOB's remit even extends to auditors of US subsidiaries incorporated in a foreign jurisdiction and audited under the laws and regulations of that jurisdiction, the auditors being subject to the regulatory requirements of that jurisdiction. Nevertheless, the Act requires such auditors also register in the US and be subject to US requirements for the regulation of auditors. Concern has been expressed in the EU and also Japan about the imposition of US regulations on auditors and companies of other jurisdictions (see Dewing and Russell 2004). Although there has been a dialogue both at EU and at member state level with the US SEC and PCAOB, the US bodies have so far resisted any relaxation in the registration requirement. The implication is that regulation is asymmetric *vis-à-vis* US and non-US accountancy firms undertaking work for companies filing accounts in the US, with firms based outside the US subject to a dual set of regulatory requirements.[18]

However, a difficulty for the US is that it cannot always be sure of having it both ways, that is, imposing US hegemony whilst reserving the power to act unilaterally. As Mann (2004: 57) has pointed out: 'Hegemony should be an invisible hand, lying behind the accepted rules of the game. The catch is that to be hegemonic, the US might have to play by the rules'. In the context of the convergence of US and international accounting standards, by accepting the roadmap for achieving equivalence between IFRS and US GAAP, US power may be restrained since the US will have to play by international rules.

Conclusion

This chapter has noted the steady rise to prominence, especially post-Enron, of hitherto obscure private actors, the IASB and the IAASB, which set international accounting and auditing standards. It has investigated the nature of the IASB and IAASB and has explored their close links with other private actors, in particular their direct and indirect links with the accountancy profession and the Big Four global accountancy practices on the one hand, and their close links with intergovernmental actors responsible for the international financial architecture, such as the BCBS, IAIS, IMF, IOSCO, the World Bank and also the European Commission, on the other. The chapter has identified the bias to mesocorporatism evident in the increasing role for private actors, particularly the IASB and IAASB, in regulatory space. The chapter has also explored the likely nature and extent of convergence between US and international accounting and auditing standards. The initial signs are that convergence could be possible under a mutually agreed objectives-oriented approach. However, this may to a large extent depend on the EU accepting international standards without further amendment. Americanization, to use Moran's term, may have received a set-back post-Enron, but US hegemony over the international financial architecture remains strong and the US is still more than capable of projecting its power in accounting and auditing, even post-Enron, as the Sarbanes-Oxley Act 2002 illustrates.

The role of public and private actors in global governance is of considerable importance. Studies of the international financial architecture have focused mainly on the roles of long established public actors, such as the IMF and the World Bank, or on the roles of significant groups of private actors, such as international banks and multinational companies. There is a danger of over-emphasizing the distinction between public and private, and not recognizing that certain key actors occupy an intermediate position. Professions and their organisations are seen, not without reason, as private actors located in civil society. However, they derive their power and influence from the state and in many instances are in effect agents of the state. In return they agree to regulate their members and to act in the public interest. In the era of global markets and an ever more complex meso-corporatist regulatory environment, it is arguably necessary to bring professions back in to re-evaluate their economic, sociological and political roles. As intermediaries located in both the private and the public they may be well placed to undertake what 'pure' private or 'pure' state actors, even though constituted as international organisations, are unable to achieve. New light may be shed on the structure of the international financial architecture by examining the role of the accountancy profession and its associated organizations and firms.

Thus, there is a need to view the IASB and IAASB not just as independent private actors, but as actors strongly linked to the accountancy profession, which in turn should be viewed in the wider context of relationships between professions and states. The worldwide accountancy and auditing profession is a case in point where the profession, or perhaps more correctly the Big Four accountancy firms and their alumni, acting in the *public* interest may play a critical, but not fully recognized, role in maintaining and improving national and international financial architectures. However, the Big Four accountancy firms and their alumni, acting in their own or their clients' *private* interests may represent a critical, but not fully recognized, threat to the stability of these architectures. In taking forward a study of the setting, monitoring and enforcing compliance with international accounting and auditing standards, it is necessary to rethink the role of the profession in international regulation, and the international regulation of the profession.

Notes

1 The extent to which such organisations are, in fact, independent of government is an interesting question that will be explored further in this chapter. In this chapter the term private actor is used but similar terms used in the literature are non-state actors (NSAs) or NGOs.
2 It is outside the scope of this chapter to describe the history of these bodies, outlines of which can be found in the relevant chapters of standard international accounting textbooks such as Nobes and Parker (2004) and Roberts *et al.* (2002), and on the IASB and IFAC websites www.iasb.org.uk and www.ifac.org respectively. This chapter concentrates on the current role of these bodies after their reform with effect from 1 April 2001 and 1 April 2002 respectively.
3 See www.iasb.org.uk/about/structure.asp, accessed 8 September 2006.
4 This includes organizations having responsibility for the international financial architecture, such as BIS, IMF, IOSCO and the World Bank, whilst the European Commission, the SEC and the Financial Services Agency, Japan have observer status, see www.iasb.org/about/sac_members.asp, accessed 8 September 2006.
5 The discrepancy is because there may be more than one professional accountancy body in a country, for example, the UK has five and the US three recognized professional accountancy bodies.
6 See www.ifac.org/MediaCenter/files/facts_about_IFAC.pdf, accessed 8 September 2006.
7 The Forum of Firms was established in 2001 to represent the interests and meet the needs of accountancy firms undertaking audits of cross-border financial statements.
8 Again, this includes organizations having responsibility for the international financial architecture, such as BIS, IMF, IOSCO and the World Bank. Interestingly, the European Commission is a member whereas on the equivalent IASB body it is an observer.
9 Accountants refer to this as the principle of economic substance taking precedence over legal form.
10 Prior to 1 April 2001 international accounting standards were set by the IASC. The IASC was reconstituted as the IASB from this date, see note 2.
11 There is a large but arguably dated literature on the sociology of the professions, and the accountancy profession has been relatively little studied by sociologists. Our discussion follows a traditional, stylised and Anglo-Saxon view of professions. It focuses mainly on the 'deal' made by the profession with the state in return for state recognition.
12 An example of where auditors are specifically agents of the state is the EU's post-BCCI banking directive which requires auditors to report to regulators if in the course of their work they become aware of circumstances 'liable to have a serious effect on the financial situation or the administrative and accounting organization of a financial undertaking' (European Parliament and European Commission 1995: Article 15).
13 There is also the European Commission which is an observer on the IASB's advisory group and a member of the IAASB's advisory group.

14 They are in alphabetical order: Deloitte & Touche Tohmatsu; Ernst &Young; KPMG; and PriceWaterhouseCoopers.

15 In the context of this chapter, an interesting example from the UK is John Tiner, Chief Executive of the UK's Financial Services Authority. Formerly he was head of Andersens worldwide financial services industry practice. In this capacity he led an investigation into the Bank of England's procedures following the failure of Barings Bank and was instrumental in introducing a risk-based approach to bank supervision. He joined the Financial Services Authority in 2001 as a managing director and became its Chief Executive in 2003. He is currently Chairman of the financial reporting group of the EU's Committee of European Securities Regulators. In this capacity he has been described as the 'Hand that guides EU accounting reform' (Parker 2004).

16 It is worth emphasizing that although the market-based, shareholder focus of the Anglo–American model is arguably dominant in international accounting and auditing practice there are some important differences between the UK and the US. For example, the UK's ASB characterizes its standards as 'principles-based' whereas the US's FASB has been criticized for being too 'rules-based', see previous discussion. However, the extent to which this distinction is real or illusory has itself been questioned, see Taub (2003).

17 It is beyond the scope of this chapter to review the debate surrounding the European Commission's adoption of IAS 39 and readers are referred to the European Commission's 'Frequently Asked Questions' on IAS 39 for further details (European Commission 2004e).

18 The Sarbanes-Oxley Act also introduced further requirements both on auditors and chief executive officers and chief financial officers in companies listed in the US. For further details see the SEC website www.sec.gov/spotlight/Sarbanes-Oxley.htm.

Part IV

Integrating emerging market economies

9 Transition through different corporate governance structures in postsocialist economies

Which convergence?

Wladimir Andreff

Seventeen years after the dawn of postsocialist economic transformation, corporate governance structures are extremely different across CEEC and CIS members. The observed differentiation is basically due to the variety of methods that have been used to privatize former State-Owned Enterprises (SOEs). The growth of the *de novo* private sector and its mushrooming start-ups as well as residual state property also had an unevenly important impact on governance structures from one postsocialist economy in transition (PET) to the other. In new private start-ups a strong corporate governance structure (being monitored entirely by a single or a few owner(s)) tends to prevail while in privatized firms (that is, former SOEs) a managerial corporate control is widespread. A privatized enterprise in CEEC today is basically a managerial firm. In our country sample, corporate governance structures change slowly since the emerging capital markets are not yet functioning properly and the set of appropriate institutions is not comprehensive and not strictly enforced. Over one decade after privatization has begun, the different corporate governance structures in CEEC can be represented by four stylized models: foreign capital controlling stake, managerial control (sometimes with the co-operation of banks), an outsider-insider coalition governing the enterprise, and a peculiar 'employee and start-up' governance. In recent years, some converging tendencies toward an 'average' Central Eastern European model of corporate governance have shown up; its two major pillars are strong foreign investor control over big corporations combined with strong governance by a single owner over genuine SMEs.

An analytical framework that goes beyond the principal–agent model

Our classification of corporate governance structures does not merely rely on the mainstream principal–agent model. The real pattern of corporate governance that is emerging in PETs is path dependent, reflecting the means used to privatize SOEs, the laws that have been enacted or revived, and the institutions that have emerged (or not) to facilitate corporate governance. The theoretical relationship postulated by the principal–agent model between privatization and an efficient ensuing corporate governance structure, and thus the firm's restructuring, is too restrictive and, in the PET context, simply wrong (Andreff 2000). In the real world of current business, this relationship is not stable due to frequent changes in the shareholding of each single corporation – share sales, take-overs, acquisitions. The same agent may unpredictably modify his/her economic behaviour depending on macro- and micro-circumstances, including the threat of a take-over, the redistribution of shareholding, the appointment of new enterprise boards, the result of a proxy fight, the emergence of a financial-industrial group (FIG), the loopholes in corporation law, the opportunities of corruption, and the claims of non-residual claimants – all factors unheeded in the mainstream model. More or less regular bonuses, premiums, perks and bribes can link insiders to outsiders (Blasi *et al.* 1997), in a not yet fully-fledged market-oriented enterprise, in a way unpredictable by the principal–agent model, so that profitability is often a meaningless variable, not to speak of profit distortions with still imperfect competition. Lower profit may reflect the existence of a coalition between outsiders and insiders involved in a profit hiding strategy, which is a widespread strategy for tax evasion purposes in PETs.

In the PET context, managers and employees have actually colluded to save insider control over privatized enterprises. Managers have purchased employee shares; some top managers have bought up stock without the employee's knowledge and have used 'pocket companies' to buy shares quietly. The shares had not been traded anonymously (Aghion and Blanchard 1998) and, at the end of the day, managers were among the main buyers. Therefore, managerial entrenchment is a widespread result of privatization in all PETs (Filatochev *et al.* 1999). Loopholes in the new legislation on joint stock companies were used by incumbent managers to avoid disclosure and, thus, alleviate small shareholders' property rights. Managers have even hidden relevant information or have circulated it after introducing some bias in order to increase the governance costs of shareholder monitoring. They have not been disciplined by the threat of bankruptcy since the law is often not yet enforced. Thus, a number of rather simplistic assumptions underlying the principal–agent model have become increasingly hard to maintain. The overall outcome of PET privatization has damaged the model.

Alternative theoretical explanations of corporate governance can dwell upon the literature on coalitions within economic organizations. In the quite peculiar ownership structures of PET firms, what matters is not only the concentration of ownership, but also the identity of owners. Who are the new owners and in how many different corporate boards are they involved? Do they behave as shameless tycoons? How many shares do they personally own? What are their alliances or interest groups, and their legal or illegal manoeuvres? All this matters as well. A part of the theory of economic organizations focuses on coalitions (Mintzberg 1983). Among the participants in a firm, some subsets or groups can coalesce around a mutual target of satisfying results under the hypothesis of a bounded rationality of economic agents. At any moment, some coalition dominates the enterprise but can be removed by another in the making. The ruling coalition should adopt management providing the highest return on assets if one wants a formally privatized firm to be transformed into a private firm maximizing its profit. The type of coalition in power and contingencies of economic environment determine the kind of target, which must reach a satisfying level in the firm: efficiency, survival, autonomy, growth, asset value, etc. The emergence of a new dominating coalition within the enterprise can obviously change the prevailing target. Although survival usually characterizes insider coalitions and profit-making outsider coalitions, the real picture in a corporation is often blurred when managers are shareholders, when employees own shares, when there is discord within the management team or the corporate board, or when alliances tie some managers to core shareholders. Once all these factors are taken into account, the objective functions of insiders and outsiders might well overlap. Although old-fashioned in mainstream economics, the analysis of intra-firm coalitions is of interest in nascent market capitalism. The principal–agent model wrongly overemphasizes the potential conflict between shareholders and managers. This is the stakeholder management nexus that is important, whoever the stakeholders (managers, employees, and shareholders) are.

There is hardly any study that systematically identifies who exactly are those involved in such coalitions or alliances in PET firms so far. However, in a work by Baltowski and Mickiewicz (2000), three types of alliances appear to be widespread across Polish privatized firms: first, alliances between a group of outsiders and representatives of the State Treasury (which holds the shares corresponding to residual state property), often opposed to the firms' personnel; second, alliances between managers and employees against the representatives of the State Treasury; and third, alliances of employees and the representatives of the State Treasury against either an outsider or the managerial team. Further studies of monitoring blockholders and interlocking directorates remain to be conducted when all information about them will be disclosed (for a first and partial attempt, see Mesnard 1999).

The impact of privatization on corporate governance structures

The corporate governance structure of a Soviet enterprise was rather simple: the state, as the single owner, assigned all management decisions to a single executive director (the *edinonatchalie* principle) who was assisted in his work by some engineers and executive managers. In charge of fulfilling the enterprise plan, the executive director was subject to different checks and controls from his tutelary industrial ministry, from the state bank (*Gosbank* in the USSR) and from the Communist Party. Due to information asymmetry, all enterprise directors were at any time capable of cheating (biasing all information transferred to controlling bodies) during both the processes of building-up and achieving the plan. Such a cybernetic weakness was one basic source of inefficiency in the former centrally planned economy (Andreff 1993).

The economic reforms launched by Gorbachev in the Soviet Union attempted to alleviate the causes of economic inefficiency through increasing the decision making autonomy given to enterprise directors and managers, that is (in terms of a property rights analysis) through fully transferring the cash flow right (or *usus fructus*) over the enterprise's assets to them. In some other socialist countries, such as Hungary and Poland, an elected employee committee was entitled to supervise the current decisions (or *usus*) made by the director and managers whereas in Yugoslavia self-management was materializing the so-called social ownership (different from state ownership) in granting supervision and cash flow rights to the enterprise personnel (however, the control right or *abusus* never got out of state hands). Thus, during the last years of the communist regime, in nearly all CEEC, corporate governance was taken over by insiders, either managers (the director included of course) or employees (or both). The only exception to insider governance was regarding the right of control over the enterprise's assets, namely the right to sell them, which was kept by the state administration, although it was partially alleviated by newly introduced schemes of leasing and renting assets.

In the early years of postsocialist transition, privatising SOEs was envisaged as the major tool for changing not only ownership, but also management and governance in order to improve economic efficiency through asset restructuring and labour shedding. However, even before a privatization law had been passed, a significant development of so-called spontaneous or *nomenklatura* privatization sprang up in all PETs. It means that the director and managers immediately used their supervision and cash flow rights in such a way as to take over all the enterprise residual revenue, tunnel it into private companies they had just set up for the purpose, and strip the most interesting assets from the SOE to their own newly established private firms. Spontaneous privatization strengthened the fans of the Washington consensus in their firm belief that the privatization drive should proceed as fast as possible, whatever the price, so that communist managers and politicians could not transform their former political power into economic ownership.

The long run consequences for corporate governance of such an accelerated, if not forced,[1] privatization process remained unheeded, at least in the mainstream economic literature, for several years. Nevertheless, some time was required to elaborate on and adopt privatization laws, but usually they were not passed soon enough to (avoid or) prevent spontaneous privatization from occurring.

On the other hand, some economists have advocated since the very beginning a (slower) development of the private sector based on new enterprises created from scratch (Kornaï 1990) or a privatization drive exclusively implemented by means of asset sales, the only way not to generate serious corporate governance problems (Andreff 1991, 1992). Their recommendations were ignored or criticized by the mainstream and rejected by international economic organizations until the late 1990s.[2] In their survey of the literature, Shleifer and Vishny (1997) conclude that an efficient and strong corporate governance structure (that triggers restructuring and turning a loss-making SOE around) requires a 'hard core' of controlling blockholders. The latter can only come about by means of firm privatization through direct asset sales to strategic investors or initial public offerings followed by the acquisition of the newly issued shares by those investors who wish to take over a majority or minority blockholding position. At odds with the previous conclusion, Washington international organizations and their experts preferred criteria such as the speed of privatization and the number of firms privatized, and assumed them to be guaranteeing the political objective of an irreversible change in ownership.

Although he demonstrated that initial conditions in PETs made it impossible efficiently to privatize SOEs through asset sales, Jeffrey Sachs (1991) nevertheless recommended to resort to non-standard methods of privatization, supposedly enabling a rapid transfer of SOE ownership to new private proprietors. The so-called non-standard methods are mass privatization, management and employee buy-out (MEBO) at preferential prices, and restitution – to former owners, before communism, or their heirs. The problem is that MEBO transfers those property rights (*usus* and *usus fructus*) previously acquired by SOE managers to the same incumbent managers while adding the *abusus* to their former rights. As for mass privatization, it generates a widespread capital dispersion since vouchers (then redeemed into shares) are allocated for free to the whole population. When the vouchers are redeemed, managers continually take benefit from their insider information in such a way as to acquire significant blocks of shares. If they succeed in such endeavour, mass privatization then has the same result as MEBO, that is the transfer of property rights from incumbent managers to incumbent managers.

Given the economic importance rapidly reached by the private sector in GDP (see Table 9.1 below) and the fact that this sector's growth is partly due to privatization, the variety of current corporate governance structures in PETs is strongly determined by those privatization methods that have been adopted in each country.

In the heat of the privatization battle, by the mid-1990s, the distribution of privatized assets according to privatization methods in PETS was as follows (Andreff 1999a): only 13 per cent had been privatized through asset sales, 43 per cent through MEBOs, 24 per cent through mass privatization and 20 per cent by means of other methods such as restitution, heirs' (financial) compensation and municipalization of assets. Since then, the distribution has more than slightly evolved toward a higher share of asset sales due, in particular, to increased participation by foreign investors. However, mass privatization is still the primary method, which has been used so far in eight PETs and MEBO in another 13. Asset sales, including to foreign investors, has really been preferred only in Hungary and Estonia, although it has become a significant privatization method in Bulgaria and Poland in recent years; it is also going to outstrip all other methods in the Czech Republic with bank privatization, very much open to foreign capital since 1999. Corporate governance structures have been diversified further in PETs by the skyrocketing growth, though uneven from one country to the other, of start-ups in the *de novo* private sector (Duchêne and Rusin 2003; Dallago and McIntyre 2003).]

On the other hand, some SOEs appear to be so 'unprivatizable' that the state has kept, willy-nilly, a significant share in their capital stock (residual state property) whereas other SOEs will remain in a state of ongoing privatization for quite a long time, and for a last group of SOEs the state has simply given up the idea of transferring (or does not wish to transfer) their assets.

Table 9.1 Major privatization methods in transition economies

Country	Share of the private sector in GDP in 2001* (%)	Direct asset sales	Mass privatization	MEBO
Albania	75	Tertiary	Secondary	Primary
Armenia	70	Tertiary	Primary	Secondary
Azerbaijan	60	Secondary	Primary	No
Belarus	20	No	Secondary	Primary
Bulgaria	70	Primary	Secondary	Tertiary
Croatia	60	Tertiary	Secondary	Primary
Czech Republic	80	Secondary	Primary	No
Estonia	80	Primary	Secondary	No
Georgia	65	Secondary	Tertiary	Primary
Hungary	80	Primary	No	Secondary
Kazakhstan	65	Secondary	Primary	No
Kyrgyzstan	60	Tertiary	Primary	Secondary
Latvia	70	Secondary	Primary	No
Lithuania	75	Secondary	Primary	No
Macedonia	60	Secondary	No	Primary
Moldova	50	Secondary	Primary	No
Poland	75	Primary	Tertiary	Secondary
Romania	65	Secondary	Tertiary	Primary
Russia**	70	Secondary	Tertiary	Primary
Slovakia	80	Tertiary	Secondary	Primary
Slovenia	65	Tertiary	Secondary	Primary
Tajikistan	50	No	No	Primary
Turkmenistan	25	Secondary	No	Primary
Ukraine	65	Tertiary	Secondary	Primary
Uzbekistan	45	Secondary	Tertiary	Primary

Source: Vagliasindi (2003).
Notes: * Estimation: EBRD (2002).
** Three-quarters of mass privatization turned out to be MEBOs.

The overall result is (insofar as various privatization methods have been experimented) a variety in the forms of ownership and in the distribution of property rights, and a diversity in corporate governance structures, both within each PET and across all PETs.

Diversified corporate governance structures

Corporate governance structures are now complex and diversified in all PETs. An overview of these structures is exhibited in Table 9.2 (below) in which they are classified from the strongest as assessed by the principal–agent model (those structures where shareholders are assumed to have the strongest monitoring power) to the weakest (where the shareholders' supervising power is the most alleviated, diluted and ineffective).

A deep economic analysis of corporate governance not carried by the principal–agent model is in limbo in the PETs so far because there is no device that compares either to the 20-F form in the US which encompasses one section about control

Table 9.2 Corporate governance structures in East European enterprises

Enterprises	Ownership acquired through	Enterprise governed by	Representative countries
Private	Creation from scratch	Owner (single)	Poland
	Small privatization: auction sale asset by asset	Owner (single)	All countries
Privatized	Restitution	Former owner, heir	Czech Republic
	Initial public offering	Institutional investors*	Rare in any country
	Direct asset sales	Foreign investors	Hungary, Estonia
		Outsiders or local FIGs**	Russia
	MEBOs	Employees	Poland, Croatia
		Managers	All countries
	Mass privatization	Investment funds	Czech Republic
		Managers	Russia, Kazakhstan
		State holdings	Poland
	Loans for shares scheme	Banks, FIGs*	Russia
Mixed	Ongoing privatization	State representatives	All countries
	(the state is the single majority shareholder) or		
	Residual state property	Unspecified	All countries
Public	Nationalized after self management	State representatives	Slovenia, Croatia
	State-owned (not yet corporatized)	State-appointed managers	Belarus
		As before	Turkmenistan

Notes: * pension funds, investment funds, insurance companies, etc. ** FIGs: Financial-industrial groups (governance) to be filled by the informant or to the European Directive 88/627/ EEC on large holdings (Becht and Mayer 2002). Therefore, a precise quantitative or qualitative analysis is now out of reach. In the future, such a study will become feasible for the eight PETs which joined the EU in May 2004, since they must now implement the aforementioned European Directive. Better information about shareholders' votes, and their possible concentration, will then be available even though information regarding the concentration of stock ownership may remain partly undisclosed – which is especially impenetrable in PET firms. Meanwhile, studying the outcome of privatization can provide an insight into the whole spectrum of governance structures that exist in postsocialist firms. In schematic form we can distinguish seven types of enterprise form and corporate governance structures.

The first configuration is one in which a private owner, often the sole owner or a few as co-associated owners, holds the entire enterprise capital stock and exerts all the prerogatives of an owner/boss, that is as chief executive officer (*usus*), as residual claimant (*usus fructus*) and as a possible vendor of his/her enterprise (*abusus*). This is the case in *private enterprises* created from scratch (start-ups) whether they are individual enterprises or SMEs. It is a strong governance structure, which foreshadows the emergence in PETs of a governance structure similar to the one of SMEs in Western market economies. Where do the assets come from in such small enterprises? Their origin can be legal or not, the assets provided to the start-up can result from primary accumulation of capital by the new entrepreneur, usually exploiting his/her rent seeking situation in newly emerging markets, or from asset stripping and tunnelling from an SOE in which he/she was previously (or still is) employed. The major problem with these new private SMEs is that their access to banking and other finance is hindered by their negligible collateral for loans. Nevertheless, the creation of start-ups has been of pervasive magnitude, especially in Poland and the Czech Republic, but also in Hungary, Slovenia, Bulgaria, Romania and Slovakia.

A variant of small private enterprises is the one owned by a single or a few co-associated owners emerging from the process of *small privatization*. The latter refers to the state releasing retail shops, hotels, restaurants, cars, lorries, buses, and small craft production through public auction sales. Small privatization also encompasses the state selling the physical assets of previously-dismantled SOEs such as machine tools, equipment goods, buildings or workshops that could be of interest for a private purchaser.

Small-scale privatization has given rise to millions of mushrooming SMEs in all the PETs. If one has to speak of a major success story in postsocialist privatization, in terms of corporate governance, small-scale privatization comes up to the fore. The dark side of the story is that private SMEs are facing high mortality rates, due to their lack of finance and/or expertise that is not always compensated by their high birth rates.

Second, strong corporate governance, with strict shareholder monitoring of managers, is rarer in *privatized firms*. When it comes to restitution to former owners or their heirs, the outcome is open-ended. In a number of cases, the former owners or heirs have fled from the communist regime long ago and have stayed abroad; they may only be interested in closing down the factory and making all workers redundant. They may intend to restructure or change the nature of the business. They may simply resell the assets they got in the restitution process. Whatever their decision, it exhibits that, when benefiting from restitution, the owner enjoys non-alleviated property rights despite possible resistance from of managers and employees. The problem lies elsewhere. In case of restitution, the owner's decision is not necessarily beneficial to the home country (factory close-down, labour shedding) so few PETs, with the exception of the Czech Republic, engage in ambitious restitution programmes. Elsewhere, in Hungary for instance, those entitled to restitution did not receive physical assets but were compensated with privatization vouchers enabling them to participate in the privatization of SOEs that were for sale (with voucher redemption into shares) at that moment. Then they entered the stockholding of privatized corporations, most often as minority shareholders excluded from corporate governance.

Third, privatization based on *initial public offering* was eventually quite rare in PETs since, when the privatization drive was launched, the stock exchange did not yet exist (except in Hungary). Thereafter, the newly emerging stock market was tiny in terms of (not even daily) transactions. All the more so, since, at the very beginning, institutional investors were few, and only came from state banks, state insurance companies and state financial institutions. Gathering a hard core of monitoring blockholders remained, in most cases, an unresolved issue because this hard core could not rally non-state shareholders and foreign investors (whose acquisitions were restricted or forbidden in most privatization programmes, except in Hungary and Estonia). Moreover, domestic or local capitalist tycoons, capable of buying a substantial block of shares, were few in number or non-existent in the first hours of transition. The most efficient corporate governance structure coming out of privatization has been revealed to be the acquisition or takeover[3] by foreign investors. A takeover has nearly always resulted from a direct asset sale negotiated by the state with a foreign firm and practically never from the latter's raid by means of the rapid acquisition of shares in the targeted domestic firm. In this case, the monitoring blockholder is a foreign transnational corporation, used to efficiently supervising its foreign subsidiaries' managers, including those subsidiaries recently acquired in PETs.

A number of assets have been sold by the state direct to domestic or local investors, that is, to domestic outsiders. However, at the dawn of the privatization process, sales to domestic outsiders were rather few and in any case undesirable because they boiled down to transferring assets to incumbent *nomenklatura* leaders and managers or, even worse, to those who had previously been able to enrich themselves illegally and accumulate enough wealth in the underground economy or in the *Mafia* to be able to invest it in a substantial share of a privatized corporation. In some PETs, the law or the programme of privatization forbade the sale of SOEs' assets to incumbent communist leaders and rulers. After some time, since the mid-1990s, circumstances have changed and privatized corporations have been acquired or taken over by domestic outsiders. The number of 'nouveaux riches' or 'new rich' has increased substantially thanks to legal, illegal and borderline transactions in formal and informal emerging markets; their capacity of investing in the property of privatized corporations has likewise increased. After the initial MEBO and mass privatization programmes, share resale transactions expanded, sometimes in the stock market, more often off the market.[4] Share resales have opened up an opportunity for domestic outsiders such as 'nouveaux riches', but also for insiders using their own private 'screen companies' and oligarchs heading the new FIGs, to acquire substantial (often controlling) blocks of shares in privatized enterprises. All these share purchasers were looking for a sizeable blockholding which, with some alliances, would enable them to take over all strategic decisions in the targeted privatized enterprise (that is, to exert strong corporate governance), in spite of the wishes, hopes and intents of both incumbent managers and minority shareholders. Although all share resales did not end up with corporate governance dominated by a hard core of monitoring blockholders, they increased the proportion of corporations under outsider and FIG control.

Fourth, the trickiest issue with corporate governance in privatized firms has surged to the forefront following MEBO and mass privatization. In PETS with a self-management tradition (former Yugoslavia, Poland), MEBO was the tool for transferring most firms to their personnel. Then, those who govern the enterprise are easily identified, that is, employees and managers, but with MEBO we should say that enterprise assets are 'socialized' rather than genuinely privatized. Of course, employees become private owners of their enterprise but their main objectives are different from those of a capitalist owner. In acquiring ownership, and the corresponding property rights, employees look for maintaining jobs, securing current wage rates and safeguarding working conditions. Assessed from the viewpoint of the principal–agent model, such a corporate governance structure is weak or inefficient; not likely to pave the way for high profitability. Most studies on enterprise samples in PETs show that on average, employee-owned firms underperform other enterprises, even SOEs, as regards to productivity and profitability, with a few noticeable exceptions in Poland (these sample studies are surveyed in Djankov and Murrell 2002; Megginson and Netter 2001). On the other hand, another interesting effect of employee ownership has been to markedly reduce, in particular in Poland, asset stripping by incumbent managers before, during and after privatization (Nellis 2002a). In their capacity of owners, employees have submitted managers to such strict supervision as to prevent any attempts at looting the firm's assets. However, the managerial discipline obtained by employees was not primarily aimed at profit or shareholder value maximization – as used to be the case with capitalist shareholders.

Anyway, a more frequent way out of MEBO is managerial governance over privatized enterprises in all PETs. In the most frequent scheme, former communist enterprise managers have transformed their political power into economic capital.[5] Either the managers altogether hold a significant share in the privatized firm's stock or they acquire it by purchasing shares from employees, after the stock has been issued to them all (by MEBO). Often, managers have simply exerted their authority over employees by taking over all governing decisions or acquiring employees' shares at low prices (managers used to threaten redundancy on those employees who intended to sell their shares to outsiders, whilst promising to reserve the remaining jobs for those who were prepared to sell them their shares). In some countries, such as the Czech Republic, employees were excluded from management buy-outs (MBOs); managers were the only ones allowed to purchase assets. Sample studies have exhibited that manager-controlled (owned) firms on average outperform employee-owned enterprises and SOEs as far as productivity and profitability are concerned, although they underperform outsider-owned firms and do markedly worse than enterprises taken over by foreign investors (Andreff 2003a). *Managerial firm* is the predominant corporate governance structure coming out of privatization so far. This is confirmed when looking at mass privatization.

Fifth, in all those PETs which have privileged *mass privatization* today, the results are disappointing, being far removed from what was expected 10 or 15 years ago. The objective was to offer for free, or nearly for free, to the whole population, privatization vouchers redeemable into shares that would give the right to anyone[6] to participate in the acquisition of state-owned assets. An *ex ante* egalitarian distribution of property rights and an *ex post* efficient redistribution of shares were supposed to evolve in accordance with the Coase theorem,[7] through share resales in the stock market, in such a way as to favour the emergence of blockholders. The latter were assumed to be willing to invest in privatized enterprises and purchase the shares of those citizens not interested or unfit for business. Contrary to these expectations, in all PETs, mass privatization has paved the way, directly or not, for corporate governance dominated by managers in privatized firms.

For instance, in Russia, three options were open in the framework of mass privatization. According to option one, 40 per cent of corporate stock was offered to the personnel at a preferential price. In option two, employees could immediately get 51 per cent of the stock at a higher (than the book value) price, and option three preserved 30 per cent of the stock for a managerial group committed to turn their respective enterprise around and avoid its bankruptcy. In each case, the remaining part of the stock was to be sold against privatization vouchers until June 1994 and for money ('cash' privatization) thereafter. Option two was chosen by over 73 per cent of the roughly 15,000 enterprises involved in the mass privatization programme while option one was adopted by 25 per cent of privatized firms, leaving less than two per cent in option three (Blasi *et al.* 1997). In nearly all circumstances, managers were able to keep a firm hand over corporate governance since the remaining stock was so dispersed. Moreover, they managed to gain control over capital by acquiring the shares held by the personnel. Thus, strong managerial entrenchment was the key result of mass privatization enforced by the opportunistic and tactical behavior of managers. In Russian privatized firms, managers exert strict supervision over those who buy their enterprise shares; most enterprises do not use independent shareholder registers; and most managers say they oppose financial disclosure and majority ownership by an outside investor with enough capital to turn the firm around. Inadequate legal and regulatory framework and poor protection of minority shareholders' rights only go to increase the benefit of holding a controlling stake. When legal rules fail to constrain the actions of controlling managers, the latter are used to engage in self-serving activity such as the transfer of assets at arbitrary prices to manager-owned private firms. This, in turn, dilutes minority claims further. Incumbent managers have also circumvented the law: we have listed (Andreff *et al.* 1996) more than 20 varieties of violations of corporate law in Russian privatized enterprises, from not convening the shareholder meeting to votes by show of hands.[8] The weakness and unpredictability of the Russian court system was not able to put a brake on these violations. When a firm is locked in managerial control, managers tend to consider shareholding as a management variable and substitute the firm to the court.

In other PETs, corporate governance was taken over by managers as an indirect result of mass privatization. In the Czech Republic, about three-quarters of all privatization vouchers have been bought from the citizens by Privatization Investment Funds (PIFs) which thereafter have redeemed them into shares. At first sight, becoming major shareholders, these newly created institutional investors (that is, the PIFs) seemed to have taken over most privatized firms. Therefore, the PIF's managers were in position to monitor the decisions made by the managers running the firms that entered into the PIF's portfolio but, as Stiglitz (2001) has stressed , the problem then became 'Who monitors the monitors?', that is, Who monitors the PIFs' managers? In the context of the Czech Republic, the response was quite clear since most PIFs had a major (often only one) shareholder, which was a state bank or a state insurance company. Thus, a Czech Minister for the Economy (Mertlik 1996) once said that mass privatization is the fastest track to transfer state property to the state. As regards corporate governance, it was transferred from former (now privatized) SOEs' managers to PIFs' managers and eventually to state banks' managers, in other words from incumbent *nomenklatura* to *nomenklatura*.

In the Polish variant of mass privatization, the state set up 15 National Investment Funds across which the assets of would-be privatized firms have been allocated. Polish citizens could not acquire shares in the privatized firms' stock but they were entitled to become shareholders of the Funds. Attempting to circumvent the issue of monitoring the monitors, each Fund was managed by a management consortium combining foreign and Polish banks and audit agencies. The resulting governance structure *a priori* seemed stronger than that of the Czech PIFs, since each management consortium was given the explicit objective of increasing asset portfolio value held by its Fund. However, all the Funds behaved in such a way as to disinvest from the least profitable firms in their portfolio and to invest in the most profitable ones instead of, as expected, restructuring and modernizing the most obsolete firms. In fact, they adopted the behaviour of an institutional investor (such as, say, an American pension fund) and did not get involved in the corporate governance of those firms they were supposed to monitor; as a result, restructuring is lagging behind in Polish mass privatized firms.

Finally, Russia has experimented with the most disavowed and criticized, in fact the worst method, the so-called 'loans for shares' scheme, even though it yielded a strong corporate governance structure. Such a scheme was suggested in 1995 to President Yeltsin by Vladimir Potanin, the Uneximbank CEO, and prescribed that the Russian State would deposit in Russian banks significant blocks of shares from the stocks of the most valuable Russian SOEs – oil companies, other energy and raw materials producers. Banks would consider the stock they held as collateral for the loans that they offered to provide in order to bail out any serious state fiscal deficit. For each company involved in this device, an auction was opened and the winning bank got a block of shares, remitted the purchase price as a loan to the state, and held the shares until September 1996. If, on this date, the state had not repaid the loan, the bank would be allowed to sell or definitively keep the shares (and the ownership in an oil trust, etc.). Since the state was obviously not capable of repaying its debt, banks gained through this scheme the ownership of the 'crown jewels' of Russian industry, for a nominal sum,[9] insofar as auctions were rigged and therefore not exempt from collusion. All the winning banks were owned by a small group of financial oligarchs well acquainted with the President of the Russian Federation (Nellis 2002b). Some of these transactions were so fraudulent that the Moscow arbitrage court invalidated them. Nevertheless, a small group of oligarchs, including Roman Abramovitch, Evgueny Ananiev, Boris Berezovski, Oleg Deripaska, Mikhaïl Fridman, Vladimir Goussinski, Mikhaïl Khodorkovski, Igor Malatchenko, Vladimir Potanin and Alexander Smolenski, appropriated the finest jewels of Russian industry. The 'loans for shares' scheme most definitely discredited the Russian privatization drive which was not only disapproved by the World Bank but was also overtly criticized by the great bulk of the Russian population, and became infamous outside Russia.[10] Absolutely questionable from a moral or business ethics point of view, the above-mentioned scheme has brought about the integration of valuable firms into oligarchic FIGs with a strong corporate governance structure (privatized enterprises are then monitored by the core bank of the FIG or by an oligarch (major shareholder) himself). It has contributed to increasing the outsiders' share in the overall control over Russian enterprises and to the emergence of a new economic and financial 'elite', although it is with the help of the most dubious, rigged and amoral device, the complete opposite of the Coase theorem (Andreff 2005b).

Sixth, until now, a number of enterprises remain in *mixed ownership* in PETs, with both private owners and the state sharing their stock. First, there are those firms whose privatization has been launched and is still ongoing, with part of the stock still in state hands. Second, there is state residual property. In several privatized enterprises, the state has kept a share in the stock ownership for one reason or another: the state may want to avoid an undesirable takeover by foreign stakeholders and so it keeps a majority share or a minority blockholding. Alternatively, the state has so far not been able to find enough purchasers to sell all stocks; or beneficiaries from MEBOs or voucher holders have not yet acquired the shares to which they are entitled which then remain in state hands. Therefore, we find some state representatives sitting on the board of directors of such firms, in proportion with the stockholding still in state ownership. A serious issue of corporate governance derives from this situation. Either incumbent managers govern the firm or state representatives on the board of directors adopt a strategy which dissuades private owners from further investment in this firm – or even incites them to sell their shares. Since the state representatives on the board are usually civil servants, academics from state universities and experts appointed by a ministry, they do not necessarily have all the required financial, juridical, accounting and managerial skills to function as effective enterprise executives. Moreover, as soon as appointed, they make up a group of stakeholders with its own interests in the board of directors. This group's interests often conflict with those of private owners, since they are leaned on to put a brake on the privatization process of the firm (of course a comprehensive privatization of the stock would entail the phasing out of their participation on the board of directors, and a loss of influence and directors' fees). Besides, the sustained relationships between these state representatives sitting on the respective boards and the state administration they come from may harm independent corporate governance in partially privatized firms. It is also the case that state residual property paves the way for an unspecified corporate governance structure due to a lack of consensus or even any missing alliances between conflicting interests of managers, private shareholders and state representatives on the board.

Seventh, the last subset of firms in PETs encompasses *public enterprises*; they still represent about 20 per cent of GDP in Hungary and up to over 80 per cent in Belarus and Turkmenistan. Their survival can be traced back to various accounts. First, in successor states of the former Yugoslavia, self-managed enterprises were in 'social ownership' so that the first step before privatization was to nationalize them in order for the state to have full ownership at its disposal and then corporatize the newly state-owned enterprises. However, since privatization has taken some time, the board of directors has meanwhile become comprized only of state representatives running the corporation according to the state agenda. On the other hand, in all PETs, primarily in Belarus, Turkmenistan and Uzbekistan, a number of SOEs have not even been corporatized. In this case, state-appointed managers dominate corporate governance as before. From the standpoint of the property rights theory and the principal–agent model, such a governance structure is assumed to be weak and inefficient, since managers are not monitored, and cannot be monitored, by too many shareholders – here the assumption is that the whole population owns each SOE. An alternative view is to regard SOEs as having a single unique shareowner (the state) which is then in a strong position to lay down governance guidelines on the managers, that is, a strong governance structure. For instance, in China (Djankov and Murrell 2002), the state is used to providing SOEs' managers with very strong incentives to keep the enterprise in the black while threatening them with heavy disciplinary and financial penalties if it falls into the red; sanctions can go as far as the death penalty in case of abuse of power. *A contrario*, sanctions are less stringent and often deferred, sometimes non existent, *vis-à-vis* SOEs' managers in Central and Eastern Europe and CIS countries.

In the same vein, we have recommended to privatize the management in public enterprises (Andreff 1992, 1995) when asset privatization is not immediately feasible or is not desirable. What does it mean? Privatization of management consists of managing a public enterprise in such a way as to put an end to current deficit, and then make profit in order to invest it into restructuring the assets, and eventually into foreign subsidiaries abroad; in other words, it means managing public enterprise according to exactly the same criteria as a private firm. Privatization of management is only feasible if the state, as the single shareholder, adopts an efficient corporate governance structure by providing appropriate incentives to SOEs' managers, that is those incentives which drive them to 'manage as in the private sector', and otherwise firing them overnight. Once profitable and efficiently managed, due to strong corporate governance exerted by a unique shareholder, privatization of SOEs' assets becomes only a question of political opportunity (depending on the color of the political party in office) and no longer one of economic efficiency, since the latter has meanwhile been restored. A World Bank report (World Bank 2002) acknowledges that often it would have been preferable to leave assets in state hands (instead of swiftly launching mass privatization and MEBOs) long enough to identify reliable strategic investors and, only then, to sell SOEs to them. Unfortunately, the World Bank was not open to such advice when it was suggested 15 years ago (Andreff 1992).

Towards a central Eastern European model of corporate governance?

Systemic change in PETs cannot be reduced to the issue of ownership transformation, although the latter is crucial. Privatization has left overall a sort of 'neither social, nor private' ownership regime. As such, PETs are mixed economies, in the sense of having mixed (private and public) ownership, often with some employee ownership. The widespread managerial control over privatized firms gives these countries a flavour of managerial capitalism but, in PETs, managers are not gaining control through acquiring a sizeable stake of property, but are acquiring it in order to keep and, indeed, strengthen the control they exercise. Now the question whether a typical Central Eastern European model of corporate governance is emerging must be addressed.

Since the dawn of the transition, the debate in PETs was about the system of corporate governance and the model of capitalism that should emerge from privatization. Most reformers in touch with Washington-based international organizations were supporting the Anglo–American model of governance while some local political leaders were openly revealing a preference for the German (Rhenish) model. In the former, corporate shareholding is dispersed; the role of capital markets is very significant; corporate governance is more geared towards short-term profitability and serves outsider interests first, in particular pension funds, insurance companies and other financial institutions – although all these institutional investors are passive minority shareholders. Furthermore, with legal protection of (minority) shareholders the frequency of raids, takeovers and proxy fights is higher than in other models making managers on average more disciplined.[11] Here, just one single objective is assigned to managers, which is to increase shareholder value. As to the German model, this is characterized by more cross-ownership relationships between firms and banks, networking in FIGs, higher capital concentration and passive behaviour of institutional investors; it also takes into better account wage earners' and stakeholders' interests by means of decision sharing with controlling blockholders. In fact their very existence reduces the opportunity of hostile takeovers and, by the same token, the financial market discipline (compared to the Anglo–American model). On the other hand, the German model maintains long-term relationships amongst all participants in such an enterprise. All these characteristics make insiders and managers more influential and increase their capacity for entrenchment despite the participation of institutional investors in the stockholding. Thus, shareholder value is not the only objective of corporate governance.

However, opposing the external monitoring of an insider system is not so clear-cut when it comes to analyzing the heterogeneous corporate governance structures that we have observed in PETs as well as those witnessed in EU countries. Sometimes, governing coalitions in PET privatized firms bring together both outsiders and insiders so that the delineation between outsider and insider control is blurred, just like it appears to be now in Western capitalism (Becht and Mayer 2002). The borderline between an outsider-dominated and an insider-controlled corporate governance structure is disrupted by the power positions acquired together by blockholders and managers (Boutillier *et al.* 2002) or, in PETs, by alliances between oligarchs and incumbent managers. From this point of view, some similarities emerge between the prevailing corporate governance structure in Western and Eastern Europe. Crowding out minority shareholders from decision making is another common feature. However, this is not enough to conclude that all corporate governance structures are converging towards a single European model, since such a conclusion is not even valid across Western European countries where there are several hybridizations of the aforementioned Anglo–American and German models. The driving force of a new hybrid model is the rising power of institutional investors (Jeffers and Plihon 2001), imposing a (15 per cent) return norm on the shareholder value. PET firms do not converge toward this new hybrid model given the low level of development of local institutional investors and the very modest investment of foreign institutional investors in local companies so far. Regarding institutional investors as 'potential agents of a (retired) employee shareholding' that determines 'a socialized property of corporate companies' (Aglietta 1997), they appear as a sort of Western counterpart of MEBOs which have *directly* transferred the company's shares to employees in PETs.

Could we at least assume that there is some sort of convergence towards a Central Eastern European model of corporate governance? During the last decade, corporate governance structures have been markedly differentiated in PETs. If we except those countries where privatization is lagging behind (Belarus, Turkmenistan, Uzbekistan), and also the issue of residual state property, it seems that the privatization drive has generated, in the context of tiny financial markets, four corporate governance models corresponding to the following stylized facts.

First, a model of *Foreign Corporate Control* (FCC) – or the 'Hungarian' model: about 150 of the biggest 200 corporations in Hungary exhibit influential foreign participation in their stockholding (and a majority blockholding in 50 of the biggest 100 corporations). Today, foreigners own 46.7 per cent of the overall stock of all corporations based in Hungary. Besides, foreign owners wholly own (that is, 100 per cent of the stock) 61 per cent of those firms with foreign participation in their stock. Still in Hungary, foreigners hold 72 per cent of the overall stock exchange capitalization value (62 per cent in Estonia) as against 34 per cent in Poland and even less in all other PETs. Hungary and Estonia are the two PETs where shareholders have the strongest supervision of managers (Vagliasindi 2003) and where monitoring shareholders are mainly foreign. The precondition for building up the FCC model is the magnitude of inward foreign direct investment (FDI) compared with GDP per capita; its emergence is facilitated when there is no regulation that prevents foreign firms from buying assets in local firms in the process of privatization (as in Hungary and Estonia from the very beginning, and contrary to all other PETs). Therefore, the great bulk of Hungarian and Estonian firms are governed by powerful foreign interests, namely well-known transnational corporations and banks, rather than by institutional investors. Such a corporate governance structure is typically strong in the capitalist vein and comes closest to the above mentioned hybrid model of corporate governance, which is fully immersed in current economic globalization.

Second, a model of banking and managerial control (BMC) – or the 'Czech' model: privatized firms are monitored by their managers who are supervised by the privatization funds' (now holdings') managers, these holdings being a proxy or a substitute to non-existent genuine institutional investors. The managers of those banks, which have set up the former privatization funds, supervize the holdings' managers, in turn. Since most of these state banks have been privatized since the late 1990s through mergers and acquisitions by foreign banks, the BMC model partly overlaps in the long run with the previous FCC model (see, for instance, the increasing significance of inward FDI in the Czech Republic, Table 9.3 (below)). On the other hand, private ownership by individual owners is not widespread, but managers in privatized firms do resist the supervision by the funds (holdings) in utilising their privileged insider information. Collusion between firms' managers and banks' managers is all but the exception. Holdings re-concentrate property that has been scattered by mass privatization and organize it into FIGs. Cross-ownership, off the market trade in shares, managerial entrenchment and corporate governance that takes care of stakeholders' interests (for years, the Czech Republic was distinguished by showing the lowest unemployment rate in PETs) position the BMC model not that far from the German model of corporate governance.

Third, a model of 'Control by an Outsider–Insider Coalition' (COIC) or the 'oligarchic–managerial' model detrimental to (small) minority shareholders is typical in Russia and several CIS countries: a great number of firms are under the inner control of insiders (primarily managers) while others are integrated in one or two hundred FIGs and holdings governed by the new tycoons, financial oligarchs and bankers. Numerous insiders are at the same time outsiders in other companies in which they have invested their new wealth (or companies that they have

Table 9.3 Inward foreign direct investment in transition economies, 1993–2002

Country	Inward FDI stock/GDP (%)			Inward FDI stock per capita ($)		
	1993	1997	2002	1993	1997	2002
CEECs						
Bulgaria	1.4	9.4	24	18.7	117.4	511.7
Czech Republic	7.7	22.8	54.8	260.2	896.5	3,733.0
Estonia	6.3	24.5	65.9	164.7	765.3	3,018.6
Hungary	13.6	34.7	38.2	514.0	1,557.1	2,417.4
Latvia	0.6	23.0	32.4	13.1	508.8	1,134.6
Lithuania	0.4	10.9	31.4	5.9	281.4	1,105.8
Poland	3.5	11.6	23.9	78.0	428.8	1,169.7
Romania	0.8	10.4	20.5	9.3	160.0	394.0
Slovakia	3.2	8.2	43.2	76.2	295.7	1,893.5
Slovenia	1.8	12.1	23.1	117.4	1,154.7	2,670.5
CIS countries						
Armenia	n.a.	8.4	28.7	n.a.	40.0	206.1
Azerbaijan	n.a.	48.8	86.4	n.a.	238.3	686.4
Belarus	0.1	2.4	11.2	1.6	31.0	155.5
Georgia	n.a.	4.2	19.9	n.a.	32.5	135.8
Kazakhstan	1.0	27.3	62.9	14.7	324.6	919.4
Kyrgyzstan	n.a.	15.7	25.9	n.a.	59.8	86.5
Moldova	0.7	9.6	45.0	6.9	40.9	163.0
Russia	0.4	3.2	6.5	9.4	97.5	155.6
Tajikistan	n.a.	2.2	14.8	n.a.	7.4	24.2
Turkmenistan	n.a.	9.5	19.1	n.a.	96.7	247.5
Ukraine	0.6	4.2	12.9	7.7	41.0	110.6
Uzbekistan	0.4	2.6	13.8	3.9	25.2	52.0

Source: Calculated from UNCTAD.

started up for that purpose) whereas interlocking directorates and outsider-insider alliances (between oligarchs, bankers, CEOs and managers) strengthen a network structure of governance. The issuance of shares off the market for the exclusive benefit of blockholders and managers is a tool for such networking. The resulting networks are the more long lasting the more they are connected to political power. Then furthermore they put a brake on FDI inflows into the stockholdings of big Russian industrial and financial trusts and hindered the emergence of new private start-ups. Generally speaking, FIGs, managerial networks and oligarchic power are not supposed to facilitate a blossoming competitive market economy. A major potential driving force which may propel this model forward into significant change might well be the globalization of Russian firms and FIGs by means of their outward FDI (Andreff 2002).

A mixed model based on 'Employee and Start Up' Control (ESUC) – or the 'Polish' model: this entails changeovers of political power between parties, followed by a stop and go economic policy (Andreff 1999b) and a mass privatization programme postponed until 1996 have created a vacuum which was soon filled by small privatization and MEBOs in the form of 'capital privatization'[12] and 'liquidation privatization'[13] both of which have enabled the creation of new start-ups and the internal supervision of the firm by its employees (and not only by managers as in Russia). The outcome is widespread dispersion of ownership among employees who are both shareholders and stakeholders. They attempt, often successfully, at locking in the existing stockholding and corporate governance and they participate in management; their success is evidenced by few social conflicts registered at the level of enterprises in Poland since 1993. On the other hand, a fairly efficient institutional framework (the 1934 commercial and bankruptcy law has come into force again, and an anti-trust law has been passed in 1990) facilitates starting up *de novo* private enterprises. New SMEs have mushroomed, mainly from 1990 to 1993 (Rusin 2002), in 1993, all these start-ups were concentrating 18.4 per cent of overall employment in Poland. Afterwards, the momentum of the new private sector relied on both the emergence of new start-ups and the increasing size of those which survived the harshness of competition; in 1996, the SME sector reached 31.7 per cent of overall employment (three times more employment than in privatized firms). In 1997, the number of Polish SMEs was 1398 million. The ESUC model paradoxically (for the principal–agent model) combines the supposedly weakest governance

Table 9.4 Small and medium-sized enterprises in Central and Eastern Europe, 1995

Country	Percentage of SMEs in total number of firms	Population density of firms*
Bulgaria	96.0	39
Czech Republic	85.6	68
Estonia	78.2	21
Hungary	83.2	56
Latvia	80.3	11
Lithuania	75.1	18
Poland	87.8	37
Romania	95.3	17
Slovakia	92.1	42
Slovenia	75.4	37

Source: Rusin (2002).
Note: * Number of active enterprises per 1,000 inhabitants.

structure (employee self-supervision) and the supposedly strongest, that is, the SME monitored by its own boss(es).

Now, we can conclude that managerial enterprise (exclusively monitored by its managers) is so widespread in all PETs, except in the FCC model, that it cannot determine, alone, a specific model of corporate governance. By the same token, it is a component of all the four suggested models, in particular the BMC and COIC models.

A sort of inertia affects corporate governance structures in PETs which is due to absent or weak institutions that would normally facilitate or trigger their improvement, causing a convergence toward a single model to slow down. However, in recent years, some omens of a possible convergence of FCC, BMC and ESUC[14] models towards a prevailing corporate governance structure have emerged in Central Eastern Europe. The latter would combine a strong foreign stake in the biggest corporations with a large number of SMEs monitored by their bosses (and fewer and fewer former privatized SOEs). In other words, it would be a hybrid of the 'Hungarian' and 'Polish' models (referring to the latter's start-ups component).

Indeed, we observe (see Table 9.3 (above)) that Poland and the Czech Republic host more FDI than Hungary in recent years. Both countries, with some delay compared to Hungary, have launched wide-ranging programmes of bank privatization (after 'cleaning' bank assets from bad debts) through selling their assets to transnational banks. Since 1998, the Czech Republic also favoured the sale of strategic enterprises to foreign investors so that FDI share in privatization has grown from one per cent in 1997 to 23 per cent in 1999 and 28 per cent in 2001. At the same time, the share of privatization funds (then holdings) has dramatically reduced in the ownership structure of Czech enterprises in which they now hold a large number of small participations and behave as sleeping partners – thus increasingly resembling West European institutional investors. In 1997, the Polish authorities decided to give more momentum to privatization and sell strategic enterprises, henceforth without any restriction on foreign investors. As a consequence, foreign-owned firms have grown from accounting for 1.8 per cent of overall employment in Poland in 1996 to 3.6 per cent in 1999. Besides increasing inward FDI, the convergence towards a common Central Eastern European model of corporate governance is influenced by spreading globalization of governance standards and, in the last few years, by outward FDI of new transnational corporations from PETs (Andreff 2003b). Adopting global strategies, PET enterprises do converge, in some sense, toward the above-mentioned hybrid model prevailing in Western economies (Plihon *et al.* 2001).

A second strong tendency is embedded in the development of new start-ups, both of individual enterprises and SMEs. Such small firms characterize the 'Polish' model (ESUC) of governance, but they are also widespread and growing in Hungary, the Czech Republic, Bulgaria, Romania and Slovakia (see Table 9.4 (above)). In 1995, one million Czech individual enterprises were employing 11.2 per cent of the overall working population; in 2000, 1,471 million individual enterprises were employing 13.2 per cent of overall working population. The same year, in Hungary, 9 per cent of overall working population was employed in 381,000 individual enterprises (51 per cent in all SMEs and individual enterprises) as against 5.6 per cent in 1992 (43 per cent in all SMEs and individual enterprises in 1994).

Therefore, the FCC, BMC and ESUC models have started exhibiting, in recent years, a convergence towards a Central Eastern European model of corporate governance that is characterized by both an important foreign stake in the ownership of (and foreign control over) big businesses and by single bosses monitoring their own SMEs. If such a converging tendency were to prevail in the future, then the FCC, BMC and ESUC models would have to be regarded as *transitory* governance structures emerging from privatization, whereby strict managerial control, employee supervision, banks' monitoring and other *ad hoc* forms (privatization investment funds, state run holdings, mixed enterprises) would pass away after some time. In the wake of convergence, the increasing significance of foreign ownership is likely to adjust the governance structure to international standards of governance, that is, the ones associated with the aforementioned hybrid model. For instance, since privatization, investment funds have eventually transformed themselves into genuine institutional investors thereby setting up a building block of the hybrid model. It remains to be seen whether it will be enough to solve all the unresolved issues of corporate governance that have accumulated during the first 15 years of transition.

Conclusion

Since the Enron suit, corporate governance has become a tremendously crucial issue in Western economies. All the more so in PETs where governance issues are intertwined with corruption, embezzlement, asset stripping and tunnelling, illegal appropriation and money laundering. Since the struggle against corruption and money laundering is a priority in PETs, namely in the new EU members, improving the corporate governance structure appears to be an immense and long-term task. Its achievement will probably not be possible without several rounds of ugly prosecutions. Beyond this, one of the major concerns today is to secure shareholder (in particular minority shareholder) protection against misuses of power from blockholders, oligarchs and managers. In this respect, the new EU members will move faster than other PETs.

Notes

1 Often managers and employees first reacted with some resistance to privatization, since they expected it to reduce overmaning in their SOE, which meant a threat to their jobs.

2 A strategy of 'organic development' (Kornaï) of the private sector and an economically efficient privatization (through asset sales) was only supported by a minor group of economists in the early 1990s, namely Wlodzimierz Brus, David Ellerman, Kasimierz Laski, Ronan McKinnon, Lubomir Mlcoch, Peter Murrell, Gérard Roland, David Stark (non-exhaustive list) and, later, Joseph Stiglitz (2001) – and of course myself.

Their economic analyses and recommendations remained unheeded until a World Bank (2002) report recognized mass privatization and MEBO (nearly for free) as inefficient privatization methods. Since this report the Bank gives its support to those basic market institutions which facilitate entry by new start-ups and privatization through direct case-by-case transactions.

3   Under certain conditions, monitoring over managers and decision making powers over other shareholders can be reached with a minority share (see Andreff 1996). A 'blocking minority', usually defined in each corporate law (for instance, it is fixed at 25 per cent of total stock (votes) in Hungary), can sometimes be enough for a foreign investor to prevail in managerial and financial decisions, but it can also bring about a conflict of interests with domestic shareholders or with the state when it keeps a share (as witnessed in Hungary and other PETs).

4   About 90 per cent of share resale in the Czech Republic and Russia occurred off the market after mass privatization.

5   According to a large EBRD survey, hardly one third of former managers have been replaced in privatized firms, in all PETs. Among the new executive managers, 40 per cent come from outside the firm while 60 per cent have been promoted within the same enterprise (European Bank for Reconstruction and Development 1999).

6   We can also see in this privatization scheme a sort of 'egalitarianism', either a strong whiff of socialism and communism or the effect of the theory of property rights regarding the whole population as the true owner of SOEs. In some circumstances, free distribution of vouchers was thought of as a tool for overcoming popular resistance against the privatization programme (Boycko *et al.* 1995) or as a means, for political parties in power, to 'purchase' their success in the next democratic elections (e.g. in the Czech Republic).

7   We elaborate elsewhere (Andreff 2005a) on a critical assessment of the Coase theorem on the grounds of both some inconsistencies between the so-called theorem and the Coasian theory of the firm and the full inaccuracy of the assumptions underlying the Coase theorem *vis-à-vis* the economic situation in post-Soviet economies (extremely high transaction costs, an absent stock market, etc.).

8   Note that remedies for illegal self-dealing by managers or board members include criminal sanctions in some OECD countries.

9   Since the auctions were rigged the shares were sold at rock bottom prices. For instance, Mikhail Khodorkovski is suspected to have paid $300 million for obtaining the ownership of assets valued at about $10 billion.

10   Keeping M. Khodorkovski in jail and circulating rumours about other oligarchs might give the feeling that President Putin's administration is now willing to put the most fraudulent acquisitions of Russian enterprises into question. An alternative assumption is that we are witnessing a harsh struggle for redistributing assets between those controlling the administration (the 'security' services and oligarchs).

11   At least until such scandals as Enron, World Com, Vivendi Universal.

12   An SOE is first corporatized and then sold through a public offering, most often to its personnel, since 'capital privatization' has a prerequisite which is the preliminary agreement of its employees; the latter can acquire 20 per cent of the stock at half price and appoint one third of the board members.

13   Liquidation privatization means the sale or a lease, at a preferential price, of an SOE's assets with a view to starting up a new enterprise whose owners are most often the SOE's employees, since the preliminary agreement of its worker council is required.

14   In Russia and CIS countries, the relative significance of inward FDI is markedly smaller and those institutions that favour the legal start up of new private enterprises are less stabilized (and more circumvented) than in Central Europe.

10 Corporate governance regulation in East Central Europe

The role of transnational forces

Arjan Vliegenthart and Henk Overbeek

Introduction

This chapter discusses the rise of corporate governance regulation as part of the establishment of capitalism in East Central Europe (ECE) after 1989.[1] In the context of the discussion on the economic transformation from a centrally planned to a market economy in this region, most of the existing literature looks at corporate governance regulation from an economic point of view. During the first years of the economic transformation in the former socialist states issues of corporate governance in a narrow sense received rather limited attention. Most emphasis was placed on price liberalization, on the opening of markets to foreign capital and on the establishment of private property, that is, privatization. From the mid-1990s onwards the institutional foundations necessary to make this process successful received increasing attention. This is partly because the unregulated emergence of capitalism caused a host of problems. An efficient allocation of resources was deemed feasible only with the 'right' regulation underpinning it. The dominant literature on the subject sees corporate governance regulation as a 'technical' solution to a 'technical' problem, and largely ignores the political dimensions (see for instance Estrin *et al.* 2001: 1; but also Boycko *et al.* 1996). It predominantly looks at the transformation process as a process of modernization, ignoring the fact that transformation entails a political struggle between various social forces (Shields 2004).

In this chapter issues of corporate governance are embedded in a broader context. In order to understand the modalities of the introduction of corporate governance regulation in ECE, it is necessary first to take a look at conditions under which the introduction of a market economy took place, and to emphasize the essentially political and contested nature of this transformation process. We will specifically address two issues that are central to this book as a whole, namely the discussion regarding 'convergence' versus 'divergence', and (related, as we will argue) the transnational nature of the process in question.

Initially policy decisions with regard to liberalization and privatization, in combination with informal networks and practices that partly 'survived' from the late communist era, differed substantially throughout the region. On the basis of an extrapolation of these early tendencies, one might have expected continued divergence (as for instance Whitley 1999; Grabher 1997; Stark 1992, 1996; Stark and Bruszt 2001 have argued) and increased differentiation over time. Presently, however, there is increasing evidence that corporate governance systems in the region are now moving in a similar direction, in some cases even converging rather than diverging (see for instance Vliegenthart forthcoming; and the contribution by Andreff to this book). We arrive at the conclusion (referring back to the discussion regarding Varieties of Capitalism (VoC) as introduced in the introductory chapter to this book) that these recent tendencies towards convergence have resulted in the emergence of something that may be called a distinct ECE VoC (see particularly section four).

In our contribution we set out to solve the puzzle (this unexpected change from initial divergence to increasing convergence) by providing an alternative interpretation that does not rely on the extrapolation of previous trends. Central to our explanation for this common trajectory is a theorization of the role of transnational factors in the process of transition towards capitalism in ECE. For us, they are a key driving force behind the current corporate governance convergence in the region.

We will argue that transnational forces have fundamentally impacted upon the establishment of these new rules both directly and indirectly. Indirectly, the search to attract foreign capital has pushed governments in the region to adopt regulation that was as favourable to the interests of foreign capital as possible. Directly, once foreign firms entered the region, they began to play a vital role in restructuring local corporate governance practices.

The remainder of this chapter is divided into three sections. In section two we develop a theoretical framework suitable to the analysis of the transformation process in ECE, in which we focus on the importance of transnational class struggle and state theory, paying particular attention to the *comprador* phenomenon. In section three the analysis turns to the dependency of these economies on foreign capital and the impact of transnational capital on the process of class formation. Having thus sketched the broader context of the transformation process, we can then in section four turn our attention to the changing character of corporate governance regulation under conditions of externally dependent capitalist development, and specifically to the role of transnationally linked managers and politicians in these developments.

Understanding class formation in ECE in the post-communist era

Much of the literature on the development of capitalism (including the creation of a regulatory framework) in ECE acknowledges the importance of external influences (in particular the activities of the IMF and the World Bank, the enlargement strategy of the EU, and the influx of foreign firms) (for example, Nölke and Stratmann 1998; Schimmelfennig and Sedelmeier 2005). However, the literature is relatively weak when it comes to theorizing the meaning and significance of this observation, and its likely future implications.

A valuable attempt to theorize the specific form of capitalist development in 1990s' Central Europe has been made by Eyal and others (1997, 1998; Eyal 2000) who observed that capitalism in ECE was being created without a true capitalist class in charge of the process. Central to their *capitalism without capitalists* thesis is the idea that privatization created a diffuse form of ownership, where managers had taken a privileged role in the chain of command. Although we find this attempt empirically rich, it is unsatisfactory to argue that capitalism can exist without capitalists (or at the very least this idea is based on a limited understanding of the capitalist mode of production). The concept is further implicitly based on an ontology that privileges the primacy of the *national* context and fails to recognize the fundamentally transnational character of contemporary capitalism. For these reasons we propose a different approach.

The transformation process through which the centrally planned economies of ECE have been recast into functioning market economies is, we would argue, a layered process in a double sense. It is first a layered process temporally (cf. Braudel 1982; Overbeek 1990): the episode of the late 1980s and early 1990s is in fact a conjuncture of crises in several different temporal dimensions. There is of course the *histoire événementielle* of the political crisis of the communist regimes and the fall of the Iron Curtain. But there is rather general agreement that this immediate political crisis must be seen in the context of a deeper layer, namely the longer term crisis of the communist system *tout court*, which can be alternatively interpreted as determined by the inherent structural defects of the centrally planned command economy (Kornai 1993, 2001) or as the consequence of the fact that the communist system was from its very inception a mercantilist project of upward mobility within the capitalist world economy rather than an autonomous alternative system (Wallerstein 1984). With this last medium-term layer we are also pointed towards a third, still deeper, layer, namely that of the capitalist world economy and the capitalist mode of production, which has its own rhythm and its own dynamic. The significance of this (we return to this theme in the next section) is of course that it enables us to understand the process of transformation not just in terms of its own contingent logic, but also as a specific phase in the underlying longer-term crisis of the communist system, and as taking place in the context of, and being in this sense overdetermined by, a specific phase in the development of global capitalism.[2]

Crosscutting this multi-layered temporality is the multi-level reality of political geography. Here, developments in ECE take place simultaneously within the politico-geographic boundaries of the individual countries and the region, as well as in the wider European macro region in which the EU with its enlargement strategy is a weighty factor, and in the global context in which such things as EU–US relations and global geopolitical rivalries play a role.

These two logics circumscribe the environment in which transformation in the former socialist states takes place, and against the background of which developments in the region must be pictured for a fuller understanding. For our purposes, it is especially relevant to address the first deeper logic, that is, the logic of the development of global capitalism in the late 1980s and 1990s, when the transformation got under way and present ECE economies were shaped. How can we understand the nature of this process and the factors responsible for the historically specific outcome?

In *The New Imperialism* David Harvey (2003) introduces the concept of 'accumulation by dispossession', which he presents as a concept expressing the present day manifestations of what Marx called 'original accumulation'. For Marx this concept referred to that form of 'accumulation, which is not the result of the capitalist mode of production, but its point of departure' (Marx 1867: 741; our translation). It needs no elaboration that the concept of original accumulation is eminently appropriate when analyzing the establishment of capitalism in the former Communist states in Europe. In his analysis of the historical process of original accumulation in Western Europe, Marx focused on the expropriation of the peasants and their separation from the land in what became known as the enclosure of the commons (Marx 1867: 744). In more general and abstract terms, original accumulation (sometimes also referred to as *primitive* accumulation) entails the separation of the direct producers from the means of production (Marx 1867: 742). Harvey speaks of 'accumulation by dispossession' to take account of new forms of dispossession that would be hard to fit into Marx's conceptualization. The more familiar ways in which primitive accumulation occurs:

> (…) include the commodification and privatization of land and the forceful expulsion of peasant populations; the conversion of various forms of property rights (common, collective, state, etc.) into exclusive private property rights; the suppression of rights to the commons; the commodification of labour power and the suppression of alternative (indigenous) forms of production and consumption; colonial, neo-colonial, and imperial processes of appropriation of assets (including natural resources); the monetization of exchange and taxation, particularly of land; the slave trade; and usury, the national debt, and ultimately the credit system as radical means of primitive accumulation. The state, with its monopoly of violence and definitions of legality, plays a crucial role in both backing and promoting these processes.
>
> (Harvey 2003: 145)

New forms of accumulation by dispossession include such phenomena as the creation of a regime of intellectual property rights, the privatization of state assets (universities, utilities) and public goods (health care, pension provision), and the rise of internal 'cannibalistic as well as predatory and fraudulent practices' (Harvey 2003: 148). This brief list makes clear (something that was always clear from Marx' own analysis as well) that original accumulation is not something of the past, of the pre-history of capitalism, but continues to occur throughout the development of the capitalist mode of production: it refers in short to all those instances where economic activity is subordinated to the discipline of capital accumulation where previously it was not.[3]

The greatest difference however between the historical process of original accumulation that Marx analyzed and accumulation by dispossession today is of course that the former was indeed an original process in the sense that it occurred in the context of a pre-capitalist world that was dominated by a wide range of national formations characterized by predominantly non-capitalist modes of production. In contrast, the original accumulation of capital in post-Cold War ECE (to stay with the region under scrutiny in this chapter) is taking place in the context of a thoroughly capitalist world economy. This difference has fundamental consequences. And here Harvey's analysis becomes innovative and helpful for our purposes. He relates the wave of accumulation by dispossession currently sweeping over the globe to the long-term overaccumulation crisis of capital, which Harvey sees as:

> (…) a condition where surpluses of capital (perhaps accompanied by surpluses of labour) lie idle with no profitable outlets in sight. The operative term here, however, is the capital surplus. What accumulation by dispossession does is to release a set of assets (including labour power) at very low (and in some cases zero) cost. Overaccumulated capital can seize hold of such assets and immediately turn them to profitable use.
>
> (Harvey 2003: 149)

The attractiveness of this approach for our purposes is that it gives us a handle to understand both the reasons for and the implications of the domination of foreign interests in the economic transition process in ECE.

For Eyal and others (1997) the fact that there were no capitalists in ECE during the transformation towards capitalism makes the region unique. However, there were no capitalists in England either when capitalism emerged through the historical process of primitive accumulation. And similarly there were no capitalists in Japan in the 1860s when the Japanese state created them. Nor was there a class of capitalists in China when the Communist state created such a class after 1978. The formation of a capitalist class, we may conclude, is the product (not the precondition) of the rise of capitalism. It is only when original accumulation is gradually overshadowed by the expanded reproduction of capital (that is, accumulation through the reinvestment of capitalist profit) that we simultaneously observe the rise of a class of capitalists and the emergence of a true proletarian working class.

In the early stages, as Harvey points out, the principal conduit for accumulation by dispossession:

> [...] has been the forcing open of markets throughout the world by institutional pressures exercised through the IMF and the WTO, backed by the power of the United States (and to a lesser extent Europe) to deny access to its own vast market to those countries that refuse to dismantle their protections.
>
> (Harvey 2003: 181)

Concretely in Central Europe, the privatization policies, different as they were from country to country (see the contribution by Andreff to this book for detailed information) were heavily influenced by the interventions of these and similar foreign actors, thus paving the way for the influx of foreign capital either immediately as buyer of privatized assets, later as investor in new greenfield operations (often assembly line production), or later still as dominant actor and investor in the financial heart of the economy (see below).

Several authors highlight the role of an elite layer in the state apparatus as being the responsible factor for the privatization trajectory and the subsequent consolidation of the power position of foreign capital (for example, Andor 2000; Janos 2001). Böröcz has proposed the titillating notion of *auctioneer elite* (Böröcz 1999): that group of state managers which was responsible for selling off state assets to foreign capital. Eyal *et al.* recognize a similar point when they introduce the concept of a *comprador intelligentsia*, defined as:

> those managerial or technocratic professionals who serve as consultants, advisors or intermediaries to foreign capital. [Such] members of the managerial or technocratic elite could, and in some cases already have, sold their firms at advantageous prices to their former foreign business connections, and at the same time they made sure that in exchange for their services they will retain their position as managers.
>
> (Eyal *et al.* 1997: 92).

The limitation of these notions (auctioneer elite, managerial elite, *comprador intelligentsia*) lies in the fact that they remain undertheorized and steer short of identifying these groups as making up a specific 'class fraction' with an identifiable place and function in the overall class structure of global capitalism.

In this chapter we propose to revitalize the concept of *comprador bourgeoisie*.[4] The concept of a *comprador bourgeoisie* originates from dependency theory. Paul Baran (1957) in his *Political Economy of Growth* was among the first to use this notion, followed by André Gunder Frank in his work on the development of underdevelopment in South America (1967). In their work it refers to those fractions of the bourgeoisie in Third World societies whose interests, by virtue of their specific role as middlemen in the import and export business, are intimately tied up with those of foreign capital. Normally, the *comprador bourgeoisie* is contrasted with the national bourgeoisie, a distinction that was first introduced by Nicos Poulantzas (1973). The comprador fraction, argued Poulantzas, does not have its own base for capital accumulation but 'is that fraction of the [bourgeois, AV/HO] class whose interests are constitutively linked to foreign imperialist capital (capital belonging to the principal foreign imperialist power) and which is thus completely bound politically and ideologically to foreign capital' (Poulantzas 1973: 39). Hence, in the Poulantzian sense the *comprador* fraction is to be discerned from other fractions of the bourgeoisie in that it does not directly possess any significant means of production itself, and its wealth does not result directly from the appropriation of surplus value in the process of production. This is eminently true in ECE as well; hence the *comprador* fraction must not be confused with a 'national' bourgeoisie.

Whereas most of the literature hardly acknowledges the constitutive role of globalization for the shaping of capitalism in ECE (as pointed out by Shields 2004: 132), the '*comprador*' concept allows us to grasp the inherently *transnational* nature of the process at hand. Transnationality, as we are reminded in the introductory chapter to this book, refers to a social space that transcends national boundaries; in this space the 'national' is no longer the primary constitutive dimension of social relations, without however being relegated to complete irrelevance. Whereas the role of 'transnational' forces (often conceived in the literature as 'external' or 'foreign') has been more widely discussed (Holman 2001, 2004; Bohle 2002), the simultaneous and concomitant national dimension remains empirically underdeveloped, as Drahokoupil has rightly argued (2005: 24). If we take the essence of the concept seriously it allows us to embed the behaviour of national agents theoretically, and transcend the artificial divide between internal and external. In the case of Poland for instance, Shields has concluded that the Polish state is 'in Poulantzas' terms, taking responsibility for the interests of the dominant capital by contributing to the endorsement of neoliberalism on a global scale' (Shields 2002: 7).

So let us now, in the next section, take a closer look at the concrete forms of domination by foreign capital in ECE.

The dependence of East Central Europe on foreign capital

The dependence on foreign capital is often quoted as a key feature of the social formations of ECE. But, when exactly is a country dependent on foreign capital?[5] The literature does not provide an unambiguous answer. Beyond the point that there is a lot of foreign direct investment (FDI) in ECE, which is a relatively uncontroversial statement, opinions diverge significantly. As Harvey argues, accumulation by dispossession can be the way to open up the route to expanded reproduction (developmentalism or socialist primitive accumulation), but it can also be a means of disrupting and destroying it (as is arguably the case with neoliberal politics) (Harvey 2003: 164). Some studies unequivocally conclude that FDI has positive effects on the development of transition economies (for example, King and Váradi 2002), and specifically on their technological capabilities (for example, Weresa 2004). Others are more skeptical, and conclude that FDI has very uneven effects 'both sectorally and geographically' (Pavlínek 2004: 63); for some there is even reason to speak of a 'new periphery' (Nesvetailova 2004). Below, we will attempt to assess to what extent aggregate data about FDI allow us to speak about ECE dependence.

Perhaps more important from the perspective of the impact on corporate governance practices in the region is the degree to which the financial sector is subject to penetration of foreign capital. In any economy, the financial sector is like 'the umbilical cord that ties together accumulation by dispossession and expanded reproduction (....) [namely] finance capital and the institutions of credit, backed, as ever, by state powers' (Harvey 2003: 152). This is even more keenly true in economies in transition (or in crisis) where social capital has to be re-allocated in order to adapt to changed conditions. Because of the role, under capitalism, of the financial sector in co-ordinating the allocation of investment, foreign investment in this sector also has a decisive impact on corporate governance practices. We will therefore pay separate attention to the degree of foreign domination in this key sector of the economy.

Foreign direct investment

How important is FDI in ECE, and how dependent is the region on foreign capital? To give a meaningful answer to such a question, we need to relate FDI statistics to comparable data for the economy as a whole. In addition, we will need to include comparative data for other relevant economies in order to determine whether data for ECE differ significantly from those for other countries. In this section, we present an overview of the FDI data most commonly used in the international literature: we will look at inward flows in relation to total capital formation, and at the stock of FDI in relation to GDP. For the purpose of this chapter, that is, to determine whether ECE is indeed dependent of foreign capital, it is most instructive to compare ECE data with data for the EU-15 where available, because that will give us insight in how externally dependent ECE is compared to those countries on which ECE is supposed to be dependent.

The first indicator is the ratio of incoming flows of FDI to gross domestic fixed capital formation, or in other words the foreign share in the overall accumulation of capital. Table 10.1 (below) shows that FDI inflows represent a significant share of fixed capital formation, which would support the notion of 'dependence' on foreign capital. However, when compared to the same data for the EU-15 we can see that the role of FDI in capital formation is not significantly different in ECE.

Table 10.1 Inward and outward FDI flows as percentage of gross fixed capital formation

Country/ region	1992–97 annual average		2000		2003	
	inward	outward	inward	outward	inward	outward
Czech Republic	9.5	0.6	32.7	0.3	11.6	1.0
Estonia	23.3	2.7	29.6	4.8	35.2	5.9
Hungary	33.0	1.0	24.5	5.5	13.5	8.7
Latvia	27.8	–3.5	21.6	0.5	13.7	1.2
Lithuania	5.8	0.4	17.7	0.2	4.7	1.0
Poland	12.2	0.1	23.8	–	11.1	1.0
Slovakia	4.6	0.7	36.6	0.4	6.8	0.3
Slovenia	4.9	–	2.8	1.4	2.9	4.8
EU-15	6.0	9.2	41.3	49.6	14.7	16.8

Source: UNCTAD, World Investment Report 2004: Annex table B.5.

A much clearer contrast emerges when we take into account FDI outflows. Not altogether surprisingly, there is very little outflow of FDI from ECE. Whereas for the EU-15 there is over time a rough balance between inward and outward FDI, in the case of ECE outward FDI has become significant only in the cases of Estonia, Hungary and Slovenia (while even in the first two still lagging very much behind inward FDI). The data thus show a strong imbalance between inward and outward FDI flows for the region – Slovenia excepted. We suggest that this imbalance could be interpreted as an indicator of 'dependence' on inward FDI in the sense that 'dependence' is not reciprocal, that is, dependence has not developed into interdependence.[6]

For a second indicator of the reliance on foreign capital as the engine of the ECE economies, let us look at FDI stocks as a percentage of GDP. As Table 10.2 (below) demonstrates, there has been a tremendous increase in FDI throughout the 1990s: in all countries in the region the ratio between inward FDI stock and GDP has at least doubled (as is the case in Slovenia), but more often trebled or quadrupled; in Slovakia it even increased nearly eightfold. But again, when compared to the EU-15, the picture is suddenly much less unambiguous as a proof of FDI-dependence.

The high inflow of foreign investment into the region is an indicator that new investments can hardly be raised domestically as Schrooten and Stephan have also argued (2001). Hence, there is a dependency on foreign capital when it comes to innovation and productive restructuring. It is important to underline that in terms of these very general statistics, the role of foreign capital is clearly significant, but it can not be argued to be significantly greater than in the case of EU-15 as a whole (let alone than in those of the EU-15 countries with a larger than average share of FDI, such as Ireland). The concept of a dependent form of capitalism in ECE can thus not be justified on this basis.

Table 10.2 Inward FDI stock as a percentage of GDP, by host region and economy

Country	1995	2000	2003
Czech Republic	14.1	42.1	48.0
Estonia	19.3	51.4	77.6
Hungary	25.3	49.3	51.8
Latvia	13.9	29.1	35.1
Lithuania	5.7	20.9	27.2
Poland	5.8	20.6	24.9
Slovakia	4.2	18.5	31.5
Slovenia	8.9	15.3	15.6
Accession-8 (unweighted average)	12.2	30.9	39.0
Ireland	60.2	144.1	129.7
EU-15	13.2	28.5	32.8

Source: UNCTAD, World Investment Report 2004: Annex Table B.6.

Foreign penetration of the financial sector

There is, however, one indicator that strongly supports the notion of one-sided dependence on foreign capital in ECE to a degree that is unheard of in EU-15: the role of foreign ownership in the financial sector. The fact that in the late 1990s the share of foreign banks, not only *vis-à-vis* domestic ones but also as a share of GDP, has rapidly expanded in ECE (see Table 10.3 (below)) means that investment decisions in these economies are decisively influenced by developments abroad.

The penetration ratio of foreign bank affiliates (a similar indicator) in the region has also increased dramatically in the most recent years, and is extremely high even in global comparison (see Table 10.4 (below)). Of all developed countries, only New Zealand shows a higher penetration of foreign banks than the ECE countries while the first six all score higher than the UK with its traditionally highly internationalized banking sector – a result of the function of the City of London as the prime financial centre of the global economy.

The origin of the banks that invest in ECE is also interesting. As *The Banker* concluded banks that invested in the region are with the exception of Citibank not the world's top players (see Table 10.5 (below)). This aspect of the predominance of foreign banks in Central Europe may be related to the ongoing process of financialization in the global economy, and in our case particularly in the EU-15.

Table 10.3 Foreign bank assets as share of commercial bank assets (A) and as a percentage of GDP (B)

Country/Year	1998		2000		2002	
	A	B	A	B	A	B
Czech Republic	28.1	31.8	72.1	81.9	85.8	94.4
Hungary	62.5	35.4	70.1	39.8	90.7	49.0
Poland	17.4	9.6	72.6	43.5	70.9	40.7
Slovakia	33.4	34.4	42.1	39.2	95.6	90.3

Source: Mérö and Valentiny (2003: 35–8).

Table 10.4 Penetration ratios of majority-owned foreign bank affiliates, 2001

East Central Europe*	%	Developed countries*	%
Estonia	98.9	New Zealand	99.1
Czech Republic	90.0	United Kingdom	46.0
Hungary	88.8	United States	20.2
Slovakia	85.5	Norway	19.2
Lithuania	78.2	Portugal	17.7
Poland	68.7	Australia	17.0

Source: UNCTAD, World Investment Report 2004, Annex table A.III.4, p. 321
Note: * Top 6 in rank.

Table 10.5 Ownership structure measured after assets of the largest ten banks in the Accession-8

Bank	Country	Total assets (millions $)	Foreign shareholder	Ownership percentage
Ceskoslovenská obchodní Banka	Czech Republic	23,641	KBC Bank (Belgium)	82
PKO Bank Polski	Poland	22,554	Polish State	100
Ceská Sporitelna	Czech Republic	21,597	Erste Bank Sparkassen (Austria)	99
Komercní banka	Czech Republic	17,801	Société Générale (France)	60
National Savings & Comm. Bank	Hungary	16,887	Widespread private ownership	n.a.
Bank Pekao	Poland	16,845	UniCredito Italiano (Italy)	54
B. Przemyslowo- Handlowy PBK	Poland	12,936	HypoVereinsBank (Germany), in 2005 acquired by UniCredito (Italy)	71
Nova Ljubljanska Banka	Slovenia	11,452	KBC Bank (Belgium)	34
Hansabank Group	Estonia	11,211	Swedbank (Sweden)	49
Bank Handlowy w Warszawie	Poland	8,893	Citibank (United States)	92

Sources: www.die-bank.de, www.thebanker.com, ownership for 2001 (all banks but Hansabank) or 2002 (Hansabank), assets for 2004.

Precisely those banks that face serious competitive disadvantages (of size for instance) in the key financial markets in Western Europe (Germany, France, the UK) are the ones that turn towards the new European semi-periphery to escape the worst competitive pressures (Raviv 2006).

Furthermore, the banks that have entered 'have made large long-term commitments to the post-Communist region' (*The Banker* 2004). Partly this long-term commitment results from the orientation of the banks involved. Both Austrian and German banks are traditionally more oriented towards long-term goals and commitments, and in the case of ECE it seems that these traditions remain intact. At the same time the fact that profits in the region are substantially higher than in many of the home countries of these banks, more specifically Germany and Austria, has given these banks extra incentives to prolong their stay, especially as a result of the liberal regulations regarding the repatriation of profits. Austrian banks for instance in 2001 made one-third of their profits in ECE, whereas they only had 10 per cent of their total assets invested there. The IMF reports that 'margins have consistently been higher and loans losses lower than in the mature banking markets of Austria' (*Financial Times* 29 October 2002: 4). The Austrian Central Bank has even begun to report periodically on the stability of the financial system in Central Europe as a service to the Austrian financial sector (www.oenb. at/en). As for KBC, the large Belgian industrial bank, it has chosen to develop Central Europe into its second home market for securities. It claims to have become the first bank in Slovenia, the second in Hungary and the Czech Republic (www.kbc.com).

This high penetration of the financial sector in ECE has had several consequences with regard to corporate governance issues. As the Committee on the Global Financial System of the BIS concluded the different host countries were pushed into distinct directions because of the diverse policy standards of the parent banks.

> Subsidiaries of foreign banks had to follow local and foreign regulations, but for business decisions the strictest rule prevailed. A host country with parent banks from different countries could end up being subject to different rules, e.g. different capital charges for the same operation. The result was an uneven playing field and a loss of liquidity in domestic markets.
>
> (Committee on the Global Financial System 2005: 7).

Altogether this implies that ECE banks had to incorporate corporate governance structures that went beyond the legal legislation in their countries. The spread of foreign practices is one of the converging tendencies with regard to corporate governance practices in ECE. This trend is further strengthened by the long-term commitments to ECE of second-tier banks from the Rhenish economies. This long-term commitment results in more day-to-day attempts to influence political issues. Müller (1998, 2001) for instance concludes that foreign banks in the region were among the most virulent advocates of the privatization of pension systems; they obviously expect to profit from participating in such private pension systems.

Now that this section has established the presence of foreign interests in the corporate world in ECE, particularly through the strong domination of foreign banks in the key financial sector, all elements are in place to allow us to take an in-depth look at the precise ways in which corporate governance has come to be regulated in the region, and what direct and indirect roles transnational actors have played in this process.

The transnational nature of the emerging corporate governance landscape in East Central Europe

How do the developments discussed in the previous section relate to developments in the field of corporate governance regulation? In this section we will turn to the increasing transnationalization of this policy field based upon an analysis of the most important corporate governance documents in the five countries under investigation and a set of interviews held with (predominantly Polish) corporate governance practitioners and experts.[7] Poland was one of the first countries in the region in which corporate governance issues made it onto the policy agenda and is often referred as a country that had dealt 'well' with this issue. At the same time, similar trajectories are observable in the other three Visegrad countries. The picture that emerges is one of significant influence by both public and private international actors on corporate governance regulation and practices and a convergence to a corporate governance model that is distinct from both the Anglo-Saxon and the Continental corporate governance model.

Foreign corporations have played a determinative role in the discussion on which corporate governance mechanisms were 'the best solution' for ECE. A substantial number of corporate governance practices have been brought into the region by foreign corporations that adhered to corporate governance rules in the US and EU member states and applied these rules to their local subsidiaries as well. Some of these developments also occur in Western Europe, where the Sarbanes-Oxley Act has impacted on the corporate governance structures of European firms that operate in the US. However, the scope and depth of these practices in ECE is far wider and deeper. Many of the investors in the region have their headquarters elsewhere and are listed in New York, London or Frankfurt, which means that they have to comply not only with the standards of the ECE region but also with those in their home countries. So while many of the foreign subsidiaries also have to comply with local regulations, their corporate governance is by no means purely a 'local business'. The introduction of international standards is not restricted to the subsidiaries of foreign firms, but through a process of socialization and best practices, domestic enterprises that are not directly under foreign control are also moving towards the models presented in the foreign-owned corporations. Igor Tham's account on the impact of foreign investment on corporate governance is an instructive illustration of many of these developments and helps us to assess the impact of these developments in the field of corporate governance. Tham, CEO of Citibank Slovakia, has argued that many changes in corporate governance practices are due to foreign pressures. Foreign corporations that entered Slovakia have introduced corporate governance principles for their subsidiaries and subsequently their practices and standards changed the attitude of the Slovakian corporations (*The Slovak Spectator* 17 September 2005). This picture is strengthened by the results of the interviews we have conducted. Senior accountants for instance change company quite regularly and introduce corporate governance codes and practices to the new companies they work for. Managers move back and forth from subsidiaries of transnational corporations to firms that do not have such links introducing what they learned in one company to the other. As subsidiaries of transnational corporations have more explicit and stricter rules with regard to corporate governance issues than 'national' firms, the spread of ideas and practices almost automatically runs from the first to the second, as one of our interviewees told us.[8]

The orientation towards international standards is further strengthened by the fact that several transnational organizations train young managers and policy makers within the region. The Centre for International Private Enterprise, one of the institutes of the American National Endowment for Democracy for instance, has set up several programmes in the region that are aimed at training leading policy makers and managers that are in the need of 'good' corporate governance. These programmes transform the orientation of leading managers and politicians towards Western codes and practices.

However, not only private organizations influence the corporate governance debates through the socialization of domestic groups; transnational public actors also impact upon them. Their influence is predominantly focussed on the formal corporate governance *regulation* and the practices of public officials. Both the OECD through its *Principles of Corporate Governance* (1999) and the European Commission in its *Modernising Company Law and Enhancing Corporate Governance in the European Union – A plan to move forward* (2003a) have introduced rules and guidelines for good corporate governance regulation. Whereas the OECD Principles are not specifically aimed at countries in economic transformation, the European Commission document directly refers to the ECE countries and declares that adherence to it will promote a 'rapid transition' to 'fully competitive modern market economies' (European Commission 2003c).

The EU has also shaped and continues to shape the ECE corporate governance landscape through informal relations with ECE officials. In the build-up to EU membership the European Commission intensively used the process of 'twinning' to socialize public officials in ECE in the 'right' practices (Vliegenthart and Horn 2005; also see Pellerin and Overbeek 2001: 148). Moreover, the European Commission has made use of a variety of mechanisms in its accession strategy, ranging from gate-keeping, benchmarking/monitoring, provision of legislative and institutional templates, technical and financial assistance to policy advice and twinning (Grabbe 2001: 1017). The criteria laid out in the *acquis* furthermore limited the policy range for the governments in the region, 'crowding out alternative pathways and domestic obstacles' (Schimmelfennig and Sedelmeier 2004: 671). This can be observed in particular in the highly complex area of financial market and corporate governance regulation. In the Czech case, Brenneman even goes so far as to argue that there is something of a standard procedure in which the 'Commission points out a problem with securities regulation in its annual report and Czech officials subsequently adopt measures designed to address that same problem' (Brenneman 2004: 52–3).

This process of the transmission of corporate governance rules and practices is highly facilitated by the reputation foreign advice has in ECE. 'A strong element in debates about economic models, in particular, is the idea that comparing Western countries' experiences could help CEE to emulate 'best practices' in areas like corporate governance' (Grabbe 2003: 248). This explains the relatively smooth introduction of foreign practices in the different national contexts. The transnational nature of the spread of corporate governance rules and practices is not only reflected in the high involvement of foreign actors in the region but equally in the greedy acceptance of their advice by local managers and policy makers. Corporate governance issues are relatively new in the region and corporate governance advice is in great demand as different scandals raised the political awareness for the issue. The high esteem for Western knowledge and advice has not changed since the corporate governance scandals that have haunted American and European firms in the early 2000s.

Many of these developments can be illustrated by the way in which ECE states drew up their corporate governance codes. These codes are an addition to the basic rules that are laid down in company laws and are considered an effective tool for bringing corporate governance practices in line with the spirit of the regulation. During the early 2000s all ECE applicant states have drawn up such codes, inspired by developments in western European countries and the US. All have done so with considerable help of transnational agents. The 2002 Polish *Corporate Governance Code for Polish Listed Firms* was drawn up with the financial support of the American Center for International Private Enterprise, the German Adenauer Stiftung, an organization closely related to the Christian-Democratic party and with expert input from ABN-AMRO Asset Management Poland and Allianz Poland Universal Pension Fund Society (Polski Forum Corporate Governance 2002). The latter two were explicitly asked for their input. The code fully followed the OECD Principles of Corporate Governance benchmarks. The Czech 2004 Corporate Governance Code, too, followed OECD principles and also referred to the aforementioned European Commission document (Czech Securities Commission 2004: 1–3). In Hungary, Ernst & Young Advisory Ltd largely drew up the Hungarian 2004 Corporate Governance Recommendations (Budapest Stock Exchange 2004: 1–2).

What kind of results did these developments have in the actual corporate governance landscape that is emerging? What kind of content is being transmitted through the involvement of transnational actors? The primary concern of many transnational actors is the observance of property rights and more in particular minority rights. Due to the experiences in the early years of economic transformation where illegal activities were widespread and many (minority) shareholders were victims of deliberate misconduct by managers or majority shareholders, many transnational investors became very wary for the safety of their investments. The safeguarding of private property has been an ongoing process since the start of the 1990s. It has been at the heart of the privatization process, which was all about creating private property and in this respect corporate governance is essentially nothing more than its safeguarding.

Table 10.6 (below) sums up the most important elements of the different privatization projects. The Czech Republic opted for a process of voucher privatization in which state property was given to the population for free. The Hungarian government chose the option of selling the former state firms to foreign investors, whereas in the Polish and Slovak case privatization started only after a couple of years, Poland choosing the option of direct sales and Slovakia opting for MEBOs. In most cases, new agencies were established that were responsible for the implementation of the privatization plans. However, these agencies had different

Table 10.6 Mode, pace and institutional setting of the privatization process

	Main method of privatization	*Private share in GDP exceeds 60%*	*Responsible institutions*	*Initial results in ownership concentration*
Czech Republic	Voucher	1994	Ministry of Privatization and Finance	Highly Dispersed
Hungary	Direct Sales	1995	State Property Agency (minister without portfolio), Ministry of Finance	Highly Concentrated
Slovakia	MEBOs	1996	Ministry of Finance	Dispersed
Poland	Direct Sales	1995	Ministry of Privatization, Finance and Industry	Dispersed

Source: European Bank for Reconstruction and Development (1992–5) Transition Reports.

institutional rights, ranging from mere advisory institutions to organizations that had substantial degree of freedom to introduce their own measures. Furthermore, the outcomes of the privatization process varied substantially. The Czech Republic opted for the most radical implementation of the privatization plans, leading to a sharp increase in the private share in GDP. Moreover, the voucher program that distributed the former state property over large parts of society led to highly dispersed ownership. In the case of Hungary, which faced a big public deficit problem, the choice for direct sales, most notably to foreign corporations, was encouraged by the need to generate income to overcome the national deficit. As a result ownership became rather concentrated in foreign hands. In Slovakia and Poland the initial plans ran out of steam in the implementation phase. As a result, the future of many state enterprises remained somewhat obscure during the first years. In terms of ownership concentration two cases hold the middle ground between the highly concentrated Hungarian situation and the widely dispersed Czech state of affairs. At the same time Poland and Slovakia were more prudent towards foreign investments.]

After the privatization process created private property proper, the need to provide legal protection of property rights came to dominate the corporate governance debates in ECE, rather than the issue of institutional structure dominating the debate in the more advanced capitalist countries. Asked for the most important corporate governance debates in Poland, one of our respondents answered quite instructively: 'Formal distinctions between a one-tier and a two-tier system do not really matter here. Corporate governance in Poland is far more about basic notions of rule of law [...] We have to make sure basic investor rights are being respected'.[9] Most of the corporate governance regulation is focused on this issue and informal rules are predominantly aimed at socializing managers with the new rules of the capitalist game. In this respect another respondent referred to the Polish corporate governance code as 'the bible for minority shareholders'.

For transnational public actors securing the safety of (international) investments also seems to be on the top agenda. Although some ECE states, notably the Czech Republic, introduced a clause in their constitution giving foreign capital the same rights as domestic capital, these clauses did not provide enough institutional safeguard. They were breached on several occasions and foreign actors have repeatedly urged the need for better protection. Especially the EU has been very active in this field and did not stop praising foreign investments for their beneficial role in the restructuring of the ECE economies (Vliegenthart forthcoming).

Yet, this process of creating enough safeguards for foreign capital is nearing its completion. Overall, transnational influence has been successful in securing these basic rights. This is amongst others reflected in the inflow of foreign investments since the late 1990s. Based on these inflows we can conclude that transnational firms find ECE safe enough to invest their money.

If we now turn to other aspects of corporate governance, we observe that there is something like an ECE 'model' emerging, displaying some specific characteristics (see also Andreff in the closing section of his contribution to this book). In its formal design this system resembles the so-called Rhineland model with its two-tier boards, low market capitalization and insider control (see Table 10.7 (below)).

With regard to other important formal corporate governance features, too, the ECE countries look rather similar. This is not too surprising given the strong influence of German and, to a lesser extent, Austrian interests since the mid-nineteenth century. The formal resemblance to the Rhineland model is however in reality only superficial. Both because of foreign influence as well as through the way in which the formal institutions are informally interpreted, the functioning of the corporate governance system is fundamentally different from the practices in the Rhenish economies. The system functions primarily to the benefit of transnational capital. Take for instance labour representation in the Board of Supervisors. Although this is formally regulated in almost all ECE countries, the practice is that 'many view board-level representation as nothing more than an opportunity to provide local union leaders and work councillors with extra income' (Kanizslai 2005: 14). Moreover organized labour was not represented in any of the commissions drawing up corporate governance codes in the region. In this respect regulation does not lead to real corporatist practices as one might be tempted to conclude but rather to an 'illusionary corporatism' (Ost 2000), or to the creation of a true labour aristocracy in the old Leninist sense of the word.

The weak position of organized labour is the result of developments at various levels that in this respect mutually strengthen each other. On the one hand it is to be explained by the position of the ECE economies in the global economy. ECE countries specialize in labour-intensive export industries, such as cars, clothing and chemicals. In this respect, the importance of the comparative advantage of low labour costs and the threat of company relocation further eastward hindered a strong labour movement that could negotiate the same kind of deals that its counterparts in Western Europe could after the Second World War (Bohle and Greskovits 2004). At the same time the development of strong trade unions is

Table 10.7 Main corporate governance features in ECE

	ECE	Czech Republic	Poland	Hungary	Slovakia
Ownership	Concentrated	Initially dispersed, now concentrating	Initially dispersed, now concentrating	Concentrated	Initially dispersed, now concentrating
Control	Insider	Insider	Insider	Insider	Insider
Dominance of 1 or 2 tier system	Two tier	Two tier	Two tier	Two tier	Two tier
Primary source of funding investments	FDI	FDI	FDI	FDI	FDI
Representation of employees	Hardly	Hardly	Hardly	Hardly	Hardly
Market capitalization as % of GDP (2003)	Low	16.5	17.2	18.7	3.5

Source: National Bank of Hungary (2006); expanded by us (AV/HO).

further hindered by their bad reputation in the domestic discourse, where they are seen as a residue of the socialist era with all kinds of bad connotations.

To sum up, increasing attractiveness for foreign investors has been at the heart of many policy initiatives in the region. Well-known examples are for instance the introduction of the flat tax in many new EU member states and other tax relieves and benefits for foreign investors (for an interesting case study on this topic see Drahokoupil 2004). In the field of corporate governance, increasing the confidence of foreign investors has been one of the driving forces behind corporate governance initiatives. Levelling the playing field for domestic and foreign investors alike, safeguarding shareholder rights and monitoring the observance of contracts have been the most prominent issues in this respect. Given the rising levels of foreign investment and the more or less long-term commitment of foreign banks to the region, we can conclude that important foreign actors find the region safe enough to invest in. In its institutional structure the different countries look remarkably similar. In all countries FDI plays a crucial role. The other characteristics of the corporate governance systems are also strikingly similar. Given the initial divergence of practices, especially in the early days of privatization, this gradual convergence represents a striking development in ECE.

Conclusion

In this chapter the leading puzzle was posed by the observation that initially, following the collapse of the Communist regimes in ECE, countries in the region followed very diverse (and diverging) pathways to the establishment of a market economy. This divergence is widely recognized in the literature, and usually ascribed, in the best traditions of historical and sociological institutionalism, to the diverse experiences under Communism and the reinforcing impact of variegated privatization strategies. However, a closer look 15 years later shows that, surprisingly, corporate governance structures in the region are converging or at least moving in similar directions and are increasingly displaying quite similar characteristics. Briefly put, our question was how to explain the emergence of this more recent common trajectory of corporate governance structures in the region.

First, our analysis in this chapter has confirmed that indeed the models of corporate governance that we find in the countries in ECE have moved in a similar direction. This emerging model is characterized by increasingly concentrated ownership, insider control, the dominance of a two-tier board structure, a dependence on foreign sources of finance, by a low degree of market capitalization, and finally by the (near) absence of substantial employee representation (formally labour is indeed represented). This model shares some of its characteristics with the prototypical Rhineland model (concentrated ownership and insider control, a two-tier board, and low market capitalization rates) while it also displays some key characteristics of the Anglo-Saxon liberal model (in particular the absence of employee representation). This specific hybrid model is completed by the very distinctive dominance of foreign sources of finance, a characteristic neither found in the Rhineland model nor in the Anglo-Saxon model. We may thus rightfully speak of a distinct Central European corporate governance model, which cannot be reduced to either of the two varieties more commonly recognized, but instead represents a truly distinct third 'model'.

In this chapter we have argued that this development is to be explained by the transnational nature of the transition process and the role of transnational actors. First, the transition process took place at a particular 'moment' in world system time: it took place at a time of fundamental restructuring of the capitalist world economy, with capital looking desperately for opportunities to raise its profit rates. Historically, the incorporation of 'new' (or previously external) regions has always provided capital with such opportunities. Concretely in the 1980s, the opening of the socialist planned economies provided capital with undreamed opportunities to appropriate productive capacity at extremely low prices, enabling an immediate contribution to improved profitability. This accumulation by dispossession (the term we borrowed from David Harvey) instilled in ECE an externally dependent mode of production. Foreign capital plays a determining role in Central European capitalism. However, we found that the simplistic idea that this predominance is reflected in the statistics on FDI does not hold without qualification. FDI is very important, but the role of foreign capital in GDP and in capital formation is on average no higher in ECE than in the rest of the EU. There does appear, until now at least, to be one respect in which ECE differs from the EU-15: capital inflows are not balanced by capital outflows of a comparable magnitude. And, more importantly, we found that the financial sector in ECE is heavily dominated by foreign banks, to a degree that is comparable to or even exceeds that in Third World countries. Given the centrality of the financial sector in any market economy (with its role in the allocation of investment throughout the economy), the predominance of foreign banks is a very strong indicator for the dependent nature of the ECE economies.

This external domination also partly explains the mechanisms of transference of external standards and practices of corporate governance. As we have shown, these external standards are introduced and disseminated by the operation of foreign firms directly (in their subsidiaries in ECE), but also by the activities of accountants and other (financial) service coordination firms (see also the contribution by Nölke and Perry to this book), and by the local managers that receive their training in subsidiaries of foreign firms or in foreign-dominated local firms. In addition, we have found that a key role was (and continues to be) played by such transnational actors as the European Commission and the OECD Secretariat, which both play key roles in drafting model corporate governance legislation and in socializing public officials in ECE in the *mores* of proper corporate governance practices. The focus in terms of the content of regulation and standard setting has clearly been on strengthening the institutional embedding of the rule of law and the sanctity of private property.

The resulting class structure in ECE, structured by the external domination of the economy through the financial sector and by the prominent role of transnational actors in shaping the regulatory standards, has strong parallels with that of 1960s Latin America, giving the concept of *comprador bourgeoisie* a new lease of life.

Notes

1   The analysis is mostly limited to a small set of countries in Central and Eastern Europe, namely the former Visegrad group (Hungary, Slovakia, Czech Republic and Poland). Occasionally we will also make reference to Slovenia which also made quick progress in introducing market reforms after 1991 (Estrin 2001: 17) and to the three Baltic states which rapidly caught up with the Visegrad countries in the course of the EU accession process.

2   This is precisely what Otto Holman has in mind when he applies the notion of 'system time' (borrowed from Anthony Giddens) to differentiate the Central European transition from the earlier transitions in Southern Europe (see Holman 2004). In terms of the prevailing conjuncture in the world economy, the international context (Cold War versus post-Cold War) and the stage of development of European integration itself, the situation of the mid-1990s was fundamentally different from that of the late 1970s and early 1980s.

3   The concept of original accumulation is similar, the reader has no doubt noticed, to that of 'commodification': as a matter of fact Harvey uses the word commodification descriptively to explain what original accumulation is about. The distinction is one of relative emphasis. Where commodification is used as a theoretical concept leaning on Polanyi in particular, as in several other contributions to this book (see van Apeldoorn and Horn in particular, as well as the introductory and concluding chapters), commodification refers primarily to the sphere of circulation: production of goods and services for sale on the market. The concept of original accumulation encompasses this aspect, but puts emphasis on the relations of production under which fruits of human labour are turned into commodities, thus making the reference historically more specific and more directly political at the same time.

4   References to a *comprador* class or *comprador elite* emerge occasionally in the literature on Central Europe (Drahokoupil 2005: 23, Shields 2002: 14, Holman 2004: 223) but not in a very systematic fashion.

5   And does dependence on foreign capital necessarily spell disaster? This question cannot be pursued in the context of this chapter, which focuses on the nature of corporate governance regulation in the region. It is necessary however to point out that dependence on foreign capital *per se* does not imply a negative assessment, as the Irish case may illustrate.

6   Further analysis would be needed to substantiate this, both of the type of investment (for the internal market or for export, manufacturing or services, assembly or production, etc.) and of the ratio of reinvestment of earnings as well as of the direction of outward flows. In general terms, such further analysis is however beyond the scope of this chapter. However, see the recent work by Dorothee Bohle in this area (Bohle 2006; Bohle and Greskovits 2006).

7   Interviews conducted in Warsaw in June 2006 with:
    - Anna Stepien, Finance and Operations Director of CVO Group Poland
    - Raimondo Eggink, former Chief Executive Officer, ABN AMRO Asset Management Poland
    - Tomasz Prusek, Correspondent on Corporate governance for the *Gazeta Wyborcza.*

8   Interview conducted in Warsaw in June 2006 with Anna Stepien, Finance and Operations Director of CVO Group Poland.

9   Interview conducted in Warsaw in June 2006 with Raimondo Eggink, former Chief Executive Officer, ABN AMRO Asset Management Poland.

Part IV
Conclusion

11 Marketization, transnationalization, commodification, and the shifts in corporate governance regulation

A conclusion

Andreas Nölke, Henk Overbeek and Bastiaan van Apeldoorn

The contributions to this book have explored the issue of corporate governance regulation in very different settings and from a wide variety of theoretical perspectives. These settings range from domestic policies via EU directives to global standards, while perspectives include, *inter alia*, regulation theory, the VoC approach and the neo-Gramscian perspective. This diversity notwithstanding, the studies presented in this book also share a common focus and a number of common concerns that run across the volume.

At the most general level, what unites these diverse contributions, and what also most clearly differentiates this book from the myriad of other studies in the field of corporate governance, is not only that they take the *regulation* of corporate governance as the main explanandum, but also that in explaining the changing regulatory framework they focus on the *politics* of these changes, that is, on the political processes and struggles shaping these policy outcomes. This is an important point because (as has been indicated in the introductory chapter) most literature that seeks to give an account of the transformation of corporate governance regulation tends to reduce the causality to such exogenous variables as the convergence pressures of globalization. The problem with such an account is that globalization is reduced to an apolitical market selection mechanism, whereas we see globalization as a politically constituted process. Furthermore, the way 'objective' pressures (to the extent that they exist) of globalization or other market forces 'translate' into regulatory change (or not) is also very much mediated by politics, that is, it requires an explanation beyond any deterministic account. We thus stress the political nature of changing corporate governance regulation and in that respect also the contingency of some of the changes. There have been and there are still alternatives to the policies actually adopted. To the extent that there might be any convergence on any particular model, there is no necessity involved here. We therefore need an account of how one option came to prevail politically over others.

A second general focal point of the preceding chapters (and what has been a major rationale of this project from the start) is the *multi-level* nature of the observed transformations in corporate governance regulation and the *transnational* dimension of the underlying political processes. The chapters have examined the politics of changing corporate governance regulation in multiple and interrelated arenas, from the national to the transatlantic and the global, with several contributions focusing on the EU arena as situated in between these two. Although most chapters individually focus on a specific level, together they provide a rather comprehensive picture of this multi-level regulation. Again, this is a major departure from a literature that overwhelmingly deals with corporate governance *practice* on the national level, or, where it studies corporate governance *regulation*, does not go beyond a cross-national perspective. The point of departure for this book has been that even though the question of convergence versus continued divergence is far from settled, there seem to be a number of similar changes going on in the regulation of corporate governance in these diverse arenas. This commonality across national boundaries and across different levels of governance in itself theoretically underlines the need for a transnational perspective to explain these 'systemic' similarities where a purely cross-national comparative perspective might only describe and explain the (persistent) differences. Indeed, several of the contributions have employed this perspective to focus on the *transnational* politics of corporate governance regulation, that is on the importance of transnational actors, embedded in transnational structures, in shaping the political processes that have led to regulatory change at multiple levels of governance.

Beyond these general commonalities we may distinguish a number of other common themes that are shared by several contributions – albeit in varying combinations. In order to discuss those, however, we go back to our three original leading questions (see the introductory chapter), and take stock of the answers that have been produced by the studies presented in this book. We thus first discuss the changing content and mode of corporate governance regulation before tackling the question of what may explain these changes. With regard to both content and mode we conclude that changes here are characterized by common trend towards marketization by which we mean 'a process of bringing about the institutional (regulatory) preconditions for markets to arise and develop, thus extending the market mechanism to areas of social life hitherto not subject to market forces' (Van Apeldoorn and Horn forthcoming). This we can observe with respect to the content of corporate governance regulation to the extent that it promotes a more market-based corporate governance regime. At the same time, however, the mode of corporate governance regulations also is affected by a trend of marketization in the sense that increasingly market-based forms of regulation are being employed. Here, an enhanced role for market actors, then, is already inherent in the mode of regulation. Of course, form and content are linked here, and we argue that both reflect a trend of deepening commodification.

The changing *content* of corporate governance regulation: remaining institutional diversity but a common trajectory towards marketization

Our first question was: *what* is the *content* of the changes taking place in corporate governance regulation in different arenas (global, EU, CEEC), and do these changes reveal convergence on a particular model or rather a continuing or increased institutional diversity?

As was indicated in the introductory chapter, the different contributions to this book describe and interpret the observed changes in the regulatory framework in which corporate governance is embedded in diverse ways, employing both familiar and less familiar analytical dichotomies (such as owner versus managerial control, dispersed versus concentrated ownership, etc.). Of these typologies, the VoC approach seems to be the most widely used to address the issue of divergence and convergence within current changes in the regulation of corporate governance. With the exception of Dewing and Russell, all authors refer to the popular comparison of Anglo-Saxon versus Rhenish capitalism. This does not necessarily mean that this dichotomy is the 'end of history' in terms of conceptualizing divergence and convergence in corporate governance regulation. In fact, this book also highlights a number of conceptual weaknesses of the VoC approach, most prominently its inability to account for changes that range across the broad variety of capitalisms. Some more specific problems are highlighted by individual contributions. Given the complexity of the VoC models they are difficult to quantify for large-scale statistical analysis. Therefore, Gourevitch uses a 'Minority Shareholder Protections Index' as a rather broad proxy for the question of diversity in corporate governance regulation. Furthermore, the VoC approach tends to downplay differences within the two broad 'families' of capitalism, as indicated by Dewing and Russell's discussion of the issue of a possible convergence *within* the Anglo-Saxon family, that is, between a rules-based emphasis in US accounting standards and a principles-based one in the UK. Finally, there are some limitations to apply the Anglo-Saxon and Rhenish models outside Western Europe and the US. Thus the introduction of a new corporate governance regime as part and parcel of the transformation of the socialist command economies into capitalist market economies appears to be producing (as both contributions in Part IV agree) convergence on a specifically 'Central European' model of corporate governance regulation, which does bear some resemblances both to the Anglo-Saxon and to the Rhenish model without however being reducible to either one, or without even representing a 'mix' of elements from both (see also Nölke and Vliegenthart 2006). Rather, it appears as if the articulation of similar historical legacies and domestic path dependencies on the one hand and similar external pressures and transnational forces on the other are leading to the emergence of a Central European model, which may (it is perhaps too early to pass a definitive judgement) result in a relatively stable form characterised by its own distinct set of institutional complementarities giving the Central European model at least some (medium range) viability.

How do we finally formulate our answer to the question of convergence or divergence in corporate governance regulation? The question is most explicitly introduced in the first part of the book, with Gourevitch and Jessop addressing the issue from different angles. Gourevitch started his chapter with an overview of the degree of share ownership concentration in 39 developed and emerging market economies. His data show an enormous variety – from 4 per cent concentration in Japan to 90 per cent in Chile. The use of the term 'divergence' for this form of variation would possibly give the wrong impression, given that the data illustrate synchronic variation (that is, *diversity*) rather than (necessarily) a movement in opposite directions over time. For the latter, we would need longitudinal data. The term *convergence* can create similar confusion depending on whether it implies (as it often does) convergence towards a pre-defined end point (for instance a 'convergence' towards the Anglo-Saxon model of corporate governance) or whether it simply implies a movement closer together over time.

Whereas the notion of co-existing varieties of capitalism (continued diversity) is discussed sympathetically by Gourevitch, with Jessop, Andreff as well as Vliegenthart and Overbeek also sharing some of his findings, other contributions rather highlight ongoing processes of convergence towards the Anglo-Saxon model with its much stronger degree of market mechanisms within corporate governance regulation. Thus the contributions by Wigger as well as by Nölke and Perry demonstrate that current changes in corporate governance regulation threaten to undermine typical features of the Rhenish variety. Similarly, the chapters by Rebérioux as well as by Van Apeldoorn and Horn argue that we can observe the increasing importance of a capital market-driven model of corporate governance throughout the variety of capitalisms, thereby arguably indicating a convergence on a form of regulation that is close to the Anglo-Saxon model.

However, we find the dichotomy between these two positions (continuing divergence or convergence) less than satisfactory. The recognition that globalising tendencies do not wipe out all variation between national formations does not logically imply that *divergence* is necessarily the dominant tendency. Colin Hay has provided a useful way of overcoming this problem by developing the notion of '*common trajectories*' (Hay 2004: 235–42). As we can read from Figure 11.1, two lines (in our case representing the direction of development over time in corporate governance models) may converge by moving closer towards each other from different directions (scenario 1) or diverge by going off in opposite directions (scenario 4). However, they may also converge (scenario 3) or diverge (scenario 2) while both moving in the same direction (or having a similar *slope*).

When we apply Hay's notion of common trajectories to corporate governance regulation, we may observe that both Anglo-Saxon and Rhineland regimes exhibit a process of extending the operation of markets, but in different measure. Thus, we find considerable diversity, and this diversity may persist for the foreseeable future. Still, a first central conclusion we draw from this book is that across all remaining diversity the content of corporate governance regulation is increasingly defined by the common trajectory of strengthening market principles. In this common trend of marketization, regulation increasingly promotes the free play

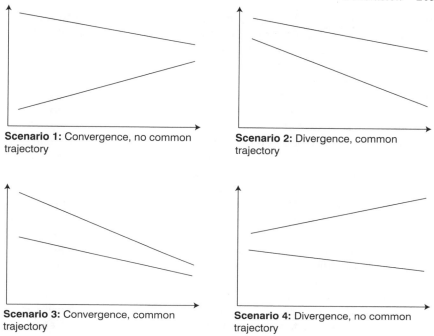

Scenario 1: Convergence, no common trajectory

Scenario 2: Divergence, common trajectory

Scenario 3: Convergence, common trajectory

Scenario 4: Divergence, no common trajectory

Figure 11.1 Convergence, divergence and common trajectories

of market forces, thus increasingly letting market actors, operating through the market mechanism, shape how and to which purpose a corporation is run. Examples of continued variation may be found in Gourevitch's chapter when he recounts the great variation in patterns of shareholding and minority shareholding protections among market economies, even among countries generally considered to be in the same category. Andreff in his chapter very clearly shows that the development of corporate governance patterns in post-socialist economies over the past decade and a half has produced great and continuing variation, especially between Central European states on the one hand and CIS states on the other.

At the same time, however, recent regulatory reforms all favour a more market-based model of corporate governance, as indicated by the chapters by Van Apeldoorn and Horn, Wigger as well as Nölke and Perry. Although the degree of ownership concentration continues to vary widely across the capitalist world (see the chapter by Gourevitch), there are strong indications that at least in the OECD area there is a trend (in part enabled through regulatory change) towards a model of outsider or market-based control (compare the contribution by Van Apeldoorn and Horn to this book).

A further important common denominator for many recent changes towards a marketization of corporate governance regulation discussed in this book is the legislation of the EU. This is obviously true for those countries within the Single Market since its inception as well as for those developed market economies that joined in 1995 (together the EU-15). It is also true, albeit in modified form, for those countries that joined the EU in the Big Bang enlargement of 2004. It may be noted that in ECE other aspects than the introduction and consolidation of an advanced system of corporate governance regulation have been the main concern in the first years of transition: establishing the conditions for security of private property, the dispossession of state-owned or collective assets via various privatization schemes and the creation of institutions necessary for the functioning of such market economies, which have until now dominated the scene (see the contribution by Andreff in particular). Full EU membership with all the implications of being part of the Internal Market will gradually assure that trends already prominent in the EU-15 will also come to dominate the corporate governance landscape in the new Member States.

But the influence of EU legislation in this field extends beyond the borders of the (old and new) Member States. EU legislation also deeply influences the regulation of corporate governance in those European countries that either aspire to full membership and as such are subject to what in Euro-speak is known as the *accession process* (Turkey, Albania and several of the independent states emerging from the dissolution of the Yugoslav Federation), or that have undertaken most of the obligations of the Internal Market by acceding to the European Economic Area (Iceland, Norway, Switzerland and a small band of micro states). Finally, there are those states that entertain the ambition of one day qualifying as a candidate member state even though that status is at the moment far beyond the limits of the possible (think of Ukraine and Georgia for instance). These instances of the (undeniably strong) influence of EU legislation however have fallen outside the scope of this volume and can only be mentioned here for the sake of completeness in a speculative fashion.

Finally, the US is of course even less affected directly by changes in the content of EU corporate governance regulation. Still, even those of our contributions that deal with the US also highlight prominent features of the common trajectory identified above. Thus Rebérioux demonstrates that the recent development towards the 'shareholder primacy' doctrine within corporate governance regulation is common to both the EU and the US. Similarly, the recent developments in international accounting standards on both sides of the Atlantic share a common direction towards market mechanisms, as far as the substance of regulation is concerned. As Nölke and Perry have shown, both IASB and US GAAP standards have increasingly moved from historic cost to fair value accounting, with the latter valuing assets at current market prices or at simulated market prices. Furthermore, both IFRS and US GAAP are primarily geared to the perspective of financial investors, in contrast to the much broader orientation of earlier norms in continental Europe (see the contribution by Rebérioux). The remaining issue of convergence between rule-based and principles-based standards, finally, concerns a less substantial feature of accounting standards and, as demonstrated by Dewing and Russell, is likely to be resolved within the next few years.

The changing *mode* of corporate governance regulation: towards marketization and transnationalization

Our second question was: *How*, or through what *modes* of regulation, and at which *levels* of governance, do these changes take place? Are there significant *shifts in governance:* from public to private and from the national to the European or global levels? The main conclusion from our contributions is that not only the content of corporate governance regulation, but also the *mode* of regulation becomes more open to market principles. At the same time, transnational regulations increasingly replace domestic ones.

The trend towards more openness to market principles is reflected in the mode of corporate governance regulation in two ways, namely in the increasing importance of private corporate governance regulation and in the growing prominence of more market-based forms of public regulation. A good example of the tendency towards market-based public regulation is that of corporate governance regulation of the EU. As the chapter by Van Apeldoorn and Horn illustrated, the EU failed with its attempt at strong *regulatory harmonization*, partly because of opposition by various Member States. As an alternative strategy (which may also be termed 'negative harmonization') the EU now seeks to introduce a looser framework allowing market forces to encourage the Member States to bring their regulation more in line, that is through *regulatory competition*.

The archetypical case of a shift from public to private corporate governance regulation is to be found in the International Accounting Standards as developed by the IASB (see the contributions by Dewing and Russell as well as by Nölke and Perry). Although we have to add that this shift affects some countries more than others (a number of countries had already private bodies for accounting standard-setting before the empowerment of the IASB, whereas others regulated accounting standards by parliament) and we also have to note that this is not complete privatisation (given the need for formal adoption of each standard by the EU), this still represents a major shift in the mode of governance. The substantial implications of this shift become most obvious if we look at how this private norm development undermines the Rhenish variety of capitalism. Similarly, in the field of banking regulation, the increasing prominence of private rating agencies considerably enhances the pressures on the Rhenish model (see the contribution by Nölke and Perry). The privatization of corporate governance regulation, however, does not stop with rule development. It also comprises later stages of the policy cycle. The role of rating agencies in the implementation of banking supervision, and even more so the growing role of law firms in the enforcement of EU competition policy (see the contribution by Wigger), are cases in point. Private sector actors provide their contribution to corporate governance regulation either on a for-profit basis (rating, law firms in competition policy) or cooperate very closely with private business (accounting standard setters).

But the shift in the mode of governance that we have observed is not only limited to the growing importance of private actors and market mechanisms, it also involves an element of transnationalization. Thus, domestic public regulation gets replaced by transnational private regulation, as in the case of accounting standards where IAS replaces the norms of the German 'Handelsgesetzbuch' in the context of new EU regulations. Even the US is contemplating a possible shift away from its entrenched national regulation towards the adoption of global rules (see the contribution by Dewing and Russell). In general, however, the EU appears to us to be the core arena where the transnationalization of corporate governance regulation is played out. Here, traditional public regulations that served to protect domestic production models are being adapted to EU-wide market-making directives and other EU regulatory policies. This may not only be observed in the case of accounting, but also for the regulation of corporate control broadly defined (Van Apeldoorn and Horn), as well as for competition policy (Wigger), although with regard to the latter, recent reforms of enforcement regulations are implicated within a complex interplay of centralization and decentralization between EU and domestic levels. In Central and Eastern Europe, as Part IV has made clear, corporate governance regulation has emerged as the result of an intense articulation of national, European and global levels of regulation. Obviously, in terms of positive regulation the existing regime is a mix of national and EU regulations. Vliegenthart and Overbeek perhaps emphasize most strongly the role of the EU level in the generation of corporate governance regulation in ECE. Andreff, on the other hand, has focused in detail on the national specificities of the different post-socialist economies, although also recognising increasing convergence within ECE. At least in the new member states of the EU, but elsewhere too, 'national' regulation is itself based on model regulation produced and propagated by such international organizations as the IMF and particularly the OECD (see Vliegenthart and Overbeek). In sum, Part IV clearly illustrates the essentially transnational and multi-level nature of the process through which the corporate governance regulatory framework in the former socialist states, especially those within the orbit of the EU, has been evolving.

Linking mode and content: deepening commodification and the de-politicization of corporate governance regulation

In a broader perspective, the marketization we observe with regard to both the changing content and changing mode of regulation may be seen as reflecting and promoting a deepening of the *commodification* of social life.

The simplest definition of commodification is 'turning something into a commodity', that is, into something for sale on the market. Commodity production is in itself a phenomenon of nearly all times and social formations, but *capitalism* is uniquely characterised by the *generalization* of commodity production. Commodification in a broader sense refers to a process or a tendency, not some fixed state of affairs, by which all spheres of human existence become increasingly subject to the commodity form. This means that an increasing number of goods and services, but also all other elements involved in production (and thus the material reproduction of social life) – such as, most critically, human labour, land or 'nature', but also knowledge (for example, intellectual property rights)

– become treated as commodities, that is, 'produced for sale' on the market (cf. Polanyi 1957; also Marx 1990).

Commodification and marketization are closely associated yet analytically distinct terms. They are closely associated inasmuch as allowing 'things' to be turned into commodities (that is, 'objects' to be transferable on a market) is one of the preconditions for capitalist markets. But as the latter phrase suggests, the existence of commodities in its turn implies the prior existence of a market. In this sense, in terms of structures that render these phenomena possible, markets and commodities are mutually constitutive. Yet we take marketization as the broader process of the social and political constitution of markets and the further extension of the market mechanism, as a result of which social relations (or production) are commodified.

In the current wave of globalization in particular (see below), spheres of human activity that were never before commodified are now increasingly subjected to the search for private profit. This trend even extends, as Van Apeldoorn and Horn have analysed in their chapter, to the capitalist firm itself. In contrast to the era in which the joint stock company became the dominant unit of capitalist production (that is in the first half of the twentieth century), in which shares in a company became commodities traded on the stock exchange as mere claims to future income streams generated by the firm, today increasingly control over the corporation as such has become a commodity. This entails a commodification of the social relations that make up the corporation: treating (control over) the corporation as a commodity (to be bought or sold on the stock market) means that these social relations, mediated by the price mechanism, increasingly come to appear as relations between things.[1] The value of a firm has become a mere exchange value, that is, determined by the laws of supply and demand in the market, and this exchange value (the share price, that is, the price tag attached to the corporation as a commodity) increasingly comes to regulate the relations between owners and management, between management and workers and between different groups of workers.

The deepening of commodification is not only generated by the marketization of corporate control and the concomitant discipline of the capital market, but (as is illustrated by the contributions to this book) extends to other aspects of changing corporate governance regulation as well. In the most general sense, the tendency towards a deepening of commodification is borne out in all those changes in corporate governance regulation and related areas (accounting standards, competition policy) that strengthen the role of market forces, enhance the global mobility of capital and extend the range of activities open to private business. Wigger provides a very telling illustration of this in her chapter: the accommodation of 'consumer interests' through what she calls the micro-economization of competition policy, and the replacement of public regulation by private litigation. Similarly, Dewing and Russell in their contribution quote the former Internal Market Commissioner Bolkestein on the move towards generally accepted international accounting standards 'which would dramatically improve the efficiency of global capital markets ...' (see p. 140). Ultimately, of course, the trend towards commodification also encompasses the internalization within the governance practices of corporations of market principles codified by new corporate governance codes, regulations, and laws and directives throughout the global economy.

The increasing commodification that we see as underlying many of the current changes in corporate governance regulation does not only relate to its *content*. To a certain extent, the *mode* of regulation too becomes more open to market principles. This trend is reflected in the mode of corporate governance regulation in two ways, namely in the increasing importance of private corporate governance regulation and in the growing prominence of more market-based forms of public regulation, as outlined above. This is most obvious in those cases where regulatory tasks de facto become outsourced to private business, as in the cases of the transnational law firms discussed in the contribution by Wigger, or of the privately financed and organized IASB as discussed by Dewing and Russell as well as by Nölke and Perry.

Finally, the changes in the content and mode of corporate governance regulation not only both follow the common trajectory of commodification, but are also causally interrelated. Political strategy is central to our argument here. The social forces that seek to open up the content of corporate governance regulation to market principles are not (yet) powerful enough to frontally assault the vestiges of established public regulation. Instead, they have gained ground through deliberately depoliticizing the regulation of core areas of corporate governance. By delegating a prominent regulatory function to some professions or expert groups, the eminent political implications become less obvious. Correspondingly, those social forces that are negatively affected by the content of regulation find it difficult to mobilize against this shift in corporate governance regulation, and in some cases may not even notice what is at stake (Dewing and Russell 2004: 300). It should not come as a surprise that attempts by the EU to introduce a more market-oriented content of corporate governance in the form of public regulations, such as the European Works Council Directive, the European Company Statute Directive and the Takeover Directive, have led to uneasy compromises, given the high visibility of these issues and the corresponding political controversy (Cernat 2004). In contrast, the more market-based modes of corporate governance regulation discussed in this book have helped to make a more market-based content of corporate governance regulation politically possible. Thus, the adoption of IASB standards allowed the harmonization of national accounting standards, which was formerly impossible. Similarly, the increased involvement of private actors in EU competition policy enforcement has made a major policy reform possible, in an issue area that is heavily contested. Finally, the involvement of a private high-level expert group has contributed to overcoming the deadlock on the Takeover Directive. While more explicit political attacks on the basic institutions of Rhenish capitalism are not (yet) feasible, the enhanced role of private actors and of market mechanisms in corporate governance regulation thus increases the chances for the erosion of these institutions – 'through the back door' (see also Wigger and Nölke 2005).

Explaining changing content and mode: the transnational politics of corporate governance regulation

The third and final question that has guided this book was: What explains both the changing content of corporate governance regulation and the changing form through which it takes place? How can we account for the fact that corporate governance regulation increasingly promotes the extension of the market mechanism, thus deepening commodification?

As Jessop as well as Van Apeldoorn and Horn have emphasised, but as equally transpires from the chapters on the introduction of corporate governance regimes in the post-socialist economies (Andreff, Vliegenthart and Overbeek), markets do not arise naturally or spontaneously but are in fact constructed socially and politically, that is, through regulation in the broad sense as defined in the introductory chapter. This does not take place without contestation – the political struggles and controversies around the EU's attempt to create a pan-European market for corporate control are a case in point. Hence, the creation of a market for corporate control can be interpreted, as Van Apeldoorn and Horn do, as a *political* project. But what kind of politics, what kind of political actors and political processes? And how is for instance the agency of these actors related to relevant structures within the global political economy? What ultimately explains certain policy outcomes? Although here our conclusions have to be tentative (in particular because more detailed and systematic research in this regard is still needed) the preceding chapters still provide a basis for a number of observations beyond our general emphasis on politics. As indicated in the introductory chapter, any comprehensive account of the changes in both the content and form of corporate governance regulation has to combine actors and structures, as well as domestic and transnational factors, beyond the close interrelationship between the market-driven content of corporate governance regulation and its market-oriented institutional underpinnings as documented above.

The confusion over the degree of convergence in corporate governance regulation has also been created by the gap between comparative and transnational approaches. Comparative research tends to concentrate on domestic politics and on the explanation of divergence, of the varied response to similar pressures, as demonstrated by the contribution by Gourevitch to this book. Thus, the VoC approach looks for answers in the differences in institutional structures and historical path-dependencies (*institutions matter*), other comparative politics approaches emphasize party or interest group politics (*politics matter*). Transnational approaches on the other hand ask what determines the commonness of the common trajectory, and what that implies for the relevance of the 'national' as the ultimate unit of analysis: if there are such strong commonalities across and beyond the boundaries of national economies, the factors explaining them must surely be *transnational* in nature. The majority of contributions to this book acknowledge the relevance of identifying common trajectories, and of transnational factors and pressures that explain why countries and national regulatory systems that exhibit diversity on many counts in fact have been moving (with different speed and intensity) in a similar direction, namely that of an extension of the scope and reach of 'the market' and of the discipline of capital in the general area of corporate governance, engendering deepening commodification.

The common trajectory of corporate governance regulation throughout the OECD world may be understood against the backdrop of what is commonly referred to as *globalization*, in particular the rise of global financial markets. Yet, these and other *structural changes* bound up with globalization, do not in and of themselves provide a sufficient explanation for regulatory change. In fact, as indicated before, the approach taken by this book has been very much to reject any such reductionist and deterministic accounts. Rather than taking globalization as something exogenously given, we should in fact see it as what Robert Cox (1981) called a *historical structure*, that is, as simultaneously shaping and being shaped by the agency of concrete social and political forces. Globalization is thus a product of social and political agency, which in turn is conditioned by it, but also capable of producing divergent responses in their strategic conduct. Thus, for some the contemporary wave of globalization is inextricably bound up with a neoliberal hegemonic interpretation of the general interest (for example, the contribution by Jessop to this book) with its indomitable belief in the market. From this perspective, such a *hegemonic project* is not a free-floating idea, but rests on a critical mass of concrete interests and actors, private and public, national and international, supranational and transnational.

Below we will, on the basis of the various contributions to this book, identify the social forces and key actors supporting (and opposing) the marketization project that is transforming corporate governance regulation in more detail – while keeping in mind that the agency of these social forces is also always shaped by the changing structural context in which these forces operate, in particular the context of globalization. In the context of neoliberal globalization we must also mention the importance of financialization in contemporary capitalism. As we have seen in the introductory chapter, financialization operates both at a macro level where it refers to the increasing importance of short-term fluctuations in financial markets for the strategic decisions of corporate actors as well as at a micro level where financialization increasingly influences the identity and consciousness of individuals (whether consumers, pensioners, mortgaged house owners, or corporate managers). Financialization thus functions to redefine the interests of major social constituencies involved in the politics of corporate governance regulation, such as, inter alia, managers, shareholders, labour and the liberal professions. In order to get a better grasp of these interests and their recent transformation, we will combine the question of the driving forces behind ongoing changes in corporate governance regulation with the question about who wins and loses from these reforms. Although the answer to the *cui bono* question is not always identical with the identification of the political supporters of a given reform, it still gives us some hints as to the interests involved.

Turning to the *actors* more specifically, let us first make an initial distinction between public and private actors. Although the former still constitute the primary group that actually makes the laws, directives, policies, etc. comprising the regulatory framework, all authors in this book recognise the importance of societal actors in the political process leading up to these policy decisions. Thus for Gourevitch the key actors are ultimately societal groups, forming different coalitions, made up of owners, managers and workers. Their struggles over political preferences (shaped by a given political institutional context) account for the corporate governance policies adopted. At the same time, we have to recognize the crucial role of the EU within recent reforms that stretch across countries, as indicated by all contributions in Parts II, III and IV as well as by Rebérioux's chapter. Since these policy decisions cannot be reduced to the 'national interests' of individual member states of the EU, we have to give considerable attention to the crucial role of the European Commission in this process; the same is true for other international organizations such as the OECD and the World Bank during the transition process in ECE.

One societal force, however, clearly appears to be at the centre of nearly all recent reforms of corporate governance regulations, that is, transnationally mobile capital, in particular global capital market actors. Recent corporate governance regulation changes are consistently meant to privilege the mobility of capital, and to privilege the interests of the owners of mobile capital (and their functionaries such as financial analysts, etc.) over the interests of those 'stakeholders' of the capitalist firm who are tied to some degree to the spatially fixed and localised concrete labour process. Thus, for instance, Van Apeldoorn and Horn identify transnationally mobile investors and other capital market actors, acting in part through seemingly apolitical expert groups, as key actors driving the marketization of European corporate control. Vliegenthart and Overbeek on the other hand stress the role of another section of transnational capital, namely big foreign (West-European) banks cornering the financial markets in Central Europe. Wigger points to the way transnationally mobile shareholders may benefit from the introduction of market-mechanisms in the EU competition control regime. Similar observations can be distilled from the contributions by Nölke and Perry, and by Dewing and Russell. All three cases of transnational private authority (accounting, auditing and rating) clearly favour the Anglo-Saxon, shareholder-driven way of governing corporations.

Returning to one of our key analytical dichotomies from the introductory chapter, commodification arguably implies a strengthening of owner control versus that of workers or other stakeholders. Of course, 'owners' do not form a homogenous category but must be broken down into different groups. The noted trend towards marketization and commodification must be seen as particularly strengthening the position of transnationally mobile shareholders, that is, individuals or institutional investors as owners of 'liquid capital' (Jackson 2001: 273), only caring about their shares as financial assets (indeed, viewing the whole corporation as such), and relying primarily on the power of exit in order to exercise control over management. This then boils down to what has been labelled the shareholder model (as opposed to network-based or co-ordinated stakeholder model), identified by Rebérioux in his chapter as bound up with a fundamental shift in global capitalism which results from ever more liquid capital markets and a concomitant rise of institutional investors within those markets. As a result, companies become engaged in a constant competition 'to attract collective savings', a competition in which they are solely 'judged on the basis of their ability to meet the financial demands imposed on them' (Rebérioux, in this book, p. 64).

Still, the contribution by Rebérioux also shows how in practice recent corporate governance reforms may not always empower shareholders in the sense of enhancing managerial accountability towards them. Van Apeldoorn and Horn indicate that even if the overall thrust of EU corporate governance regulation is clearly one of marketization, the market-liberal content of the key EU Takeover Directive, which was intended as a major step towards the completion of a European market for corporate control, in the end has been watered down. Even more strongly, Gourevitch warns us that changing corporate governance regulations may not necessarily mean changing corporate governance practice, the more so where regulations have a private, voluntary character. Thus transnationally mobile capital may in the end benefit less from recent reforms, also indicated by the general rhetoric that is strongly geared to investor needs. He also points out that not all financial institutions share the same narrow focus on shareholder value activism – while some public employee and union based funds are also committed to social considerations, major investment banks might profit more from consulting contracts awarded by management. Finally, changing corporate governance regimes in ECE cannot be seen in terms of strengthening (through the market) the control of (minority) shareholders (see in particular the contribution by Andreff). Still, the commodification that is promoted in other respects as a result of the transformation in the overall regulatory framework in which corporate governance is embedded nevertheless does benefit some more than others. The winners here appear to be foreign capital and those indigenous groups whose interests are bound up with this transnational capital – the *comprador* fraction of the bourgeoisie (as discussed by Vliegenthart and Overbeek; see also the also the 'Hungarian' and 'Czech' models as discussed by Andreff).

As particularly Part III demonstrates, these capital market actors are joined by some *professions*, such as legal experts, rating analysts and auditors. As both the contributions by Nölke and Perry and by Dewing and Russell show, private actors such as rating agencies and auditing companies not only lobby or otherwise influence public policy-makers, they are themselves often the policy-makers, the ones who both draw up and (often via the market) enforce the regulations or standards, similar to the law firms highlighted by Wigger. She points to the role of the law firms as the prime beneficiaries of a system in which compliance with competition rules forces firms to buy their legal advice. Wigger also demonstrates that the law firms have been among the driving forces for recent changes in EU competition policy, closely cooperating with the European Commission. In the case of creating the conditions for a European market for corporate control Van Apeldoorn and Horn have also noted the involvement of company law experts, particularly in preparing the ground for a new compromise on the Takeover Directive.

This appears to be a more general pattern, where the regulatory role of the professions is backed up by *international institutions* such as the Basle II regime (discussed by Nölke and Perry), or, more specifically the European Commission. Thus, Dewing and Russell have demonstrated that the European Commission was (and is) among the most prominent driving forces for the global accounting standards harmonization. As Van Apeldoorn and Horn have shown, this model of an Anglo-Saxon shareholder capitalism has since the 1990s been consistently promoted by the European Commission as part of its overall neoliberal marketization project. The two chapters (Van Apeldoorn and Horn, and Wigger) in Part II, dealing with the European arena, in the first instance emphasize the agency of the European Commission and its important role in constructing a market-based and market-enhancing regime with respect to corporate control and competition control. But these chapters also stress the importance of the neoliberal discourse in which these regulatory changes are embedded. Whereas Wigger has identified neoliberalism primarily with the US model of competition control and the Chicago School, Van Apeldoorn and Horn have interpreted it in terms of a European political project as advanced by the European Commission. Thus, for them the marketization of corporate control is a political project bound up with the broader neoliberal marketization project that has shaped the socio-economic content of the integration process since the late 1980s. However, the European Commission is not the only public actor beyond the realm of the national state that is playing a leading role in the drive towards marketization in the realm of corporate governance regulation. As demonstrated by Vliegenthart and Overbeek, particularly the OECD has provided an important input into the drafting of ECE corporate governance regulations, whereas the imprint of other organizations such as the World Bank has been particularly obvious during earlier stages of transition, for example, regarding the design of privatization programmes. If compared with the pro-active role of these international institutions, it is remarkable that many national governments have been somewhat reserved about the commodification project, as indicated by the opposition against a pan-European market for corporate control (mentioned by Van Apeldoorn and Horn), as well as the diversity of existing domestic regulation documented by Gourevitch.

Organized labour might arguably be identified as being on the losing side with regard to the commodification trend as we have observed it in its different manifestations. Thus, in rising shareholder capitalism, as several previous studies have shown, increasing exposure to capital markets through the primacy of shareholder value may translate into a corporate strategy of 'downsize and distribute', to the shareholders, that is (Lazonick and O'Sullivan 2000; see also De Jong 1997). Nevertheless, this general argument about labour being on the losing side also needs to be qualified: as Jessop has pointed out in this book, we need to differentiate between different groups of workers. Some may actually benefit (at least financially) from the industrial restructuring engendered by the re-orientation of firms to the maximization of shareholder value (for example, by boosting the value of their pension fund assets), whereas others may either lose their job or accept that they have to work harder for less. We also have to notice that some recent corporate governance reforms, such as those by the Red-Green coalition in Germany, have been driven forward by 'transparency coalitions' (see the contribution by Gourevitch) that unite organised labour and mobile capital against management and other major stakeholders. What employees are actually getting out of this alliance is another matter. Fact is that in terms of regulatory change, the corporate governance model promoted emphasizes the primacy of (minority) shareholders at the expense of, if not management (see below) or of all workers individually, then certainly of labour as a collective force – reducing its traditionally significant role in what Rebérioux views as the continental European model that is now under threat.

Finally, as indicated above, the shareholder model promoted by current changes in corporate governance regulation (for instance with Europe emulating the US) does not always do in practice what it is supposed to do in theory – indeed, paradoxically, it arguably tends to achieve the opposite result, that is *enhance managerial discretion* (Rebérioux). Although not everyone might subscribe to this rather unorthodox view, the point that managers may not necessarily be the losers of this process is an important one. Indeed, what managers may lose in autonomous control (that is, unaffected by the demands of capital markets) over the production process, they may very well win in income (through, for example, stock options), prestige and international career mobility (that is at least as long as they manage to push the market value of their firm upwards). Rebérioux argues that the trend of rising executive pay (no longer restricted to the US) is a direct effect of the doctrine of shareholder primacy and arguably represents a process of rent extraction. This trend deepens the inequality both within the firm and in society at large.

In conclusion, we have identified a coalition of powerful forces that is driving current changes towards a regulatory framework of corporate governance premised on market principles. At the core of this coalition are global capital market actors (for example, pension funds, hedge funds and other institutional investors); a range of professional service firms that sell their services to these actors, and a small number of supranational and international public agencies, namely the European Commission, the OECD and the World Bank. This coalition is potentially facing a powerful opposition, including large sections of the work force that do not benefit from the current process of financialization, and those managers and representatives of productive capital that do not want to submit corporate strategy to the control of short-term capital market considerations. Still, this opposition is lacking a similar operational coherence than the pro-market coalition and is restrained in its ability for political mobilization by the choice of depoliticized modes of regulation, and thus has hardly been able to reverse the commodification trend inherent in the transformation of corporate governance regulation. Forces seeking to resist the current marketization trend in corporate governance regulation moreover have to contend with the ideological dominance (fitting with a broader neoliberal discourse) of the 'shareholder model' thus promoted, that is, the dominance (or, as some would prefer, *hegemony*) of the idea that the general interest (equated with the 'competitiveness' in for instance current EU policy discourse (as argued by Van Apeldoorn and Horn)) is best served if the firm only serves the interests of its (liquid) owners operating through liberalized transnational capital markets.

Conclusion and research perspectives

In sum, this book has broken new ground by addressing the public and private regulation of corporate governance, and particularly its multi-level character. We have highlighted an increasing openness of corporate governance regulation to market forces as a common trajectory across the remaining diversity of capitalisms. Together with the increasing utilization of private corporate governance regulation and the growing prominence of more market-based and market-induced forms of public regulation we have subsumed the current changes in corporate governance regulation under the heading of 'commodification'. At the same time, we have observed an increasing transnationalization of corporate governance regulation, both regarding the type of actors involved, and the simultaneity of regulatory changes. Correspondingly, our explanation of the commodifying content and mode of corporate governance regulation as well as of its increasing transnationalization has sought to integrate an account of the role of transnational structures, such as engendered by globalization, with an account of transnational actors, embedded within those structures and strategically responding to the structural changes facing them. In highlighting the struggles between these actors we have added a new facet to the study of corporate governance, namely the politics of regulatory changes, whereas the overwhelming majority of existing studies assume that these changes are due to the functional requirements of globalization or to the alleged self-evident superiority of the shareholder model.

As major driving forces behind these changes we have identified capitalist interests, primarily those of transnational financial capital, some professions (such as transnational law firms and the Big Four auditing companies), and a number of public authorities, most notably the European Commission, but also the World Bank and the OECD as far as the transition economies in ECE are concerned. The (potential) opposition to these changes, in contrast, is internally divided, since managers and workers can both gain and loose from current reforms, depending on their individual circumstances. They thus fail to mobilize effectively against current reforms, although the outcome of these reforms will hurt some of them quite substantially.[2] While many managers may gain in income, due to the linkage of their remuneration with stock prices, they may lose in freedom of manoeuvre, due to the increased scrutiny of their activities by capital market actors. And while some workers may gain from regulatory changes that favour their pension funds, many others may suffer from the economic restructuring that goes hand in hand with an increased emphasis on capital market actors in regulatory reforms. In this way, the transformation of corporate governance regulation reflects, as well as helps to bring about a changing balance of power between the different 'stakeholders' of the modern corporation.

Still, this book does not close the book on the transnational politics of corporate governance regulation. First of all, this book has a strong *empirical* focus on continental Europe and the OECD region in more general. While this is a major strength of the volume in comparison with a general corporate governance literature that is overwhelmingly focused on the US and the UK, it still raises the question whether our results on the content and mode of corporate governance regulation as well on its explanation hold true for corporate governance regulation outside of the OECD world, although we do cover the specific case of transition economies in ECE. Still, any discussion of corporate governance regulation in the global South would need to take account of a number of specific factors, including a far more prominent role of supranational agencies such as the World Bank (Soederberg 2003). Finally, our approach has strongly focused on the relationship between owners and managers. Although we did cover the position of labour to a certain extent, a full discussion of the transnational politics of corporate governance regulation would need a more comprehensive discussion of the role of labour and broader social constituencies.

While future research on the politics of corporate governance regulation should try to compensate for these empirical shortcomings, there is also a need for further *theoretical* development. Regarding the three core questions at stake we have been able, within the empirical limitations outlined above, to show most clearly a common trajectory towards marketization and commodification in the *content* of corporate governance regulation. Our conclusion with respect to a common trajectory as regards the *mode* of corporate governance regulation is somewhat weaker. The existing work on the emergence of forms of private governance in the global economy as well as work on the shifting level of governance are still primarily descriptive and aimed at refining existing categorizations. What is needed most of all is further theorization of the linkages between form and content. Only on the basis of a better understanding of these linkages can we improve our ability to *explain* current changes in both the content and the mode of corporate governance regulation. In this book we have attempted to provide the basis for a better understanding by embedding the empirical analysis of changing corporate governance regulation explicitly in such a theoretically informed framework. From our findings it has become clear that we consider as most promising those contributions coming from what might collectively be labelled *critical political economy*. Questioning the status quo and historicizing contemporary developments (two key imperatives we accept from critical theory) are preconditions for such an ongoing enterprise of theoretical work.

Finally, we have shown that political contestation plays a key role in the final outcome of processes of restructuring and (re-)regulation. The trend towards deepening commodification and further marketization, undeniable as it is, is not an inevitable and irreversible process. The process is full of internal contradictions, the hegemonic project driving it is unstable, and the social forces supporting the neoliberal project will find it increasingly difficult to keep the presently quite fragmented oppositional forces divided as the consequent polarizing effects (in terms of unequal distribution of income and political influence) continue to deepen those internal contradictions.

Notes

1 That 'social relations between persons' come to appear (in capitalism) as 'material [dinglich] relations between persons and social relations between things' is what Marx called the fetishism of the commodities (Marx 1990: 166).

2 History is of course open-ended, and the politics of corporate governance in this respect may yet change. As observed in note 1 of Chapter 1, some aspects of current changes in corporate governance, especially in continental Europe, in fact have sparked quite some political controversy and debate. Occasionally, top managers do speak out against what they view as the short-termism of the capital market (although it has to be added that these are usually managers close to retirement). Politicians sometimes echoe these concerns as well (see note 1, Chapter 1). Even more rarely in the public debate, but arguably increasingly so, some trade unions have also joined these critical voices (for the Dutch case, see, for example, *NRC Handelsblad*, 26 August, 2006). Yet apart from the fact that any real coalition (for example, a cross-class coalition between some sections of the managerial elite on the one hand and employees' interests on the other) is far from in the making, what is striking about these public interventions is also that they focus on criticizing corporate governance *practice*, laying the blame above all on the doorstep of 'predatory' Anglo-Saxon investors. What is much less recognized is the role played by changing corporate governance *regulation* in enhancing the mobility of these new type of investors, and thus in enabling and promoting this increased capital market discipline. It should therefore maybe also not surprise us that recent controversies around the role of, for example, hedge funds so far have resulted in little, if any, concrete regulatory action. So far, then, the marketization inherent in most of the current regulatory changes continues to make its inroads in what used to be much more non-liberal corporate governance regimes.

Bibliography

Acemoglu, D. and Johnson, S. (2005) 'Unbundling Institutions', *Journal of Political Economy*, 113 (5), pp. 949–95.

Acemoglu, D. and Robinson, J. (2005) *Origins of Dictatorship and Democracy*, Cambridge University Press, Cambridge, MA.

Acemoglu, D., Johnson, S. and Robinson, J. (2001) 'The colonial origins of comparative development: an empirical investigation', *American Economic Review*, 91 (5), pp. 1369–401.

Aghion, P. and Blanchard, O. (1998) 'On privatization methods in Eastern Europe and their implications', *Economics of Transition*, 6 (1), pp. 87–99.

Aglietta, M. (1997) 'Le capitalisme au tournant du siècle', in Aglietta, M. (ed.) *Régulation et crises du capitalisme*, Odile Jacob, Paris.

—— (2000) 'Shareholder value and corporate governance: some tricky questions', *Economy and Society*, 29 (1), pp. 146–59.

Aglietta, M. and Rebérioux, A. (2005) *Corporate Governance Adrift: A Critique of Shareholder Value*, Edward Elgar, Cheltenham and Northampton, MA.

Aguilera, R.V. and Federowicz, M. (2003) *Corporate Governance in a Changing Economic and Political Environment: Trajectories of Institutional Change on the European Continent*, Palgrave Macmillan, London.

Aguilera, R.V. and Jackson, G. (2002) 'Institutional changes in European corporate governance', *Economic Sociology*, 3, pp. 17–26.

—— (2003) 'The cross-national diversity of corporate governance: dimensions and determinants', *Academy of Management Review*, 28 (3), pp. 447–65.

Albert, M. (1991) *Capitalism Against Capitalism*, Whurr Publishers, London.

—— (1993) *Capitalism vs. Capitalism: How America's Obsession with Individual Aachievement and Short-term Profit has Led it to the Brink of Collapse*, Four Wall Eight Windows, New York.

Alexander, C.R. (1999) 'On the nature of the reputational penalty for corporate crime', *Journal of Law and Economics*, 42 (1), pp. 489–526.

Allen, T. (2005) 'Interest in class action grows outside the U.S.', *Securities Litigation Watch*. Internet magazine. Available online at http://slw.issproxy.com/securities_litigation_blo/2005/06/the_state_of_fo.html (accessed 14 June 2005).

Andor, L. (2000) *Hungary on the Road to the European Union: Transition in Blue*, Praeger, London.

Andreff, W. (1991) 'A francia privatizalas tanulsagai Kelet-Europa szamara' (The French privatization experience and Eastern Europe), (Part 1) *Külgazdasag* (Budapest), XXXV (9), pp. 53–66; (Part 2) *Külgazdasag*, XXXV (10), pp. 24–44.

—— (1992) 'French privatization techniques and experience: a model for Central-Eastern Europe?', in Targetti, F. (ed.) *Privatization in Europe: West and East Experiences*, Dartmouth, Aldershot, pp. 135–53.

—— (1993) *La crise des économies socialistes. La rupture d'un système*, Presses Universitaires de Grenoble, Grenoble.

—— (1995) 'Les entreprises du secteur public: conditions du succès de la transition', in Andreff, W. (ed.) *Le secteur public à l'Est. Restructuration industrielle et financière*, L'Harmattan, Paris, pp. 13–52.

—— (1996) 'Corporate governance of privatized enterprises in transforming economies: a theoretical approach', *MOCT-MOST*, 6 (2), pp. 59–80.

—— (1999a) 'Privatisation et gouvernement d'entreprise dans les économies en transition', *Économie internationale*, 1Q, pp. 97–129.

—— (1999b) 'Nominal and real convergence: at what speed?', in Van Brabant, J. (ed.) *Remaking Europe: The European Union and the Transition Economies*, Rowman & Littlefield, Lanham, MD, pp. 111–38.

—— (2000) 'Privatization and corporate governance in transition countries: beyond the principal-agent model', in Rosenbaum, E.F., Bönker, F. and Wagener, H.-J. (eds) *Privatization, Corporate Governance and the Emergence of Markets*, Macmillan, Basingstoke, pp. 123–38.

—— (2002) 'The new multinational corporations from transition countries', *Economic Systems*, 25 (4), pp. 371–9.

—— (2003a) 'Twenty lessons from the experience of privatization in transition Economies', in Kalyuzhnova, Y. and Andreff, W. (eds) *Privatization and Structural Change in Transition Economies*, Palgrave, London.

—— (2003b) 'The newly emerging TNCs from economies in transition: a comparison with Third World outward FDI', *Transnational Corporations*, 12 (2), pp. 73–118.

—— (2005a) 'Post-Soviet privatization in the light of the *Coase theorem*: transaction costs and governance costs', in Oleynik, A. (ed.) *The Institutional Economics of Russia's Transformation*, Ashgate, Aldershot, pp. 191–212.

—— (2005b) 'Russian privatization at bay: some unresolved transaction and governance costs issues in post-Soviet economies', in Oleynik, A. (ed.) *The Institutional Economics of Russia's Transformation*, Ashgate, Aldershot, pp. 213–44.

Andreff, W., Radygin, A. and Malginov, G. (1996) *The Typical Ownership of Russian Enterprises: Main Investors and Corporate Governance*, Institute for the Economy in Transition, mimeo, Moscow.

Armour, J. (2005) 'Who should make corporate law? EC legislation versus regulatory competition', *ECGI Law Working Paper* 54/2005, European Corporate Governance Institute, Brussels.

Arrighi, G. (1994) *The Long Twentieth Century: Money, Power, and the Origins of Our Times*, Verso Books, London.

Arrighi, G. and Silver, B.J. (1999) *Chaos and Governance in the Modern World System*, University of Minnesota Press, Minneapolis, MN.

Bainbridge, S. (1993) 'In defence of the shareholder wealth maximization norm', *Washington & Lee Law Review*, 50, pp. 1423–47.

Baltowski, M. and Mickiewicz, T. (2000) 'Privatization in Poland: ten years after', *Post-Communist Economies*, 12 (4), pp. 425–43.

Banker, The (2003) *Top 100 CEE Banks*, 4 October, p. 90.

Baran, P.A. (1957) *The Political Economy of Growth*, Monthly Review Press, London.

Barlev, B. and Haddad, J. (2003) 'Fair value accounting and the management of the firm', *Critical Perspectives on Accounting*, 14 (4), pp. 383–415.

Batsch, L. (1999) *Finance et stratégie*, Economica, Paris.

Baums, T. and Buxbaum, K.J. (1994) *Institutional Investors and Corporate Governance*, W. de Gruyter, Berlin and New York.

Baums, T. and Scott, K.E. (2003) 'Taking Shareholder protection seriously? Corporate governance in the United States and Germany', *ECGI Working Paper Series in Law*, No. 17, European Corporate Governance Institute, Brussels.

Bebchuk, L.A. and Fried, J. (2004) *Pay Without Performance: The Unfulfilled Promise of Executive Compensation*, Harvard University Press, Cambridge, MA.

Bebchuk, L.A. and Hamdani, A. (2002) 'Vigorous race or leisurely walk: reconsidering the competition over corporate charters', *Yale Law Journal*, 112 (3), pp. 553–613.

Bebchuk, L.A. and Roe, M.J. (1999) 'A theory of path dependence in corporate ownership and governance', *Stanford Law Review*, 52 (1), pp. 127–70.

—— (2004) 'A theory of path dependence in corporate ownership and governance', in Gordon, J.N. and Roe, M.J. (eds) *Convergence and Persistence in Corporate Governance*, Cambridge University Press, Cambridge, pp. 69–113.

Becht, M. and Mayer, C. (2002) 'Corporate control in Europe', *Revue d'Économie Politique*, 112 (4), pp. 471–512.

Becht, M., Bolton, P. and Roëll, A. (2002) 'Corporate governance and control', *ECGI Working Paper Series in Finance*, European Corporate Governance Institute, Brussels.

—— (2003/Revised 2005) 'Corporate governance and control', in Constantides, G.M., Arris, M. and Stulz. R. (eds) *Handbook of Economic of Finance*, Elsevier, Amsterdam.

Beck, T., Clarke, G., Groff, A., Keefer, P. and Walsh, P. (2001) 'New tools in comparative political economy: the database of political institutions', *World Bank Economic Review*, 15 (1), pp. 165–76.

Berger, S. (2003) *The First Globalization: Lessons from the French*, Seuil, Paris.

Berger, S. and Dore, R. (eds) (1996) *National Diversity and Global Capitalism*, Cornell University Press, Ithaca, NY.

Berglöf, E. and Burkart, M. (2003) 'European takeover regulation', *Economic Policy*, 18 (36), pp. 171–213.

Berkowitz, D., Pistor, K. and Richard, J.-F. (2003) 'Economic development, legality, and the transplant effect', *European Economic Review*, 47 (1), pp. 165–95.

Berle, A.A. and Means, G.C. (1991 and 1967 [1932]) *The Modern Corporation and Private Property*, Transaction Publishers, New Brunswick, NJ; Harcourt, Brace and World, New York.

Bhagat, S., Bizjak, J. and Coles, J.L. (1998) 'The shareholder wealth implications of corporate lawsuits', *Financial Management*, 27 (4), pp. 5–27.

Bhagat, S., James, A. and Coles, J.L. (1994) 'The wealth effects of interfirm lawsuits', *Journal of Financial Economics*, 35 (2), pp. 221–47.

Bieling, H.-J. (2003) 'Social forces in the making of the new European economy: the case of financial market integration', *New Political Economy*, 8 (2), pp. 203–24.

Bieling, H.-J. and Steinhilber, J. (2002) 'Finanzmarktintegration und corporate governance in der Europäischen Union', *Zeitschrift für Internationale Beziehungen*, 9 (1), pp. 39–74.

Bittlingmayer, G. (1998) 'The market for corporate control (including takeovers)', in Bouckaert, B. and Geest, G.D. (eds) *JAAR Encyclopedia of Law and Economics*, Edward Elgar, Cheltenham.

Bittlingmayer, G. and Hazlett, T. (2000) 'DOS Kapital: has antitrust action against Microsoft created value in the computer industry?', *Journal of Financial Economics*, 55 (March), pp. 329–35.

Bizjak, J.M. and Coles, J.L. (1995) 'The effect of private antitrust litigation on the stock-market valuation of the firm', *The American Economic Review*, 85 (3), pp. 436–59.

Black, B.S. (1992) 'Institutional investors and corporate governance: the case for institutional voice', *Journal of Applied Corporate Finance*, Fall (5), pp. 19–32.

—— (2001) 'The legal and institutional preconditions for strong securities markets', *UCLA Law Review*, 48 (April), pp. 781–805.

Blair, M.M. (1995) *Ownership and Control: Rethinking Corporate Governance for the Twenty-first Century*, Brookings Institution Press, Washington, DC.

—— (2003) 'Post-Enron reflections on comparative corporate governance', *Journal of Interdisciplinary Economics*, 14 (2), pp. 113–24.

Blasi, J., Kroumova, M. and Kruse, D. (1997) *Kremlin Capitalism: Privatizing the Russian Economy*, Cornell University Press, Ithaca, NY.

Bohle, D. (2002) 'Erweiterung und Vertiefung der EU: Neoliberale Restrukturierung und transnationales Kapital', *Prokla*, 3 (28), pp. 353–76.

—— (2006) 'Race to the bottom? Complementary institutional advantages? Competition and its consequences in the enlarged European Union', paper presented to the ESA Critical Political Economy Workshop, 31 August–2 September, Vrije Universiteit, Amsterdam.

Bohle, D. and Greskovits, B. (2004) 'Ein Sozialmodel an der Grenze', *Osteuropa*, 5–6, pp. 372–86.

—— (2006) 'Capitalism without compromise: strong business and weak labour in Eastern Europe's new transitional industries', *Studies in Comparative International Development*, 41 (1), pp. 3–25.

Böhm, F. (1980) *Freiheit und Ordnung in der Marktwirtschaft*, Nomos, Baden-Baden.

Bolkestein, F. (2000) 'Speech at presidency conclusion, European Council', Lisbon, 23–24 March 2000.

—— (2003a) 'Corporate governance in Europe', speech at the FESE Conference at Clifford Chance, 30 January, Amsterdam.

—— (2003b) 'Keynote speech', speech at the FESE Convention, 23 June, London.

—— (2004) 'Corporate governance in the European Union', speech at the European Corporate Governance Forum, 18 October, The Hague.

Böröcz, J. (1999) 'From comprador state to auctioneer state: property change, realignment, and peripheralization in post-state-socialist central and eastern Europe', in Smith, D.A., Solinger, D.J. and Topik, S.C. (eds) *States and Sovereignty in the Global Economy*, Routledge, London, pp. 193–209.

Botero, J.C., Djankov, S., La Porta, R. and Lopez-De-Silanes, F.C. (2004) 'The regulation of labor', *The Quarterly Journal of Economics*, 119 (4), pp. 1339–82.

Botzem, S. and Quack, S. (2005) 'Contested rules and shifting boundaries: international standard setting in accounting', *Discussion Paper SP III 2005-201*, Wissenschaftszentrum Bonn für Sozialforschung, Berlin.

—— (2006) 'Contested rules and shifting boundaries: international standard setting in accounting', in Djelic, M. and Sahlin-Andersson, K. (eds) *Transnational Governance: Institutional Dynamics of Regulation*, Cambridge University Press, Cambridge.

Boutillier, M., Labaye, A., Lagoutte, C., Lévy, N. and Oheix, V. (2002) 'Financement et gouvernement des entreprises: exceptions et convergences européennes', *Revue d'Économie Politique*, 112 (4), pp. 499–544.

Boycko M., Shleifer, A. and Vishny, R.W. (1995) *Privatizing Russia*, MIT Press, Cambridge, MA.

—— (1996) 'Second-best economic policy for a divided government', *European Economic Review*, 3 (5), pp. 767–74.

Boyer, R. (1990) *Regulation Theory: A Critical Introduction*, Columbia University Press, New York.

—— (2000a) 'The political in the era of globalization and finance: focus on some régulation school research', *International Journal of Urban and Regional Studies*, 24 (2), pp. 274–322.

—— (2000b) 'Is a finance-led growth regime a viable alternative to Fordism?', *Economy and Society*, 29 (1), pp. 111–45.

—— (2001) 'The diversity and future of capitalism: a regulationist analysis', in Hodgson, G.M., Itoh, M. and Yokokawa, N. (eds) *Capitalism in Evolution: Global Contentions-East and West*, Edward Elgar, Cheltenham.

Boyer, R. and Saillard, Y. (eds) (2002) *Régulation Theory: State of the Art*, Routledge, London.

Bratton, W. (2002) 'Enron and the dark side of shareholder value', *Tulane Law Review*, 76 (May), pp. 1275–362.

—— (2005) 'The academic tournament over executive compensation', *California Law Review*, 93 (5). Available online at SSRN: http://ssrn.com/abstract=678165.

Braudel, F. (1982) *On History*, University of Chicago Press, Chicago, IL.

Brenneman, D. (2004) *The Role of Regional Integration in the Development of Securities Markets: A Case Study of the EU Accession Process in Hungary and the Czech Republic*. Manuscript available online at www.law.harvard.edu/programs/pifs/pdfs/david_brenneman.pdf (accessed 12 January 2007).

Brenner, N. and Theodore, N. (2002) 'Cities and the geographies of "actually existing neoliberalism"', *Antipode*, 34 (3), pp. 349–79.

Buck, T. (2006) 'Doubts grow on efficacy of takeover directive', *Financial Times*, 12 June 2006.

Budapest Stock Exchange (2004) *Corporate Governance Recommendations*. Available online at www.ecgi.org/codes/documents/cg_recommendations.pdf (accessed 1 May 2006).

Budzinski, O. (2003) 'Pluralism of competition policy paradigms and the call for regulatory diversity', Working paper No. 14, Volkswirtschaftliche Beiträge Universität, Marburg.

Burnham, J. (1975 [1941]) *The Managerial Revolution*, Greenwood Press, Westport, CT.

Cadbury Report (1992) *Report of the Committee on Financial Aspects of Corporate Governance* (Chairman: Sir Adrian Cadbury), Gee, London.

Callaghan, H. (2006) 'European integration and the clash of capitalisms: British French and German disagreement over corporate governance, 1970–2003', PhD Dissertation, Northwestern University, Chicago, IL.

Callaghan, H. and Höpner, M. (2005) 'European Integration and the clash of capitalisms: political cleavages over takeover liberalization', *Comparative European Politics*, 3 (3), pp. 307–32.

Caporaso, J.A. (1996) 'The European Union and forms of state: Westphalian, regulatory or post-modern?', *Journal of Common Market Studies*, 34 (1), pp. 29–51.

Cernat, L. (2004) 'The emerging European corporate governance model: Anglo-Saxon, continental, or still the century of diversity?', *Journal of European Public Policy*, 11 (1), pp. 147–66.

—— (2006) *Europeanization, Varieties of Capitalism and Economic Performance in Central and Eastern Europe*, Palgrave, Basingstoke.

Chandler, A. (1977) *The Visible Hand: The Managerial Revolution in American Business*, Greenwood, Westport, CT.

Chatterjee, S. (2003) 'Enron's incremental descent into bankruptcy: a strategic and organisational analysis', *Long Range Planning*, 36 (2), pp. 133–49.

Cheffins, B. (2001) 'Does law matter? The separation of ownership and control in the United Kingdom', *Journal of Legal Studies*, 30, p. 459.

—— (2002) 'Putting Britain on the Roe map: the emergence of the Berle-Means corporation in the United Kingdom', in McCahery, J.A., Moerland, P., Raaijmakers, T. and Renneboog, L. (eds) *Corporate Governance Regimes: Convergence and Diversity*, University of Chicago Press, Chicago, IL.

Cini, M. and McGowan, F. (1998) *Competition Policy in the European Union*, St Martins Press, New York.

Cioffi, J.W. (2000) 'Governing globalisation? The state, law, and structural change in corporate governance', *Journal of Law and Society*, 27 (4), pp. 572–600.

—— (2005) 'Corporate governance reform, regulatory politics, and the foundations of finance capitalism in the United States, and Germany', *Law Research Institute Research Paper Series*, CLPE Research Paper 6/2005, Vol. 1 (1), Osgoode Hall Law School, York University, Toronto, Canada.

Cioffi, J.W. and Höpner, M. (2006) 'The political paradox of finance capitalism: interests, preferences, and center-left party politics in corporate governance reform', *Politics & Society*, 34 (4), pp. 463–502.

Coates, D. (2000) *Models of Capitalism: Growth and Stagnation in the Modern Era*, Polity Press, Cambridge.

Coffee, J.C. (1991) 'Liquidity versus control: the institutional investor as corporate monitor', *Columbia Law Review*, 91 (6), pp. 1277–366.

—— (1999a) 'The future as history: the prospects for global convergence in corporate governance and its implications', *Northwestern University Law Review*, 93 (3), pp. 641–708.

—— (1999b) 'Privatization and corporate governance: the lessons from securities market failure', *Journal of Corporation Law*, 1 (Working paper No. 158), pp. 1–39.

—— (2001) 'The rise of dispersed ownership: the roles of law and the state in the separation of ownership and control', *Yale Law Journal*, 1 (111), p.1.

—— (2002) 'Understanding Enron: it's about the gatekeepers, stupid', *Columbia Law School*, Working Paper No. 207, July, Columbia Law School, New York.

—— (2003) 'Gatekeeper failure and reform: the challenge of fashioning relevant reforms', *Columbia Law School: The Center for Law and Economic Studies*, Working Paper No. 237, Columbia Law School, New York.

—— (2005) 'A theory of corporate scandals: why the US and Europe differ', *The Center for Law and Economics Studies*, Working Paper No. 274, Columbia Law School, New York.

Collier, D. (1993) 'The comparative method', in Finifter, A. (ed.) *Political Science: The State of the Discipline II*, American Political Science Association, Washington, DC.

Committee on the Global Financial System (CBFS) (2005) *Foreign Direct Investment in the Financial Sector: Experiences in Asia, Central and Eastern Europe and Latin America*, Bank of International Settlements, Basel.

Cooper, S., Crowther, D., Davies, M. and Davis, E. (2000) 'The adoption of value-based management in large UK companies: a case for diffusion theory', 23rd Annual Congress of the European Accounting Association, March, Munich, pp. 29–31.

Cox, G. (1997) *Making Votes Count: Strategic Coordination in the World's Electoral Systems*, Cambridge University Press, New York.

Cox, R.W. (1981) 'Social forces, states and world orders: beyond international relations theory', *Millennium: Journal of International Studies*, 10 (2), pp. 126–55.

—— (1987) *Production, Power, and World Order: Social Forces in the Making of History*, Columbia University Press, New York.

Crouch, C. (2005) *Capitalist Diversity and Change: Recombinant Governance and Institutional Entrepreneurs*, Oxford University Press, Oxford.

Crouch, C. and Streeck, W. (eds) (1997) *The Political Economy of Modern Capitalism*, Sage Publications, London.

Cuervo-Cazurra, A. and Aguilera, R. (2004) 'The worldwide diffusion of codes of good governance', in Grandori, A. (ed.) *Corporate Governance and Firm Organization*, Oxford University Press, Oxford.

Culpepper, P., Hall, J.A. and Palier, B. (eds) (2006) *Changing France: The politics that markets make French Politics, Society and Culture*, Palgrave Macmillan, New York.

Cutler, C. (1992) 'Canada and the private international trade law regime', in Cutler, C. and Zacher, M. (eds) *Canadian Foreign Policy and International Economic Regimes*, University of British Columbia Press, Vancouver.

—— (2002) 'Private international regimes and interfirm cooperation', in Hall, R.B. and Biersteker, T.J. (eds) (2002) *The Emergence of Private Authority in Global Governance*, Cambridge University Press, Cambridge, pp. 23–42.

—— (2003) *Private Power and Global Authority: Transnational Merchant Law in the Global Political Economy*, Cambridge University Press, Cambridge.

Cutler, C., Haufler, V. and Porter, T. (eds) (1999a) *Private Authority and International Affairs*, SUNY Press, New York.

—— (1999b) 'Private authority and international affairs', in Cutler, C., Haufler, V. and Porter, T. (1999) *Private Authority and International Affairs*, SUNY Press, New York.

Czech Securities Commission (2004) *Corporate Governance Code based on the OECD Principles*. Available online at www.ecgi.org/codes/documents/czech_code_2004_en.pdf (accessed 1 May 2006).

Dahrendorf, R. (1959) *Class und Class Conflict in Industrial Society*, Stanford University Press, Stanford, CA.

Dallago, B. and McIntyre, R.J. (eds) (2003) *Small and Medium Enterprises in Transition Economies*, Palgrave, Basingstoke.

Davis, G.F. (1991) 'Agents without principles? The spread of the poison pill through the intercorporate network', *Adminstrative Science Quarterly*, 36, pp. 583–613.

—— (1996) 'The significance of board interlocks for corporate governance', in *Corporate Governance*, 4 (3), pp. 154–9.

Davis, G.F. and MacAdam, D. (2000) 'Corporations, classes, and social movements', in Straw, B. and Sutton, R.I. (eds) *Research in Organizational Behavior 22*, Elsevier Science, Oxford.

Davis, G.F. and Robbins, G.E. (2005) 'Nothing but net? Networks and status in corporate governance', in Knorr-Cetina, K. and Preda, A. (eds) *The Sociology of Financial Markets*, Oxford University Press, Oxford, pp. 290–311.

Davis, G.F. and Useem, M. (2002) 'Top management, company directors, and corporate control', in Pettigrew, A., Thomas, H. and Whittington, R. (eds) *Handbook of Strategy and Management*, Sage Publications, London.

Davis, G.F., Diekmann, K.A. and Tinsley, C. H. (1994) 'The decline and fall of the conglomerate firm in the 1980s: the de-institutionalization of an organizational form', *American Sociological Review*, 59 (4), pp. 547–70.

De Bernis, G.D. (1988) 'Les contradictions des relations financières internationales dans la crise', *Économies et Sociétés*, Série R, No. 3, 22 (5), pp. 101–32.

De Jong, A., De Jong, D., Mertens, G. and Roosenboom, P. (2005) 'Royal Ahold: a failure of corporate governance', *ECGI Working Paper Series in Finance*, No. 67, European Corporate Governance Institute, Brussels.

De Jong, H.W. (1989) 'The takeover market in Europe: control structures and the performance of large companies compared', *Review of Industrial Organization*, 6, pp. 1–18.

—— (1996) 'European capitalism: between freedom and social justice', in Bratton, W., MacCahery, J.A., Picciotto, S. and Scott, C. (eds) *International Regulatory Competition and Coordination: Perspectives on Economic Regulation in Europe and the United States*, Oxford University Press, Oxford, pp. 186–206.

—— (1997) 'The governance structure and performance of large European companies', *Journal of Management and Governance*, 1 (1), pp. 5–27.

Deakin, S. (2002) 'Squaring the circle? Shareholder value and corporate social responsibility in the UK', *Washington Law Review*, 70 (5/6), pp. 976–87.

Dewing, I. and Russell, P.O. (2002) 'The developing role of actuaries and auditors in UK insurance supervision', *Journal of Insurance Regulation*, 21 (1), pp. 3–27.

—— (2004) 'Accounting, auditing and corporate governance of European listed countries: EU policy developments before and after Enron', *Journal of Common Market Studies*, 42 (2), pp. 289–319.

Djankov, S. and Murrell, P. (2002) 'Enterprise restructuring in transition: a quantitative survey', in *Journal of Economic Literature*, 40 (3), pp. 739–92.

Djankov, S., La Porta, R., Lopez-De-Silanes, F. and Shleifer, A. (2002) 'The regulation of entry', *Quarterly Journal of Economics*, 117 (1), pp. 1–37.

Djelic, M.L. (2001) *Exporting the American Model: The Postwar Transformation of European Business*, Oxford University Press, Oxford.

Djelic, M.L. and Quack, S. (eds) (2003) *Globalization and Institutions: Redefining the Rules of the Economic Game*, Edward Elgar, Cheltenham.

Dobbin, F. (ed.) (2004) *The New Economic Sociology: A Reader*, Princeton University Press, Princeton, NJ.

Dobbs, I.M. (2002) 'The assessment of market power and market boundaries using the hypothetical monopoly test', Department of Accounting and Finance and Newcastle School of Management, University of Newcastle. Available online at www.staff.ncl.ac.uk/i.m.dobbs/Files/market%20definition%20general%20case.pdf (accessed 14 September 2006).

Dombey, D. (2003) 'Watered-down EU Takeover Directive is a missed opportunity for open markets', *Financial Times*, 20 December.

—— (2004) 'EU Antitrust reforms will see rulings decentralized: the balance of competition power is set to shift dramatically when the European Union enlarges next month', *Financial Times*, 21 April, p. 7.

Dore, R. (2002) 'Pensioners to the casino', in d. Cecco, M. and Lorentzen, J. (eds) *Markets and Authorities: Global Finance and Human Choice*, Edward Elgar, Cheltenham.

Dore, R., Lazonick, W. and O'Sullivan, M. (1999) 'Varieties of Capitalism in the twentieth century', *Oxford Review of Economic Policy*, 15 (4), pp. 102–20.

Drache, D. and Boyer, N. (eds) (1996) *States Against Markets: The Limits of Globalization*, Routledge, London.

Drahokoupil, J. (2004) 'Post-Fordist capitalism in the Czech Republic: the investment of Flextronics in Brno', *Czech Sociological Review*, 3 (3), pp. 343–62.

—— (2005) 'On the state of the state: the Czech transformation and the moment of convergence in the Visegrad region', paper presented at the ESA conference, September, Torun.

Duchêne, G. and Rusin, P. (2003) 'New private sector and growth. A tale of two economies in transition: Poland and Romania compared', in Kalyuzhnova, Y. and Andreff, W. (eds) *Privatization and Structural Change in Transition Economies*, Palgrave, London, pp. 139–57.

Dunsire, A. (1996) 'Tipping the balance: autopoiesis and governance', *Administration and Society*, 28 (3), pp. 299–334.

Easterbrook, F. and Fischel, D. (1993) *The Economic Structure of Corporate Law*, Harvard University Press, Cambridge, MA and London.

Eaton, S. (2005) 'Crisis and the consolidation of international accounting standards: Enron, the IASB and America', *Business and Politics*, 7(3), article 4.

Ensminger, J. (1992) *Making a Market: The Institutional Transformation of an African Society*, Cambridge University Press, New York.

Erturk, I., Froud, J., Johal, S. and Williams, K. (2004) 'Corporate governance and disappointment', *Review of International Political Economy*, 11 (4). pp. 677–713.

Erturk, I., Froud, J., Solari, S. and Williams, K. (2005a) 'The reinvention of prudence: household savings, financialisation and forms of capitalism', *CRESC Working Papers*, No. 11, University of Manchester, Manchester.

Erturk, I., Froud, J., Johal, S., Leaver, A. and Williams, K. (2005b) 'The democratisation of finance? Promises, outcomes and conditions', *CRESC Working Papers*, No. 9, University of Manchester, Manchester.

Estrin, S. (2001) 'Competition and corporate governance in transition', *Journal of Economic Perspectives*, 16 (1), pp. 101–24.

Estrin, S., Nuti, D.M. and Uvalic, M. (2000) 'The impact of investment funds on corporate governance in mass privatization schemes: Czech Republic, Poland and Slovania', *MOCT-MOST*, 10 (1), pp. 1–26.

EU–US Initiative (2005) *The European Union and the Unites States Initiative to Enhance Transatlantic Economic Integration and Growth*, EU–US Summit, 20 June, Washington, DC.

European Bank for Reconstruction and Development (EBRD) (1992) *Transition Report*, EBRD, London.

—— (1993) *Transition Report*, EBRD, London.

—— (1994) *Transition Report*, EBRD, London.

—— (1995) *Transition Report*, EBRD, London.

—— (1996) *Transition Report*, EBRD, London.

—— (1999) *Transition Report*, EBRD, London.

—— (2002) *Transition Report*, EBRD, London.

European Commission (1965) *Eighth General Report on the Activities of the Community* (June 1965) European Commission, Brussels.

—— (1985) *Completing the Internal Market*, Commission White Paper, COM (85) 310 final, European Commission, Brussels.

—— (1995) *Communication from the Commission. Accounting Harmonisation: A New Strategy vis-à-vis International Harmonisation*, European Commission, Brussels.

—— (1996a) *EC Competition Policy Newsletter*, 2 (Spring) (1), European Commission, Brussels.

—— (1996b) *The Role, the Position and the Liability of the Statutory Auditor within the European Union*, Green Paper, European Commission, Brussels.

—— (1999a) *White Paper on Modernisation of the Rules Implementing Articles 85 and 86 of the EC Treaty*, Commission Programme No. 99/027, 28 April 1999, European Commission, Brussels.

—— (1999b) *Financial Services: Implementing the Framework for Financial Markets: Action Plan*, COM (1999) 232, 11 May 1999, European Commission, Brussels.

—— (2000) *The Czech Republic and the Enlargement of the European Union*, report to the European Parliament, European Commission, Brussels.

—— (2002a) *Financial Reporting: Commission Welcomes IASB/FASB Convergence Agreement*, Press Release, IP/02/1576, 29 October 2002, European Commission, Brussels.

—— (2002b) *Commission Adopts Comprehensive Reform of EU Merger Control*, Press Release IP/02/1856, 11 December. Available online at http://europa.eu.int/rapid/pressReleasesAction.do?reference=IP/02/1856&format=HTML&aged=0&language=EN&guiLanguage=en (accessed 14 September 2006).

—— (2002c) *Proposal for a Directive on Takeover Bids*, COM (2002) 534, Official Journal of the European Union 45 E, European Commission, Brussels.

—— (2003a) *Modernising Company Law and Enhancing Corporate Governance in the European Union: A Plan to move Forward*, COM (2003) 284 final, 21 May, European Commission, Brussels.

—— (2003b) *Commission Appoints Consumer Liaison Officer*, Press Release DG Competition, Brussels. Available online at http://europa.eu.int/rapid/pressReleasesAction.do?reference=IP/03/1679&format=HTML&aged=0&language=EN&guiLanguage=en (accessed 14 September 2006).

—— (2003c) *Communication from the Commission to the Council and the European Parliament – Modernising Company Law and Enhancing Corporate Governance in the European Union – A Plan to Move Forward*, Mimeo, Brussels.

—— (2004a) *Delivering Lisbon: Reforms for the Enlarged Union*, Report from the Commission to the Spring European Council, COM (2004) 29 final/2, 20 February 2004, European Commission, Brussels.

—— (2004b) *Turning the Corner: Preparing the Challenge of the next Phase of European Capital Market Integration*, Tenth FSAP Progress Report. Available online at http://europa.eu.int/comm/internal_market/finances/docs/actionplan/index/progress10_en.pdf.

—— (2004c) *Financial Services Action Plan: Good Progress but Real Impact Depends on Good Implementation*, Commission Press Release IP/04/696, European Commission, Brussels.

—— (2004d) *Audit of Company Accounts: Commission Proposes Directive to Combat Fraud and Malpractice*, Press Release IP/04/340, 16 March, European Commission, Brussels.

—— (2004e) *IAS 39 Financial Instruments: Recognition and Measurement – Frequently Asked Questions (FAQ)*, Memo/04/265, 19 November, European Commission, Brussels.

—— (2005a) *Accounting Standards: EU Commissioner McCreevy Sees Agreement with S.E.C. as Progress Towards Equivalence*, Press Release IP/05/469, 22 April, European Commission, Brussels.

—— (2005b) *Fostering an Appropriate Regime for Shareholders' Rights. Consultation Document of DG Markt*. Available online at http://europa.eu.int/comm/internal_market/company/docs/shareholders/consultation_en.pdf (accessed 12 January 2007).

—— (2005c) 'Damages actions for breach of the EC antitrust rules', Green Paper. Available online at http://europa.eu.int/comm/competition/antitrust/others/actions_for_damages/gp_en.pdf (accessed 16 November 2006).

—— (2006) 'Contributions received in response to the public consultation on the "modernization package"'. Available online at http://europa.eu.int/comm/competition/antitrust/legislation/procedural_rules/comments/ (accessed 16 November 2006).

European Council (2000) Presidency Conclusions Lisbon European Council, 23 and 24 March 2000.

European Parliament and European Commission (1995) *European Parliament and Council Directive 95/26/EC of 29 June 1995 Amending Directives 77/780/EEC and 89/646/EEC in the Field of Credit Institutions, Directives 73/239/EEC and 92/49/EEC in the Field of Non- Life Insurance, Directives 79/267/EEC and 92/96/EEC in the Field of Life Assurance, Directive 93/22/EEC in the Field of Investment Firms and Directive 85/611/EEC in the Field of Undertakings for Collective Investment in Transferable Securities (Ucits), With a View to Reinforcing Prudential Supervision*, European Commission, Brussels.

—— (2002) *Regulation (EC) No 1606/2002 of the European Parliament and of the Council of 19 July 2002 on the Application of International Accounting Standards*, European Commission, Brussels.

European Round Table of Industrialists (ERT) (1998) *Job Creation and Competitiveness through Innovation*, ERT, Brussels.

—— (2001) *Response to the 'Green Paper on the Review of Council Regulation (EEC)'*, ERT, Competition Policy Task Force, Brussels.

—— (2002) *Proposals for Reform of EU Competition Policy*. ERT. Available online at www.ert.be/pe/ene02.htm (accessed 14 September 2006).

Eyal, G.I. (2000) 'Anti-politics and the spirit of capitalism: dissidents, monetarists, and the Czech transition to capitalism', *Theory and Society*, 29 (1), pp. 49–92.

Eyal, G.I., Selényi, I. and Townsley, E. (1997) 'The theory of post-communist managerialism', *New Left Review*, 222, pp. 60–92

—— (1998) *Making Capitalism Without Capitalists: The New Ruling Elites in Eastern Europe*, Verso, London.

Fama, E.F. and Jensen, M. (1983a) 'Agency problems and residual claims', *Journal of Law and Economics*, 26 (2), pp. 327–49.

—— (1983b) 'Separation of ownership and control', *Journal of Law and Economics*, 26 (2), pp. 301–26.

Filatochev, I., Wright, M. and Bleaney, M. (1999) 'Privatization, insider control and managerial entrenchment in Russia', *Economics of Transition*, 7 (2), pp. 481–504.

Financial Accounting Foundation (2005) *2004 Annual Report*, Financial Accounting Standards Board/Governmental Accounting Standards Board, Norwalk, CT.

Financial Accounting Standards Board (1999) *The IASC–US Comparison Project: A Report on the Similarities and Differences Between IASC Standards and US GAAP*, Financial Accounting Standards Board, Stamford, CT.

Financial Accounting Standards Board/International Accounting Standards Board (2002) *FASB and IASB Agree to Work Together toward Convergence of Global Accounting Standards*, News release, 29 October, Financial Accounting Standards Board, Stamford, CT.

—— (2006) *US FASB and IASB Reaffirm Commitment to Enhance Consistency, Comparability and Efficiency in Global Capital Markets*, News release, 27 February, Financial Accounting Standards Board, Norwalk, CT.

Fiss, P. and Zajac, E. (2004) 'The diffusion of ideas over contested terrain: the non adoption of shareholder value orientation among German firms', *Administrative Science Quarterly*, 49 (4), pp. 501–34.

Fligstein, N. (2001) *The Architecture of Markets: An Economic Sociology of Twenty-first Century Capitalist Societies*, Princeton University Press, Princeton, NJ.

Fligstein, N. and Markowitz, L. (1993) 'Financial reorganization of American corporations in the 1980s', in Wilson, W.J. (ed.) *Sociology and the Public Agenda*, Sage Publications, Newbury Park, CA.

Foot, R., MacFarlane, S. and Mastanduno, M. (eds) (2003) *US Hegemony and International Organisations: The United States and Multilateral Institutions*, Oxford University Press, Oxford.

Forwood, N. (2003) *The Content and Meaning of Article 81(3) EC*, paper for The Role of the National Judge Within Regulation 1/2003, 8–9 May, Trier. Available online at www.era.int/web/en/resources/5_1990_300_file.323.pdf (accessed 14 September 2006).

Fox, E. (1997) 'US and EU competition law: a comparison', in Graham, E.M. and Richardson, J.D. (eds) *Global Competition Policy*, Institute for International Economics, Washington, DC.

Frank, A.G. (1967) *Capitalism and Underdevelopment in Latin-America: Historic Studies of Chile and Brazil*, Monthly Review Press, New York.

Franks, J.R. and Mayer, C. (1997) 'Corporate ownership and control in the UK, Germany, and France', *Bank of America Journal of Applied Corporate Finance*, 9 (4), pp. 30–45.

Froud, J., Haslam, C., Johal, S. and Williams, K. (2000) 'Shareholder value and financialization: consultancy promises, management moves', *Economy and Society*, 29 (1), pp. 80–110.

Galbraith, J.K. (1967) *The New Industrial State*, Penguin, Harmondsworth.

Gande, A. and Lewis, C.M. (2005) 'Shareholder initiated class action lawsuits: shareholder wealth effects and industry spillovers', Working Paper, Owen Graduate School of Management, Vanderbilt University Nashville, TN. Available online at www.sauder.ubc.ca/faculty/divisions/finance/conference2005/papers/CraigLewis-class_action_July2005.pdf (accessed 14 September 2006).

Garrett, G. (1998) *Partisan Politics in the Global Economy*, Cambridge University Press, Cambridge.

Gaughan, P.A. (2002) *Mergers, Acquisitions, and Corporate Restructurings*, John Wiley & Sons, New York.

Gavil, A.I., Kovacic, W.E. and Baker, J.B. (2002) *Antitrust Law in Perspective: Cases, Concepts and Problems in Competition Policy*, Thomson West, St Paul Minneapolis, MN.

Geithner, T. (2006) 'Hedge funds and derivatives and their implications for the financial system', Federal Reserve Bank of New York, speech to Hong Kong Monetary Authority, 15 September.

Gerber, D.J. (1998) *Law and Competition in Twentieth Century Europe: Protecting Prometheus*, Oxford University Press, Oxford.

Gerschenkron, A. (1962) *Economic Backwardness in Historical Perspective*, Harvard University Press, Cambridge, MA.

Gill, S.R. (1995) 'Globalisation, market civilisation and disciplinary neoliberalism', *Millennium: Journal of International Studies*, 24 (3), pp. 299–332.

Gilson, R.J. (2004) 'Globalizing corporate governance: convergence of form or function', in Gordon, J.N. and Roe, M.J. (eds) *Convergence and Persistence in Corporate Governance*, Cambridge University Press, Cambridge, pp. 128–58.

Glaeser, E., Johnson, S. and Shleifer, A. (2001) 'Coase vs. the coasians', *Quarterly Journal of Economics*, 116 (3), p. 853.

Gordon, J.N. and Roe, M.J. (eds) (2004) *Convergence and Persistence in Corporate Governance*, Cambridge University Press, Cambridge.

Gourevitch, P.A. (1978) 'The second image reversed: the international sources of domestic politics', *International Organization*, 32 (Autumn), pp. 881–911.

—— (1986) *Politics in Hard Times: Comparative Responses to International Economic Crises*, Cornell University Press, Ithaca, NY.

—— (2003) 'The politics of corporate governance regulation', *Yale Law Journal*, 112 (7), pp. 1829–80.

Gourevitch, P.A. and Hawes, M.B. (2002) *The Politics of Choice Among National Production Systems, L'Annee de la regulation*, Presses de Sciences Po, Paris.

Gourevitch, P.A. and Shinn, J. (2005) *Political Power and Corporate Control: The New Global Politics of Corporate Governance*, Princeton University Press, Princeton, NJ.

Gourevitch, P.A., Shinn, J.P. and Allen, J. (2006) 'Financial institutions, pensions, and corporate governance: some comparative linkages', unpublished mimeo.

Goyer, M. (2002) *The Transformation of Corporate Governance in France and Germany: The Role of Workplace Institutions*, MPIfG Working Paper 02/10, Max-Planck-Institut für Gesellschaftsforschung, Cologne.

Grabbe, H. (1999) *A Partnership for Accession? The Implications of EU Conditionality for the Central and East European Applicants*, Robert Schuman Centre Working Paper 12/99, European University Institute, Florence, Italy.

—— (2001) 'How does Europeanization affect CEE governance? Condionality, diffusion and diversity', *Journal of European Public Policy*, 8 (6), pp. 1013–31.

—— (2003) 'European integration and corporate governance in Central Europe: trajectories of institutional change', in Federocwicz, M. and Aguilera, R.V. (eds) *Corporate Governance in a Changing Economic and Political Environment. Trajectories of Institutional Change*, Palgrave, Basingstoke, pp. 247–66.

Grabher, G. and Stark, D. (1997) *Restructuring Networks in Post-Socialism: Legacies, Linkages and Localities*, Oxford University Press, Oxford.

Gramsci, A. (1971) *Selections from the Prison Notebook*, Lawrence and Wishart, London.

Graz, J.-C. (2002) 'Between global markets and *lex republica*: the hybrid power of standards', paper prepared for the British International Studies Association conference, London.

—— (2005) 'Beware of global hybrids: defining authority in global political economy', paper presented at the Afdeling Politicologie, Vrije Universiteit, Amsterdam, 11 February.

Grossman, G.M. and Helpman, E. (2002) *Outsourcing in a Global Economy*, National Bureau of Economic Research, Cambridge, MA.

Guillen, M. (2000) 'Corporate governance and globalization: is there a convergence across countries?, *Advances in International Comparative Management*, 13, pp. 175–204.

Guttman, R. (2002) 'Money and credit in régulation theory', in Boyer, R. and Saillard, Y. (eds) *Régulation Theory*, Routledge, London, pp. 57–63.

Hall, P.A. and Soskice, D. (eds) (2001) *Varieties of Capitalism: Institutional Foundations of Comparative Advantage*, Oxford and Cambridge University Press, Oxford and Cambridge.

Hall, R. and Biersteker, T. (eds) (2002a) *The Emergence of Private Authority in Global Governance*, Cambridge University Press, Cambridge.

—— (2002b) 'The emergence of private authority in the international system', in Hall, R. and Biersteker, T. (eds) *The Emergence of Private Authority in Global Governance*, Cambridge University Press, Cambridge.

Hancke, B. (2002) *Large Firms and Institutional Change: Industrial Renewal and Economic Restructuring in France*, Oxford University Press, Oxford.

Hansmann, H. (1996) *The Ownership of Enterprise*, The Belknap Press of Harvard University, Cambridge, MA.

Hansmann, H. and Kraakman, R. (2000) 'The end of history for corporate law', *Law and Economics Working Paper* No. 235, Yale Law School, New Haven, CT.

—— (2001) 'The end of history for corporate law', *Georgetown Law Journal*, 89 (2), pp. 439–68.

Harmes, A. (2001a) 'Mass investment culture', *New Left Review*, 9 (May–June), pp. 103–24.

—— (2001b) 'Institutional investors and Polanyi's double movement: a model of contemporary currency crises', *Review of International Political Economy*, 8 (3), pp. 389–437.

Harvey, D. (2003) *The New Imperialism*, Oxford University Press, Oxford.

Haufler, V. (1993) 'Crossing the boundary between public and private', in Rittberger, V. (ed.) *Regime Theory and International Relations*, Clarendon Press, Oxford.

—— (1997) *Dangerous Commerce: Insurance and the Management of International Risk*, Cornell University Press, Ithaca, NY.

—— (1999) 'Self-regulation and business norms: political risk, political activism', in Cutler, C., Haufler, V. and Porter, T. (eds) *Private Authority and International Affairs*, SUNY Press, New York.

—— (2001) *A Public Role for the Private Sector: Industry Self-Regulation in a Global Economy*, Carnegie Endowment, Washington, DC.

—— (2002) 'Public and private authority in international governance: historical continuity and change', paper prepared for the conference on New Technologies and International Governance, 11–12 February, Washington, DC.

Hay, C. (2004) 'Common trajectories, variable paces, divergent outcomes? Models of European capitalism under conditions of complex economic interdependence', *Review of International Political Economy*, 11 (2), pp. 231–62.

Held, D. and McGrew, A. (eds) (2002) *Governing Globalization: Power, Authority and Global Governance*, Polity Press, Cambridge.

Henning, L. (2003) 'Big firms begin hiring for upturn', *Legal Times*, ALM Media, Inc. Available online at www.law.com/jsp/article.jsp?id=1059980446042 (accessed 14 September 2006).

Hewson, M. and Sinclair, T. (eds) (1999) *Approaches to Global Governance Theory*, SUNY Press, Albany, NY.

Higgott, R., Underhill, G. and Bieler, A. (eds) (2000) *Non-State Actors and Authority in the Global System*, Routledge, London and New York.

High Level Group of Company Experts (2002) 'Report of the High Level Group of Company Law Experts on issues related to takeover bids'. Available online at: http:// europa.eu.int/comm/internal_market/en/company/company/news/hlg01-2002.pdf (accessed 13 April 2006).

Hillebrand, E. (2001) 'Schlüsselstellung im globalisierten Kapitalismus: der Einfluss privater Rating-Agenturen auf Finanzmärkte und Politik', in Brühl, T., Debiel, T., Hamm, B., Hummel, H. and Martens, J. (eds) (2001) *Die Privatisierung der Weltpolitik: Entstaatlichung und Kommerzialisierung im Globalisierungsprozess*, Dietz, Bonn, pp. 150–73.

Hirschman, A. (1970) *Exit, Voice and Loyalty: Responses to Decline in Firms, Organizations and States*, Harvard University Press, Cambridge, MA.

Hiscox, M.J. (2002) *International Trade and Political Conflict: Commerce, Coalitions, and Mobility*, Princeton University Press, Princeton, NJ.

Hollinger, P. (2005), 'France mulls allowing class-action suits', *Financial Times*, 6 January, p. 7.

Holman, O. (2001) 'The enlargement of the European Union towards Central and Eastern Europe: the role of supranational and transnational actors', in Bieler, A. and Morton, A.D. (eds) *Social Forces in the Making of the New Europe: The Restructuring of European Social Relations in the Global Political Economy*, Palgrave, Basingstoke.

—— (2004) 'Integrating peripheral Europe: the different roads to "security and stability" in Southern and Central Europe', *Journal of International Relations and Development*, 7 (2), pp. 208–36.

Holmström, B. and Kaplan, S. (2003) 'The state of US corporate governance: what's right and what's wrong?', *ECGI Working Paper Series in Finance*, No. 23, European Corporate Governance Institute, Brussels.

Hölscher, J. and Stephan J. (2004) 'Competition policy in Central and Eastern Europe in the light of EU accession', *Journal of Common Market Studies*, 42 (2), pp. 321–45.

Hooghe, L. and Marks, G. (2001) *Multi-Level Governance and European Integration*, Rowman & Littlefield, Lanham, MD.

Hooghe, L. and Nugent, N. (2002) 'The Commission's services', in Peterson, J. and Shackleton, M. (eds) *The Institutions of the European Union*, Oxford University Press, Oxford.

Höpner, M. (2001) *Corporate Governance in Transition: Ten Empirical Findings on Shareholder Value and Industrial Relations in Germany*, MPIfG Discussion Paper 01/05, Max-Planck-Institut für Gesellschaftsforschung, Cologne.

—— (2003a) *Wer beherrscht die Unternehmen? Shareholder Value, Managerherrschaft und Mitbestimmung in Deutschland*, Campus Verlag, Frankfurt.

—— (2003b) *European Corporate Governance Reform and the German Party Paradox*, Max-Planck-Institute für Gesellschaftsforschung, Cologne.

—— (2006) 'Corporate governance reform and the German party paradox', *Comparative Politics*.

Höpner, M. and Jackson, G. (2001) *An Emerging Market for Corporate Control? The Mannesmann Takeover and German Corporate Governance*, MPIfG Discussion Paper 01/04, Max-Planck-Institut für Gesellschaftsforschung, Cologne.

Hopt, K. (2002) 'Modern company law and capital market problems: improving European corporate governance after Enron', *ECGI Working Paper Series in Law*, European Corporate Governance Institute, Brussels.

—— (2005) 'European company law and corporate governance: where does the action plan of the European Commission lead?', *ECGI Working Paper Series in Law*, 52/2005, European Corporate Governance Institute, Brussels.

Hopt, K., Kanada, H., Roe, M., Wymeersch, E. and Prigge, S. (1999) *Comparative Corporate Governance: The State of the Art and Emerging Research*, Oxford University Press, Oxford.

Horn, L. and Van Apeldoorn, B. (2004) 'Levelling the playing field for whom? The European Takeover Directive and the European marketisation project', paper prepared for the International Studies Association Annual Meeting, Honolulu 2005.

Hossfeld, C. and Klee, L. (2003) 'Performance reporting on EVA by French and German companies', Second workshop on Performance and Management Control, September, Nice.

Huber, E. and Stephens, J. (2001) *Development and Crisis of the Welfare State*, University of Chicago Press, Chicago, IL.

Hudson, R. (2002) 'Global production systems and European integration', *ESRC 'One Europe or Several?'* Working Papers, 43 (2), Sussex European University, Brighton.

International Accounting Standards Committee Foundation (2005a) *Constitution*, IASC Foundation, New York.

—— (2005b) *Annual Report 2004*, IASC Foundation, London.

International Association for Statistical Computing (IASC) (1998) *IAS 39 Financial Instruments: Recognition and Measurement*, IASC, London.

International Auditing and Assurance Standards Board (2006) *Annual Report 2005*, International Federation of Automatic Control, New York.

International Federation of Accountants (IFAC) (2006) *Annual Report 2005*, IFAC, New York.

International Organization of Securities Commissions (IOSCO) (2000) *A Resolution on IASC Standards – Passed by the Presidents' Committee*, IOSCO, Madrid.

Ireland, P. (1996) 'Corporate governance, stakeholding, and the company: towards a less degenerate capitalism', *Journal of Law and Society*, 23 (3), pp. 287–320.

Jackson, G. (1998) 'International capital markets and regime competition in corporate governance', paper presented at the Twelfth International Conference of the Society for the Advancement of Socio-Economics, 14–18 July, Vienna.

—— (2001) 'Comparative corporate governance: sociological perspectives', in Gamble A., Parkinson, J. and Kelly, G. (eds) *The Political Economy of the Company*, Hart Publishers, Oxford, pp. 265–87.

James, A.J. (1999) *Private Enforcement of Antitrust Law in the EU, UK and USA*, Oxford University Press, Oxford.

James, C. (2001) 'Reconciling Divergent enforcement policies: where do we go from here?', paper for Address by the Assistant Attorney General, Antitrust Division US Department of Justice at the 28th Annual Conference on International Law and Policy, 25 October, Fordham Corporate Law Institute, New York. Available online at www.usdoj.gov/atr/public/speeches/9395.pdf (accessed 14 September 2006).

Janos, A.C. (2001) 'From eastern empire to western hegemony: East Central Europe under two international regimes', *East European Politics and Societies*, 15 (2), pp. 221–49.

Jarman-Williams, P. (2001) 'Social and economic policy objectives of the European Union and European Competition Law', *Scots Law Student Journal* (3).

Jeffers, E. and Plihon, D. (2001) 'Investisseurs institutionnels et gouvernance des entreprises', *Revue d'Economie Financière*, 63 (November), pp. 137–52.

Jensen, M.C. (1988) 'Takeovers: their causes and consequences', *Journal of Economic Perspectives* 2 (1), pp. 21–48.

—— (1993) 'The modern industrial revolution, exit, and the failure of internal control systems', *Journal of Finance*, 48 (3), pp. 831–80.

Jensen, M.C. and Meckling, W.H. (1976) 'Theory of the firm: managerial behavior, agency costs and ownership structure', *Journal of Financial Economics*, 3 (4), pp. 305–60.

Jensen, M.C. and Murphy, K. (2004) 'Remuneration: where we've been, how we got to here, what are the problems, and how to fix them', *ECGI Working Paper Series in Finance*, No. 44, European Corporate Governance Institute, Brussels.

Jessop, B. (1990) *State Theory*, Polity Press, Cambridge.

—— (1998) 'The rise of governance and the risks of failure: the case of economic development', *International Social Science Journal*, 50 (155), pp. 29–46.

—— (2002a) *The Future of the Capitalist State*, Polity Press, Cambridge.

—— (2002b) 'Governance and meta-governance', in Bang, H. (ed.) *Governance as Social and Political Communication*, Manchester University Press, Manchester, pp. 110–16.

Jessop, B. and Sum, N.L. (2006) *Beyond the Regulation Approach: Putting Capitalist Economies in their Place*, Edward Elgar, Cheltenham.

Kahan, M. and Kamar, E. (2002) 'The myth of state competition in corporate law', *Stanford Law Review*, 55 (3), pp. 679–87.

Kahan, M. and Rock, E.B. (2006) 'Hedge funds in corporate governance and corporate control', *Working Paper* 99, University of Pennsylvania Law School. Available online at: http://lsr.nellco.org/cgi/viewcontent.cgi?article=1102&context=upenn/wps (accessed 14 September 2006).

Kalyuzhnova, Y. and Andreff, W. (eds) (2003) *Privatization and Structural Change in Transition Economies*, Palgrave, London.

Kamar, E. (2005) 'Beyond competition for incorporations', American Law & Economics Association Annual Meetings, New York University School of Law.

Kanizslai, L. (2005) 'Hungary: practitioner report', in Social Development Agency and European Trade Union Institute for Research, Education and Health and Safety (eds) *Worker board-level representation in the new EU Member States: Country Reports on the National Systems and Practices*, Presens, Brussels, pp. 15–17.

Katz, M. (2004) 'Is it time for the US to abandon its horizontal merger guidelines?', paper for Competition Commission Lecture on Competition Policy, 7 April, Victoria House Bloomsbury Square, London. Available online at www.competition-commission.org.uk/our_role/cc_lectures/lecture_transcript.pdf (accessed 14 September 2006).

Katzenstein, P. and Shiraishi, T. (2006) 'Remaking Asia: Americanization and Japanization', in Katzenstein, P. and Shiraishi, T. (eds) *Beyond Japan: East Asian Regionalism*, Cornell University Press, Ithaca, NY.

Kemper, R.A.P. (2004) 'Private enforcement of EU and national competition law', paper for European Competition Day, 21–22 October, Amsterdam.

Keohane, R.O. and Nye, J.S. (eds) (1971) *Transnational Relations and World Politics*, Harvard University Press, Cambridge, MA.

Kerwer, D. (2001) *Standardising as Governance: The Case of Credit Rating Agencies*, Max Planck Project Group Common Goods – Law, Politics and Economics, Bonn (Preprint).

King, L.P. and Váradi, B. (2002) 'Beyond Manichean economics: foreign direct investment and growth in the transition from socialism', *Communist and Post-Communist Studies*, 35 (1), pp. 1–21.

King, M. and Sinclair, T. (2001) 'Grasping at straws: a ratings downgrade for the emerging international financial architecture', paper prepared for the American Political Science Association Annual Meeting, San Francisco.

Kollman, K. (2003) 'Marketing good behavior: the role of transnational business networks in promoting standards of corporate responsibility', paper prepared for the CEEISA/ISA International Convention, Budapest.

Kooiman, J. (2003) *Governing as Governance*, Sage Publications, London.

Kornai, J. (1979) 'Resource-Constrained versus demand-constrained systems', *Econometrica*, 47 (4), pp. 801–19.

—— (1986)'The soft budget constraint', *Kyklos*, 39 (1), pp. 3–30.

—— (1990) *The Road to a Free Economy: Shifting from a Socialist System. The Example of Hungary*, W.W. Norton, New York.

—— (1993) 'The Evolution of financial discipline under the postsocialist system', *Kyklos*, 46 (3), pp. 315–36.

—— (2001) 'Hardening the budget constraint: the experience of the post-socialist countries', *European Economic Review*, 45 (9), pp. 1573–99.

Kroes, N. (2005a) 'Building a competitive Europe: competition policy and the relaunch of the Lisbon Strategy', paper for speech 5/78 at Conference at the Bocconi University, Milan, 7 February. Available online at http://europa.eu.int/rapid/pressReleasesAction.do?reference=SPEECH/05/78&format=HTML&aged=0&language=EN&guiLanguage=en (accessed 14 September 2006).

—— (2005b) 'Effective competition policy: a key tool for delivering the Lisbon Strategy', paper for speech 05/73 at EMAC Open Meeting of Coordinators, 2 February, Brussels. Available online at http://europa.eu/rapid/pressReleasesAction.do?reference=SPEECH/05/73&format=HTML&aged=0&language=EN&guiLanguage=en (accessed 14 September 2006).

—— (2005c) 'Taking competition seriously: anti-trust reform in Europe', speech 05/157. Available online at http://europa.eu.int/rapid/pressReleasesAction.do?reference=SPEECH/05/157&format=HTML&aged=0&language=EN&guiLanguage=en (accessed 14 September 2006).

—— (2006) 'Actions for damages'. Available online at http://ec.europa.eu/comm/competition/antitrust/others/actions_for_damages/index_en.html (accessed 14 September 2006).

Krozsner, R. (2000) 'The economics and politics of financial modernization', *Economic Policy Review of the Federal Reserve Bank of New York* (October), pp. 25–37.

La Porta, R., Lopez-de-Silanes, F., Shleifer, A. and Vishny, R. (1997) 'Legal determinants of external finance', *The Journal of Finance*, 52 (3), p. 1131.

—— (1998) 'Law and finance', *Journal of Political Economy*, 106 (6), p. 1113–55.

—— (1999) 'Corporate ownership around the world', *The Journal of Finance*, 54 (2), p. 471.

—— (2000) 'Investor protection and corporate governance', *Journal of Financial Economics*, 58 (1), p. 3.

Lamfalussy, A. *et al.* (2000) *Initial Report of the Committee of Wise Men on the Regulation of European Securities Markets*, European Commission, Brussels.

Lane, C. (2003) 'Changes in corporate governance of German corporations: convergence to the Anglo-American model?', *Competition and Change*, 7 (2–3), pp. 79–100

Lane, D. and Myant, M. (2006) *Varieties of Capitalism in Post-Communist Countries*, Palgrave, Basingstoke.

Lannoo, K. (1999) 'A European perspective on corporate governance', *Journal of Common Market Studies*, 37 (2), pp. 269–94.

Lannoo, K. and Khachaturyan, A. (2003) *Reform of Corporate Governance in the EU*, Centre for European Policy Studies Papers, Brussels.

Lazonick, W. and O'Sullivan, M. (2000) 'Maximizing shareholder value: a new ideology for corporate governance?', *Economy and Society*, 29 (1), pp. 13–35.

Lev, B. and Zarovan, P. (1999) 'The boundaries of financial reporting and how to extend them', *Journal of Accounting Research*, 37 (2), pp. 353–85.

Lijphart, A. (1999) *Patterns of Democracy: Government Forms and Performance in Thirty-six Countries*, Yale University Press, New Haven, CT and London.

Lipietz, A. (1982) 'Towards global Fordism?', *New Left Review*, 132 (1), pp. 33–47.

—— (1987) *Mirages and Miracles: The Crisis of Global Fordism*, Verso Books, London.

Litan, R.E. and Shapiro, C. (2001) 'Antitrust policy and the Clinton Administration', Harvard University, Center for Business and Government, John F. Kennedy School of Government, Massachusetts MA.

Lowe, P. (2003) 'Interview', *Europolitix*. Available online at http://www.eupolitix.com/EN/Interviews/200309/26545d22-8f11-46b2-abb2-cfd2029e0f4b.htm (accessed on 11 January 2007).

MacCreevy, C. (2005a) 'Company Law Action Plan: setting future priorities', speech at the European Corporate Governance Forum, 14 November, London.

—— (2005b) 'The future of the Company Law Action Plan', Listed Companies and Legislators in Dialogue Conference, 17 November, Copenhagen.

MacIntyre, A. (2001) 'Institutions and investors: the politics of the financial crisis in Southeast Asia', *International Organization*, 55 (1), p. 81.

McKinsey (2002) *Global Investor Opinion Survey. Available online at* http://mckinsey.com/clientservice/organizationleadership/service/corpgovernance/research.asp or directly at http://mckinsey.com/clientservice/organizationleadership/service/corpgovernance/pdf/GlobalInvestorOpinionSurvey2002.pdf (accessed 12 January 2007).

Mann, M. (2004) 'The first failed empire of the twenty-first century', in Held, D. and Koenig-Archibugi, M. (eds) *American Power in the 21st Century*, Polity Press, Cambridge.

Manne, H. (1965) 'Mergers and the market for corporate control', *The Journal of Political Economy*, 73 (2), pp. 110–20.

March, J.G. and Olsen, J.P. (1998) 'The institutional dynamics of international political orders', *International Organization*, 52 (4), pp. 943–69.

Martinez-Diaz, L. (2005) 'Strategic experts and improvising regulators: explaining the IASC's rise to global influence, 1973–2001', *Business and Politics*, 7 (3), article 3.

Marx, K. (1867) *Das Kapital. Kritik der politischen Ökonomie*, Meisner, Hamburg.

—— (1990) *Capital*, Vol. 1, Penguin, London.

—— (1996) *Capital*, volume 1, Lawrence & Wishart, London

Maul, S. and Kouloridas, A. (2004) 'The takeover bids directive', *German Law Journal*, 5 (4), pp. 355–66.

Mayntz, R. (1993) 'Governing failures and the problem of governability: some comments on a theoretical paradigm', in Kooiman, J. (ed.) *Modern Governance*, Sage Publications, London, pp. 9–20.

Meaney, C.S. (1995) 'Foreign Experts, capitalists, and competing agendas. privatization in Poland, the Czech Republic, and Hungary', *Comparative Political Studies*, 28 (2), pp. 275–305.

Megginson, W.L. and Netter, J.M. (2001) 'From state to market: a survey of empirical studies on privatization', *Journal of Economic Literature*, 39 (2), pp. 321–89.

Merö, K. and Valentinyi, M.E. (2003) *The Role of Foreign Banks in Five Central and Eastern European Countries*, November, National Bank of Hungary, Budapest.

Mertlik, P. (1996) 'Czech privatization: from public ownership to public ownership in five years?', in Blaszczyk, B. and Woodward, R. (eds) *Privatization in Post-Communist Countries*, Vol. 1, CASE, Warsaw, pp. 103–22.

Mesnard, M. (1999) 'Emergence des groupes et *corporate governance* en Russie', *Économie internationale*, 77 (1), pp. 131–60.

Meyer, J.W. and Rowan, B. (1977) 'Institutionalized organizations: formal structure as myth and ceremony', *American Journal of Sociology*, 83 (2), pp. 340–63.

Milgrom, P. and Roberts, J. (1990) 'The economics of modern manufacturing: technology, strategy and organization', *American Economic Review*, 80 (3), pp. 511–28.

Mintzberg, H. (1983) *Power In and Around Organizations*, Prentice Hall, Englewood Cliffs, NJ.

Monti, M. (2001) 'Antitrust in the US and Europe: a history of convergence, Speech/01/540', paper for General Counsel Roundtable in Front of the American Bar Association (ABA), 14 November, Washington, DC. Available online at http://europa.eu.int/rapid/pressReleasesAction.do?reference=SPEECH/01/540&format=HTML&aged= 0&lang uage=EN&guiLanguage=en (accessed 14 November 2006).

—— (2002) 'Merger control in the European Union. a radical reform', paper for European Commission/IBA Conference on EU Merger Control, 7 November, Brussels. Available online at http://europa.eu.int/comm/competition/speeches (accessed 25 December 2002).

—— (2004a) 'The EU gets new competition powers for the 21st century', *Competition Policy Newsletter*, Special Edition.

—— (2004b) 'Private litigation as a key complement to public enforcement of competition rules and the first conclusions on the implementation of the new merger regulation', paper for speech 04/403 at IBA Eighth Annual Competition Conference, Fiesole, 14 September. Available online at http://europa.eu.int/rapid/pressReleasesAction. do?reference=SPEECH/04/403&format=HTML&aged=0&language=EN& guiLanguage=en (accessed 14 September 2006).

—— (2004c) 'A reformed competition policy: achievements and challenges for the future', paper for speech 04/477 at the Centre for European Reform, Brussels, 28 October. Available online at http://europa.eu.int/rapid/pressReleasesAction.do?reference=SPEECH/ 04/477&format=HTML&aged=0&language=EN&guiLanguage=en (accessed 14 September 2006).

Moore, M. and Rebérioux, A. (2007) 'The corporate governance of the firm as an entity; old issue for the new debate', in Biondi, Y., Canziani, A. and Kyrat, T. (eds) *The Firm as an Entity: Implications for Economics, Accounting, and Law*, Routledge, London.

Moran, M. (1991) *The Politics of the Financial Services Revolution: the USA, UK and Japan*, Macmillan, Basingstoke.

Morck, R. (2005) *A History of Corporate Governance Around the World: Family Business Groups to Professional Managers*, University of Chicago Press, Chicago, IL.

Morgan, G., Whitley, R. and Moen, E. (2005) *Changing Capitalisms? Institutional Change and Systems of Economic Organization*, Oxford University Press, Oxford.

Motta, M. (2004) *Competition Policy: Theory and Practice*, Cambridge University Press, Cambridge.

Müller, K. (1998) 'Transformation als Lateinamerikanisierung? Die neue rentenpolitische Orthodoxie in Ungarn und Polen', *Prokla. Zeitschrift für kritische Sozialwissenschaft*, 3, pp. 459–83.

—— (2001) *The Political Economy of Pension Reform in Central-Eastern Europe*, Edward Elgar, Cheltenham.

—— (2002) 'Beyond privatization: pension reform in the Czech Republic and Slovenia', *Journal of European Social Policy*, 4 (4), pp. 293–306.

National Bank of Hungary (2006) Different statistical sources. Available online at http://english.mnb.hu/Engine.aspx (accessed 10 March 2006).

Nellis, J. (2002a) 'The World Bank, privatization, and enterprise reform in transition economies. a retrospective analysis', *Transition Newsletter*, 13 (1), pp. 17–21.

—— (2002b) *The World Bank, Privatization and Enterprise Reform in Transition Economies: A Retrospective Analysis*, Center for Global Development, mimeo, Washington, DC.

Nesvetailova, A. (2004) 'From "transition" to dependent development: the new periphery in global financial capitalism', in Robinson, N. (ed.) *Reforging the Weakest Link*, Ashgate, Aldershot.

Nicolaisen, D. (2004) 'Remarks before the IASB meeting with world standard-setters', speech, 28 September, SEC, Washington, DC.

Nobes, C. and Parker, R. (2004) *Comparative International Accounting* (8th edn), Prentice Hall/Financial Times, Harlow.

Nölke, A. (1999) 'Transnational economic relations and national models of capitalism', paper for ECPR Joint Sessions of Workshops, 26–31 March, Mannheim.

—— (2003) 'The relevance of transnational policy networks: some examples from the European Commission and the Bretton Woods Institutions', *Journal of International Relations and Development*, 6 (3), pp. 267–98.

—— (2004a) 'Transnationale Politiknetzwerke: eine Analyse grenzüberschreitender politischer Prozesse jenseits des regierungszentrischen Modells', *Habilitationsschrift*, Universität Leipzig, Leipzig.

—— (2004b) 'Transnational private authority and corporate governance', in Schirm, S. (ed.) *New Rules for Global Markets: Public and Private Governance in the World Economy*, Palgrave Macmillan, Basingstoke.

—— (2006) 'Private Norms in the global political economy', in Giesen, K.-G. and Van der Pijl, K. (eds) *Global Norms*, Cambridge Scholars Press, Cambridge.

Nölke, A. and Stratmann, G. (1998) 'Filling the transitional void: the crucial role of international financial institutions in assisting Eastern European reforms', in Reinalda, B. and Verbeek, B. (eds) *Autonomous Policy Making by International Organizations*, Routledge, London, pp. 163–77.

Nölke, A. and Vliegenthart, A. (2006) 'Varieties of capitalism meet world system theory: which type of capitalism for the East Central European semi-periphery?', paper prepared for presentation at the Annual Convention of the International Studies Association, 22–25 March, San Diego.

Nölke, A., Overbeek, H. and Van Apeldoorn, B. (2003) 'The transnational political economy of corporate governance regulation: a research outline', *Working Papers Political Science 2003* (5), Vrije Universiteit, Amsterdam.

Nooteboom, B. (1999) 'Voice- and exit-based forms of corporate control: Anglo-American, European, and Japanese', *Journal of Economic Issues*, 13 (4), pp. 845–60.

North, D.C. (1981) *Structure and Change in Economic History*, W.W. Norton & Co, New York.

Nugent, N., Paterson, W.E. and Wright, V. (eds) (2001) *The European Commission*, Palgrave, Basingstoke.

O'Sullivan, M. (2000a) 'Corporate governance and globalisation', *Annals of the American Academy of Political and Social Sciences*, 570 (July), pp. 153–72.

—— (2000b) *Contests for Corporate Control: Corporate Governance and Economic Performance in the United States and Germany*, Oxford University Press, Oxford.

Organization for Economic Co-operation and Development (OECD) (1999) *Principles of Corporate Governance*, OECD, Paris.

—— (1998) 'Shareholder value and the market for corporate control in OECD countries', *Financial Market Trends*, 69 (1), pp. 15–37.

—— (2004) *OECD Principles of Corporate Governance*, OECD, Paris.

Ost, D. (2000) 'Illusory corporatism in Eastern Europe: neoliberal tripartism and postcommunist class identities', *Politics & Society*, 4 (4), pp. 503–30.

Overbeek, H.W. (1990) *Global Capitalism and National Decline: The Thatcher Decade in Perspective*, Unwin Hyman, London.

—— (2000) 'Transnational historical materialism: theories of transnational class formation and world order', in Palan, R.P. (ed.) *Global Political Economy. Contemporary Theories*, Routledge, London and New York, pp. 168–83.

—— (2003) 'Transnational political economy and the politics of European (un)employment: introducing the themes', in Overbeek, H.W. (ed.) *The Political Economy of European Employment: European Integration and the Transnationalization of the (un)Employment Question*, Routledge, London and New York, pp. 1–10.

—— (2004a) 'Transnational class formation and concepts of control: towards a genealogy of the Amsterdam Project', *Journal of International Relations and Development*, 7 (2), pp. 113–41.

—— (2004b) 'Global governance, class, hegemony: a historical materialist perspective', *Working Papers Political Science*, 2004 (1), Vrije Universiteit, Amsterdam.

Pagano, M. and Volpin, P. (2001) 'The political economy of finance', *Oxford Review of Economic Policy*, 17 (4), p. 502.

—— (2005) 'Workers, managers, and corporate control', *Journal of Finance*, 60 (April), p. 841.

Parker, A. (2004) 'Hand that guides EU accounting reform', *Financial Times*, 9 August, p. 23.

Parkinson, P., Gamble, A. and Kelly, G. (eds) (2001) *The Political Economy of the Company*, Hart, Oxford, pp. 265–87.

Pattberg, P. (2004) 'Private environmental governance and the changing nature of authority', paper prepared for the International Studies Association Annual Meeting, Montreal.

Paulis, E. and De Smijter, E. (2005) 'Enhanced enforcement of the EC competition rules Since 1 May 2004 by the Commission and the NCAs. The Commission's view', paper for IBA Conference on the Antitrust Reform in Europe, 9–11 March.

Pavlínek, P. (2004) 'Regional development implications of foreign direct investment in Central Europe', *European Urban and Regional Studies*, 11 (1), pp. 47–70.

Peck, J.A. and Tickell, A. (2002) 'Neoliberalizing space', *Antipode*, 34 (3), pp. 380–404.

Pellerin, H. and Overbeek, H.W. (2001) 'Neoliberal regionalism and the management of people's mobility', in Bieler, A. and Morton, A.D. (eds) *Social Forces in the Making of the 'New Europe': The Restructuring of European Social Relations in the Global Political Economy*, Palgrave, Basingstoke, pp. 137–57.

Permanent Subcommittee on Investigations of the Committee of the Governmental Affairs United States Senate (2002) *The Role of the Board of Directors in Enron's Collapse*, Report 107–70, July, US Senate, Washington, DC.

Perotti, E. and Von Thadden, L. (2003) *The Political Economy of Bank and Market Dominance*, European Corporate Governance Institute Finance, CEPR Discussion Paper No. 3914. Available online at SSRN: http://ssrn.com/abstract=427140.

Perry, J. and Nölke, A. (2005) 'International accounting standard setting: a network approach', *Business and Politics*, 7 (3), article 5.

—— (2006) 'The political economy of international accounting standards', *Review of International Political Economy*, 13 (4), pp. 559–86

Persson, T. and Tabellini, G. (2003) *The Economic Effects of Constitutions: What do the Data Say?*, MIT Press, Cambridge, MA.

Picciotto, S. (2004) Presentation to the ARCCGOR inaugural workshop, December, Amsterdam.

Pirrung, M. (2004) 'EU enlargement towards cartel paradise? An economic analysis of the reform of European Competition Law', *Erasmus Law and Economics Review*, February (1), pp. 77–109.

Plihon, D., Ponssard, J.-P. and Zarlowski, P. (2001) 'Quel scénario pour le gouvernement d'entreprise? Une hypothèse de double convergence', *Revue d'Economie Financière*, 63 (3), pp. 35–51.

Polanyi, K. (1957) *The Great Transformation*, Beacon Press, Boston, MA.

Pollack, M.A. (1998) 'The engines of integration? Supranational autonomy and influence in the European Union', in Sandholtz, W. and Stone Sweet, A. (eds) *European Integration and Supranational Governance*, Oxford University Press, Oxford.

Polski Forum Corporate Governance (2002) *The Corporate Governance Code for Polish Listed Firms* Available online at www.ecgi.org/codes/documents/code_final_complete.pdf (accessed 1 May 2006).

Porter, T. (1993) *States, Markets and Regimes in Global Finance*, St Martin's Press, New York.

—— (2005) 'Private authority, technical authority, and the globalization of accounting standards', *Business and Politics*, 7 (3), article 2.

Porter, T. and Coleman, W. (2002) 'Transformations in the private governance of global finance', paper prepared for the International Studies Association Annual Meeting, New Orleans.

Poulantzas, N. (1973) 'On social classes', *New Left Review*, 1/78 (March–April), pp. 27–54.

Powers, W. (ed.) (2002) *Report of Investigation by the Special Investigate Committee of the Board of Directors of Enron Corp*, 1 February 2002, Counsel: Wilmer, Cutler & Pickering, Houston, TX.

Public Company Accounting Oversight Board (PCAOB) (2006) *2005 Annual Report*, PCAOB, Washington, DC.

Rajan, R.G. and Zingales, L. (2003a) *Saving Capitalism from the Capitalists*, Random House, New York.

—— (2003b) 'The great reversals: the politics of financial development in the 20th century', *Journal of Financial Economics*, 69 (1), p. 5.

Rappaport, A. (1986) *Creating Shareholder Value: The New Standard for Business Performance*, Free Press, New York and Collier Macmillan, London.

Raviv, O. (2006) 'Predatory finance and the financialization of the new European periphery', paper presented to the ESA Critical Political Economy Workshop, 31 August–2 September, Vrije Universiteit, Amsterdam.

Rebérioux, A. (2002) 'European style of corporate governance at the crossroads: the role of worker involvement', *Journal of Common Market Studies*, 40 (1), pp. 111–34. Reprinted in Clarke, T. (ed.) (2005) *Corporate Governance, Volume III: European Corporate Governance*, Routledge, London, pp. 64–87.

Rhodes, M. and Van Apeldoorn, B. (1998) 'Capital unbound? The transformation of European corporate governance', *Journal of European Public Policy*, 5 (3), pp. 406–27.

Rieth, L. (2004) 'Corporate social responsibility in global economic governance: a comparison of the OECD guidelines and the UN global compact', in Schirm, S. (ed.) *New Rules for Global Markets: Public and Private Governance in the World Economy*, Palgrave Macmillan, Basingstoke.

Risse-Kappen, T. (1995) 'Bringing transnational relations back in: introduction', in Risse-Kappen, T. (ed.) (1995) *Bringing Transnational Relations Back In: Non-State Actors, Domestic Structures, and International Institutions*, Cambridge University Press, Cambridge, pp. 3–36.

—— (2002) 'Transnational actors and world politics', in Carlsnaes, W., Risse-Kappen, T. and Simmons, B. (eds) *Handbook of International Relations*, Sage Publications, London.

Roberts, C., Weetman, P. and Gordon, P. (2002) *International Financial Accounting: A Comparative Approach* (2nd edn), Pearson Education, Harlow.

Roberts, J., McNulty, T. and Stiles, P. (2005) 'Beyond agency conceptions of the work of the non-executive director: creating accountability in the boardroom', *British Journal of Management*, 16 (1), pp. 5–26.

Roe, M.J. (1994) *Strong Managers, Weak Owners: The Political Roots of American Corporate Finance*, Princeton University Press, Princeton, NJ.

—— (2003) *Political Determinants of Corporate Governance : Political Context, Corporate Impact*, Oxford University Press, Oxford and New York.

—— (2004) 'Modern politics and ownership separation', in Gordon, J.N. and Roe, M.J. (eds) *Convergence and Persistence in Corporate Governance*, Cambridge University Press, Cambridge, pp. 252–90.

Rogowski, R. (1989) *Commerce and Coalitions: How Trade Affects Domestic Political Alignments*, Princeton University Press, Princeton, NJ.

Röller, L.H. (2005) 'Using economic analysis to strengthen competition policy enforcement in Europe', 21 March, Chief Competition Economists at the European Commission, Brussels.

Röller, L.H. and Friederiszick, H.W. (2005) *Ökonomische Analyse in der EU Wettbewerbspolitik*, European Commission, Brussels.

Romano, R. (1993) 'Public pension fund activism in corporate governance reconsidered', *Columbia Law Review*, 93 (May), pp. 795–853.

—— (2005) 'The Sarbanes-Oxley Act and the making of quack corporate governance', *Yale Law Journal*, 114 (7), pp. 1521.

Ronit, K. and Schneider, V. (eds) (2000) *Private Organizations in Global Politics*, Routledge, London and New York.

Roy, W. (1997) *Socializing Capital: The Rise of the Large Industrial Corporation in America*, Princeton University Press, Princeton, NJ.

Rusin, P. (2002) 'La privatisation de l'économie par création d'entreprises: une nouvelle approche de la transition. Le cas de la Pologne', PhD dissertation, University Paris 1.

Ryner, M. (2002) *Capitalist Restructuring, Globalisation and the Third Way: Lessons from the Swedish Model*, Routledge, London and New York.

Sachs, J.D. (1991) 'Accelerating privatization in Eastern Europe', World Bank Conference on Development Economics, 25–26 April, Washington, DC.

Sally, R. (1995) *States and Firms: Multinational Enterprises in Institutional Competition*, Routledge, London and New York.

Sandholtz, W. and Stone Sweet, A. (eds) (1998) *European Integration and Supranational Governance*, Oxford University Press, Oxford.

Scharpf, F.W. and Schmidt, V.A. (2000a) *Welfare and Work in the Open Economy. Vol I. From Vulnerability to Competitiveness*, Oxford University Press, Oxford.

—— (2000b) *Welfare and Work in the Open Economy. Vol II. Common Challenges and Diverse Responses*, Oxford University Press, Oxford.

Schaub, A. (2002) 'Antitrust law enforcement: a shared trans-Atlantic vision', paper for Bi-Annual Conference of the Council for the United States and Italy, 25 January, New York.

—— (2004) *Regulatory Competition and Subsidiarity in Corporate Governance in a Transatlantic Perspective*, Transatlantic Corporate Governance Dialogue, 12 July, Brussels.

Scheffman, D. and Coleman, M. (2001) 'Dialogue and Consultation facilitates convergence in the analyses of mergers in the US and EU', Federal Trade Commission. Available online at www.ftc.gov/be/convergence.pdf (accessed 14 September 2006).

Schimmelfennig, F. and Sedelmeier, U. (2004) 'Governance by conditionality: EU rule transfer to the candidate countries of Central and Eastern Europe', *Journal of European Public Policy*, 11 (4), pp. 661–79.

—— (eds) (2005) *The Europeanization of Central and Eastern Europe*, Cornell University Press, Ithaca, NY.

Schmidt, I. and Rittaler, J.B. (1986) *Die Chicago School of Antitrust Analysis*, Nomos, Baden-Baden.

Schmidt, R.H. and Spindler, G. (2004) 'Path dependance and complementarity in corporate governance', in Gordon, J.N. and Roe, M.J. (eds) *Convergence and Persistence in Corporate Governance*, Cambridge University Press, Cambridge, pp. 114–27.

Schmidt, V.A. (2001) 'The politics of adjustment in France and Britain: when does discourse matter?', *Journal of European Public Policy*, 8 (2), pp. 247–64.

—— (2002) 'Does discourse matter in the politics of welfare state adjustment?', *Comparative Political Studies*, 35 (2), pp. 168–93.

Schmitthof, C. (ed.) (1973) *The Harmonisation of European Company Law*, The United Kingdom National Committee of Comparative Law, London.

Schonfeld, A. (1965) *Modern capitalism: The Changing Balance of Public and Private Power*, Oxford University Press, New York.

Schrooten, M. and Stephan, S. (2001) *Savings in Central Eastern Europe*, DIW Discussion Paper Nr. 250, DIW, Berlin.

Schumpeter, J.A. (1942) *Capitalism, Socialism, and Democracy*, Harper and Brothers, New York.

Scott, J. (1997) *Corporate Business and Capitalist Classes*, Oxford University Press, Oxford.

Securities and Exchange Commission (SEC) (2000) *SEC Concept Release: International Accounting Standards*, SEC, Washington, DC.

—— (2003) *Study Pursuant to Section 108(d) of the Sarbanes-Oxley Act of 2002 on the Adoption by the United States Financial Reporting System of a Principles-Based Accounting System*, SEC, Washington, DC.

—— (2005) *Chairman Donaldson Meets with EU Internal Market Commissioner McCreevy*, Press Release 2005-62, 21 April, SEC, Washington, DC.

—— (2006) *SEC and CESR Launch Work Plan Focused on Financial Reporting*, Press Release, 2006-130, 2 August, SEC, Washington, DC.

Sherwood, B. and Tait, N. (2005) 'Class actions across the Atlantic Group litigation', *Financial Times*, 16 June, p. 14.

Shields, S. (2002) *Global Restructuring and the Transnationalization of the Polish State, IPEG Working Papers in Global Political Economy 2*, British International Studies Association. Available online at http://www.bisa.ac.uk/groups/ipeg/papers/StuartShields.pdf (accessed 12 January 2007.

—— (2004) 'Global restructuring and the Polish state: transition, transformation, or transnationalization?', *Review of International Political Economy*, 1 (1), pp. 132–54.

Shleifer, A. and Vishny, R.W. (1996) 'A survey of corporate governance', *NBER Working Paper*, No. 5554, National Bureau of Economic Research, Cambridge, MA

—— (1997) 'A survey of corporate governance', *Journal of Finance*, 52 (2), pp. 737–83.

Shonfield, A. (1965) *Modern Capitalism: The Changing Balance of Public and Private Power*, Oxford University Press, Oxford.

Shugart, M.S. and Carey, J.M. (1992) *Presidents and Assemblies: Constitutional Design and Electoral Dynamics*, Cambridge University Press, Cambridge, MA.

Simmons, B. (2001) 'The international politics of harmonization: the case of capital market regulation', *Industrial Organization*, 55 (3), pp. 589–620.

Sinclair, T. (1994) 'Passing judgement: credit rating processes as regulatory mechanisms of governance in the emerging world order', *Review of International Political Economy*, 1(1), pp. 133–59.

—— (1995) 'Economic and financial analysis considered as knowledge dynamics of global governance', paper prepared for the International Studies Association Annual Meeting, Chicago.

—— (1999) 'Bond-rating agencies and coordination in the global political economy', in Cutler, C., Haufler, V. and Porter, T. (eds) (1999a) *Private Authority and International Affairs*, SUNY Press, New York.

—— (2001) 'The infrastructure of global governance: quasi-regulatory mechanisms and the new global finance', *Global Governance*, 7 (4), pp. 441–51.

—— (2003) 'Global monitor: credit rating agencies', *New Political Economy*, 8 (1), pp. 147–61.

—— (2005) *The New Masters of Capital: American Bond Rating Agencies and the Politics of Creditworthiness*, Cornell University Press, Ithaca, NY and London.

Skog, R. (2002) 'The Takeover Directive: an endless saga?', *European Business Law Review*, 13 (4), pp. 301–12.

Slaughter, A.M. (2004) *New World Order*, Princeton University Press, Princeton, NJ.

Social Development Agency (SDA) European Trade Union Institute for Research, Education and Health and Safety (ETUIREHS) (eds) (2005) *Worker Board-level Representation in the New EU Member States: Country Reports on the National Systems and Practices*, Presens, Brussels.

Soederbergh, S. (2003) 'The promotion of "Anglo–American" corporate governance in the south: who benefits from the new international standard?', *Third World Quarterly*, 24 (1), pp. 7–27.

Stark, D. (1992) 'Path dependence and privatization strategies in East Central Europe', *Eastern European Politics and Societies*, 6 (1), pp. 17–54.

—— (1996) 'Recombinant property in East European capitalism', *American Journal of Sociology*, 4 (1), pp. 993–1028.

Stark, D. and Bruszt, L. (2001) 'One way or multiple paths: for a comparative sociology of East European capitalism', *American Journal of Sociology*, 106 (4), pp. 1129–37.

Stiglitz, J. (2001) '*Quis custodiet ipsos custodes?* (Who is to guard the guards themselves?)', in Stiglitz, J.E. and Muet, P.-A. (eds) *Governance, Equality, and Global Markets, The Annual Bank Conference on Development Economics, Europe*, World Bank, Washington, DC, pp. 22–54.

Story, J. and Walter, I. (1997) *Political Economy of Financial Integration in Europe*, Manchester University Press, Manchester.

Strange, S. (1994) *States and Markets* (2nd edn), Pinter, London.

—— (1996) *The Retreat of the State: The Diffusion of Power in the World Economy*, Cambridge University Press, Cambridge.

Streeck, W. (1984) *Industrial relations in West Germany: A Case Study of the Car Industry*, Heinemann, London.

—— (2001) 'The transformation of corporate organization in Europe: an overview', *MPIfG Working Paper* 01/08, Max-Planck-Institut für Gesellschaftsforschung, Cologne.

Streeck, W. and Yamamura, K. (eds) (2002) *The Origins of Non-Liberal Capitalism*, Cornell University Press, Ithaca, NY.

Suchman, M.C. and Cahill, M.L. (1996) 'The hired gun as facilitator: lawyers and the suppression of business disputes in Silicon Valley', *Law & Social Inquiry*, 21 (3), pp. 679–712.

Sum, N.L. (2005) 'Globalization and paradoxes of ethical transnational production', *Competition and Change*, 9 (2), pp. 181–200.

Sundgren, J. (1997) 'Self-regulatory initiatives in the global economy: exploring the concept of private regimes', Paper prepared for the International Studies Association Annual Meeting, 18–22 March, Toronto, Canada.

Swenson, P.A. (1989) *Fair shares: Unions, Pay and Politics in Sweden and West Germany*, Cornell University Press, Ithaca, NY.

—— (2002) *Capitalists and Markets: The Making of Labor Markets and Welfare States in the United States and Sweden*, Oxford University Press, New York.

Taub, S. (2003) 'Remarks before the 2003 Thirty-first AICPA National Conference on Current SEC Developments', speech, 11 December, SEC, Washington, DC.

Thomson, T.A. and Davis, G.F. (1997) 'The politics of corporate control and the future of shareholder activism in the United States', *Corporate Governance*, 5 (3), pp. 152–9.

Tiberghein, Y. (2002) 'State mediation of global financial forces: different paths of structural reforms in Japan and South Korea', *Journal of East Asian Studies*, 2, pp. 103–41.

—— (2003) 'Veto players, financial globalization, and policy making: a political analysis of the pathway of structural reforms in Japan 1993–2002', Annual Meeting of the American Political Science Association, Philadelphia, PA.

—— (2007 forthcoming) *The Corporate Restructuring Dilemma: France, Korea, Japan*, Cornell University Press, Ithaca, NY.

Tirole, J. (2001) 'Corporate governance', *Econometrica*, 69 (1), 1–35.

Tomand, W.K. and Lister, P.M. (2001) 'Antitrust enforcement in the new administration', in Newsletter from the Antitrust Practice Group of Morganlewis. Available online at www.morganlewis.com/pdfs/7F501625-1565-4302-9CCB7AC3372DC444_Publication.pdf (accessed 14 September 2006).

Tweedie, D. and Seidenstein, T. (2005) 'Setting a global standard: the case for accounting convergence', *Northwestern Journal of International Law & Business*, 25 (3), pp. 589–608.

Ullrich, H. (2003) 'Competitor cooperation and the evolution of competition law: issues for research in a perspective of globalization', in Drexl, J. (ed.) *The Future of Transnational Antitrust: From Comparative to Common Competition Law*, Staempfli Publishers Ltd, Berne.

Union of Industrial and Employers' Confederation of Europe (UNICE) (1995) 'Modernizing EU competition policy: refocusing the scope and administration of article 85', UNICE Discussion Paper, Brussels.

—— (1999) 'UNICE comments, executive summary on the modernization of EC competition law', Position Paper, Brussels.

—— (2001) 'UNICE comments on the modernization of EC competition law. Proposal for a council regulation implementing Articles 81 and 82 of the Treaty. COM (2000) 582 Final', Position Paper, Brussels.

—— (2002) 'UNICE supplementary comments on the modernization of EC competition law. Proposal for a council regulation implementing Articles 81 and 82 of the Treaty. Status: 26 July 2002', Position Paper, Brussels.

United Nations Conference on Trade and Development (2004) *World Investment Report 2004*, United Nations, New York.

—— (2005) *World Investment Report 2005*, United Nations, New York.

United States General Accounting Office (2003) *Public Accounting Firms: Mandated Study on Consolidation and Competition*, Report to the Senate Committee on Banking, Housing, and Urban Affairs, and the House Committee on Financial Services, Washington, DC.

Useem, M. (1993) *Executive Defense: Shareholder Power and Corporate Reorganization*, Harvard University Press, Cambridge, MA.

—— (1996) *Investor Capitalism: How Money Managers are Changing the Face of America*, Harper Collins, New York.

—— (2004) 'Corporate leadership in a globalizing equity market', in Clarke, T. (ed.) *Theories of Corporate Governance: The Philosophical Foundations of Corporate Governance*, Routledge, London and New York, pp. 206–22.

Vagliasindi, M. and Vagliasindi, P. (2003) 'Privatization methods and enterprise governance in transition economies', in Kalyuzhnova, Y. and Andreff, W. (2003) *Privatization and Structural Change in Transition Economies*, Palgrave, London, pp. 60–92.

Van Apeldoorn, B. (2002) *Transnational Capitalism and the Struggle over European Integration*, Routledge, London.

—— (2003) 'European unemployment and transnational capitalist class strategy: the rise of the neoliberal competitiveness discourse', in Overbeek, H. (ed.). *The Political Economy of European Employment: European Integration and the Transnationalization of the (un)Employment Question*, Routledge, London and New York, pp. 113–34.

—— (2004a) 'Theorizing the transnational: a historical materialist approach', *Journal of International Relations and Development*, 7 (2), pp. 142–76.

—— (2004b) (ed.) 'Transnational historical materialism: the Amsterdam International Political Economy Project', *Journal of International Relations and Development*, 7 (2), Special Issue.

—— (2006) 'The Lisbon Agenda and the legitimacy crisis of European socio-economic governance: the future of "embedded neo-liberalism"', paper presented at the Fourth

Convention of the Central and East European International Studies Association (CEEISA), 25– 27 June, University of Tartu, Estonia.

Van Apeldoorn, B. and Horn, L. (2005) 'The European marketization project and the struggle over the Takeover Directive', paper presented at the Annual Conference of the International Studies Association, 1–5 March, Hawaii.

—— (2007 forthcoming) 'The marketisation of European corporate control: a critical political economy perspective', *New Political Economy*, 12 (2).

Van Apeldoorn, B., Overbeek, H. and Ryner, M. (2003) 'Theories of European integration: a critique', in Cafruny, A. and Ryner, M. (eds) *A Ruined Fortress? Neoliberal Hegemony and Transformation in Europe*, Rowman and Littlefield, Lanham, MD, pp. 17–45.

Van der Pijl, K. (2006) 'A Lockean Europe', *New Left Review*, 37 (February–March), pp. 9–37.

Venit, J.S. and Kolasky, W.J. (2000) 'Substantive convergence and procedural dissonance in merger review', in Evenett, S., Lehmann A. and Steil B. (eds) *Antitrust Goes Global. What Future for Transatlantic Cooperation?*, Royal Institute of International Affairs Brookings Institution Press, London and Washington, DC.

Vitols, S. (2001) 'Varieties of corporate governance: comparing Germany and the UK', in Hall, P. and Soskice, D. (eds) *Varieties of Capitalism. Institutional Foundations of Comparative Advantage*, Oxford University Press, Oxford, pp. 337–60.

Vliegenthart, A. (2005) 'EU Membership and the rise of a foreign-led type of capitalism in the Czech Republic', paper prepared for the ISA Annual Conference, Honolulu.

—— (2007 forthcoming) 'Transnational actors and corporate governance in ECE: the case of the EU and the Czech Republic', in Pickles, J. and Jenkins, R. (eds) *Rethinking the State and Society in Soviet and Post-socialist Economies*, Palgrave, London.

Vliegenthart, A. and Horn, L. (2005) 'Corporate governance in Central Eastern Europe: the role of the European Union', paper presented at the ESA Conference, Torun, September.

Waelbroeck, D., Slater, D. and Even-Shoshan, G. (2004) 'Study on the conditions of claims for damages in case of infringement of EC competition rules', Comparative and Economics Reports by Ashurst for the European Commission's DG Competition, European Community, Brussels.

Wallerstein, I. (1984) 'Socialist states: mercantilist strategies and revolutionary objectives', in Wallerstein, I. (ed.) *The Politics of the World Economy: The States, the Movements and the Civilizations*, Cambridge University Press, Cambridge, pp. 86–96.

Watson, M. and Hay, C. (2003) 'The discourse of globalisation and the logic of no alternative: rendering the contingent necessary in the political economy of New Labour', *Policy & Politics*, 31 (1), pp. 289–305.

Weresa, M.A. (2004) 'Can foreign direct investment help Poland catch up with the EU?', *Communist and Post-Communist Studies*, 37 (3), pp. 413–27.

Whitley, R. (1999) *Divergent Capitalisms: The Social Structuring and Change of Business Systems*, Oxford University Press, Oxford.

Whittington, G. (2005) 'The adoption of international accounting standards in the European Union', *European Accounting Review*, 14 (1), pp. 127–53.

Wigger, A. (2004) 'Revisiting the European competition reform: the toll of private self-enforcement', *Working Papers Political Science*, 2004(7), Vrije Universiteit, Amsterdam.

—— (2005) 'The convergence crusade. the politics of global competition laws and practices', paper presented at the 46th Annual International Studies Association (ISA) Convention, 1–6 March, Honolulu, Hawaii.

Wigger, A. and Nölke, A. (2005) 'Private Selbstregulierung in der EU und ihre Konsequenzen für den Rheinischen Kapitalismus: das Beipiel der Wettwerbspolitik', paper prepared for presentation at the Meeting of the International Relations Section of the German Political Science Association, 6–7 October, Mannheim.

Wilks, S. (2004) 'Markets and law: competition policy and the juridification of the economic sphere', paper for SASE Conference, 8 July, George Washington University, Washington, DC.

Williamson, O. (1985) *The Economic Institutions of Capitalism*, Free Press, New York.

Wils, W.P.J. (2003) 'Should private antitrust enforcement be encouraged in Europe?', *World Competition*, 26 (3), pp. 473–88.

Windolf, P. (1994) 'Die neuen Eigentümer: eine Analyse des Marktes für Unternehmens-kontrolle', *Zeitschrift für Soziologie*, 23 (2), pp. 79–92.

Winter, J. (ed.) (2002a) *Report of the High Level Group of Company Law Experts on Issues Related to Takeover Bids in the European Union*, High Level Group of Company Law Experts, Brussels, January.

—— (ed.) (2002b) *A Modern Regulatory Framework for Company Law in Europe*, High Level Group of Company Law Experts, Brussels, November.

—— (2004) 'EU company law on the move', *Legal Issues of Economic Integration*, 31 (2), pp. 97–114.

Wolf, K. (2002) 'Civil society and the legitimacy of governance beyond the state: conceptional outlines and empirical explorations', paper prepared for the International Studies Association Annual Meeting, New Orleans.

Wooldridge, F. (2004) 'The recent directive on takeover bids', *European Business Law Review*, 15 (2), pp. 147–58.

World Bank (2002) *Transition: The First Ten Years: Analysis and Lessons for Eastern Europe and the Former Soviet Union*, Washington, DC, January.

Wouters, J. (2000) 'European company law: *quo vadis?*', *Common Market Law Review*, 37 (2), pp. 257–307.

Zingales, L. (1998) 'Corporate governance', in Newman, P. (ed.) *The New Palgrave Dictionary of Economics and the Law*, Stockton Press, London, pp. 497–502.

—— (2000) 'In search of new foundations', *Journal of Finance*, 55 (4), pp. 1623–53.

Zorn, D., Dobbin, F., Dierkes, J. and Kwok, M. (2004) 'Managing investors: how financial markets reshaped the American firm', in Knorr-Cetina, K. and Preda, A. (eds) *The Sociology of Financial Markets*, Oxford University Press, Oxford, pp. 269–89.

Index